ViZ MANGA

Descendants of Darkness™

Yami no Matsuei

WELCOME TO THE MINISTRY OF HADES!

10

Story & Art by **YOKO MATSUSHITA**

Descendants of Darkness
Yami no Matsuei
Vol. 10
Shôjo Edition

Story & Art by
Yoko Matsushita

English Adaptation/Lance Caselman
Translation/David Ury
Touch-Up & Lettering/Gia Cam Luc
Graphics & Cover Design/Courtney Utt
Editor/Nancy Thistlethwaite

Managing Editor/Annette Roman
Director of Production/Noboru Watanabe
VP of Publishing/Alvin Lu
Sr. Director of Acquisitions/Rika Inouye
VP of Sales & Marketing/Liza Coppola
Publisher/Hyoe Narita

Published by VIZ Media, LLC
P.O. Box 77064
San Francisco, CA 94107

Shôjo Edition
10 9 8 7 6 5 4 3 2 1
First printing, March 2006

For advertising rates or media kit, e-mail advertising@viz.com

www.viz.com   store.viz.com

Table of Contents

Chapter 37 3

Chapter 38 25

Chapter 39 46

Chapter 40 65

Chapter 41 84

Chapter 42 103

Chapter 43 127

Chapter 44 147

Chapter 45 167

Afterword 187

闇(やみ)の末裔(まつえい)

DESCENDANTS OF DARKNESS
YAMI NO MATSUEI

CHAPTER 37

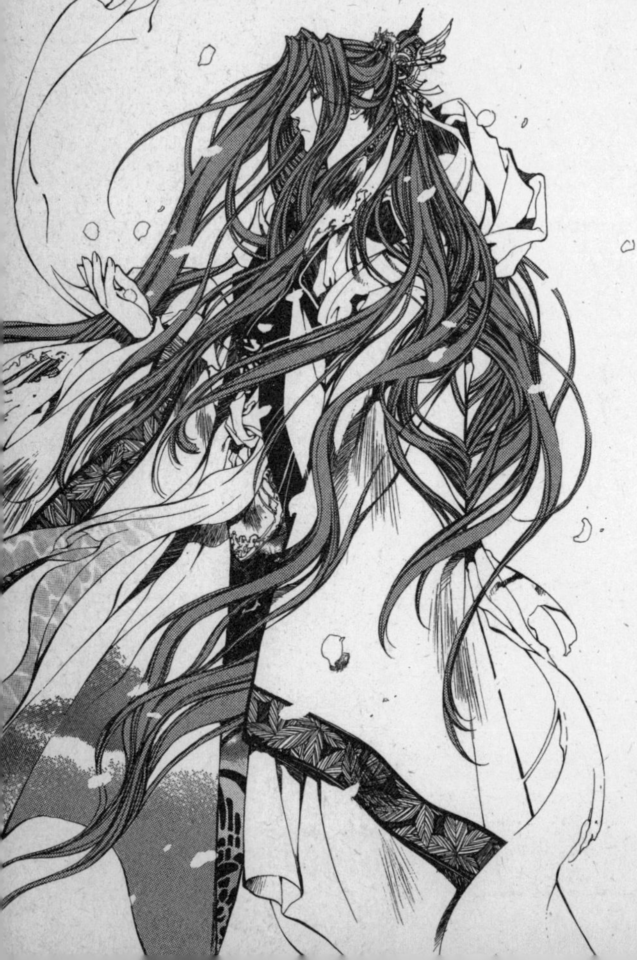

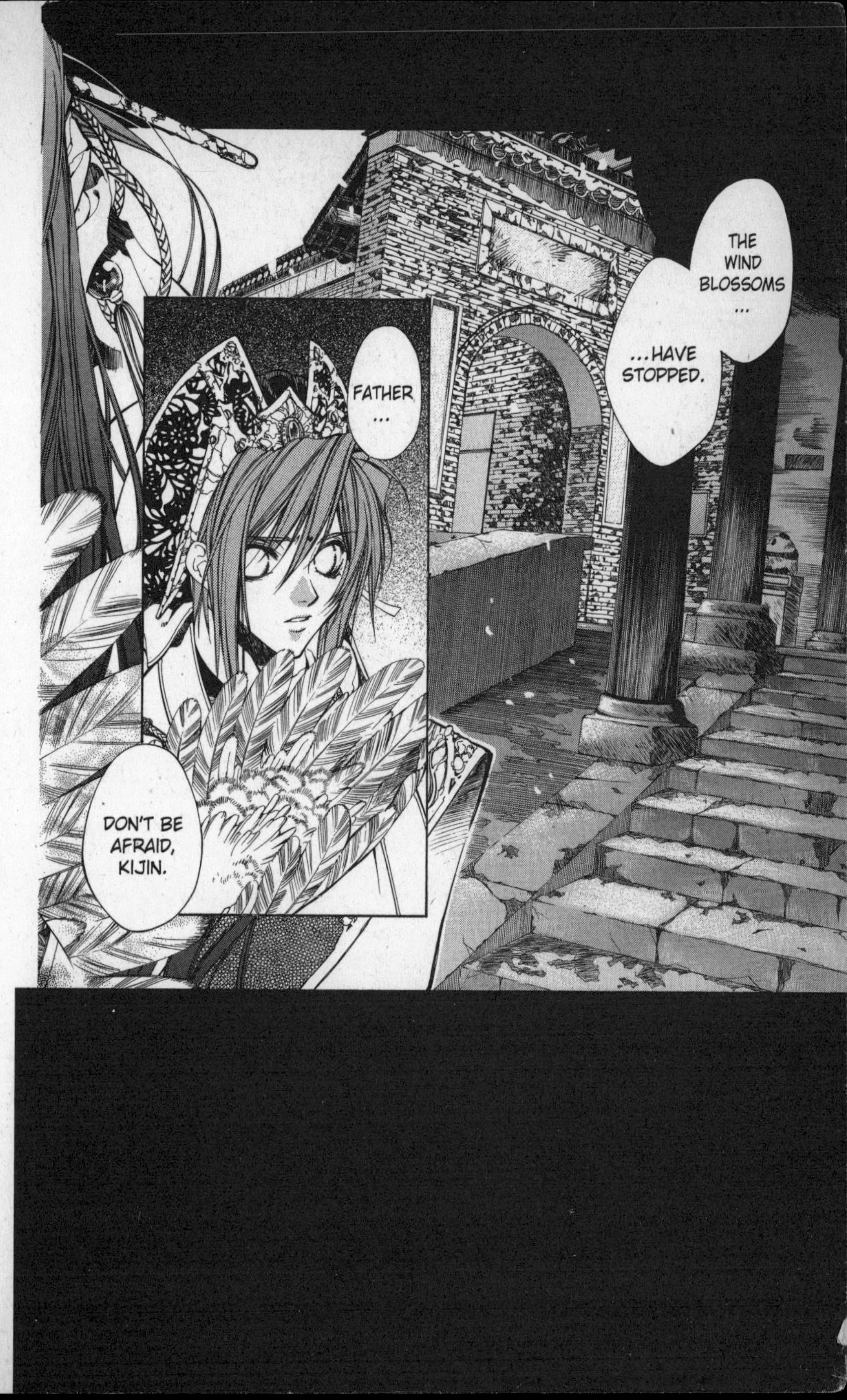
THE WIND BLOSSOMS...
...HAVE STOPPED.
FATHER...
DON'T BE AFRAID, KIJIN.

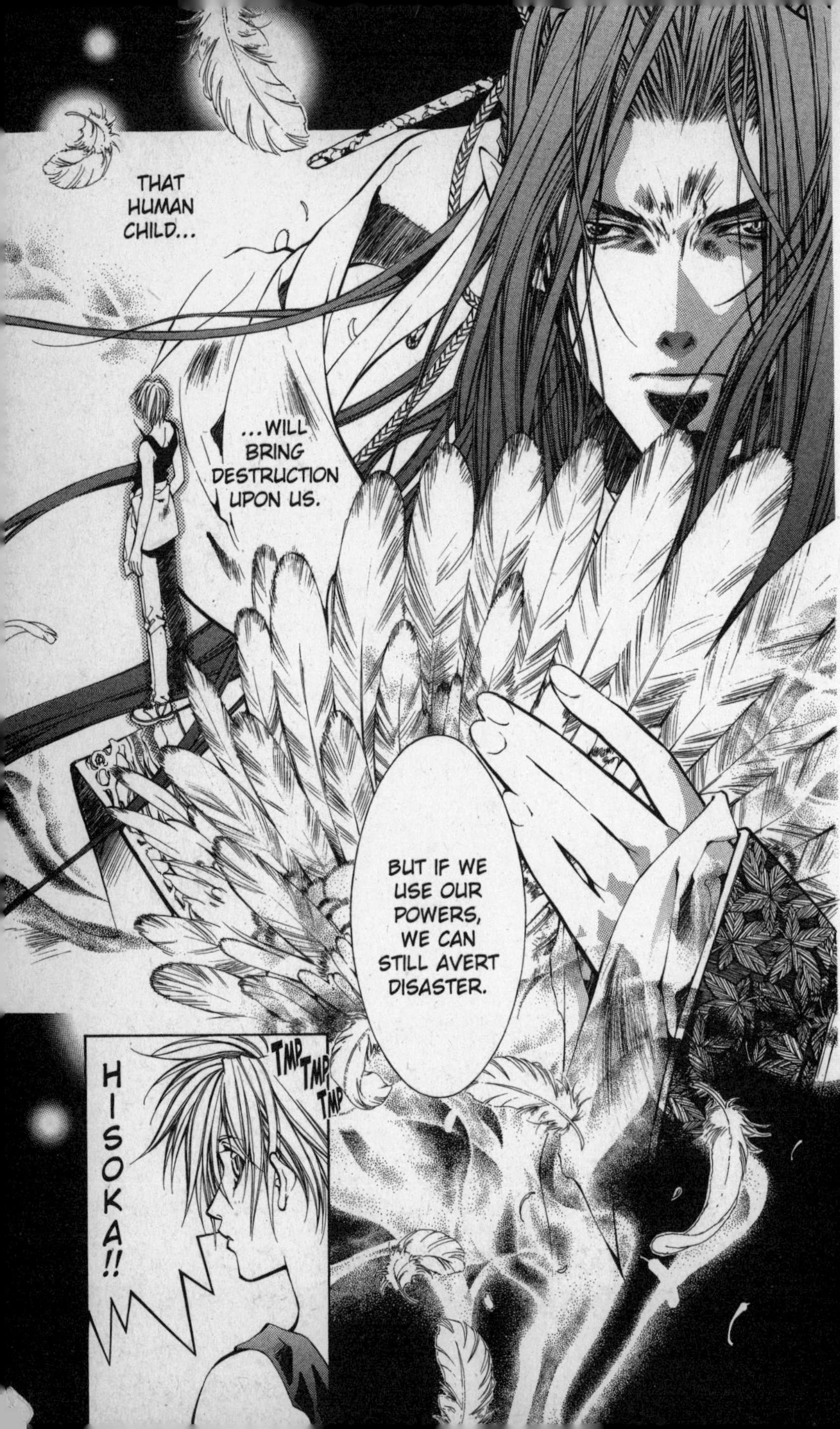
THAT HUMAN CHILD...
...WILL BRING DESTRUCTION UPON US.
BUT IF WE USE OUR POWERS, WE CAN STILL AVERT DISASTER.
TMP TMP TMP
HISOKA!!

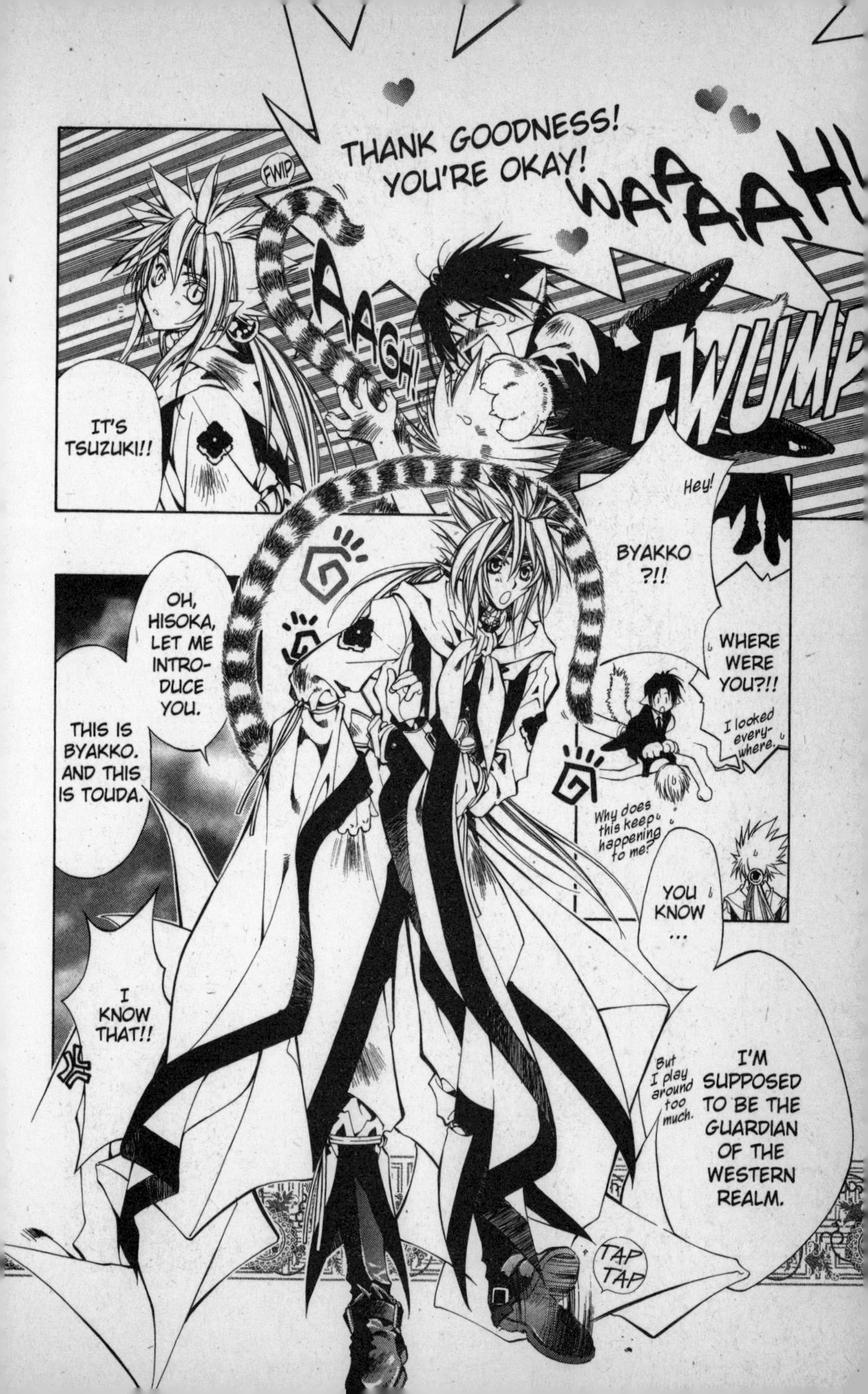
WAAAAH!
THANK GOODNESS! YOU'RE OKAY!
FWUMP
AAGH!
FWIP
IT'S TSUZUKI!!
Hey!
BYAKKO?!!
WHERE WERE YOU?!!
I looked every-where.
Why does this keep happening to me?
YOU KNOW...
I'M SUPPOSED TO BE THE GUARDIAN OF THE WESTERN REALM.
But I play around too much.
TAP TAP
OH, HISOKA, LET ME INTRO-DUCE YOU.
THIS IS BYAKKO. AND THIS IS TOUDA.
I KNOW THAT!!

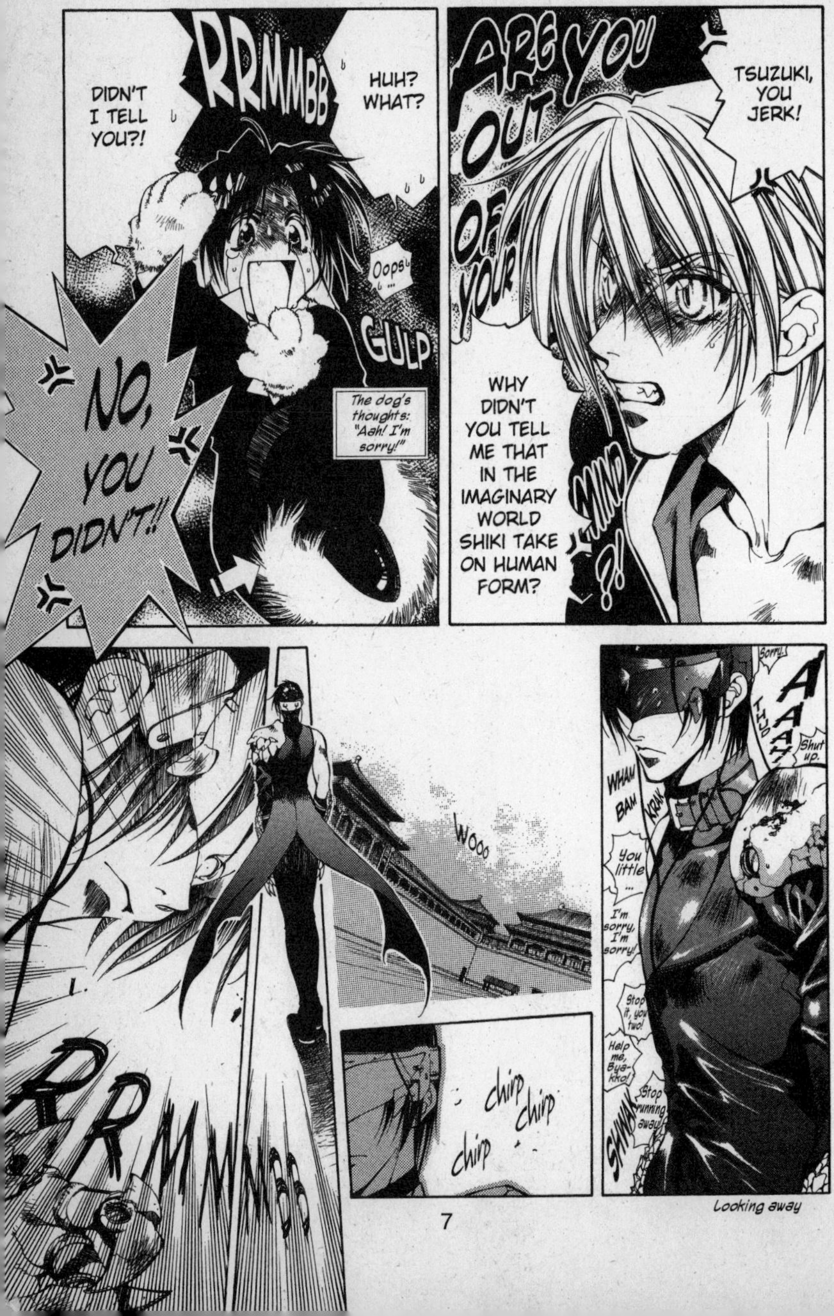

TSUZUKI, YOU JERK!
ARE YOU OUT OF YOUR MIND?!
WHY DIDN'T YOU TELL ME THAT IN THE IMAGINARY WORLD SHIKI TAKE ON HUMAN FORM?
HUH? WHAT?
RRMMBB
DIDN'T I TELL YOU?!
Oops...
GULP
The dog's thoughts: "Aah! I'm sorry!"
NO, YOU DIDN'T!!
Sorry.
AAAH!
THUD
Shut up.
WHAM
BAM
KRAK
You little...
I'm sorry, I'm sorry!
Stop it, you two!
Help me, Byakko!
Stop running away!
Looking away
WOOO
chirp chirp
chirp

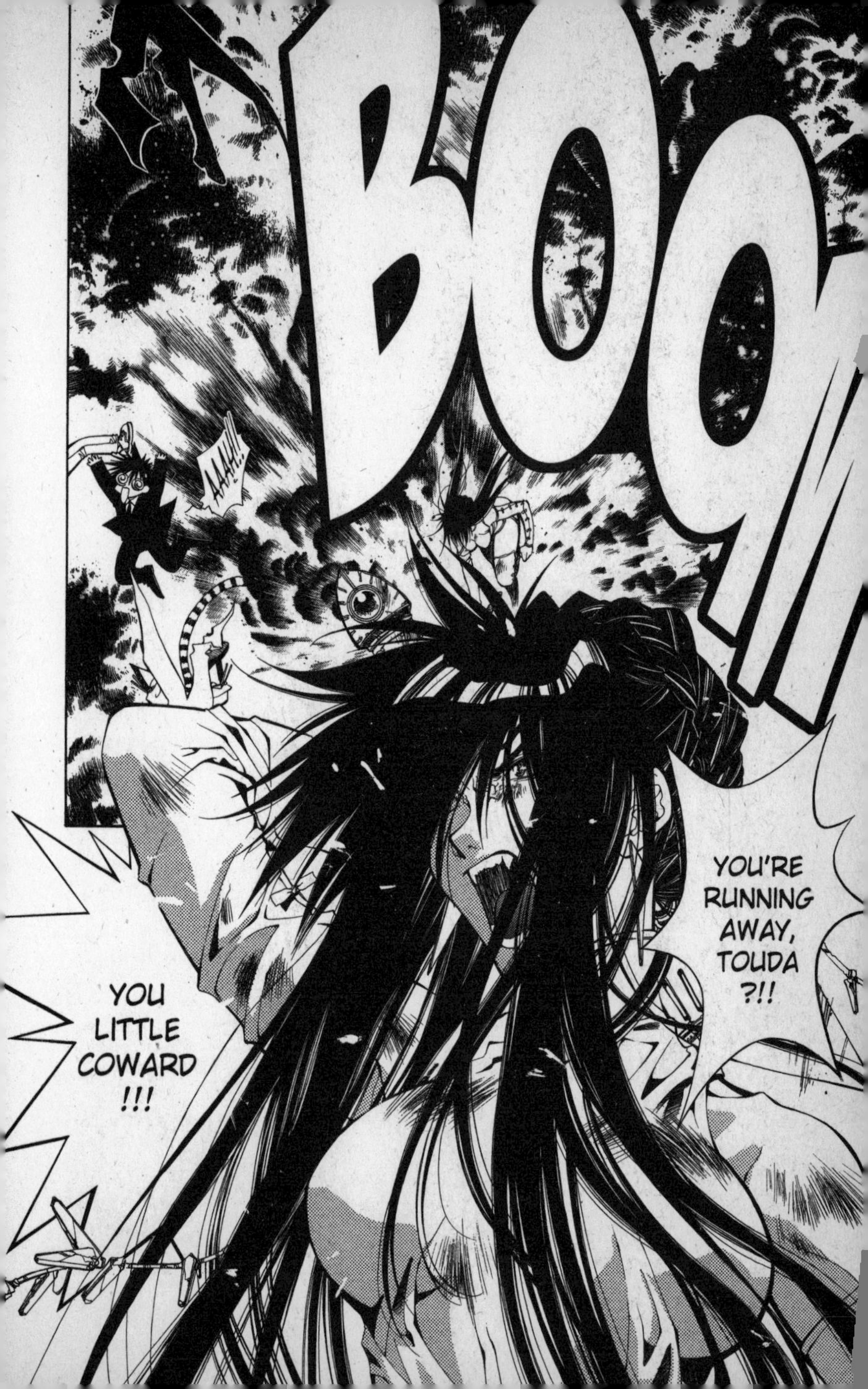
BOOM!!
AAAH!!
YOU'RE RUNNING AWAY, TOUDA ?!!
YOU LITTLE COWARD !!!

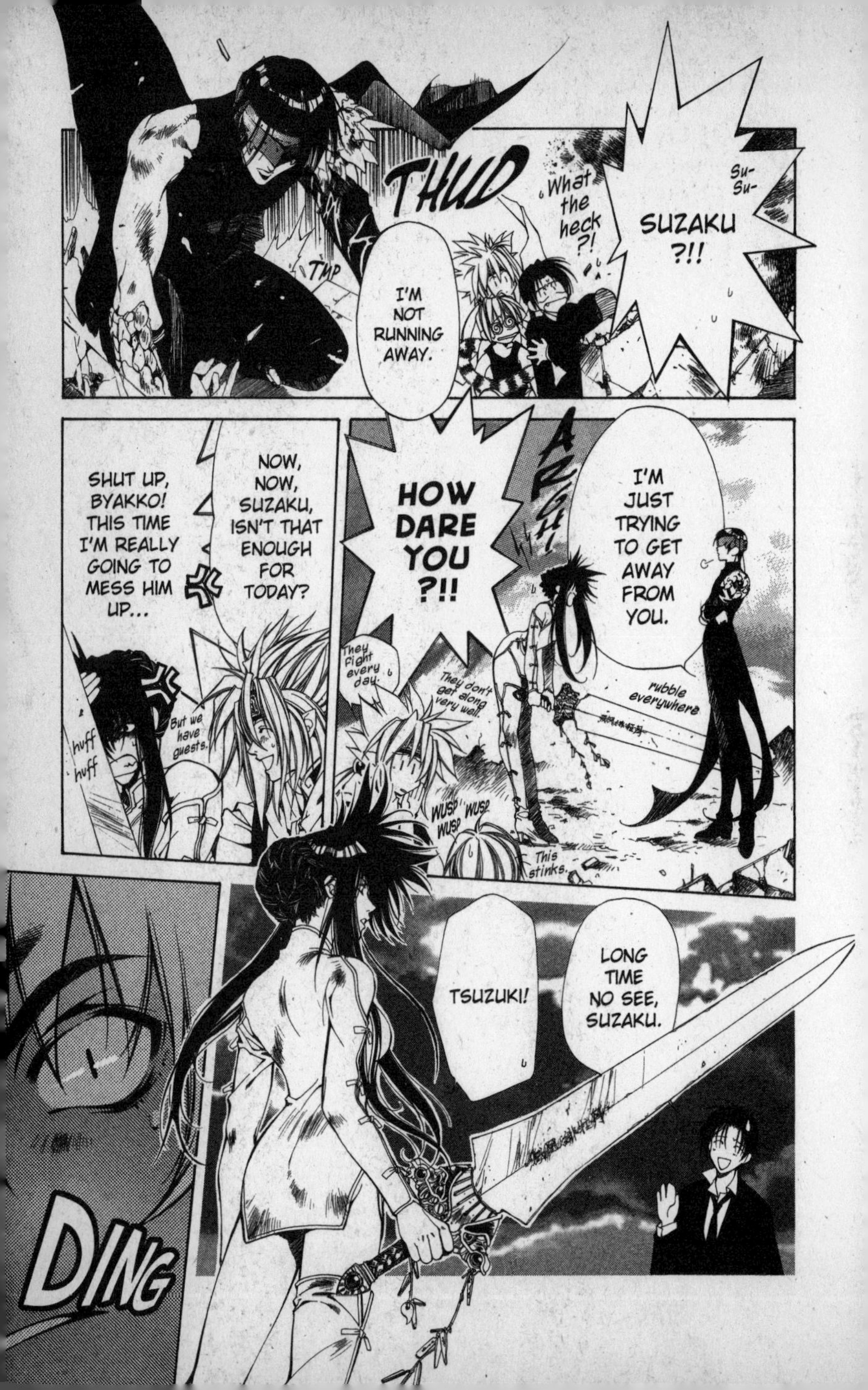

Su- Su-
SUZAKU ?!!
What the heck ?!
THUD
I'M NOT RUNNING AWAY.
TMP
I'M JUST TRYING TO GET AWAY FROM YOU.
ARGH!
HOW DARE YOU ?!!
rubble everywhere
They don't get along very well.
They fight every day.
WUSP WUSP WUSP
This stinks.
NOW, NOW, SUZAKU, ISN'T THAT ENOUGH FOR TODAY?
SHUT UP, BYAKKO! THIS TIME I'M REALLY GOING TO MESS HIM UP...
But we have guests.
huff huff
LONG TIME NO SEE, SUZAKU.
TSUZUKI!
DING

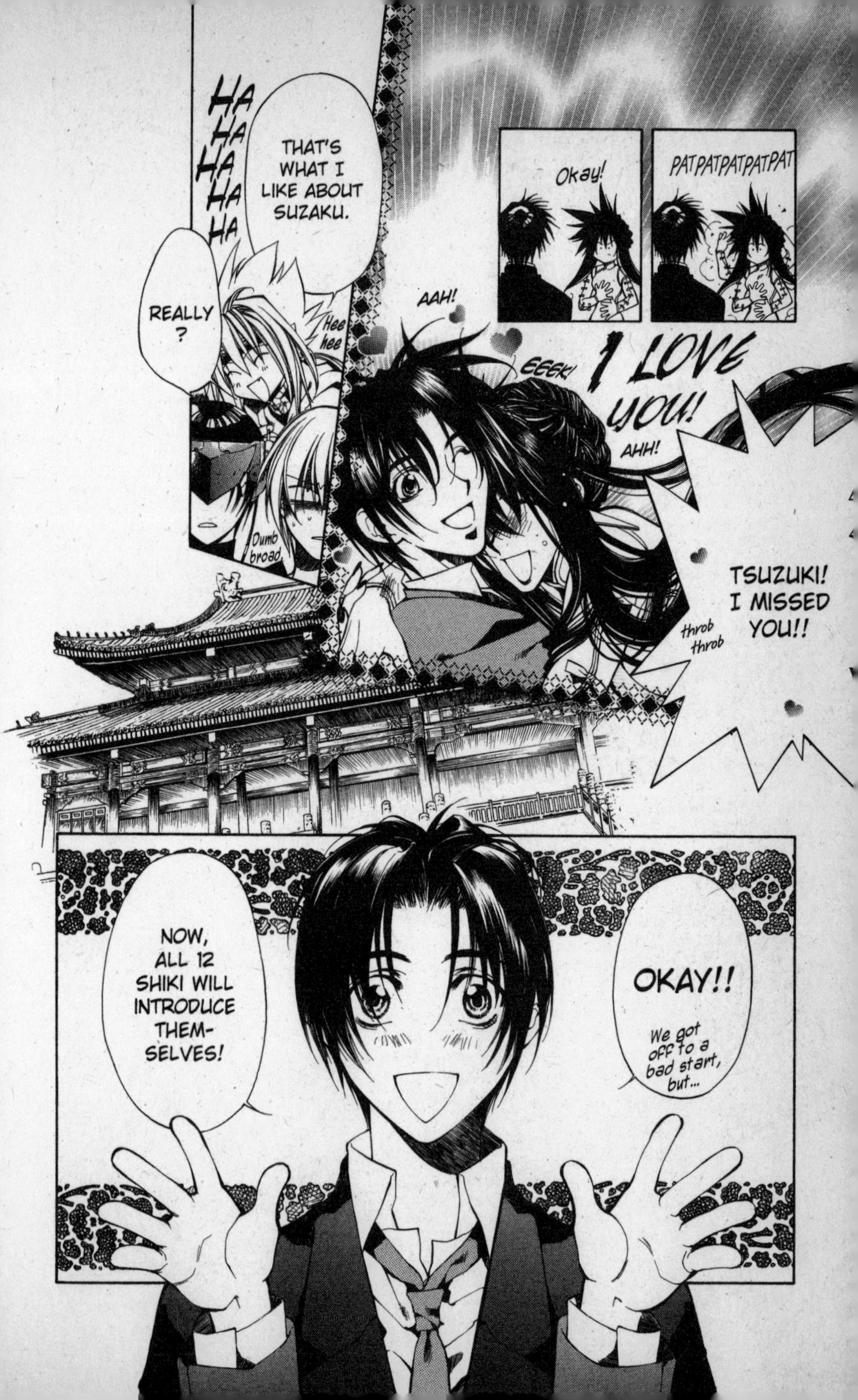
PATPATPATPATPAT
Okay!
TSUZUKI! I MISSED YOU!!
I LOVE YOU!
AHH!
EEEK!
AAH!
throb throb
THAT'S WHAT I LIKE ABOUT SUZAKU.
HA HA HA HA HA
REALLY?
Hee hee
Dumb broad.
OKAY!!
We got off to a bad start, but...
NOW, ALL 12 SHIKI WILL INTRODUCE THEM-SELVES!

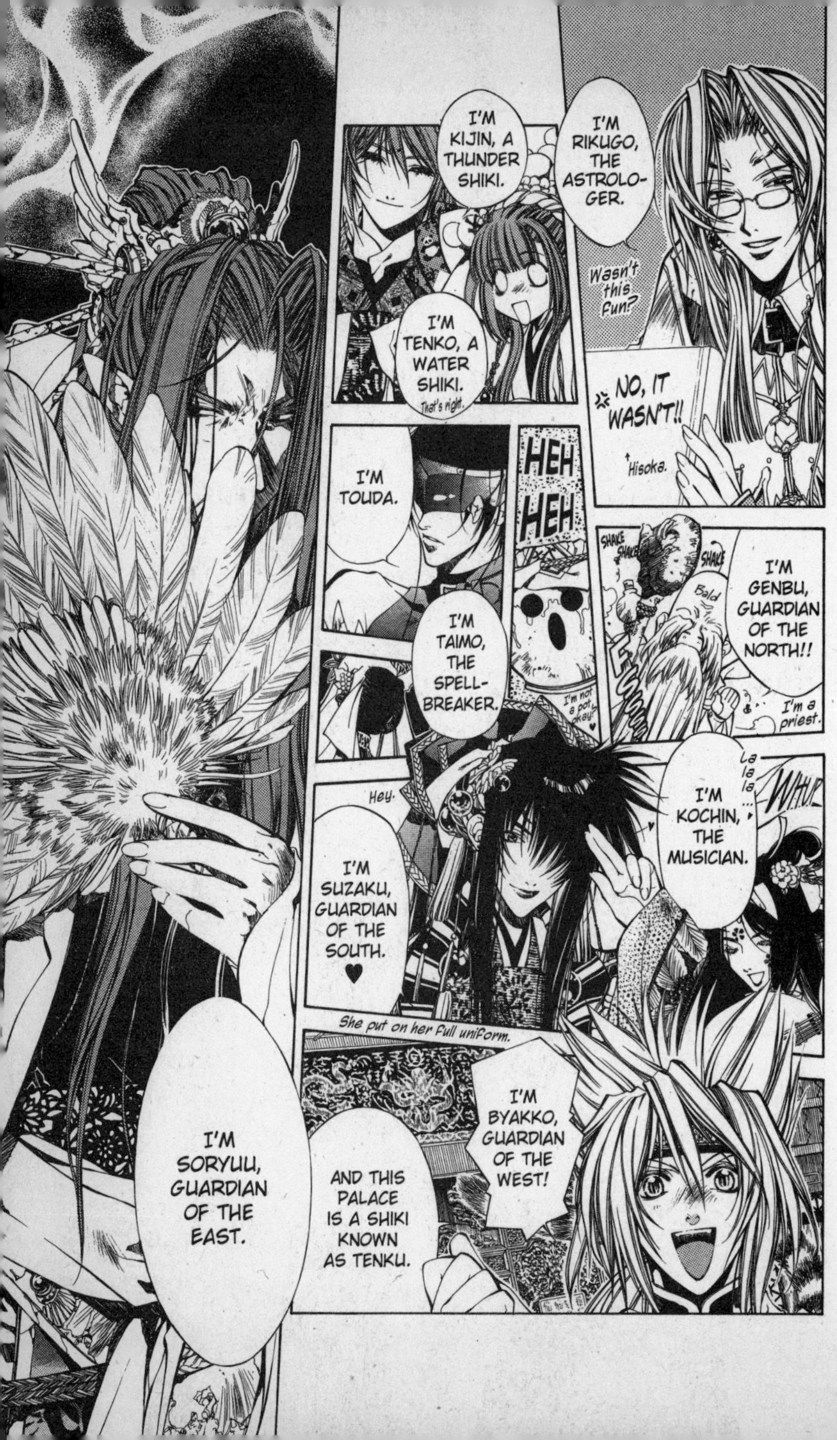
I'M RIKUGO, THE ASTROLOGER.
Wasn't this fun?
NO, IT WASN'T!!
Hisoka.
I'M KIJIN, A THUNDER SHIKI.
I'M TENKO, A WATER SHIKI.
That's right.
SHAKE SHAKE SHAKE
I'M GENBU, GUARDIAN OF THE NORTH!!
Bald
I'm a priest.
HEH HEH
I'm not a pot, okay?
I'M TOUDA.
I'M TAIMO, THE SPELL-BREAKER.
La la la...
WHUR
I'M KOCHIN, THE MUSICIAN.
Hey.
I'M SUZAKU, GUARDIAN OF THE SOUTH. ♥
She put on her full uniform.
I'M BYAKKO, GUARDIAN OF THE WEST!
I'M SORYUU, GUARDIAN OF THE EAST.
AND THIS PALACE IS A SHIKI KNOWN AS TENKU.

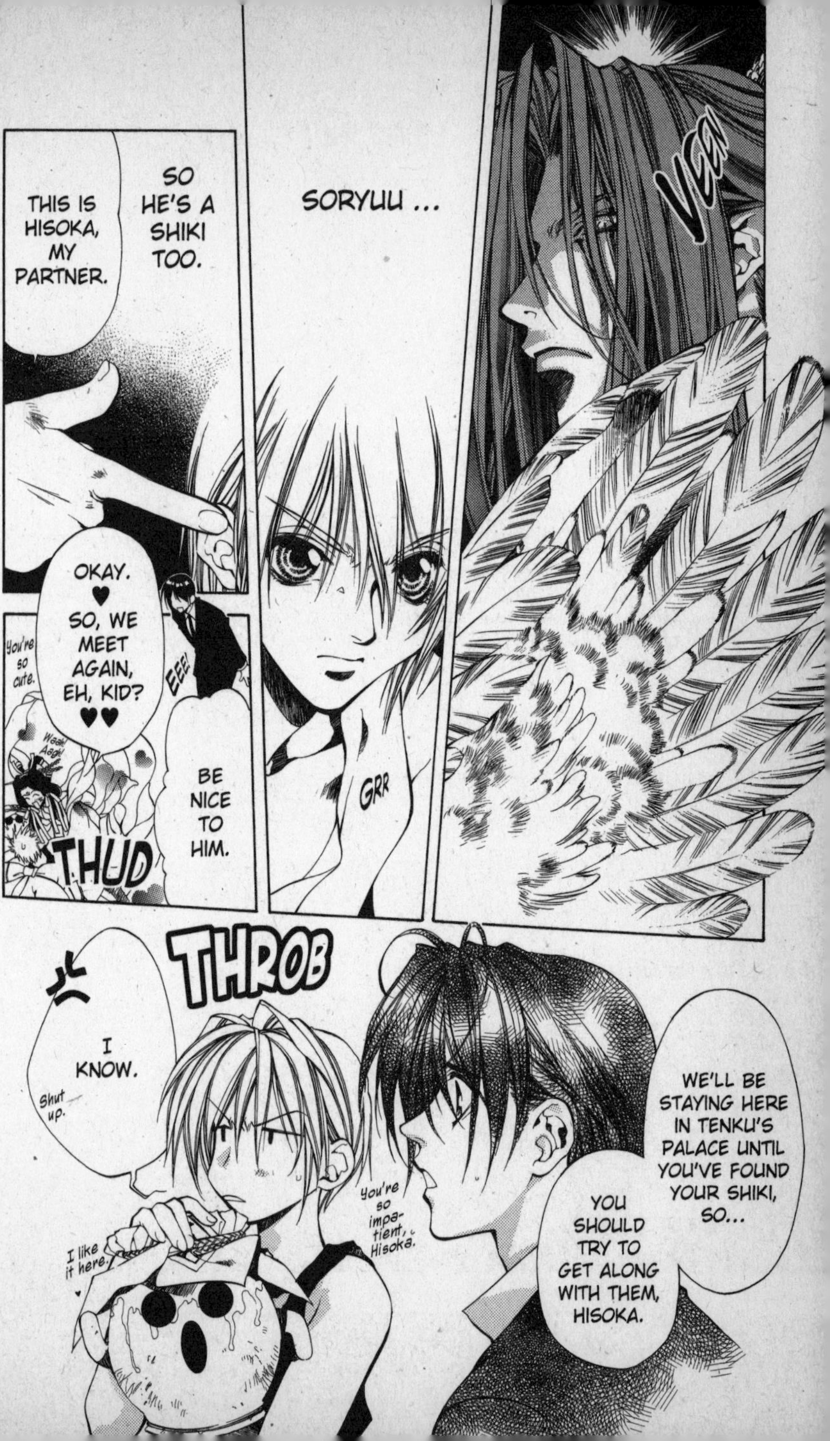
SORYUU ...
GRR
SO HE'S A SHIKI TOO.
THIS IS HISOKA, MY PARTNER.
OKAY. ♥ SO, WE MEET AGAIN, EH, KID? ♥♥
EEE!
BE NICE TO HIM.
You're so cute.
Waah! Aagh!
THUD
THROB
WE'LL BE STAYING HERE IN TENKU'S PALACE UNTIL YOU'VE FOUND YOUR SHIKI, SO...
YOU SHOULD TRY TO GET ALONG WITH THEM, HISOKA.
You're so impa-tient, Hisoka.
I KNOW.
Shut up.
I like it here.

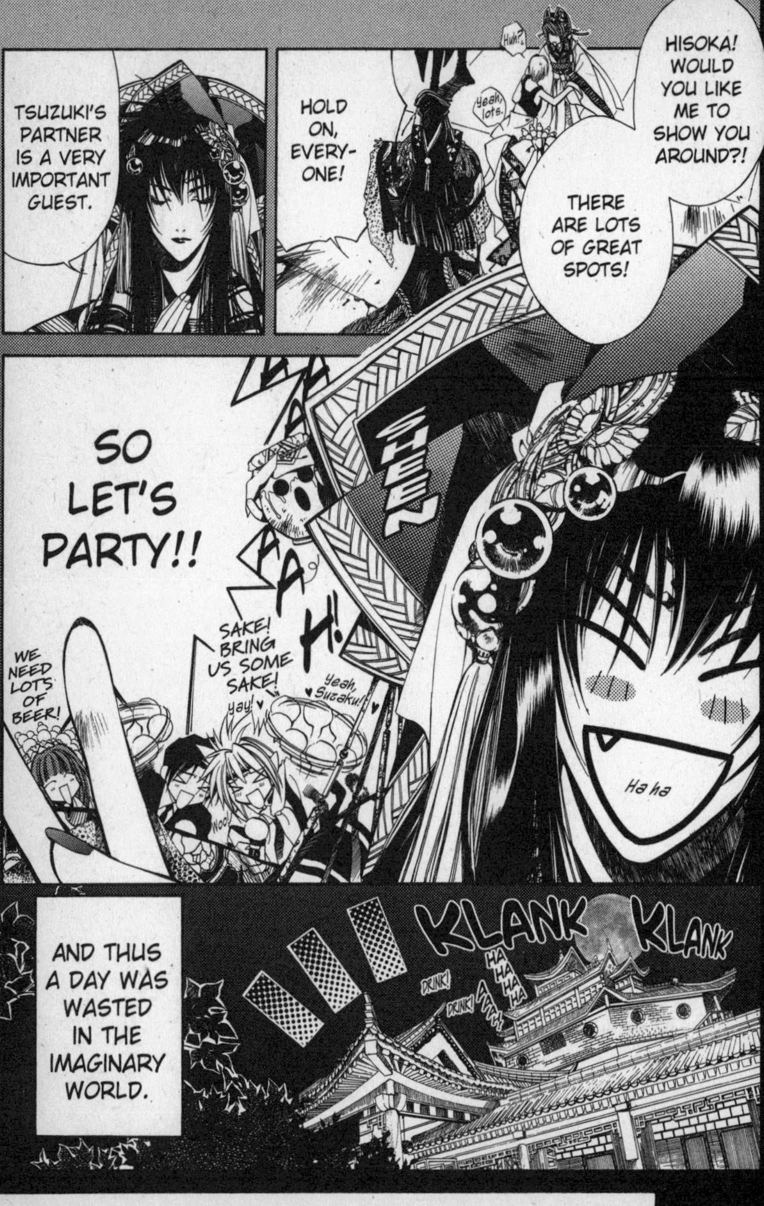
HISOKA! WOULD YOU LIKE ME TO SHOW YOU AROUND?!
Huh?
THERE ARE LOTS OF GREAT SPOTS!
Yeah, lots.
HOLD ON, EVERYONE!
TSUZUKI'S PARTNER IS A VERY IMPORTANT GUEST.
Ha ha
SO LET'S PARTY!!
Yeah, Suzaku!
yay!
SAKE! BRING US SOME SAKE!
WE NEED LOTS OF BEER!
Woo!
KLANK KLANK
HA HA HA HA
DRINK!
DRINK!
AND THUS A DAY WAS WASTED IN THE IMAGINARY WORLD.

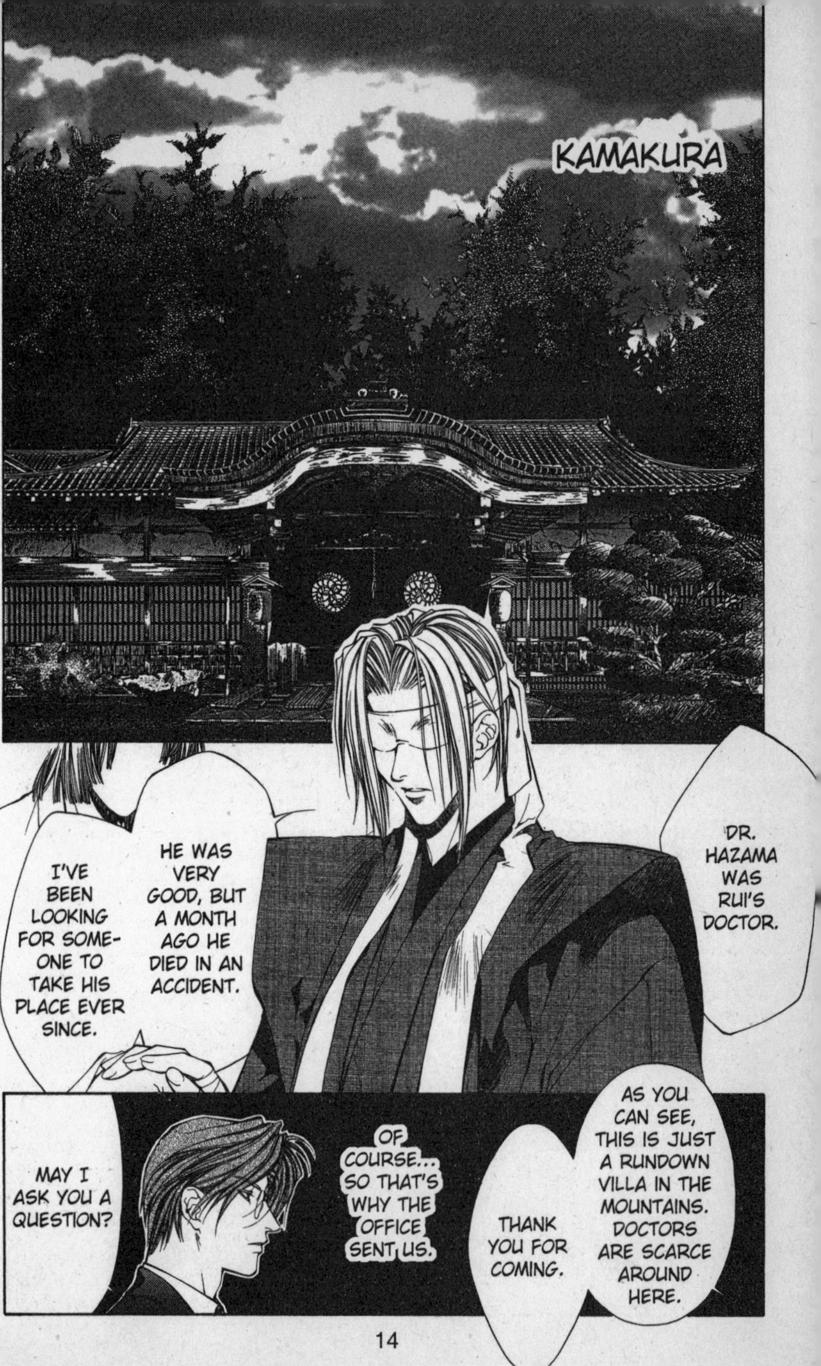
KAMAKURA
DR. HAZAMA WAS RUI'S DOCTOR.
HE WAS VERY GOOD, BUT A MONTH AGO HE DIED IN AN ACCIDENT.
I'VE BEEN LOOKING FOR SOME-ONE TO TAKE HIS PLACE EVER SINCE.
AS YOU CAN SEE, THIS IS JUST A RUNDOWN VILLA IN THE MOUNTAINS. DOCTORS ARE SCARCE AROUND HERE.
THANK YOU FOR COMING.
OF COURSE... SO THAT'S WHY THE OFFICE SENT US.
MAY I ASK YOU A QUESTION?

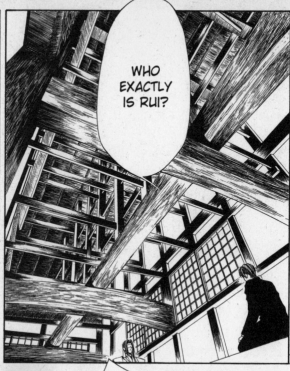

WHO EXACTLY IS RUI?
YACK
IT'S TRUE THAT WE'VE COME TO REPLACE DR. HAZAMA ...
BUT WE WEREN'T TOLD ANYTHING ABOUT THE PATIENT.
IF DR. HAZAMA LEFT ANY FILES, I'D LIKE TO SEE THEM.
YACK
YACK
YACK
YACK
YACK
So we're getting right down to business.
Getting into playing a doctor's assistant.
...
THERE ARE NO FILES.

CONGRATULATIONS TO ME!

Hooray! I made it to double digits (laugh)! Yes, this is volume 10! My schedule was very busy, but I still managed to make corrections. I had to give up playing Final Fantasy and Dragon Quest, so I was drawing through my tears. The time when I was supposed to do the corrections corresponded with the release date of some games, so it was really terrible. I wanted to play, but I couldn't. It was torture. It's times like those when I wish I were a public servant (laugh). If only they gave manga writers two weeks' vacation. (Impossible.) I really wanted to talk about the anime right now, but as I write this, it's only September and it hasn't even aired yet, so what can I say about it? Well, there are a lot of things I'd like to say about it (laugh). But I'll wait until next time. So anyway, for the subject of these quarter-page columns, I'm going to go with video games. Yeah. I don't have anything else to write about (laugh). Sorry to all of you who have no interest in them. Next time, I think I'll talk about mysteries and dramas, so let me know if you have any requests (laugh).

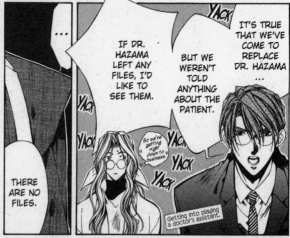

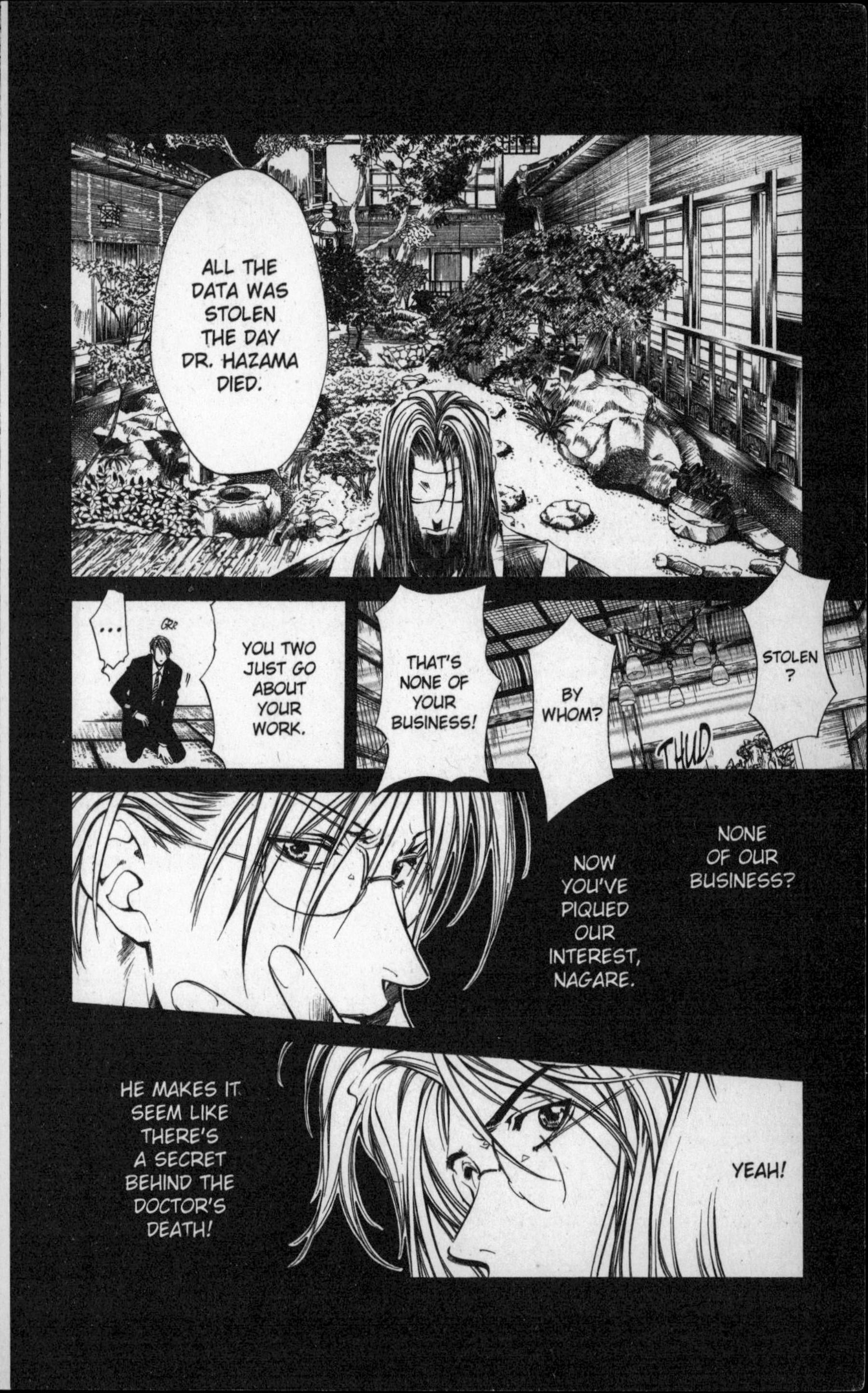
ALL THE DATA WAS STOLEN THE DAY DR. HAZAMA DIED.
STOLEN ?
THUD
BY WHOM?
THAT'S NONE OF YOUR BUSINESS!
YOU TWO JUST GO ABOUT YOUR WORK.
...
GRR
NONE OF OUR BUSINESS?
NOW YOU'VE PIQUED OUR INTEREST, NAGARE.
YEAH!
HE MAKES IT SEEM LIKE THERE'S A SECRET BEHIND THE DOCTOR'S DEATH!

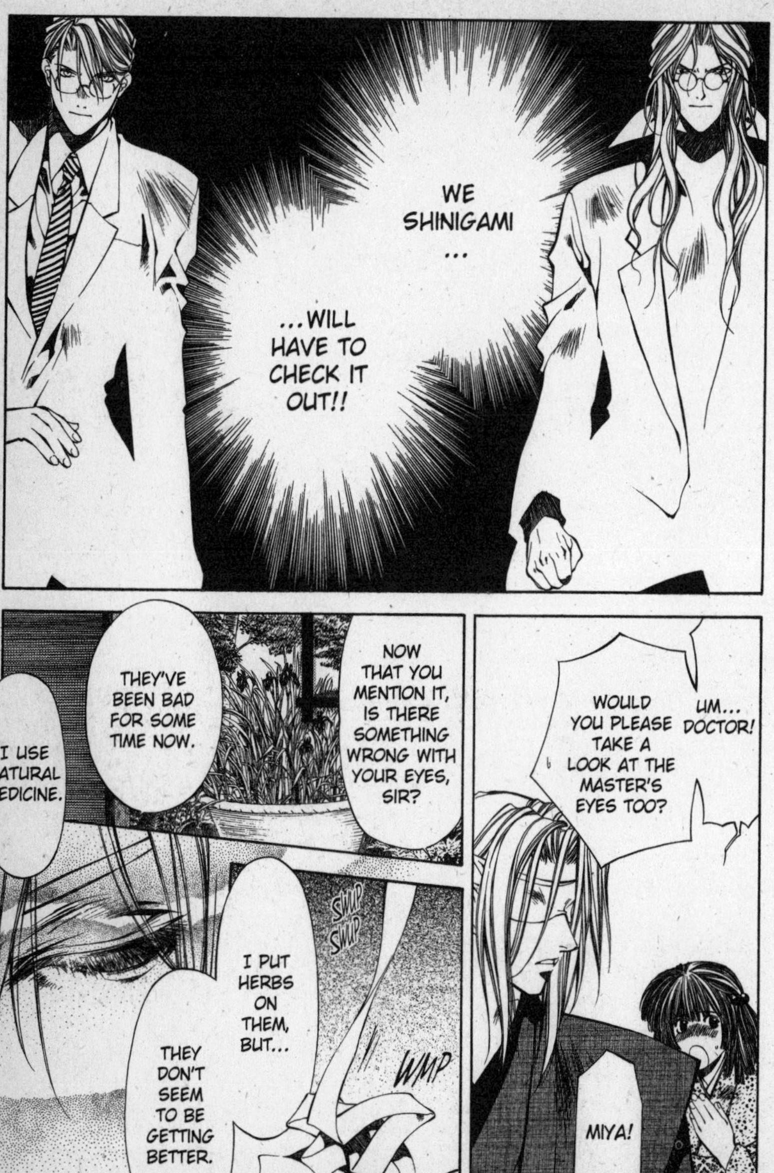
WE SHINIGAMI ...
...WILL HAVE TO CHECK IT OUT!!
UM... DOCTOR!
WOULD YOU PLEASE TAKE A LOOK AT THE MASTER'S EYES TOO?
MIYA!
NOW THAT YOU MENTION IT, IS THERE SOMETHING WRONG WITH YOUR EYES, SIR?
THEY'VE BEEN BAD FOR SOME TIME NOW.
I USE NATURAL MEDICINE.
SWIP SWIP
I PUT HERBS ON THEM, BUT...
WMP
THEY DON'T SEEM TO BE GETTING BETTER.

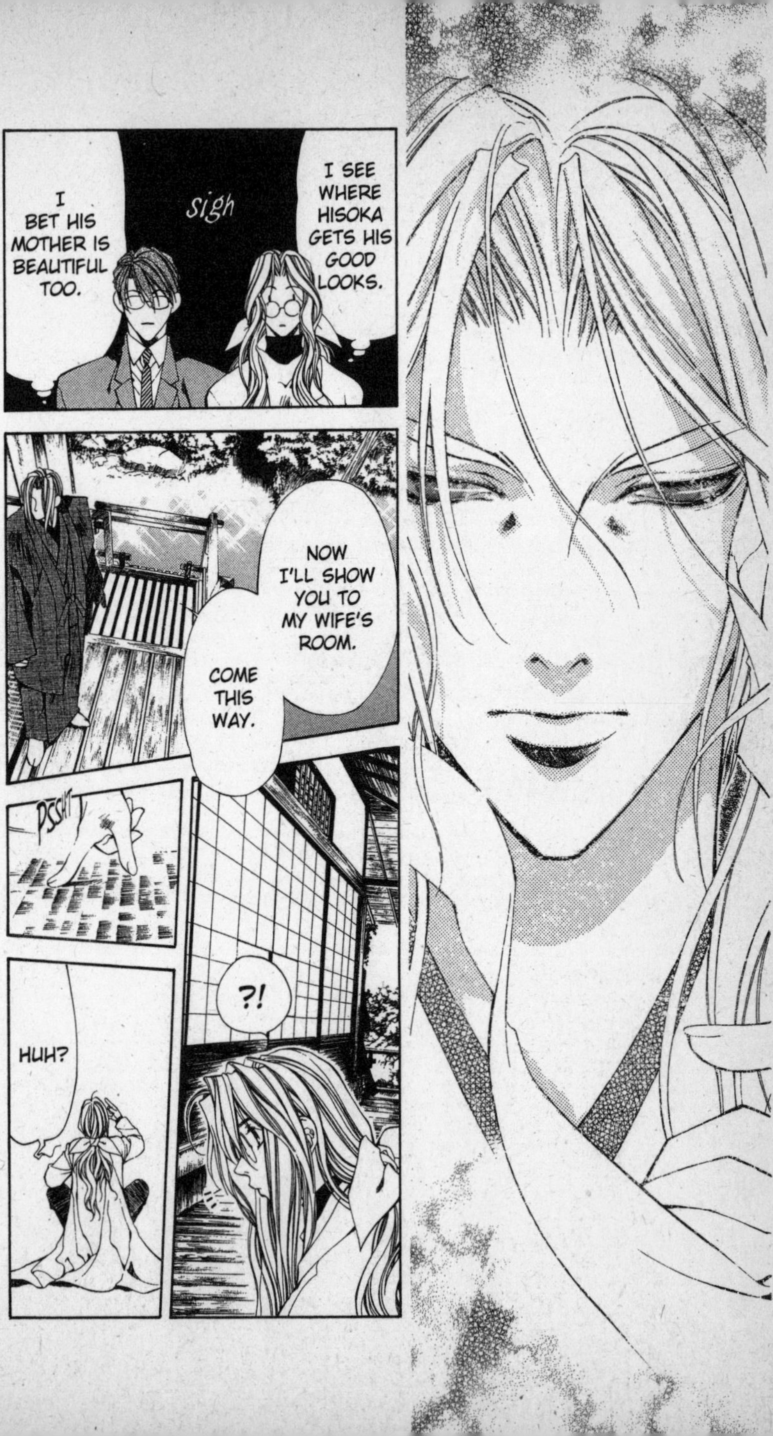
I SEE WHERE HISOKA GETS HIS GOOD LOOKS.
sigh
I BET HIS MOTHER IS BEAUTIFUL TOO.
NOW I'LL SHOW YOU TO MY WIFE'S ROOM.
COME THIS WAY.
?!
PSSHT
HUH?

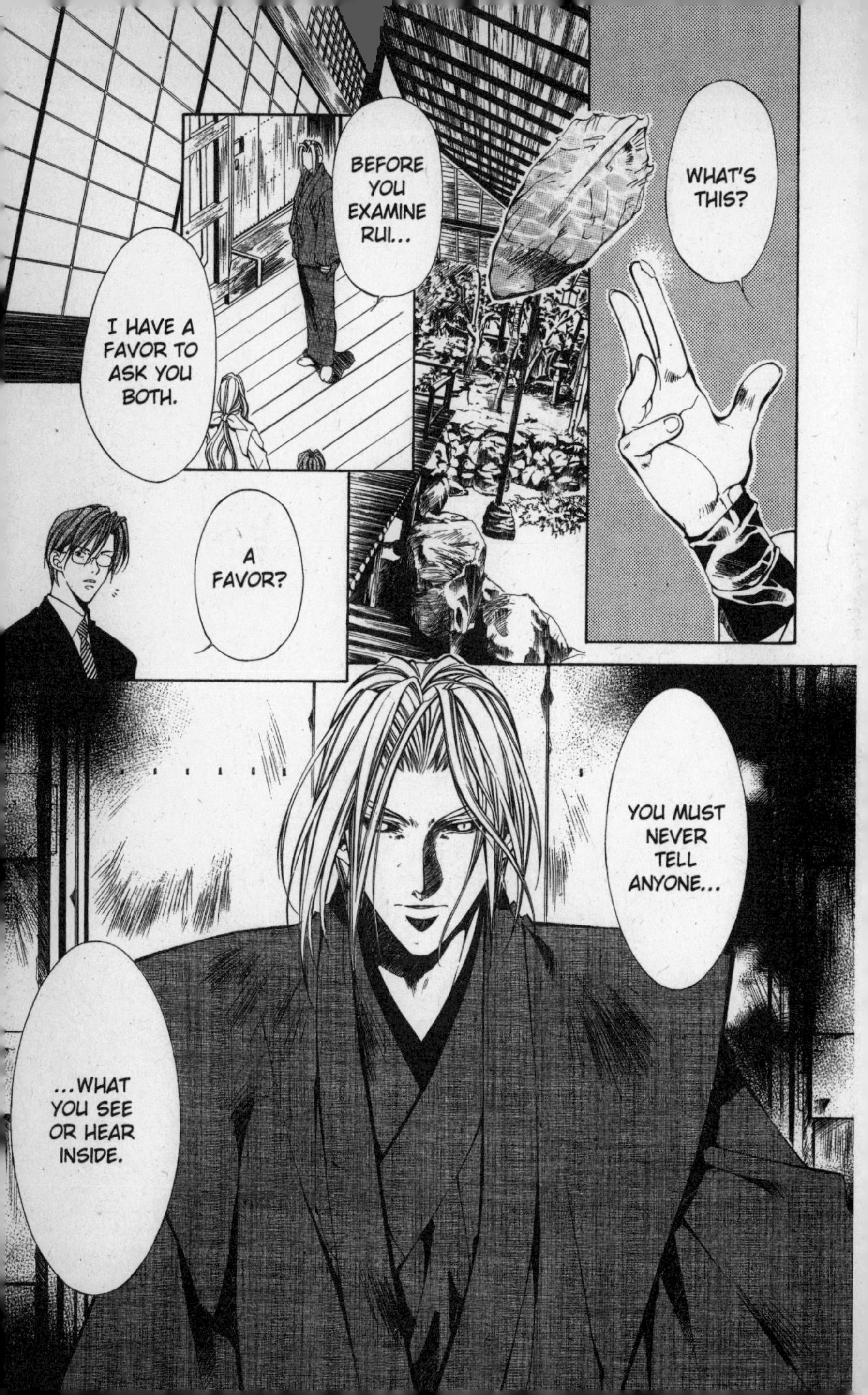
WHAT'S THIS?
BEFORE YOU EXAMINE RUI...
I HAVE A FAVOR TO ASK YOU BOTH.
A FAVOR?
YOU MUST NEVER TELL ANYONE...
...WHAT YOU SEE OR HEAR INSIDE.

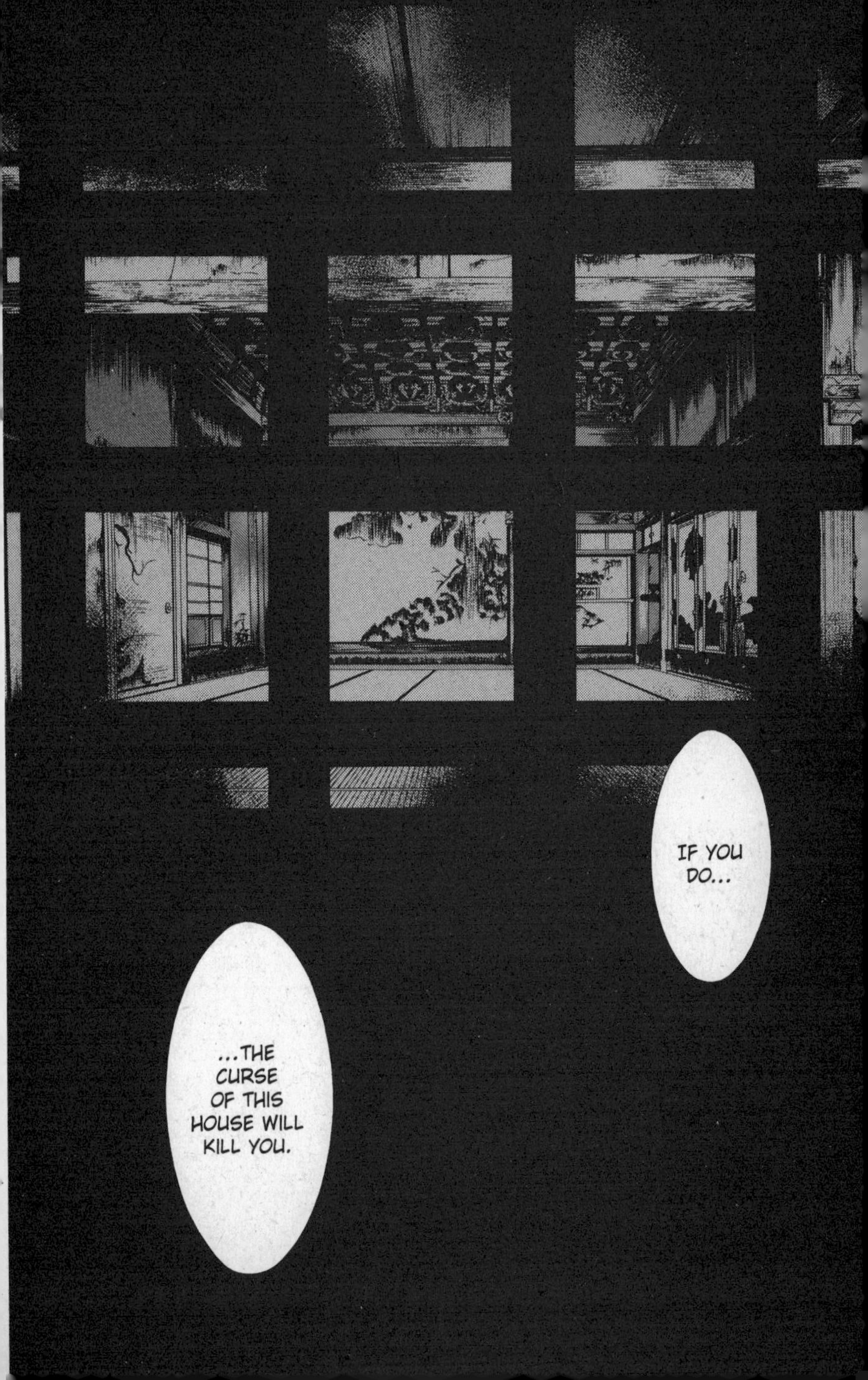
IF YOU DO...
...THE CURSE OF THIS HOUSE WILL KILL YOU.

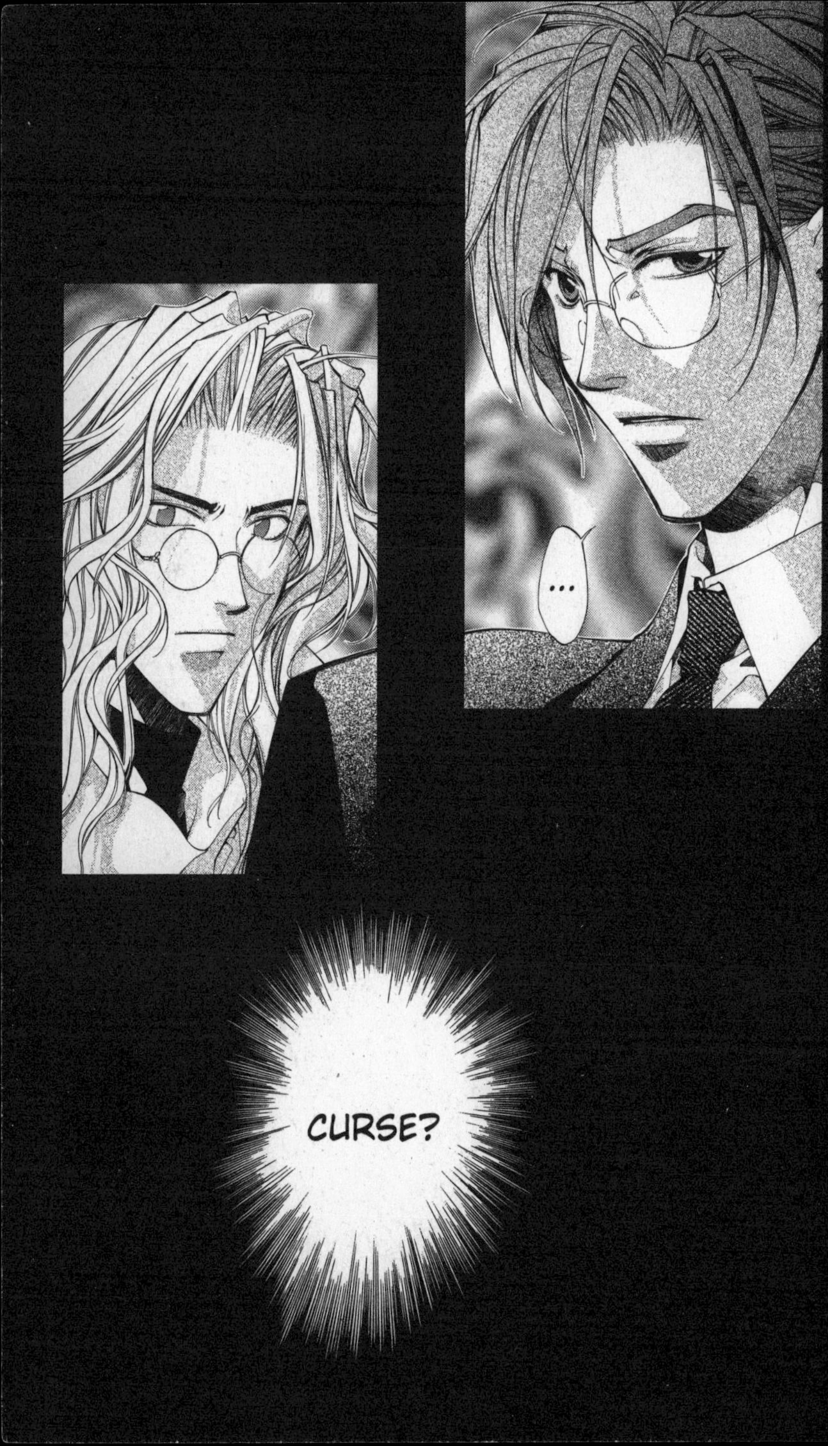
...
CURSE?

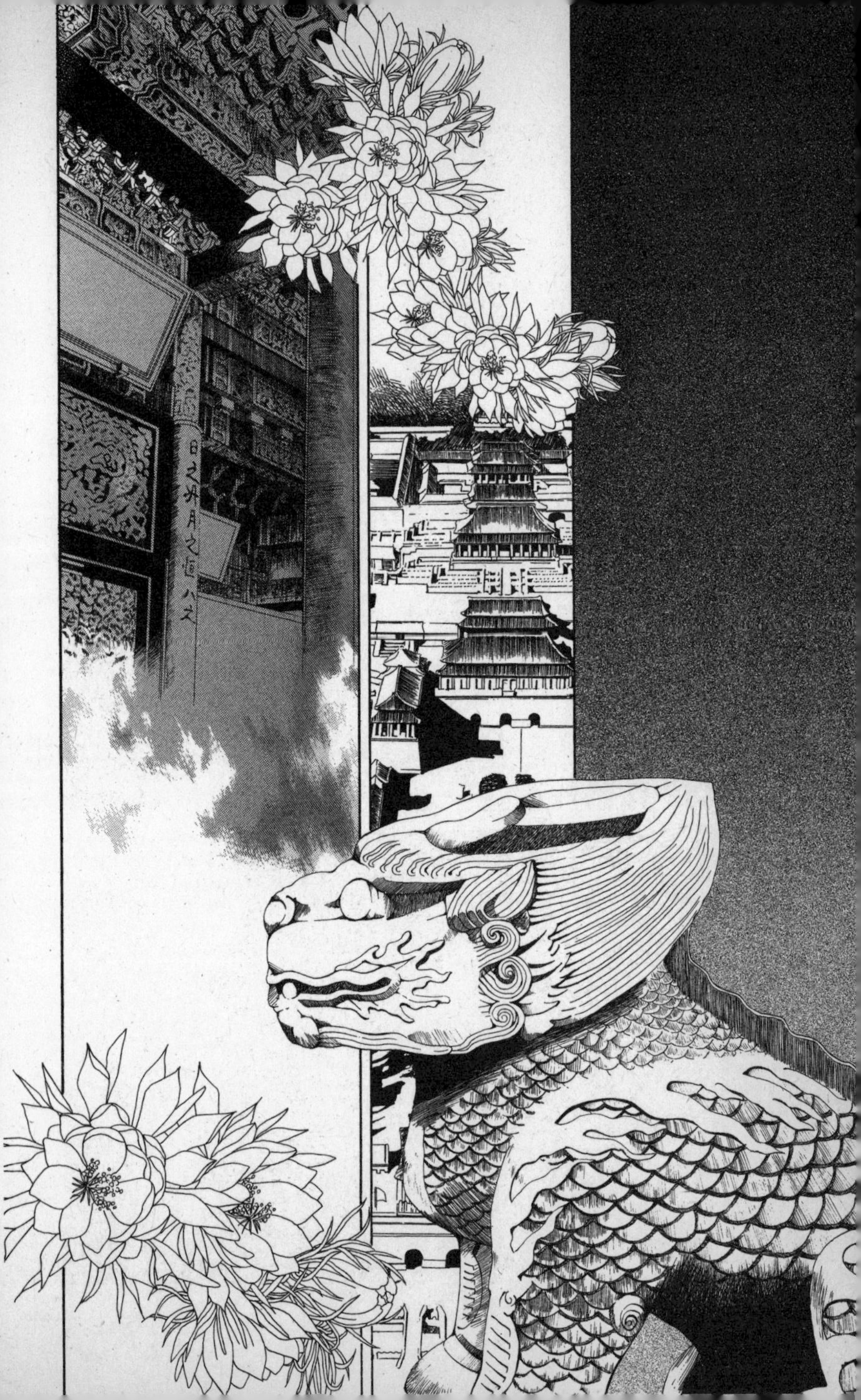
日之升月之恒八之

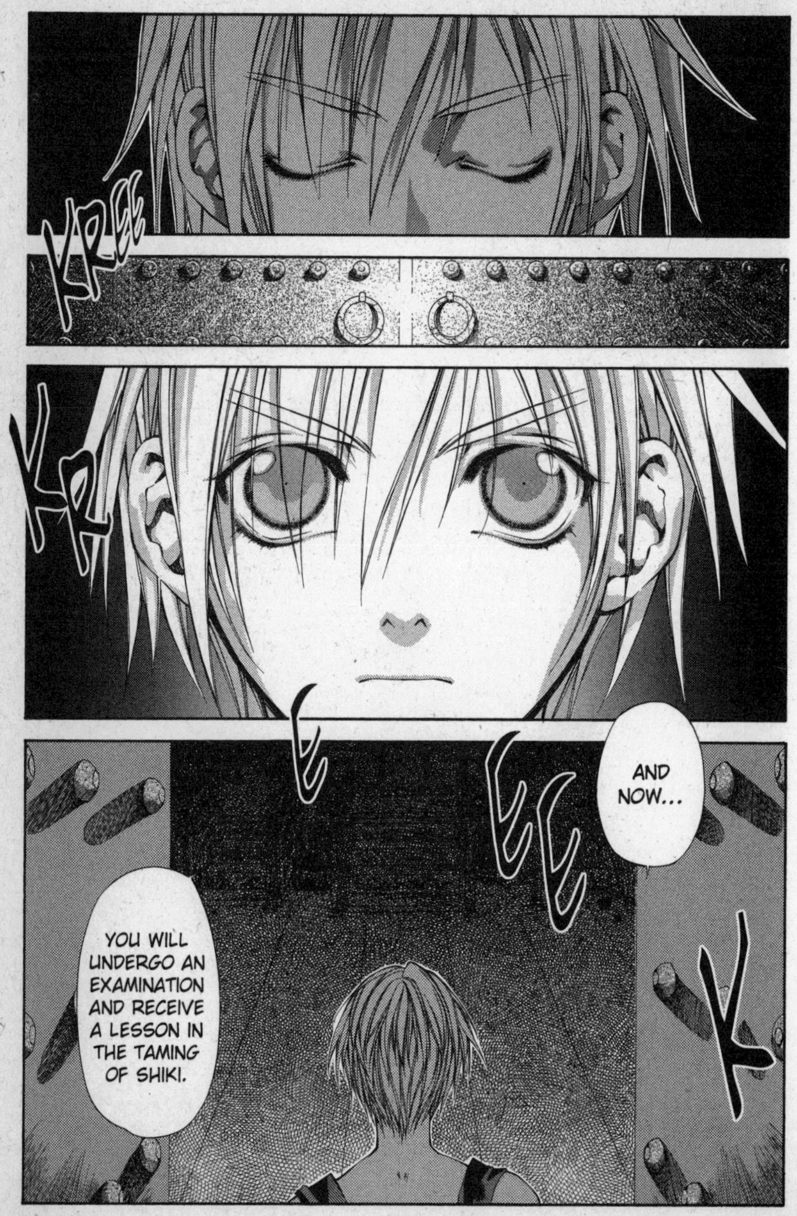
KREE
KR
EEEE
AND NOW...
K
YOU WILL UNDERGO AN EXAMINATION AND RECEIVE A LESSON IN THE TAMING OF SHIKI.

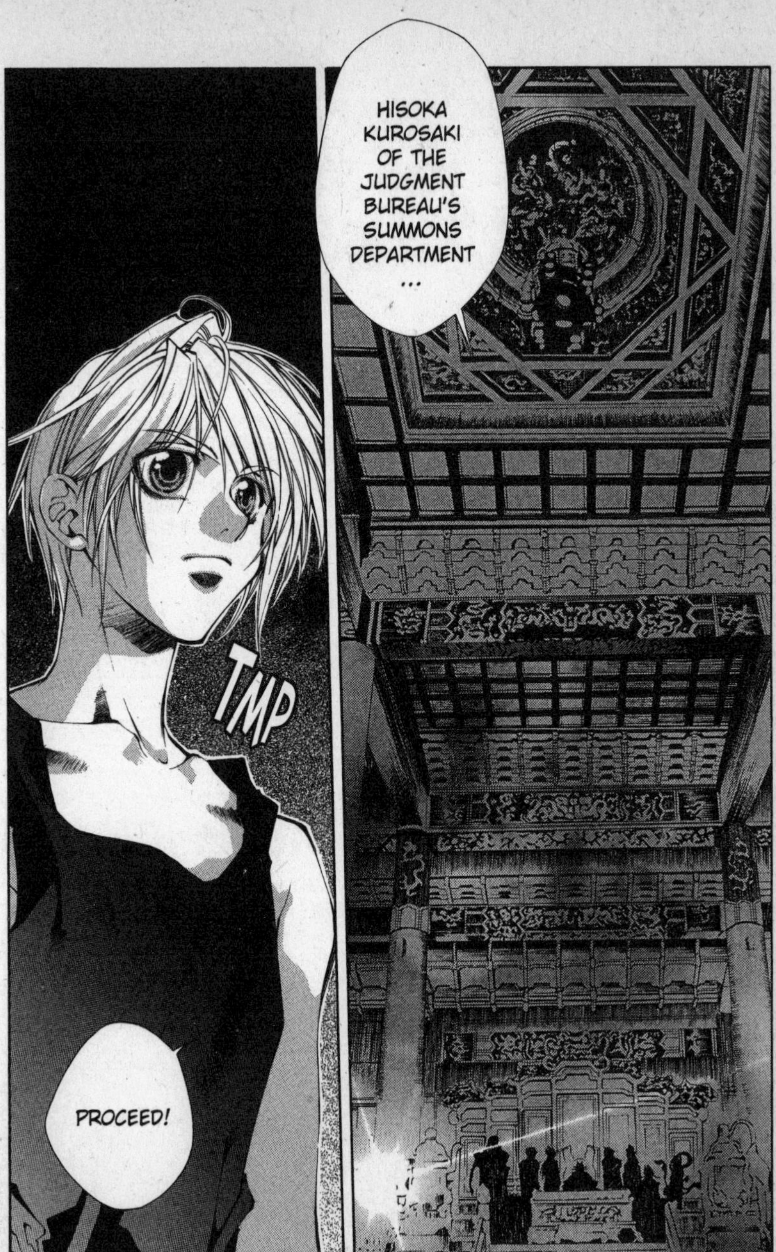
HISOKA KUROSAKI OF THE JUDGMENT BUREAU'S SUMMONS DEPARTMENT ...
TMP
PROCEED!

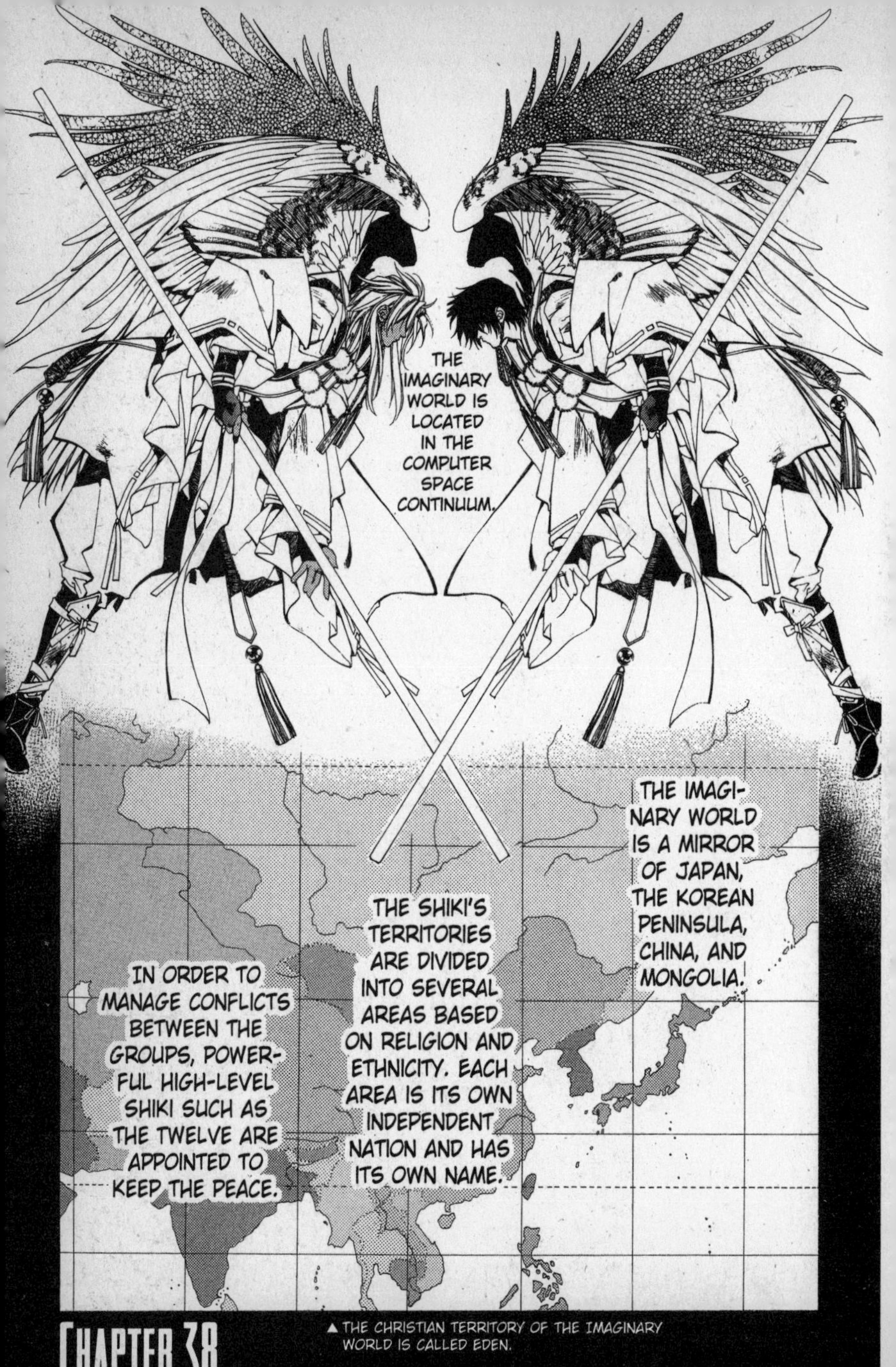
THE IMAGINARY WORLD IS LOCATED IN THE COMPUTER SPACE CONTINUUM.
THE IMAGINARY WORLD IS A MIRROR OF JAPAN, THE KOREAN PENINSULA, CHINA, AND MONGOLIA.
THE SHIKI'S TERRITORIES ARE DIVIDED INTO SEVERAL AREAS BASED ON RELIGION AND ETHNICITY. EACH AREA IS ITS OWN INDEPENDENT NATION AND HAS ITS OWN NAME.
IN ORDER TO MANAGE CONFLICTS BETWEEN THE GROUPS, POWERFUL HIGH-LEVEL SHIKI SUCH AS THE TWELVE ARE APPOINTED TO KEEP THE PEACE.

▲THE CHRISTIAN TERRITORY OF THE IMAGINARY WORLD IS CALLED EDEN.

CHAPTER 38

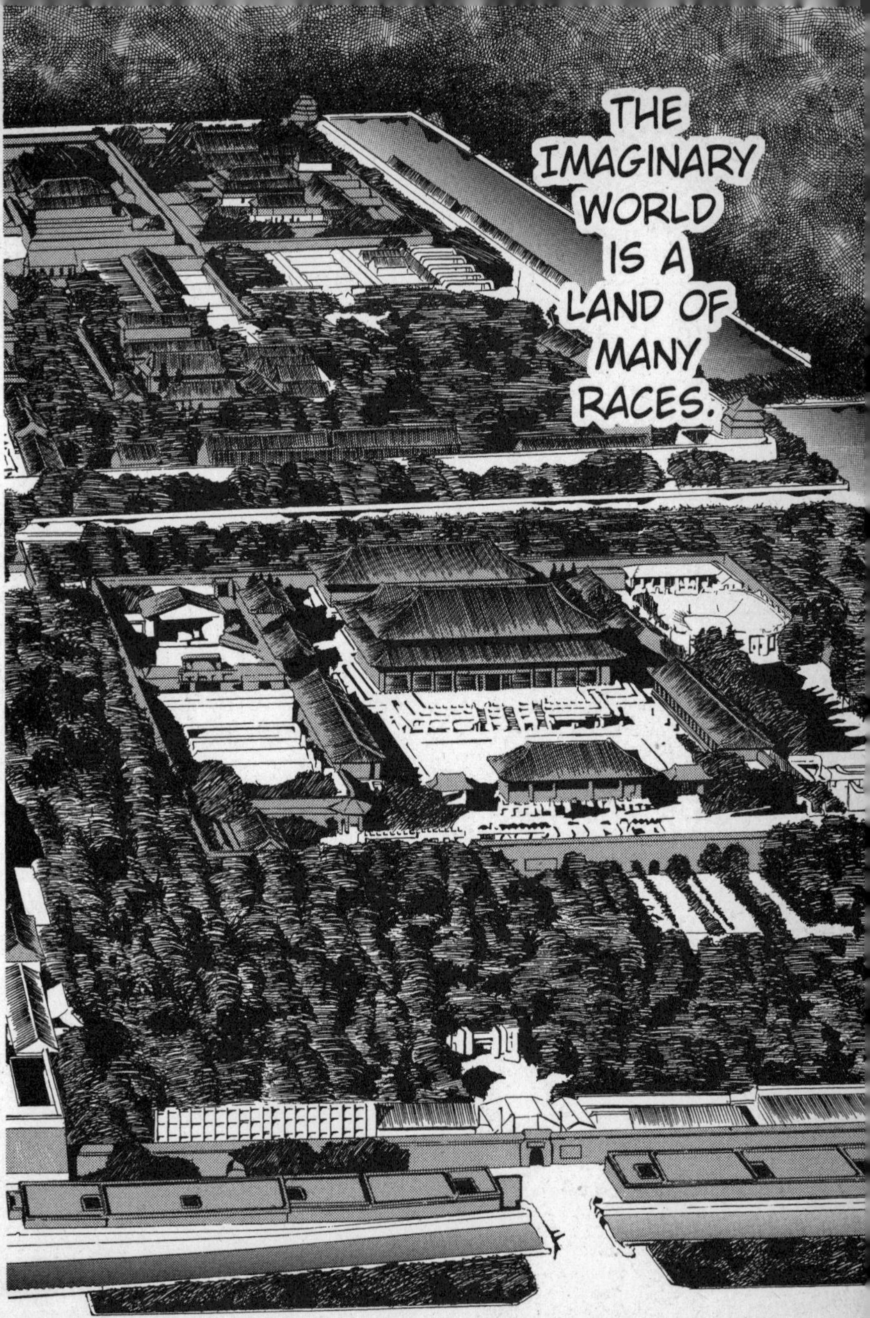
THE IMAGINARY WORLD IS A LAND OF MANY RACES.

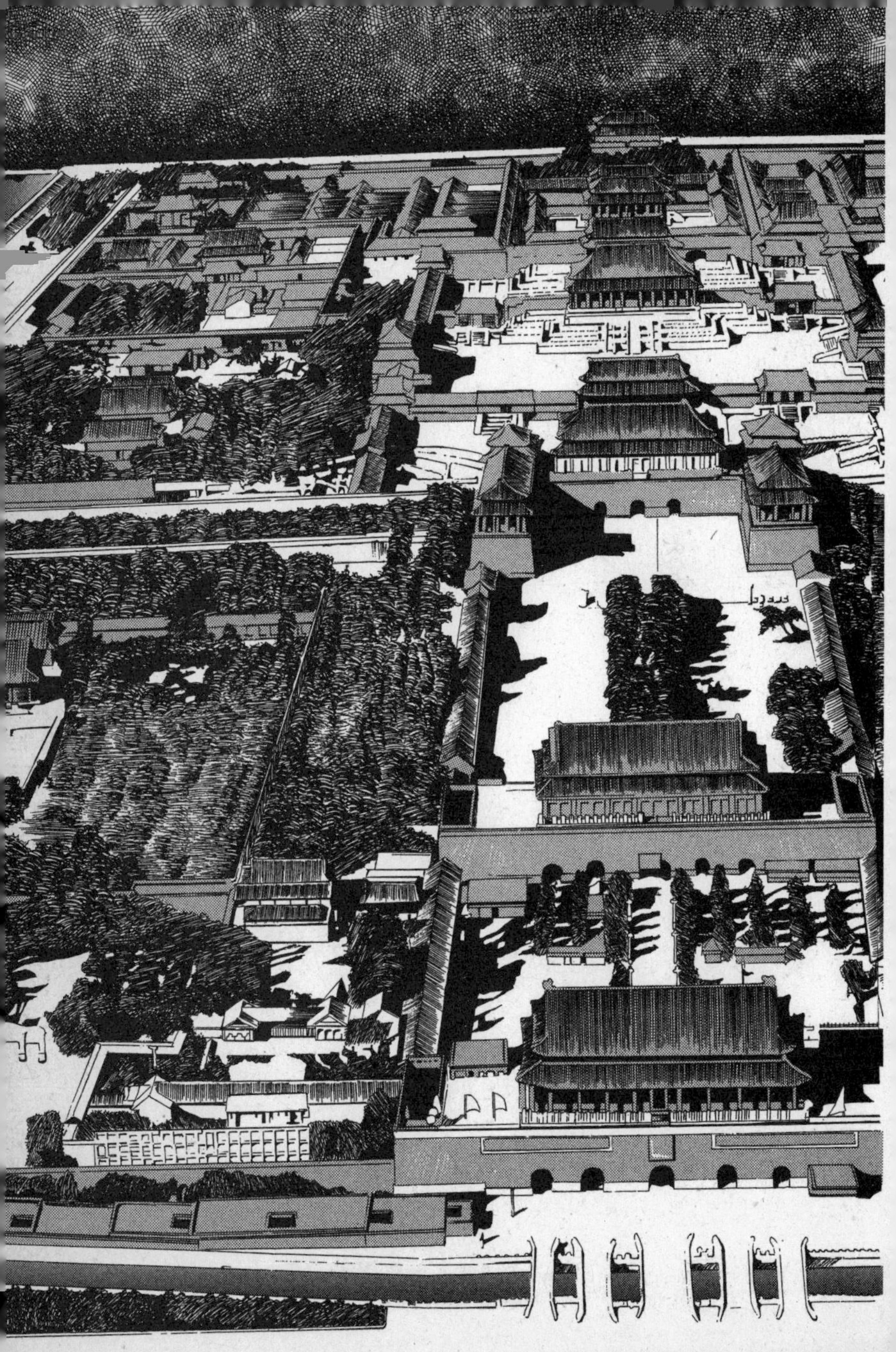

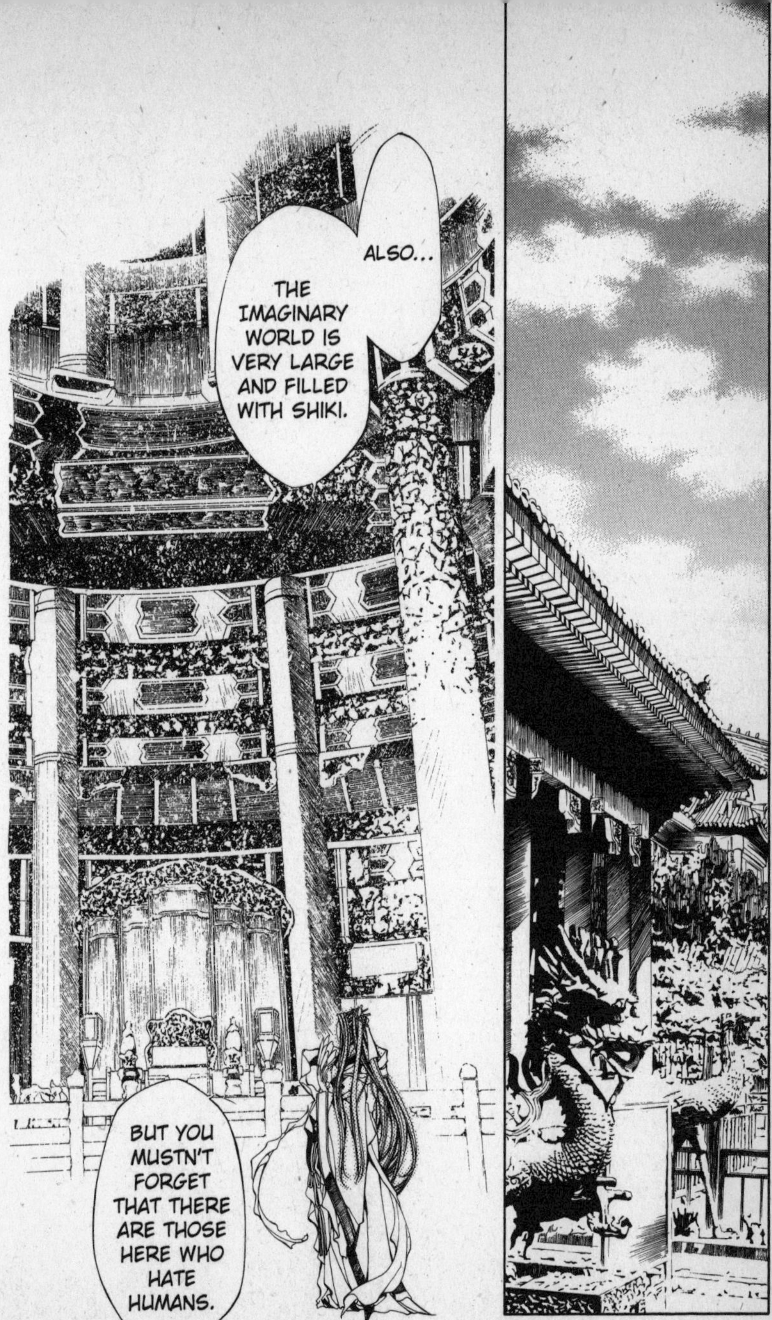
ALSO...
THE IMAGINARY WORLD IS VERY LARGE AND FILLED WITH SHIKI.
BUT YOU MUSTN'T FORGET THAT THERE ARE THOSE HERE WHO HATE HUMANS.

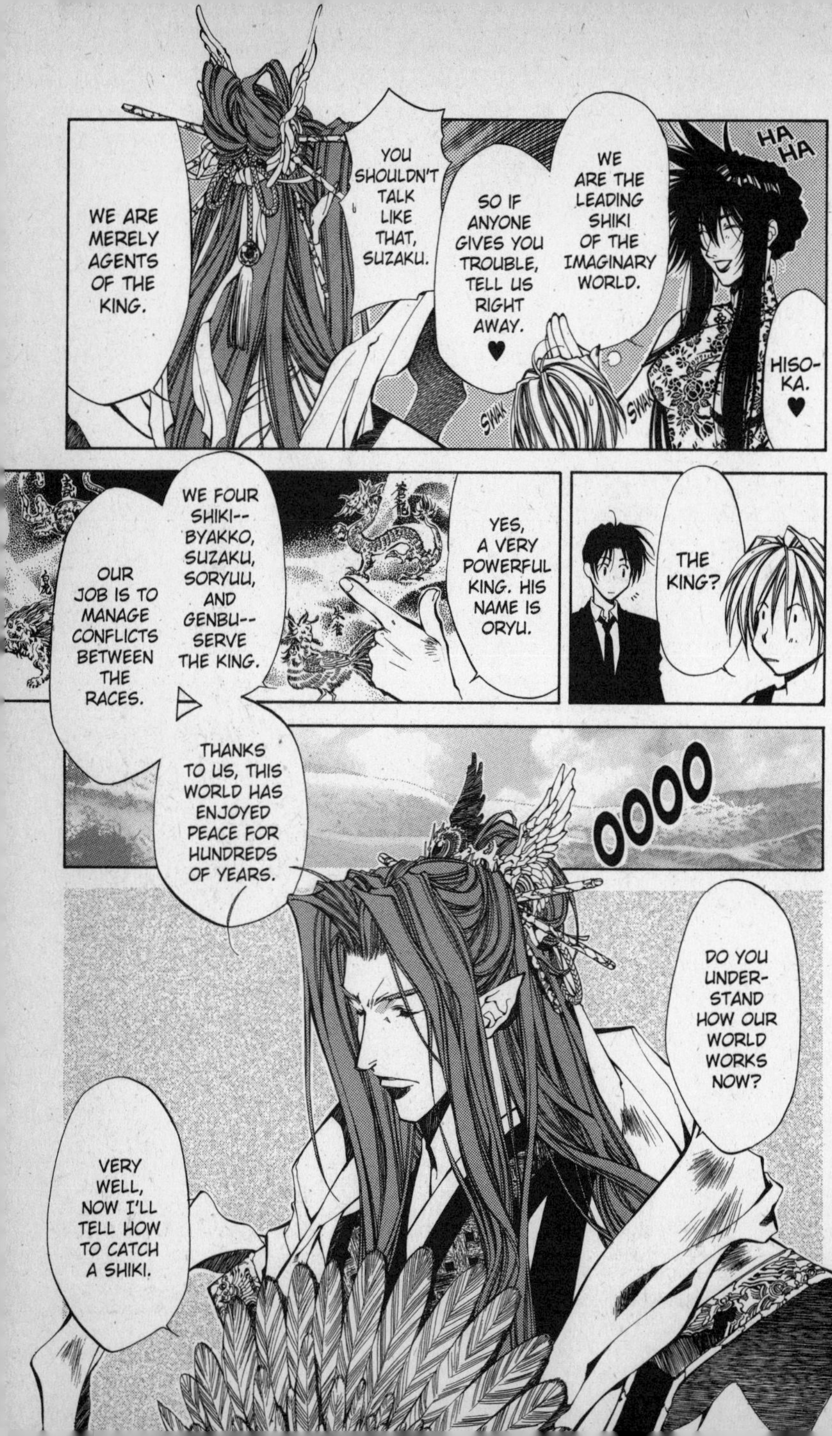
HA HA
HISO-KA. ♥
WE ARE THE LEADING SHIKI OF THE IMAGINARY WORLD.
SO IF ANYONE GIVES YOU TROUBLE, TELL US RIGHT AWAY. ♥
SWAK SWAK
YOU SHOULDN'T TALK LIKE THAT, SUZAKU.
WE ARE MERELY AGENTS OF THE KING.
THE KING?
YES, A VERY POWERFUL KING. HIS NAME IS ORYU.
WE FOUR SHIKI--BYAKKO, SUZAKU, SORYUU, AND GENBU--SERVE THE KING.
OUR JOB IS TO MANAGE CONFLICTS BETWEEN THE RACES.
OOOO
THANKS TO US, THIS WORLD HAS ENJOYED PEACE FOR HUNDREDS OF YEARS.
DO YOU UNDERSTAND HOW OUR WORLD WORKS NOW?
VERY WELL, NOW I'LL TELL HOW TO CATCH A SHIKI.

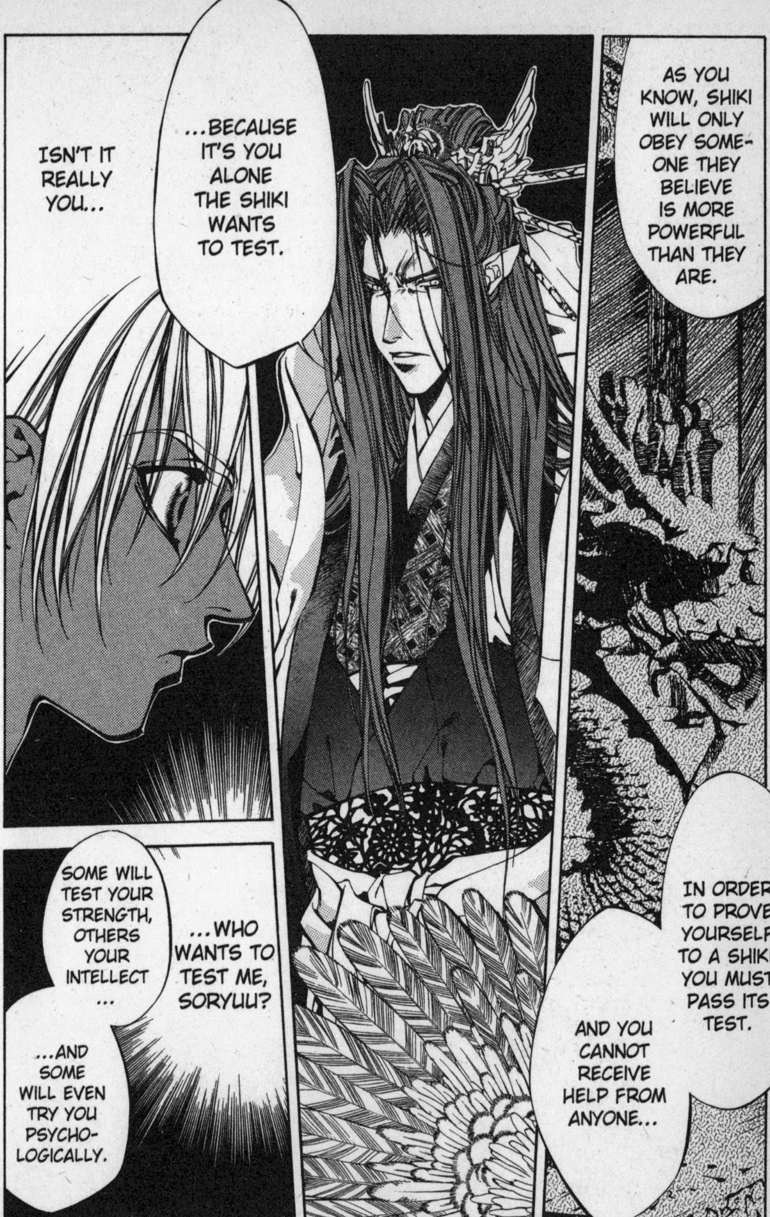
AS YOU KNOW, SHIKI WILL ONLY OBEY SOME-ONE THEY BELIEVE IS MORE POWERFUL THAN THEY ARE.
IN ORDER TO PROVE YOURSELF TO A SHIKI, YOU MUST PASS ITS TEST.
AND YOU CANNOT RECEIVE HELP FROM ANYONE...
...BECAUSE IT'S YOU ALONE THE SHIKI WANTS TO TEST.
ISN'T IT REALLY YOU...
...WHO WANTS TO TEST ME, SORYUU?
SOME WILL TEST YOUR STRENGTH, OTHERS YOUR INTELLECT ...
...AND SOME WILL EVEN TRY YOU PSYCHO-LOGICALLY.

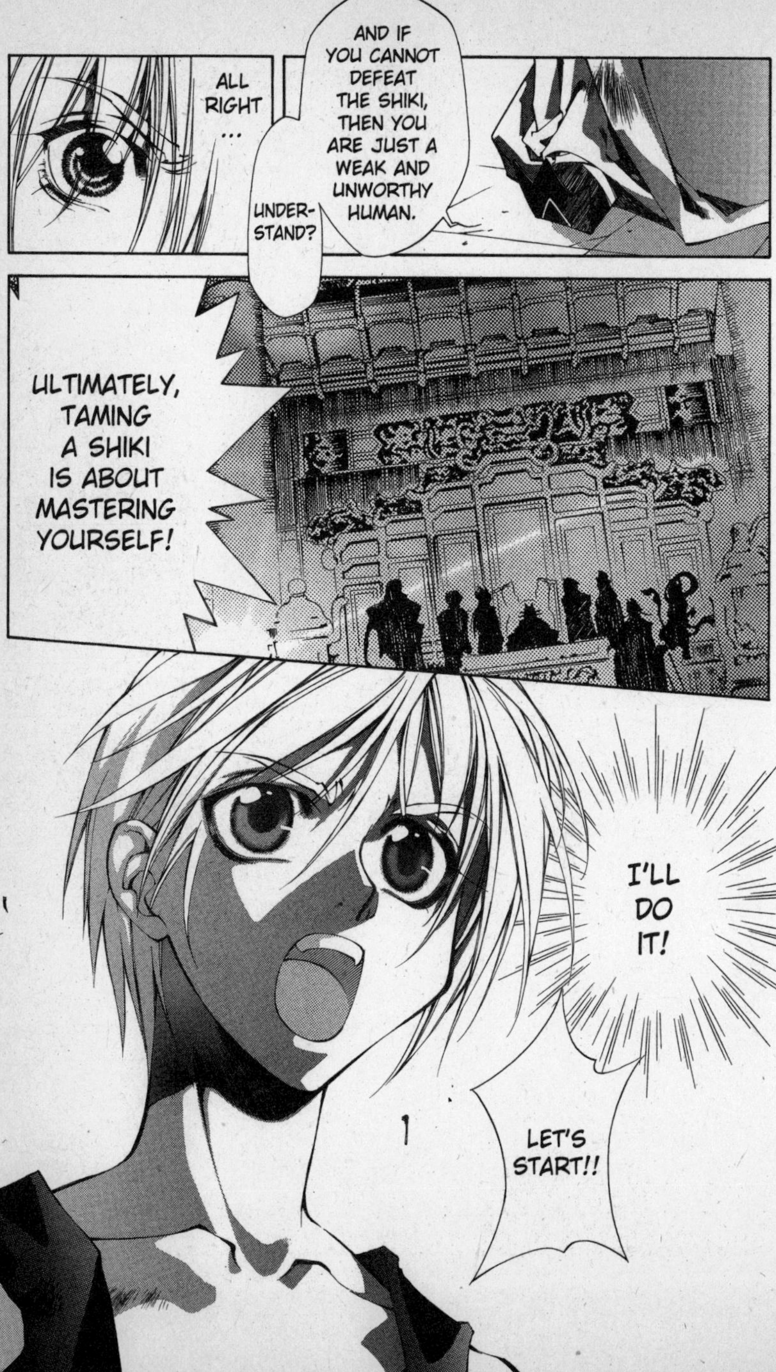
AND IF YOU CANNOT DEFEAT THE SHIKI, THEN YOU ARE JUST A WEAK AND UNWORTHY HUMAN.
UNDER-STAND?
ALL RIGHT ...
ULTIMATELY, TAMING A SHIKI IS ABOUT MASTERING YOURSELF!
I'LL DO IT!
LET'S START!!

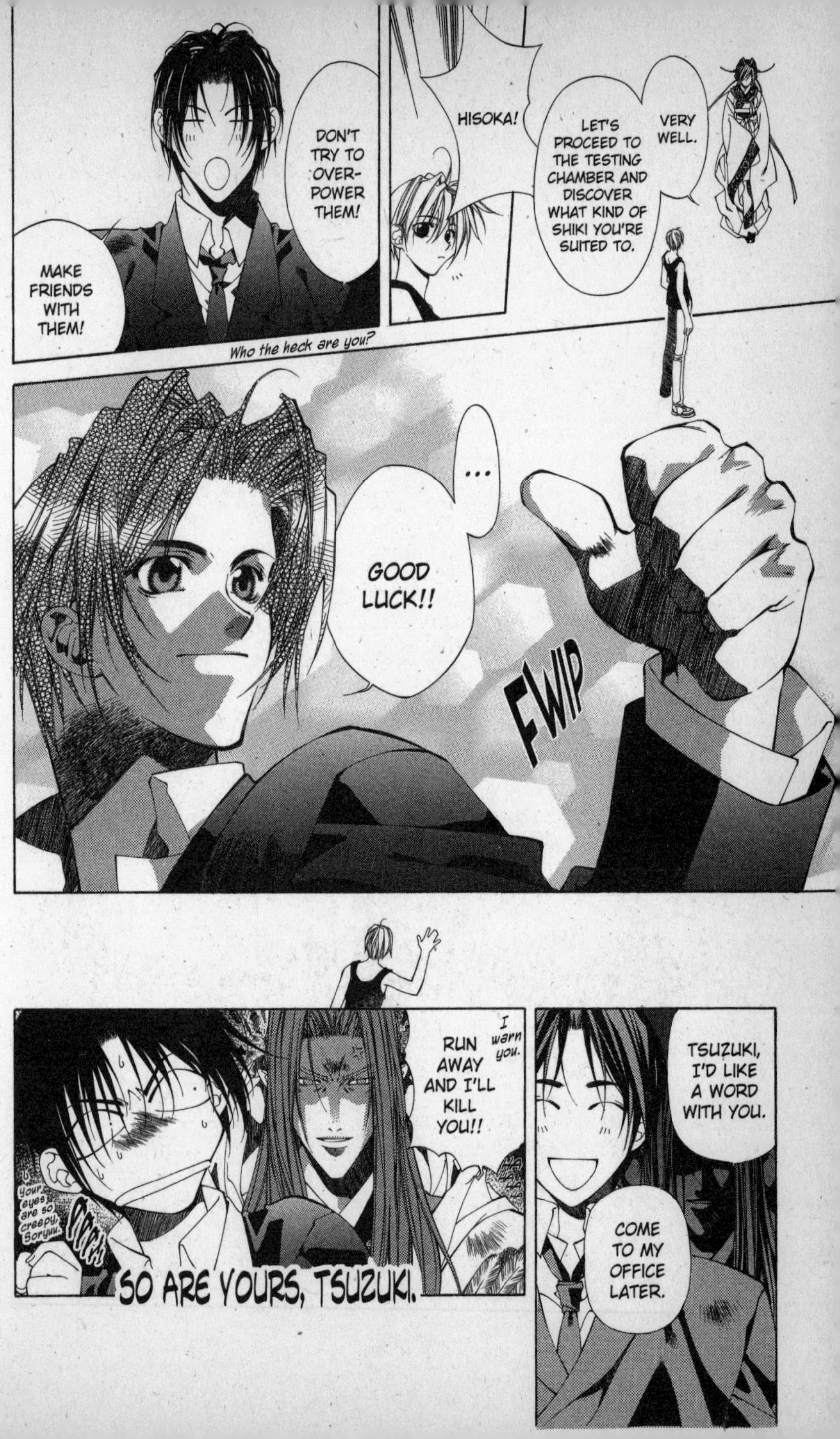
VERY WELL.
LET'S PROCEED TO THE TESTING CHAMBER AND DISCOVER WHAT KIND OF SHIKI YOU'RE SUITED TO.
HISOKA!
DON'T TRY TO OVER-POWER THEM!
MAKE FRIENDS WITH THEM!
Who the heck are you?
...
GOOD LUCK!!
FWIP
TSUZUKI, I'D LIKE A WORD WITH YOU.
COME TO MY OFFICE LATER.
I warn you.
RUN AWAY AND I'LL KILL YOU!!
Your eyes are so creepy, Soryuu.
SO ARE YOURS, TSUZUKI.

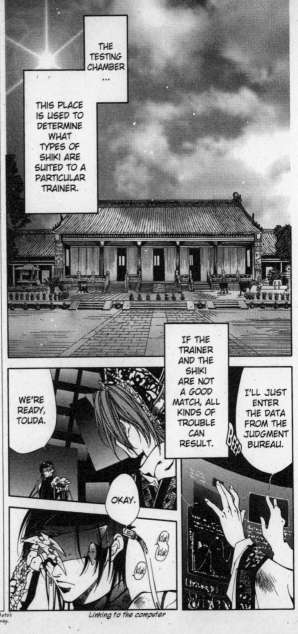

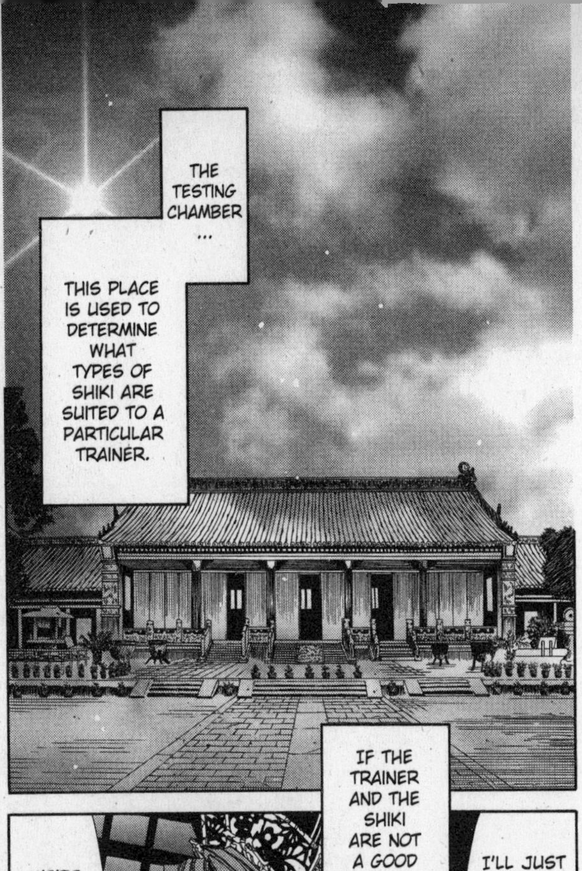
THE TESTING CHAMBER ...
THIS PLACE IS USED TO DETERMINE WHAT TYPES OF SHIKI ARE SUITED TO A PARTICULAR TRAINER.
I'LL JUST ENTER THE DATA FROM THE JUDGMENT BUREAU.
BEEP
IF THE TRAINER AND THE SHIKI ARE NOT A GOOD MATCH, ALL KINDS OF TROUBLE CAN RESULT.
WE'RE READY, TOUDA.
OKAY.
klak
klak
klak

Linking to the computer

Topic 1: Dragon Quest III

I'm talking about the Roto series. To me this is the only true Dragon Quest. After four, they're all the same (unbelievably). I've been playing games since I was in grade school, but Dragon Quest is still my favorite (laugh). It's the game that first got me interested in video games. Number three is especially good. The Super Family Computer version is no good. Game purists prefer the original version. I love it so much, it makes me want to scream: "I can't believe you brought Roto's father back to life!" (laugh). I think the story works better with his father dead. I like to think that Roto's following in his great father's footsteps. Once he surpasses his dead father's skill level, he beats the demon, and it all ties in with Dragon Quest I. It's so moving...sniff...I'm gonna cry. All in all, it's a great game. Really. And I love Sugiyama's music. I like Toriyama's characters too, and Horii's scenario was perfect for me. Dragon Quest III--banzai! Roto series--banzai! Let's keep his father dead.

Otherwise, it's not as poignant. Sorry, Roto's father. It's just more dramatic that way.

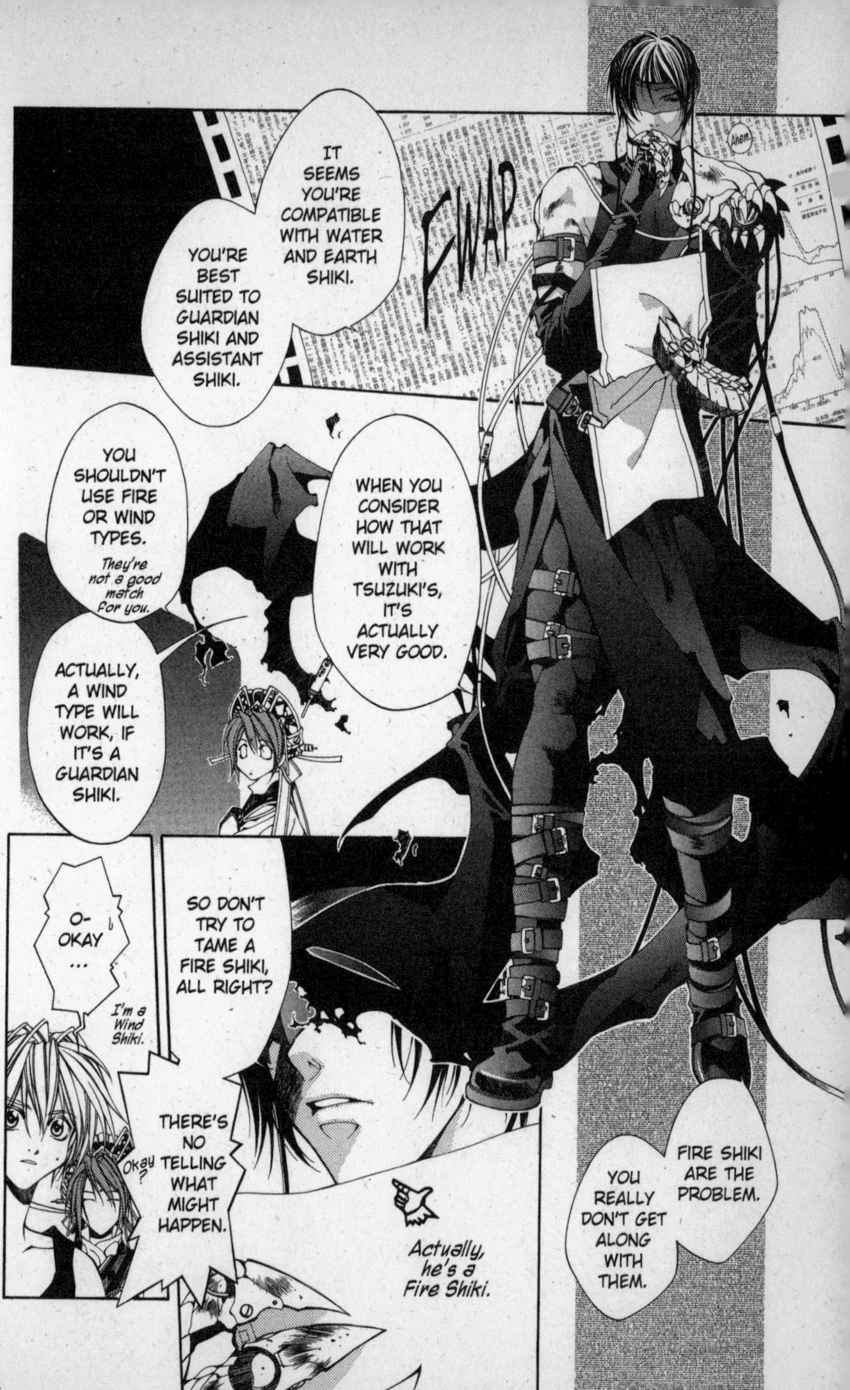
Ahem.
CWAP
IT SEEMS YOU'RE COMPATIBLE WITH WATER AND EARTH SHIKI.
YOU'RE BEST SUITED TO GUARDIAN SHIKI AND ASSISTANT SHIKI.
WHEN YOU CONSIDER HOW THAT WILL WORK WITH TSUZUKI'S, IT'S ACTUALLY VERY GOOD.
YOU SHOULDN'T USE FIRE OR WIND TYPES.
They're not a good match for you.
ACTUALLY, A WIND TYPE WILL WORK, IF IT'S A GUARDIAN SHIKI.
FIRE SHIKI ARE THE PROBLEM.
YOU REALLY DON'T GET ALONG WITH THEM.
Actually, he's a Fire Shiki.
SO DON'T TRY TO TAME A FIRE SHIKI, ALL RIGHT?
THERE'S NO TELLING WHAT MIGHT HAPPEN.
O-OKAY ...
I'm a Wind Shiki.
Okay?

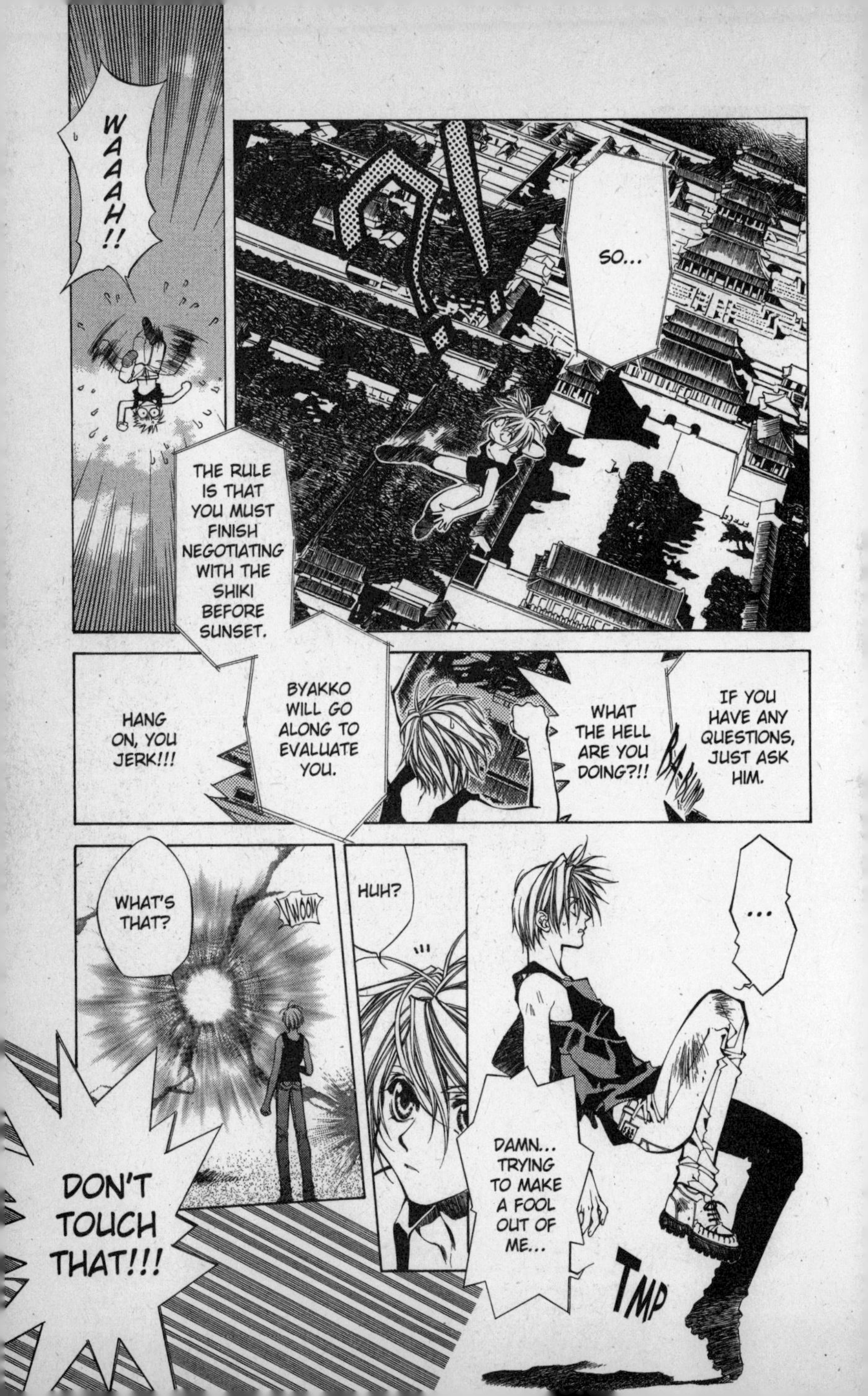
SO...
THE RULE IS THAT YOU MUST FINISH NEGOTIATING WITH THE SHIKI BEFORE SUNSET.
WAAAAH!!
IF YOU HAVE ANY QUESTIONS, JUST ASK HIM.
BA-BUMP
WHAT THE HELL ARE YOU DOING?!!
BYAKKO WILL GO ALONG TO EVALUATE YOU.
HANG ON, YOU JERK!!!
...
DAMN... TRYING TO MAKE A FOOL OUT OF ME...
TMP
HUH?
WHAT'S THAT?
VWOOM
DON'T TOUCH THAT!!!

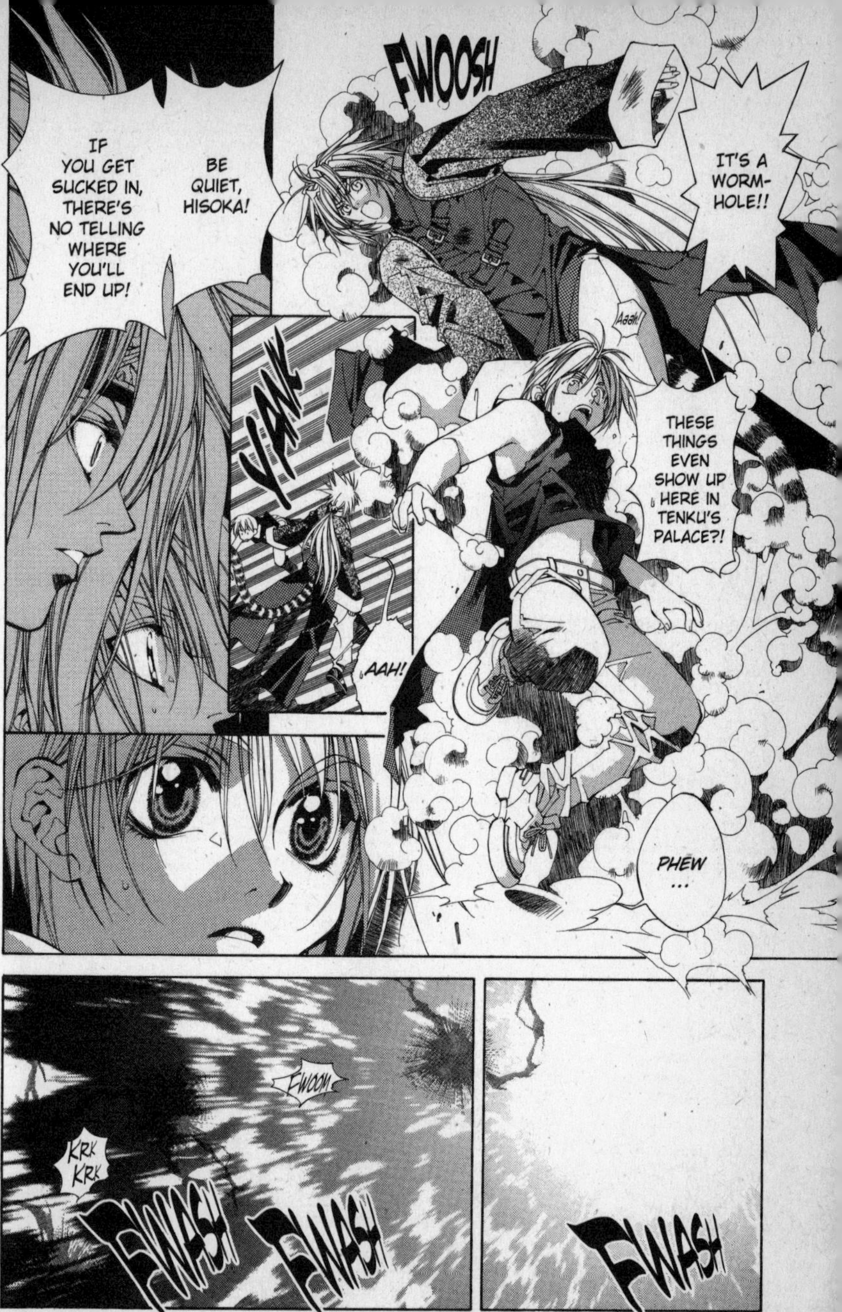
FWOOSH
IT'S A WORM-HOLE!!
Aaah!
THESE THINGS EVEN SHOW UP HERE IN TENKU'S PALACE?!
BE QUIET, HISOKA!
IF YOU GET SUCKED IN, THERE'S NO TELLING WHERE YOU'LL END UP!
YANK
AAH!
PHEW ...
FWASH
FWOOM
KRK KRK
FWASH FWASH

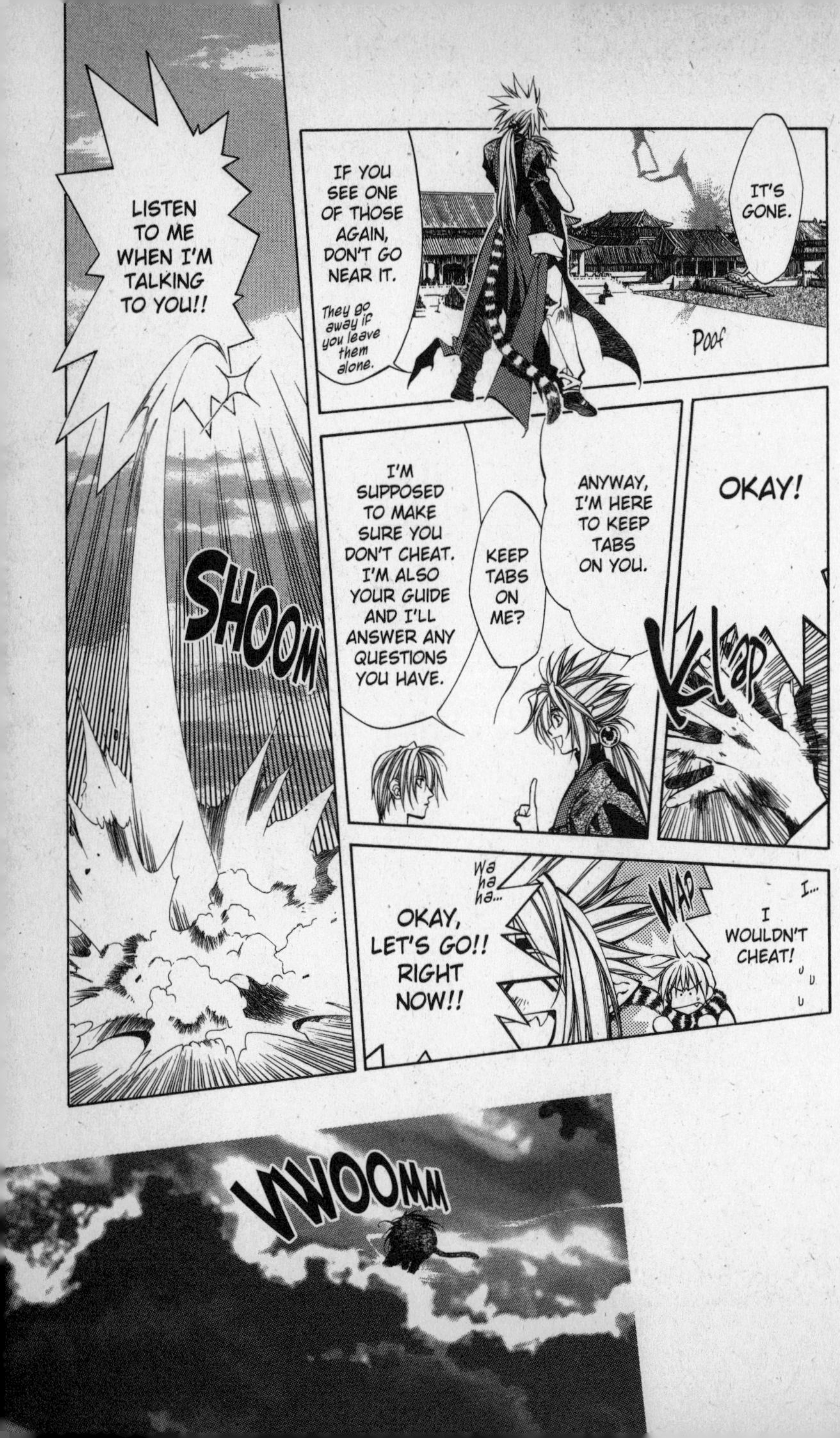
IT'S GONE.
Poof
IF YOU SEE ONE OF THOSE AGAIN, DON'T GO NEAR IT.
They go away if you leave them alone.
OKAY!
KLAP
ANYWAY, I'M HERE TO KEEP TABS ON YOU.
KEEP TABS ON ME?
I'M SUPPOSED TO MAKE SURE YOU DON'T CHEAT. I'M ALSO YOUR GUIDE AND I'LL ANSWER ANY QUESTIONS YOU HAVE.
I...
I WOULDN'T CHEAT!
WAP
Wa ha ha...
OKAY, LET'S GO!! RIGHT NOW!!
LISTEN TO ME WHEN I'M TALKING TO YOU!!
SHOOM
VWOOMM

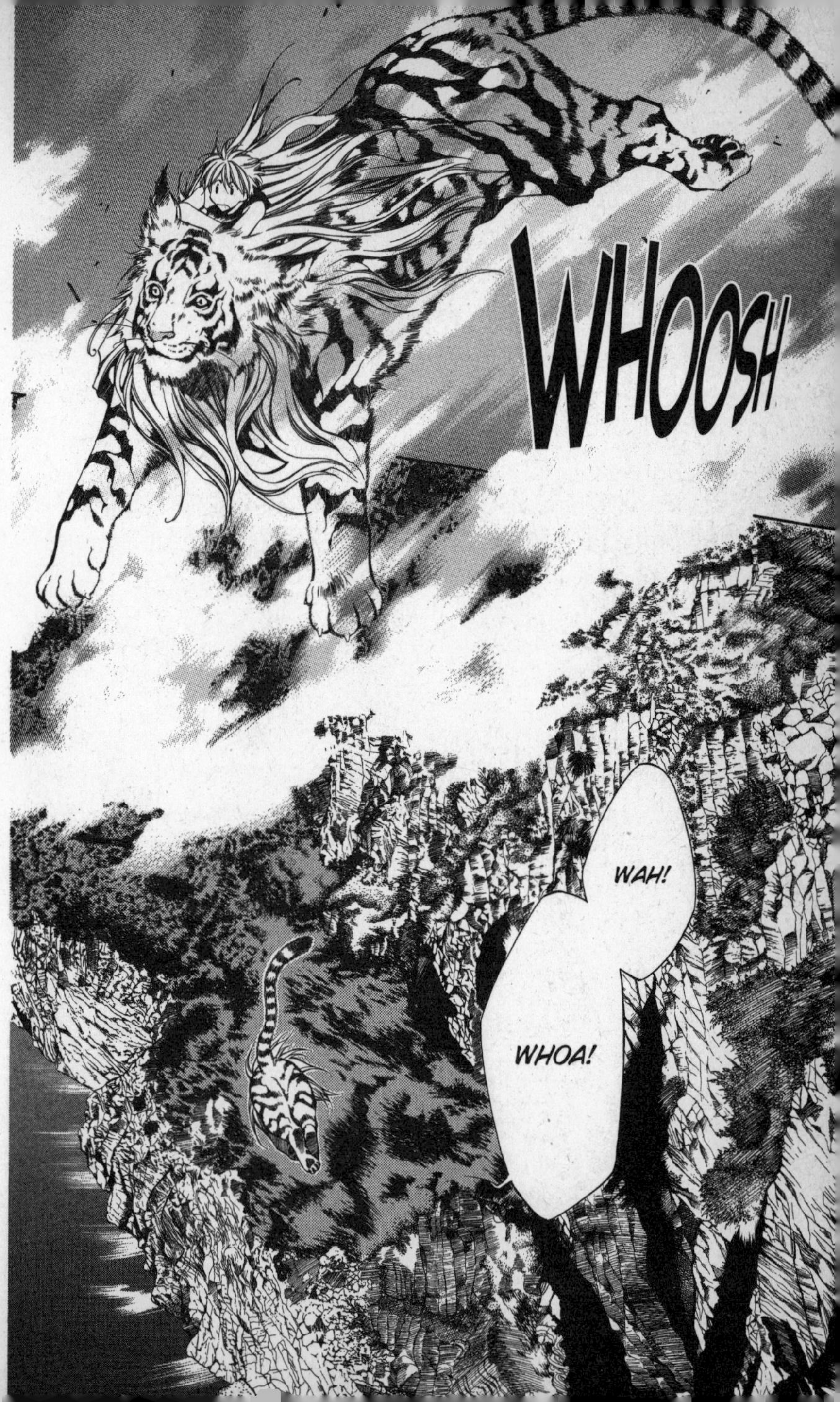
WHOOSH
WAH!
WHOA!

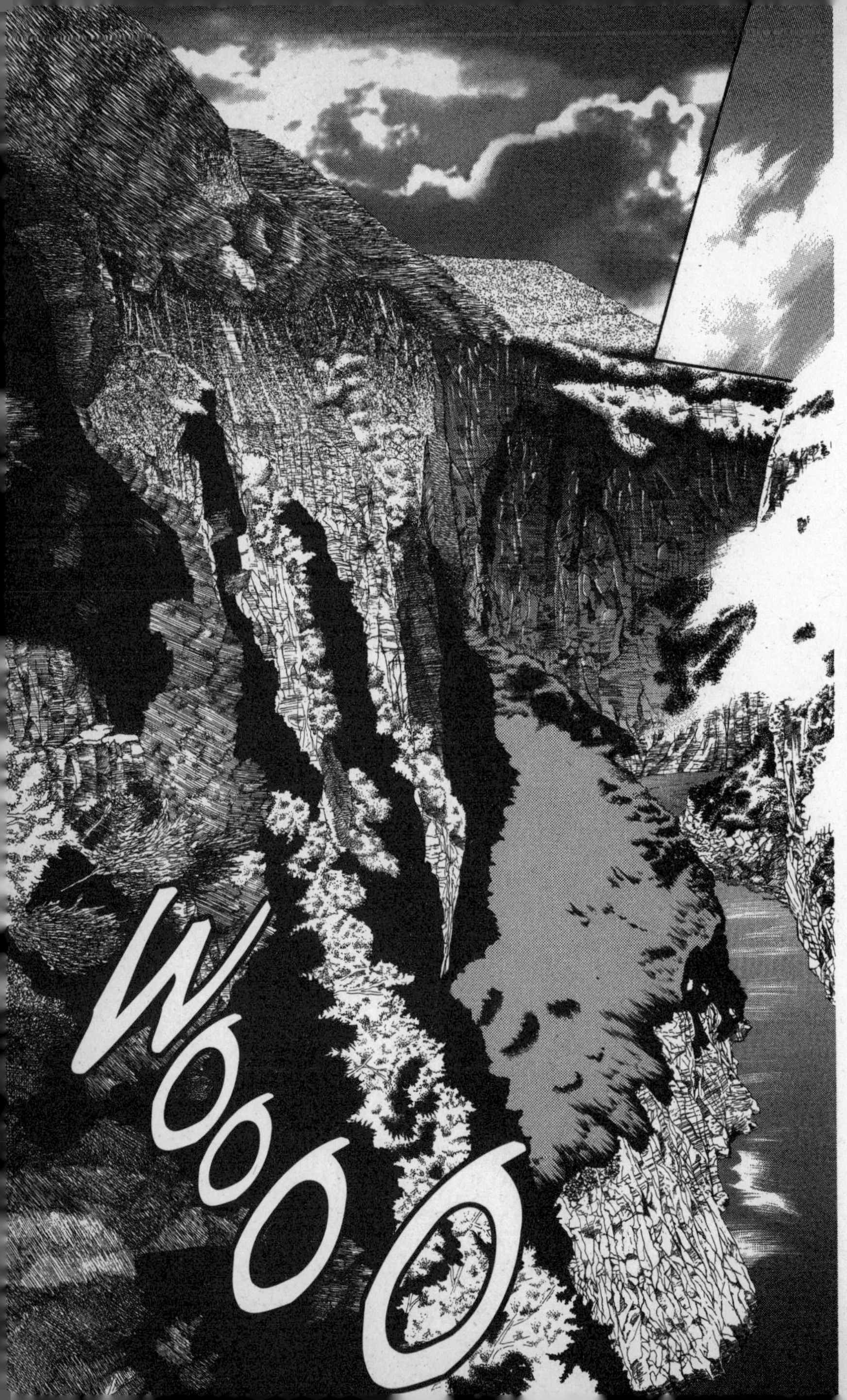
WOOOO

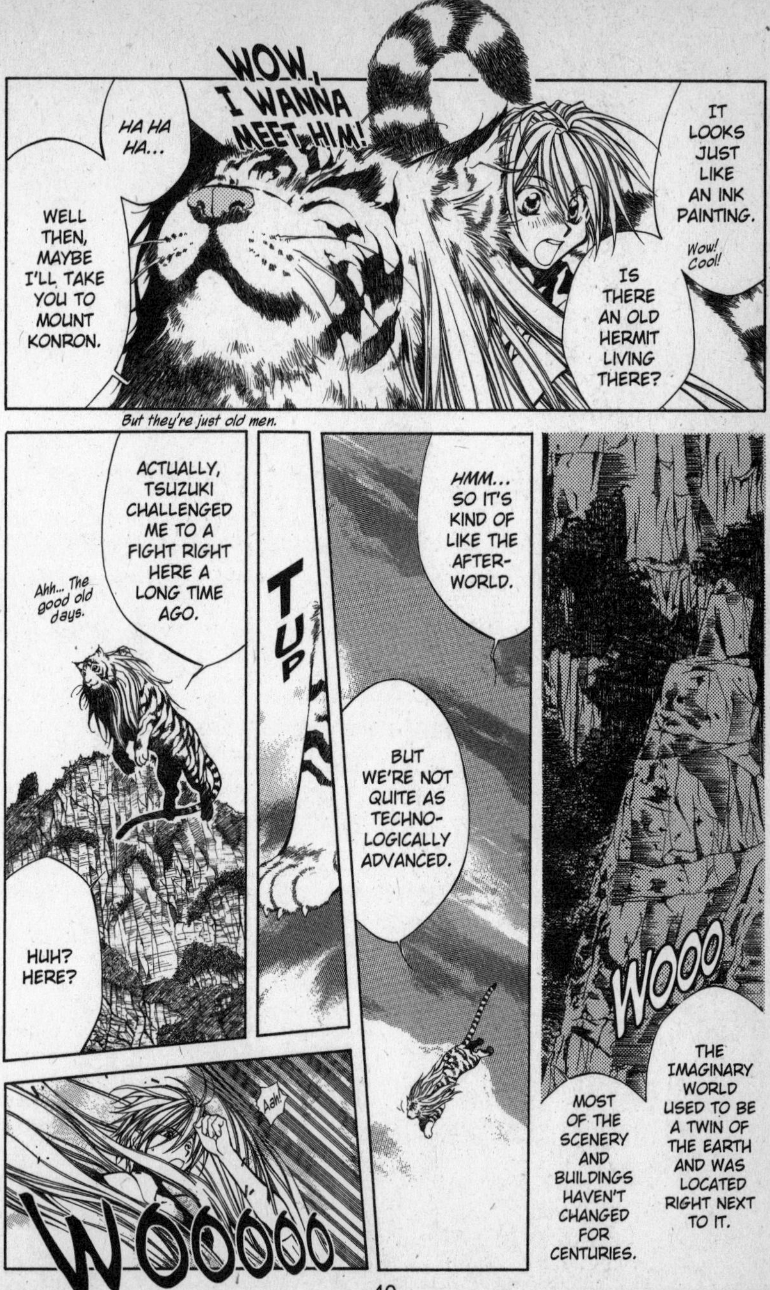
IT LOOKS JUST LIKE AN INK PAINTING.
Wow! Cool!
IS THERE AN OLD HERMIT LIVING THERE?
WOW, I WANNA MEET HIM!
HA HA HA...
WELL THEN, MAYBE I'LL TAKE YOU TO MOUNT KONRON.
But they're just old men.
WOOO
THE IMAGINARY WORLD USED TO BE A TWIN OF THE EARTH AND WAS LOCATED RIGHT NEXT TO IT.
MOST OF THE SCENERY AND BUILDINGS HAVEN'T CHANGED FOR CENTURIES.
HMM... SO IT'S KIND OF LIKE THE AFTER-WORLD.
BUT WE'RE NOT QUITE AS TECHNO-LOGICALLY ADVANCED.
TUP
ACTUALLY, TSUZUKI CHALLENGED ME TO A FIGHT RIGHT HERE A LONG TIME AGO.
Ahh... The good old days.
HUH? HERE?
Aah!
WOOOOO

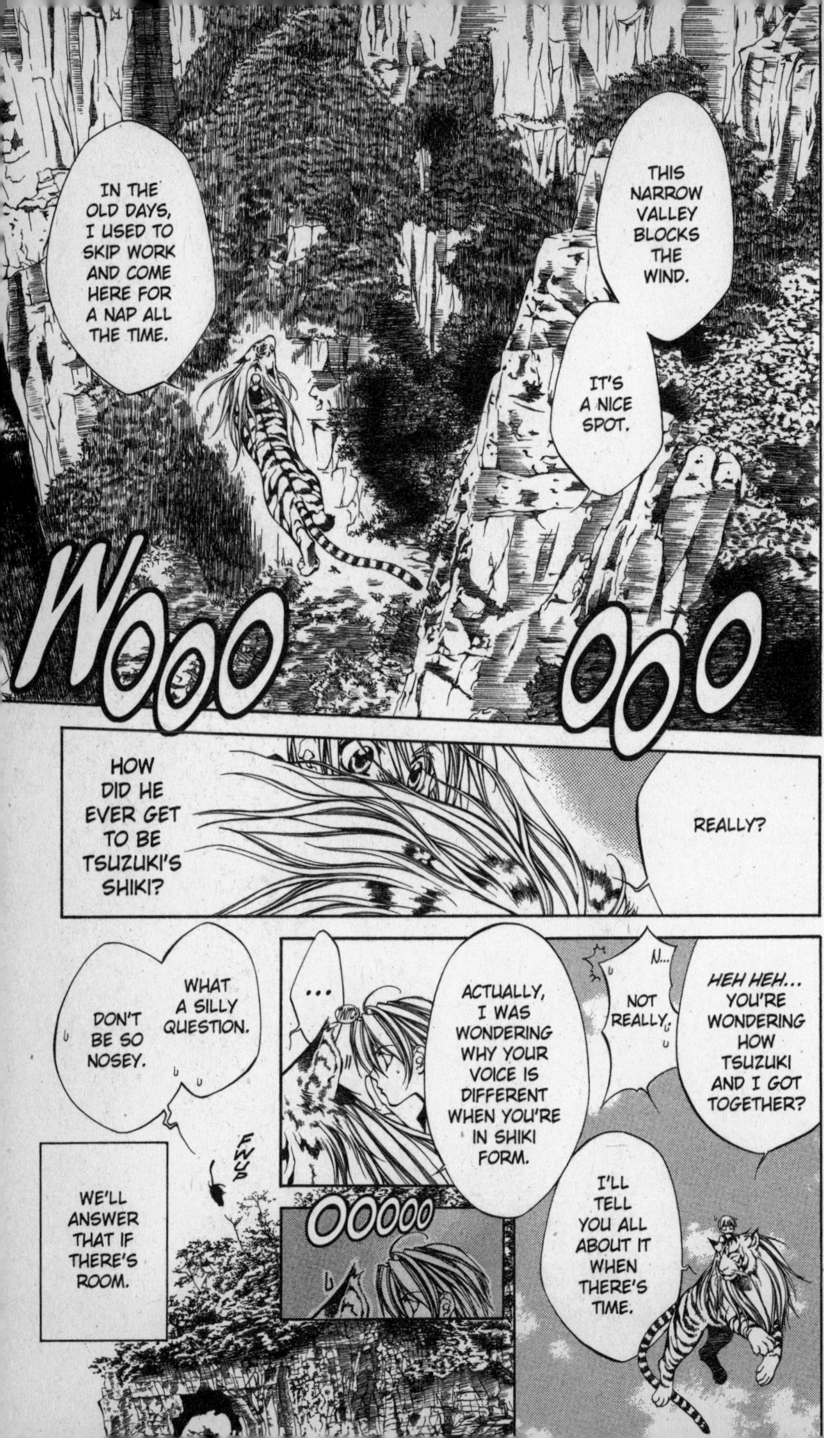
THIS NARROW VALLEY BLOCKS THE WIND.
IT'S A NICE SPOT.
IN THE OLD DAYS, I USED TO SKIP WORK AND COME HERE FOR A NAP ALL THE TIME.
WOOO
OOO
REALLY?
HOW DID HE EVER GET TO BE TSUZUKI'S SHIKI?
HEH HEH... YOU'RE WONDERING HOW TSUZUKI AND I GOT TOGETHER?
N...
NOT REALLY.
ACTUALLY, I WAS WONDERING WHY YOUR VOICE IS DIFFERENT WHEN YOU'RE IN SHIKI FORM.
...
I'LL TELL YOU ALL ABOUT IT WHEN THERE'S TIME.
OOOOO
WHAT A SILLY QUESTION.
DON'T BE SO NOSEY.
FWUP
WE'LL ANSWER THAT IF THERE'S ROOM.

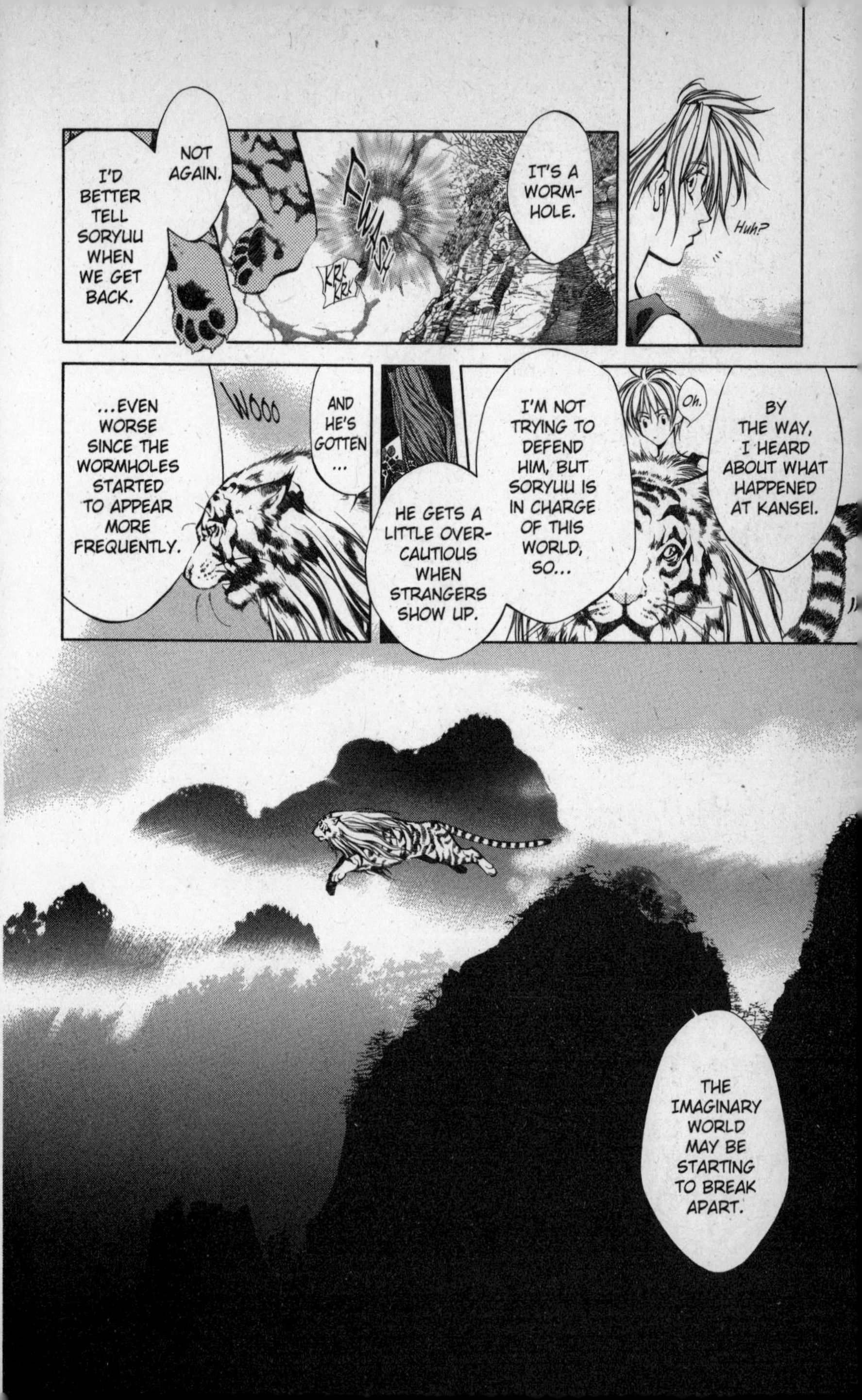
Huh?
IT'S A WORM-HOLE.
FWASH
KRK KRK
NOT AGAIN.
I'D BETTER TELL SORYUU WHEN WE GET BACK.
BY THE WAY, I HEARD ABOUT WHAT HAPPENED AT KANSEI.
Oh.
I'M NOT TRYING TO DEFEND HIM, BUT SORYUU IS IN CHARGE OF THIS WORLD, SO...
HE GETS A LITTLE OVER-CAUTIOUS WHEN STRANGERS SHOW UP.
AND HE'S GOTTEN...
WOOO
...EVEN WORSE SINCE THE WORMHOLES STARTED TO APPEAR MORE FREQUENTLY.
THE IMAGINARY WORLD MAY BE STARTING TO BREAK APART.

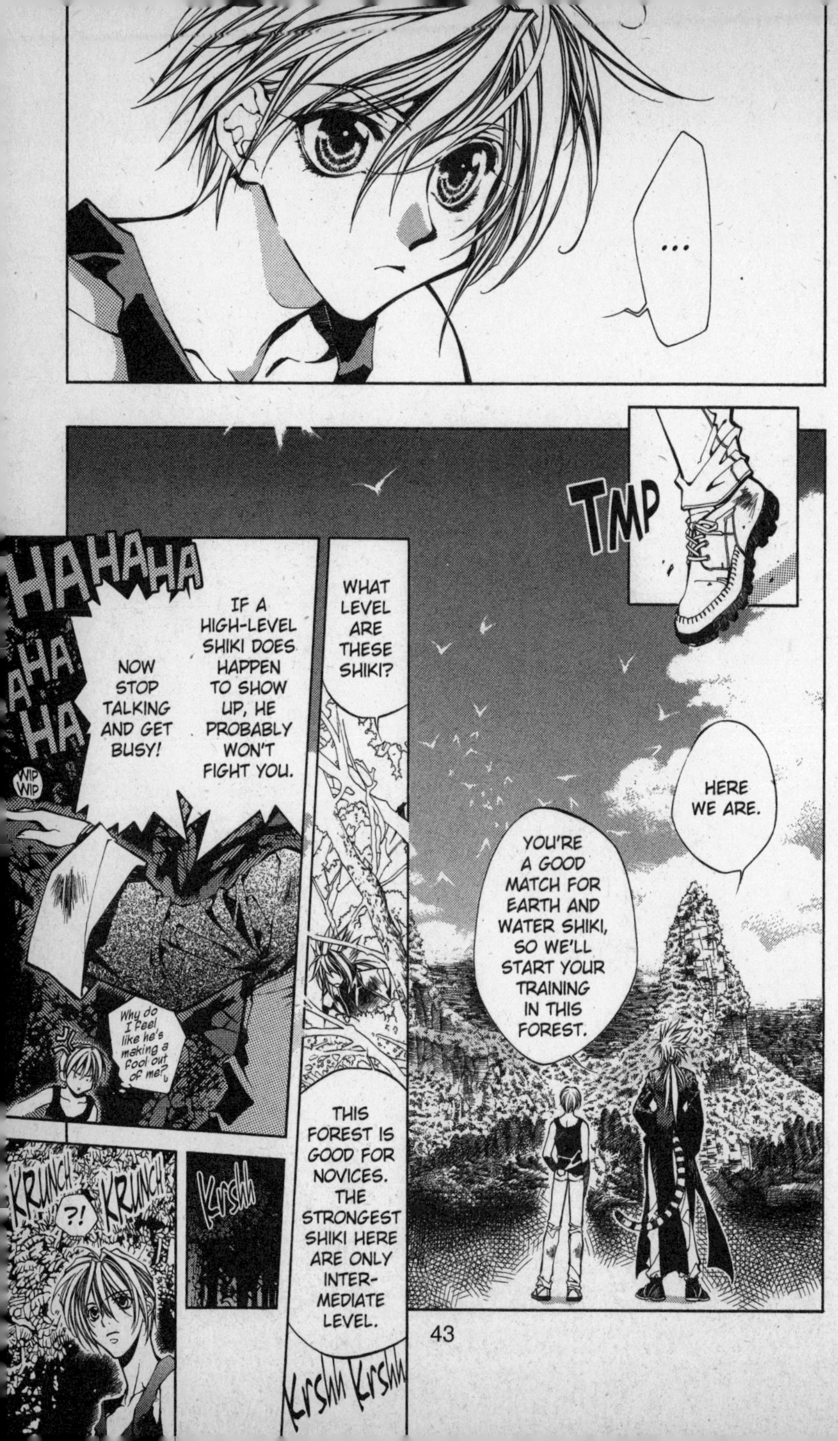
...
TMP
HERE WE ARE.
YOU'RE A GOOD MATCH FOR EARTH AND WATER SHIKI, SO WE'LL START YOUR TRAINING IN THIS FOREST.
WHAT LEVEL ARE THESE SHIKI?
THIS FOREST IS GOOD FOR NOVICES. THE STRONGEST SHIKI HERE ARE ONLY INTER-MEDIATE LEVEL.
Krshh Krshh
IF A HIGH-LEVEL SHIKI DOES HAPPEN TO SHOW UP, HE PROBABLY WON'T FIGHT YOU.
NOW STOP TALKING AND GET BUSY!
HAHAHA HAHAHA
WIP WIP
Why do I feel like he's making a fool out of me?
Krshh
KRUNCH KRUNCH
?!

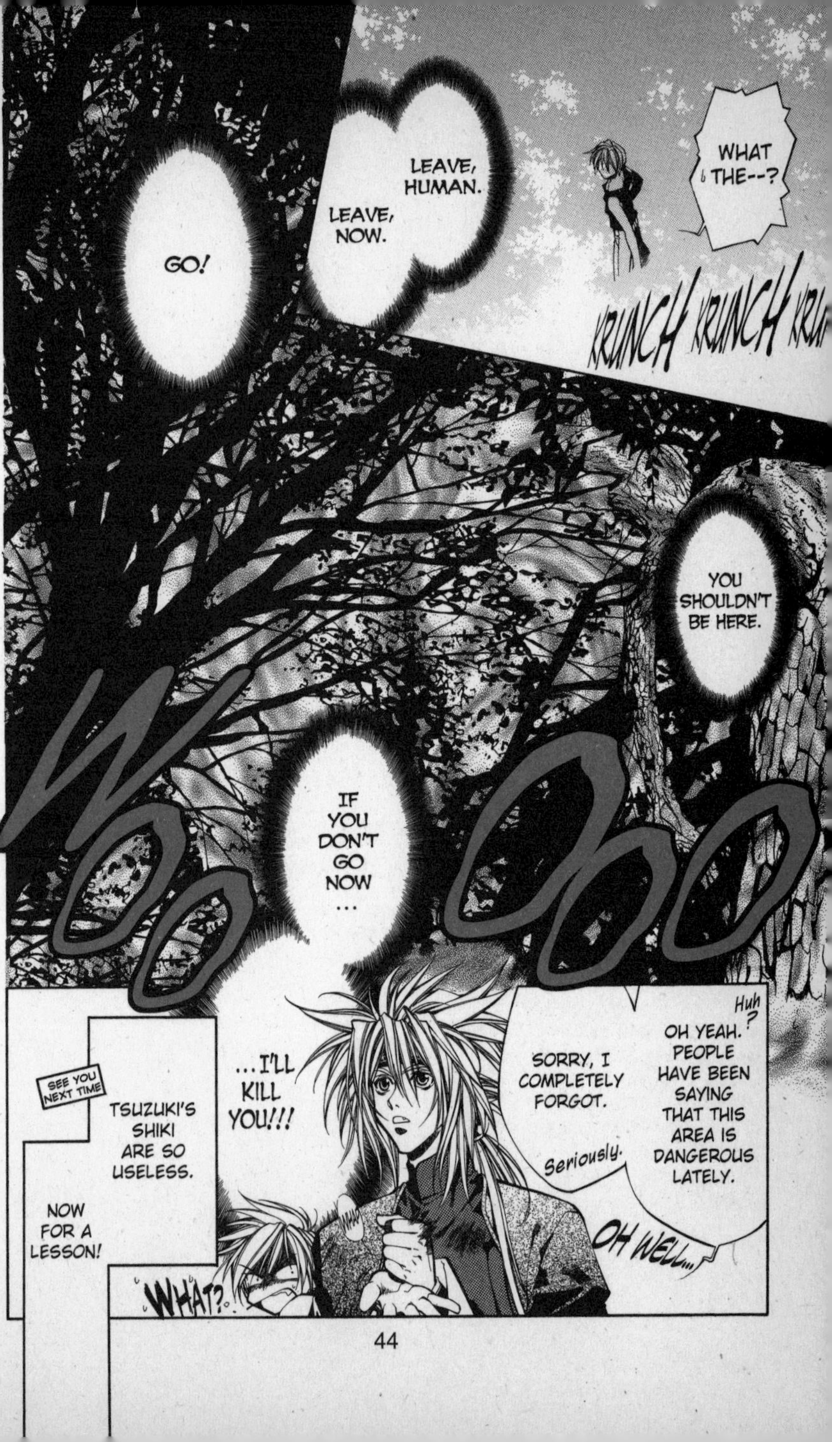
WHAT THE--?
KRUNCH KRUNCH KRU
LEAVE, HUMAN.
LEAVE, NOW.
GO!
YOU SHOULDN'T BE HERE.
IF YOU DON'T GO NOW ...
WOOOOO
Huh?
OH YEAH. PEOPLE HAVE BEEN SAYING THAT THIS AREA IS DANGEROUS LATELY.
SORRY, I COMPLETELY FORGOT.
Seriously.
OH WELL...
...I'LL KILL YOU!!!
WHAT?
SEE YOU NEXT TIME
TSUZUKI'S SHIKI ARE SO USELESS.
NOW FOR A LESSON!

HEI HEI

THE HEI HEI IS SORT OF LIKE A FOX, BUT WITH WINGS ON ITS BACK. WHEN IT APPEARS, IT BRINGS DROUGHT WITH IT. IT DWELLS ON MT. KOHO. (I CHANGED IT INTO A CAT.)

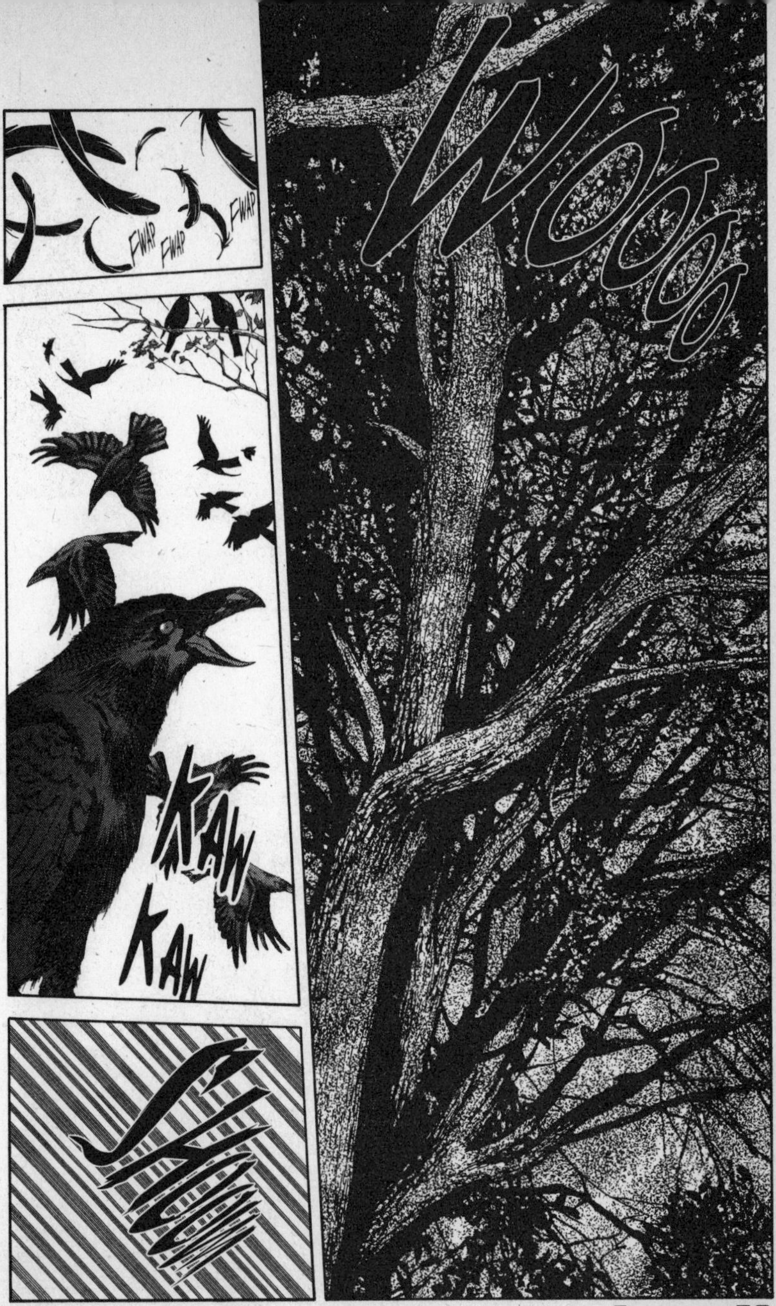
WOOOO
FWAP
FWAP
FWAP
KAW
KAW
KAW

CHAPTER 39

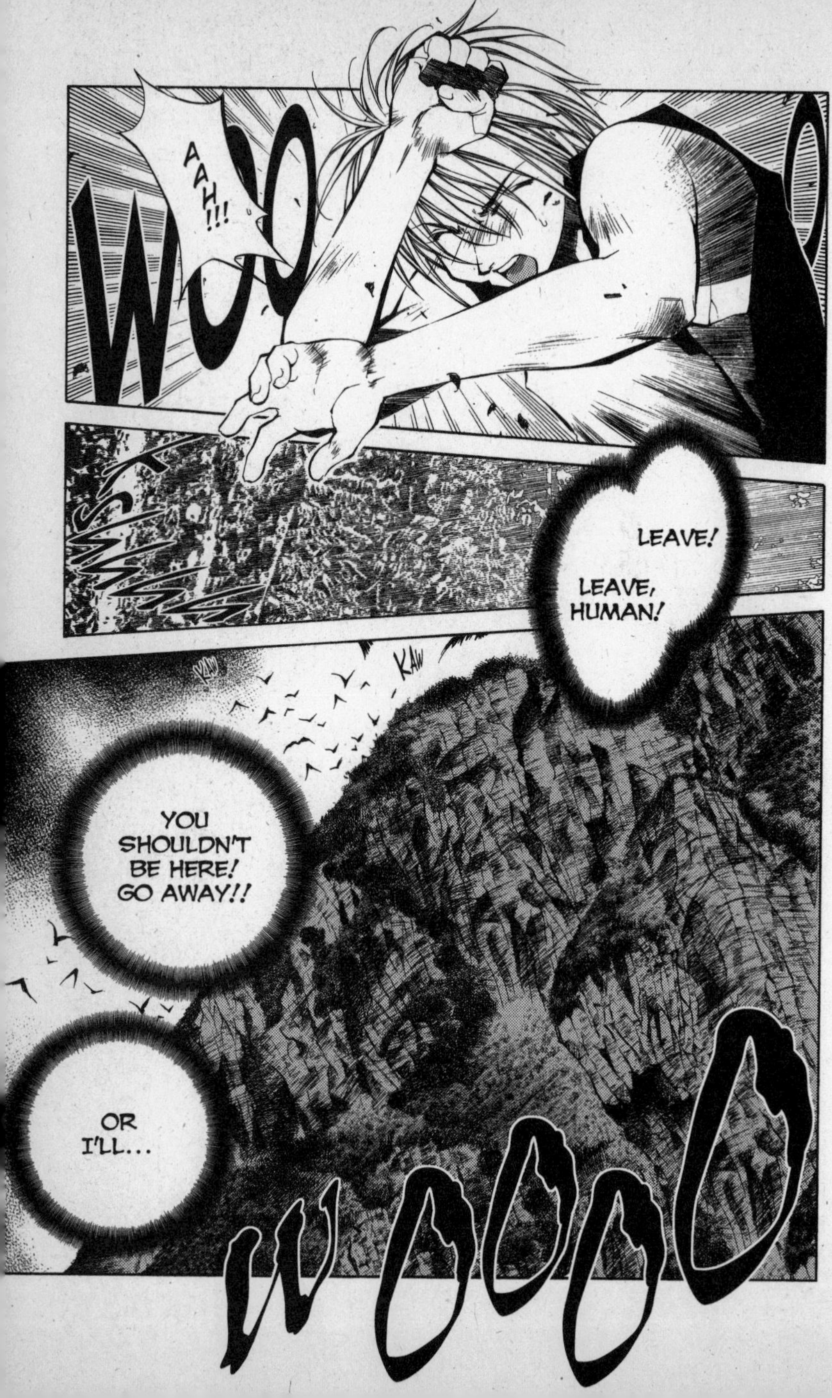
AAH!!!
LEAVE!
LEAVE, HUMAN!
KAW
YOU SHOULDN'T BE HERE! GO AWAY!!
OR I'LL...

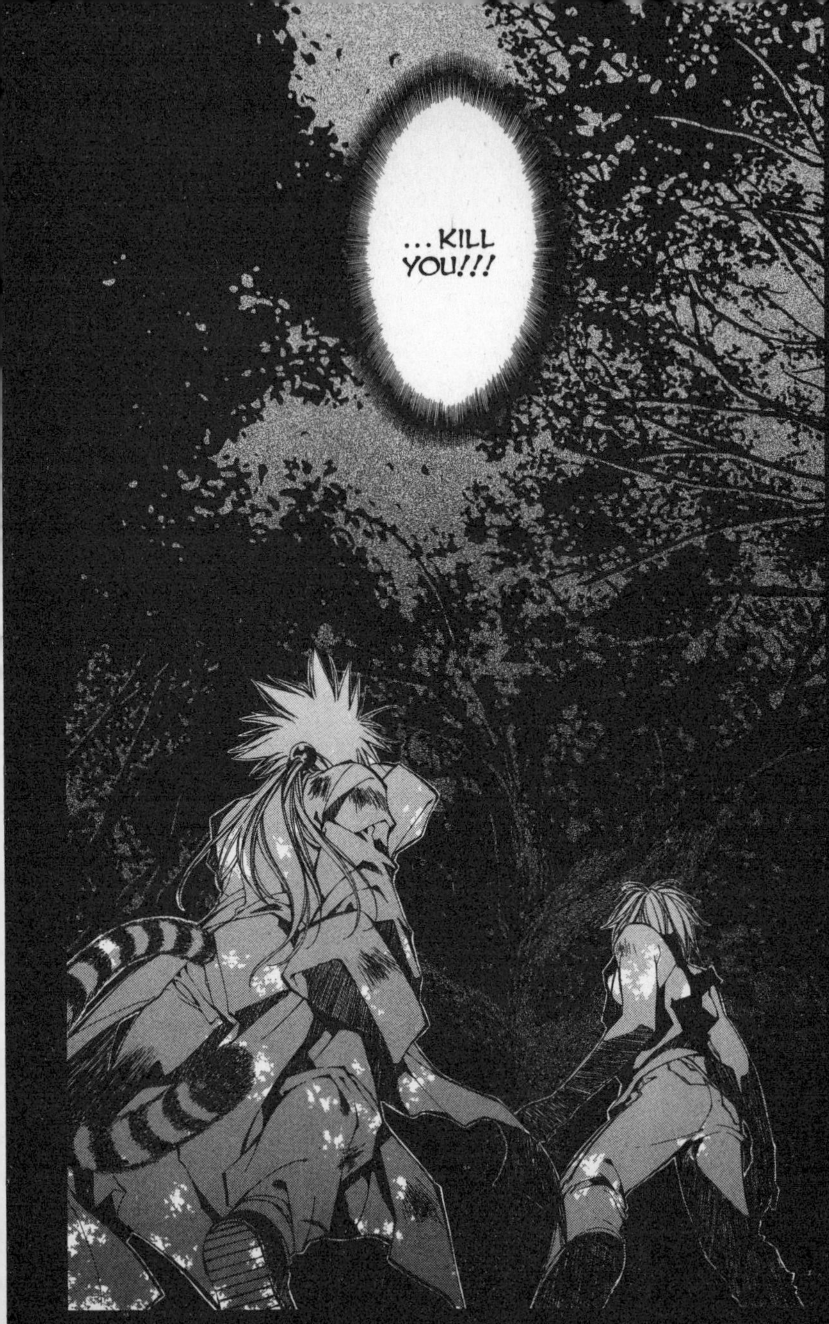
...KILL YOU!!!

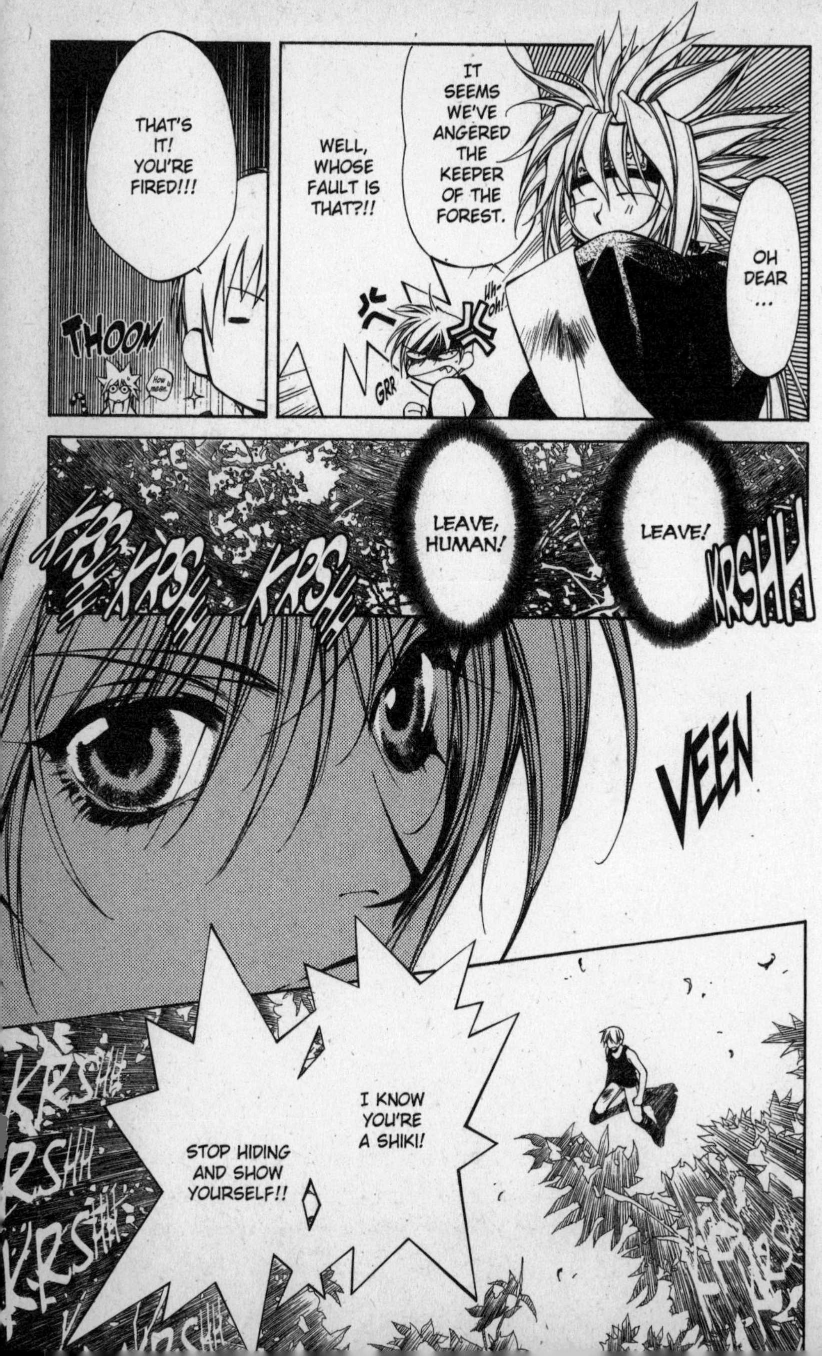

OH DEAR ...
IT SEEMS WE'VE ANGERED THE KEEPER OF THE FOREST.
Uh-oh!
WELL, WHOSE FAULT IS THAT?!!
GRR
THAT'S IT! YOU'RE FIRED!!!
THOOM
How mean.
KRSHH
LEAVE!
LEAVE, HUMAN!
KRSHH KRSHH KRSHH
VEEN
I KNOW YOU'RE A SHIKI!
STOP HIDING AND SHOW YOURSELF!!
KRSHH
KRSHH
KRSHH
KRSHH

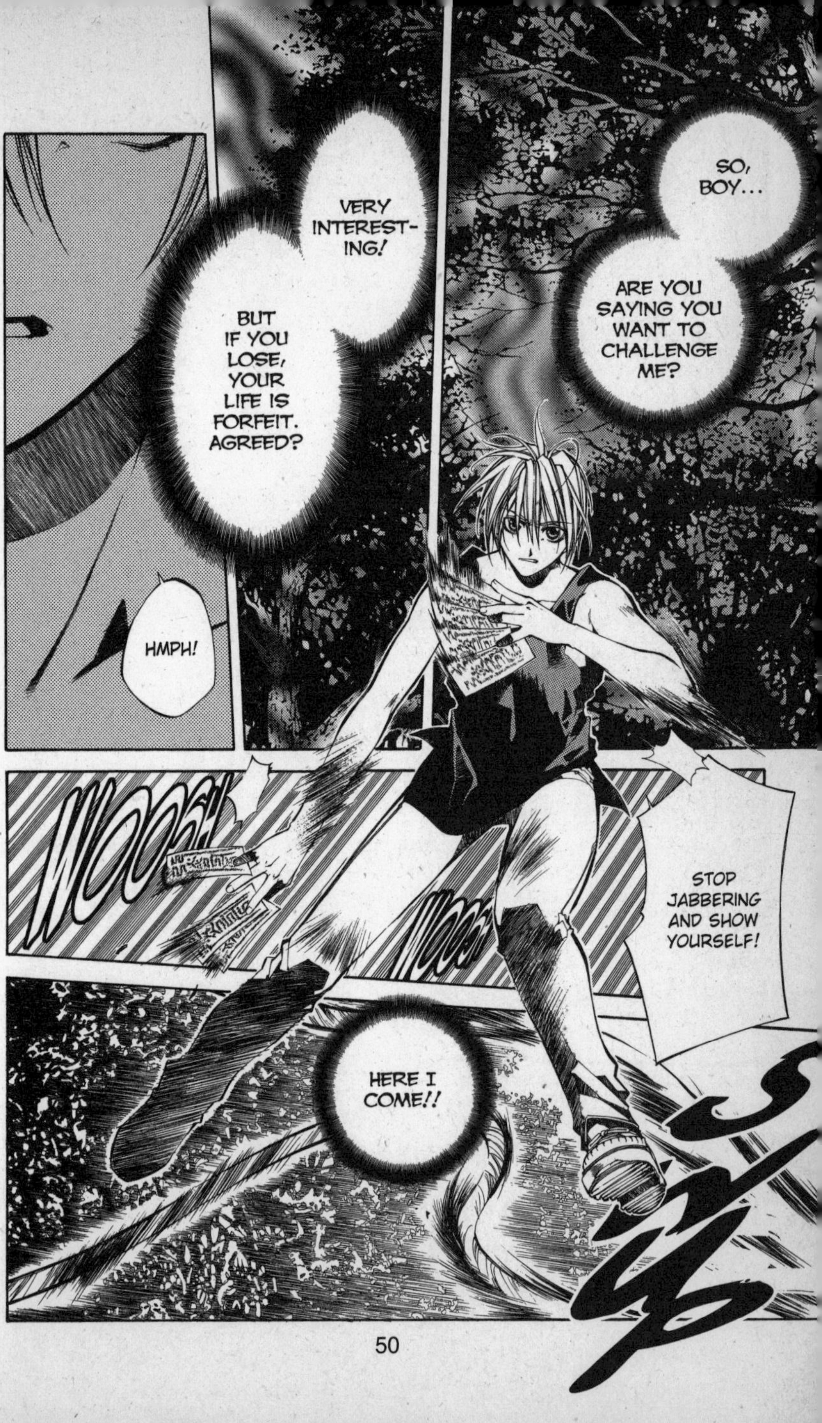
SO, BOY...
ARE YOU SAYING YOU WANT TO CHALLENGE ME?
VERY INTERESTING!
BUT IF YOU LOSE, YOUR LIFE IS FORFEIT. AGREED?
HMPH!
STOP JABBERING AND SHOW YOURSELF!
WHOOSH!
WHOOSH
HERE I COME!!

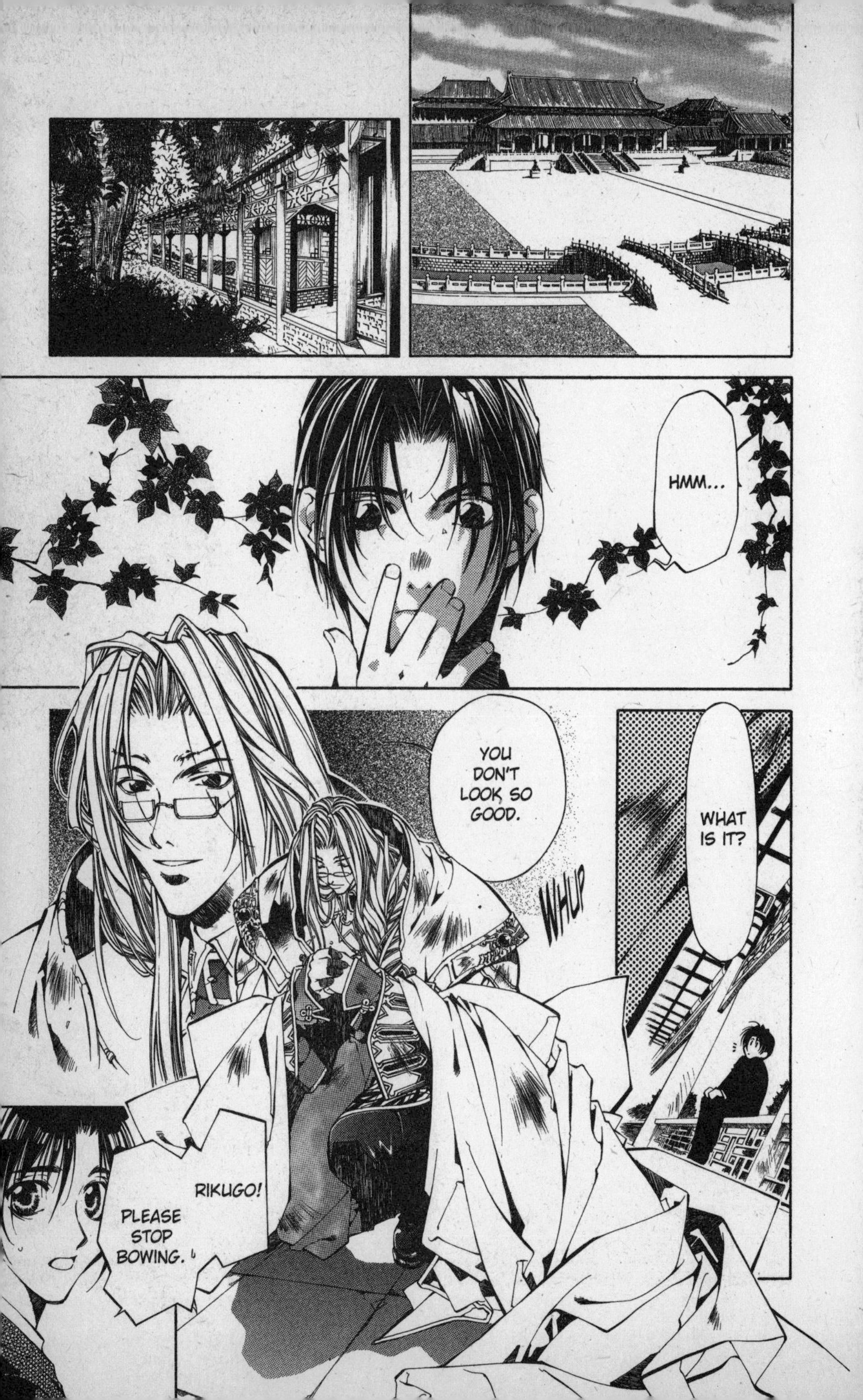
HMM...
WHAT IS IT?
YOU DON'T LOOK SO GOOD.
WHUP
RIKUGO! PLEASE STOP BOWING.

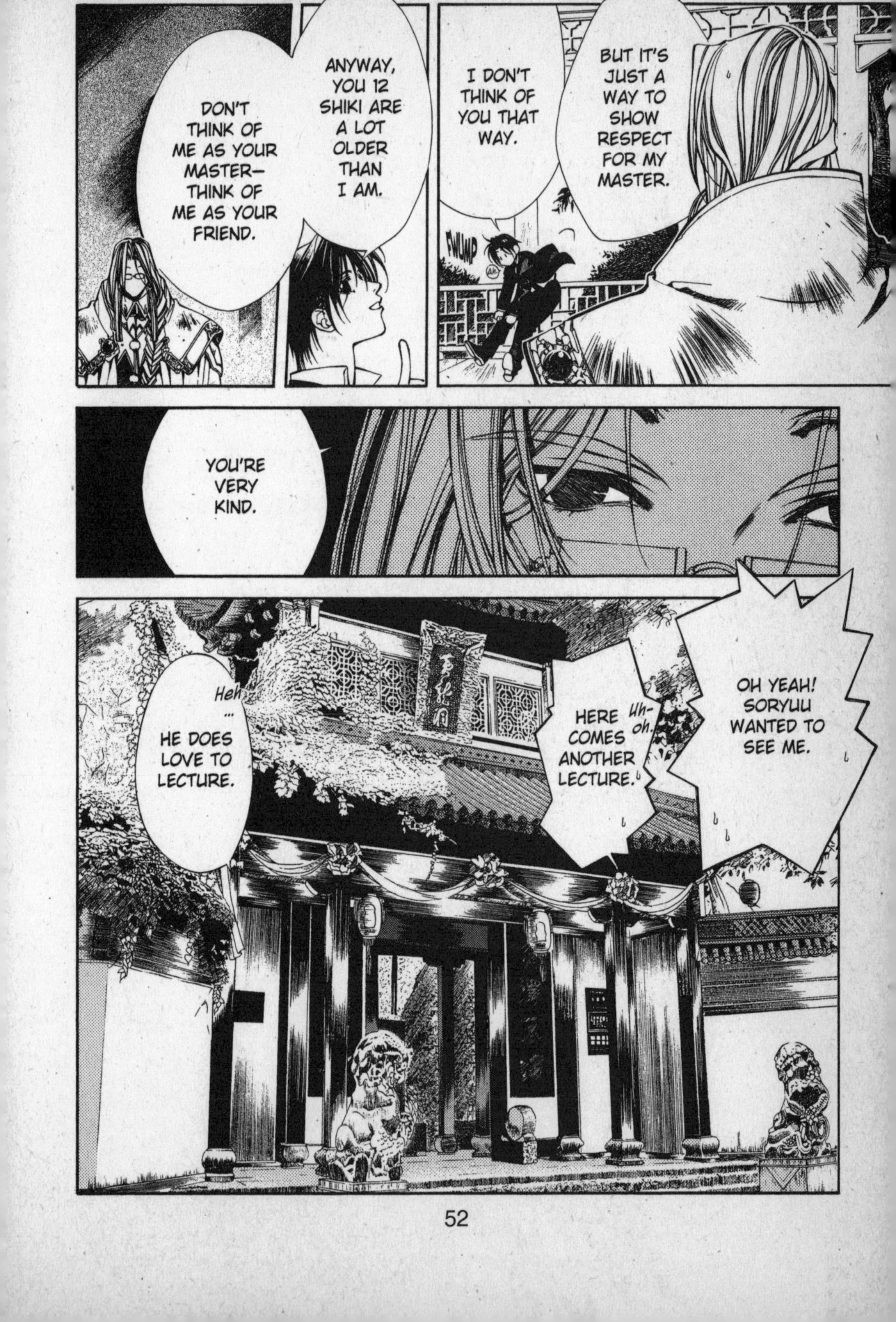
BUT IT'S JUST A WAY TO SHOW RESPECT FOR MY MASTER.
I DON'T THINK OF YOU THAT WAY.
FWUMP
Ah.
ANYWAY, YOU 12 SHIKI ARE A LOT OLDER THAN I AM.
DON'T THINK OF ME AS YOUR MASTER—THINK OF ME AS YOUR FRIEND.
YOU'RE VERY KIND.
OH YEAH! SORYUU WANTED TO SEE ME.
Uh-oh.
HERE COMES ANOTHER LECTURE.
Heh...
HE DOES LOVE TO LECTURE.

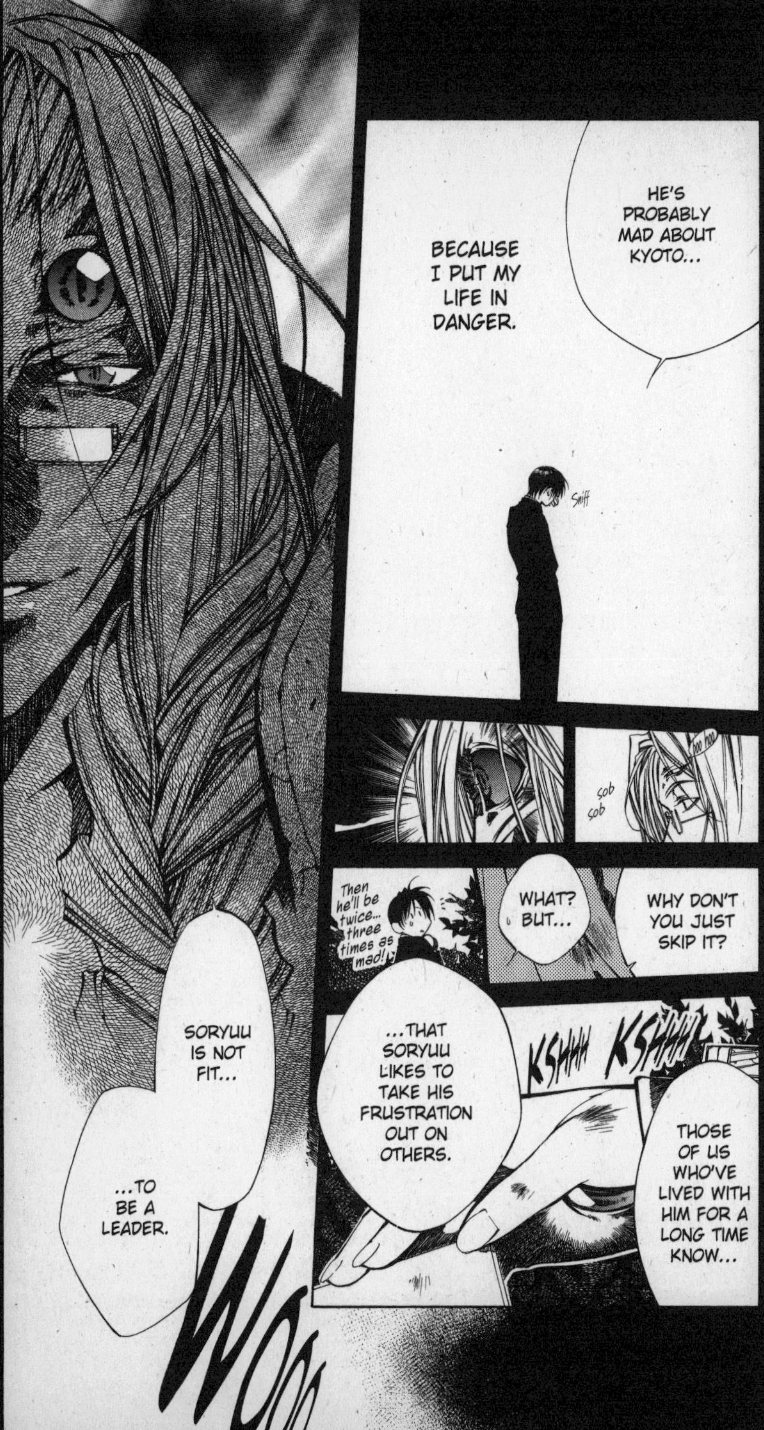
HE'S PROBABLY MAD ABOUT KYOTO...
BECAUSE I PUT MY LIFE IN DANGER.
Sniff
boo hoo
sob sob
WHY DON'T YOU JUST SKIP IT?
WHAT? BUT...
Then he'll be twice... three times as mad!
THOSE OF US WHO'VE LIVED WITH HIM FOR A LONG TIME KNOW...
KSHHH KSHHH
...THAT SORYUU LIKES TO TAKE HIS FRUSTRATION OUT ON OTHERS.
SORYUU IS NOT FIT...
...TO BE A LEADER.
WOOO

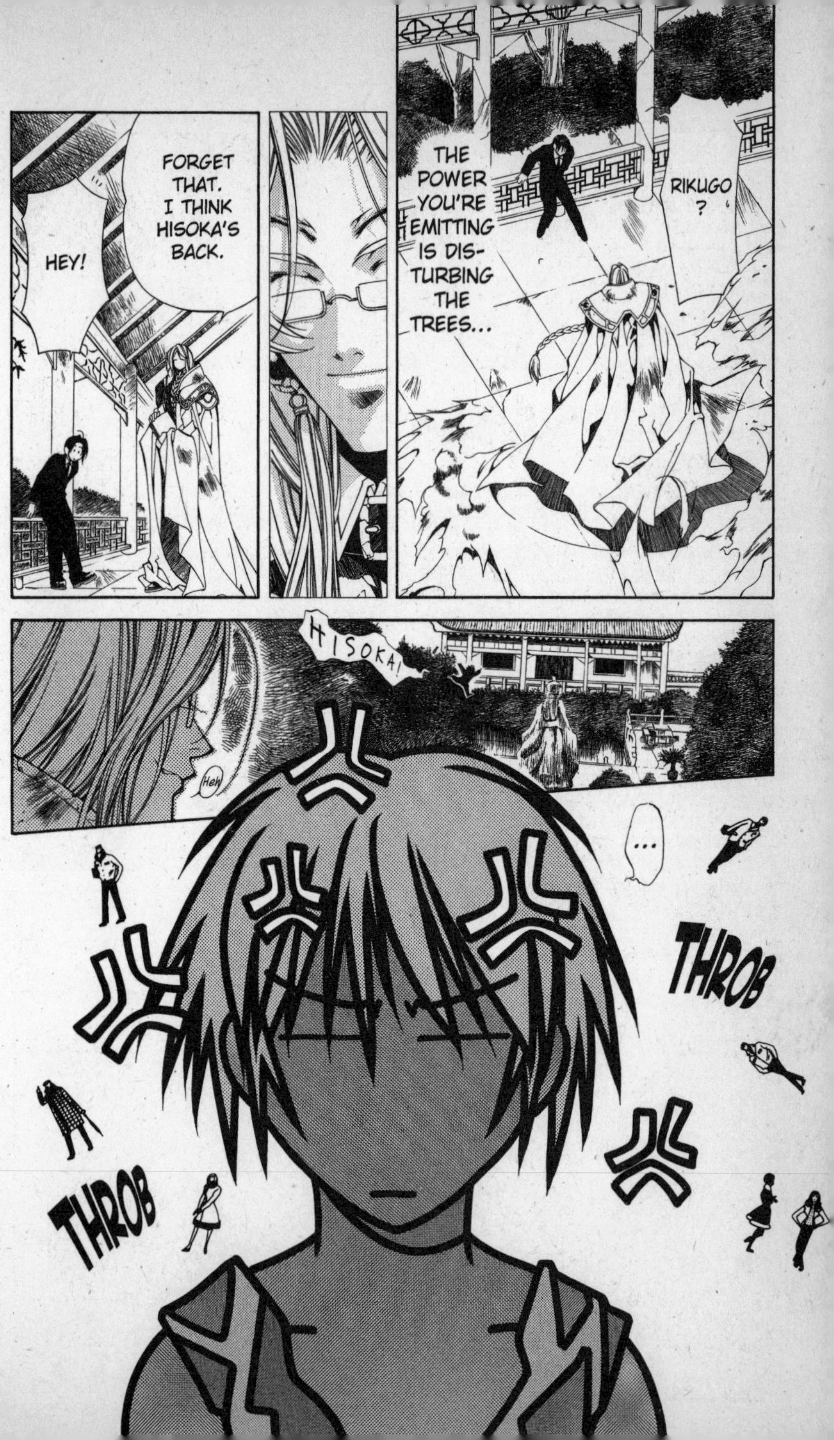
RIKUGO ?
THE POWER YOU'RE EMITTING IS DISTURBING THE TREES...
FORGET THAT. I THINK HISOKA'S BACK.
HEY!
HISOKA!
Heh
...
THROB
THROB

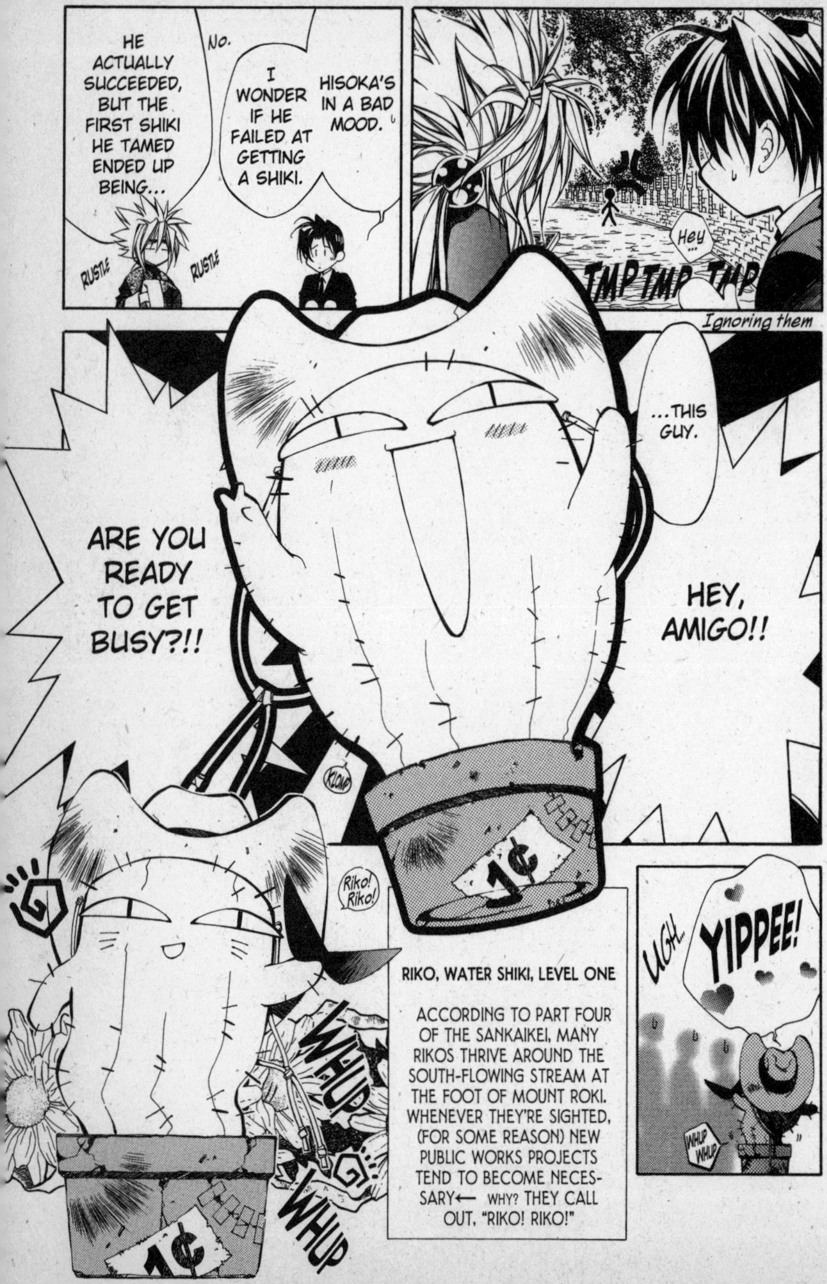
Hey...
TMP TMP TMP
Ignoring them
HISOKA'S IN A BAD MOOD.
I WONDER IF HE FAILED AT GETTING A SHIKI.
NO.
HE ACTUALLY SUCCEEDED, BUT THE FIRST SHIKI HE TAMED ENDED UP BEING...
RUSTLE RUSTLE
...THIS GUY.
HEY, AMIGO!!
ARE YOU READY TO GET BUSY?!!
KLOMP
1¢
Riko! Riko!
WHUP WHUP
UGH
YIPPEE!
WHUP WHUP
RIKO, WATER SHIKI, LEVEL ONE
ACCORDING TO PART FOUR OF THE SANKAIKEI, MANY RIKOS THRIVE AROUND THE SOUTH-FLOWING STREAM AT THE FOOT OF MOUNT ROKI. WHENEVER THEY'RE SIGHTED, (FOR SOME REASON) NEW PUBLIC WORKS PROJECTS TEND TO BECOME NECES-SARY← WHY? THEY CALL OUT, "RIKO! RIKO!"

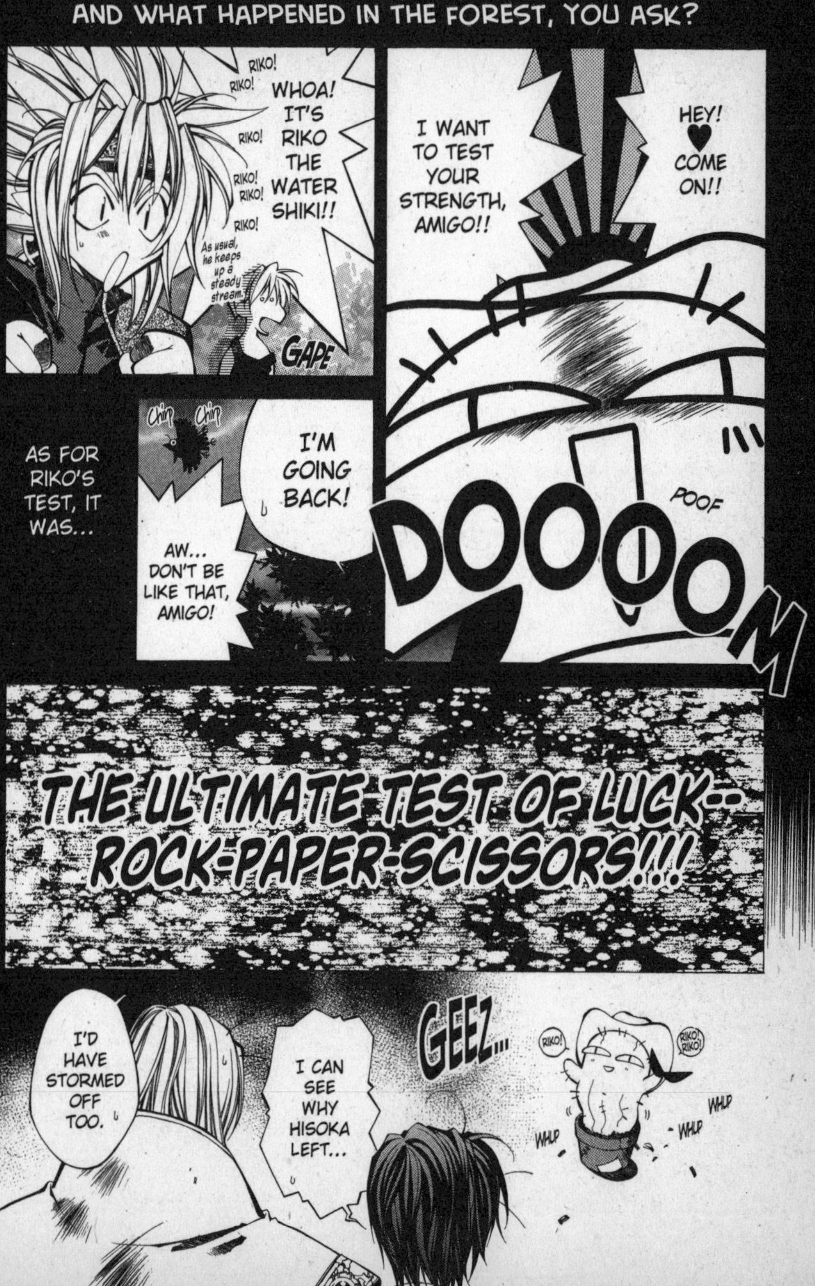
AND WHAT HAPPENED IN THE FOREST, YOU ASK?
HEY! ♥ COME ON!!
I WANT TO TEST YOUR STRENGTH, AMIGO!!
DOOOOOM
POOF
RIKO! RIKO!
WHOA! IT'S RIKO THE WATER SHIKI!!
RIKO!
RIKO! RIKO!
RIKO!
As usual, he keeps up a steady stream.
GAPE
Chirp Chirp
I'M GOING BACK!
AW... DON'T BE LIKE THAT, AMIGO!
AS FOR RIKO'S TEST, IT WAS...
THE ULTIMATE TEST OF LUCK-- ROCK-PAPER-SCISSORS!!!
RIKO! RIKO!
RIKO!
WHUP
WHUP
WHUP
GEEZ...
I CAN SEE WHY HISOKA LEFT...
I'D HAVE STORMED OFF TOO.

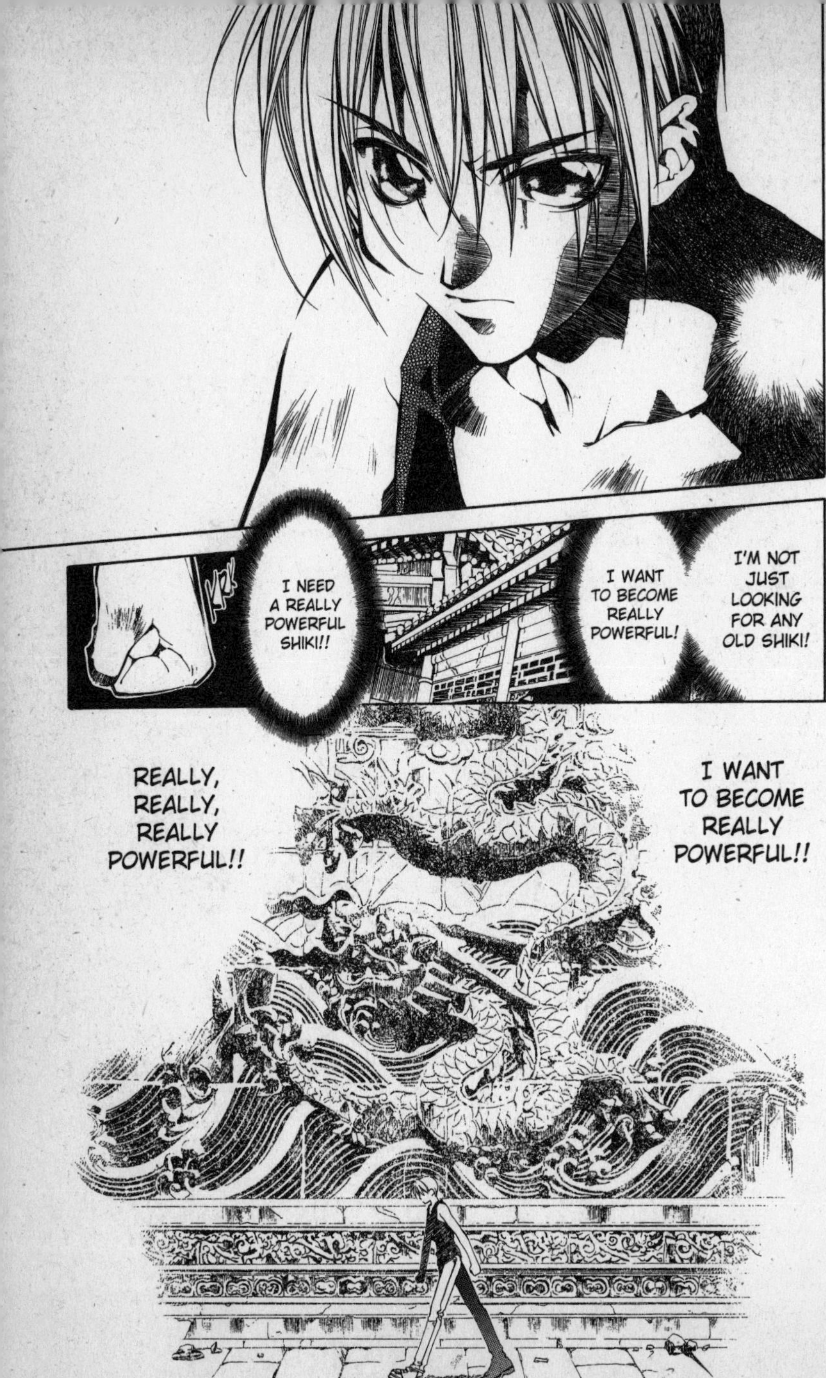
I'M NOT JUST LOOKING FOR ANY OLD SHIKI!
I WANT TO BECOME REALLY POWERFUL!
I NEED A REALLY POWERFUL SHIKI!!
I WANT TO BECOME REALLY POWERFUL!!
REALLY, REALLY, REALLY POWERFUL!!

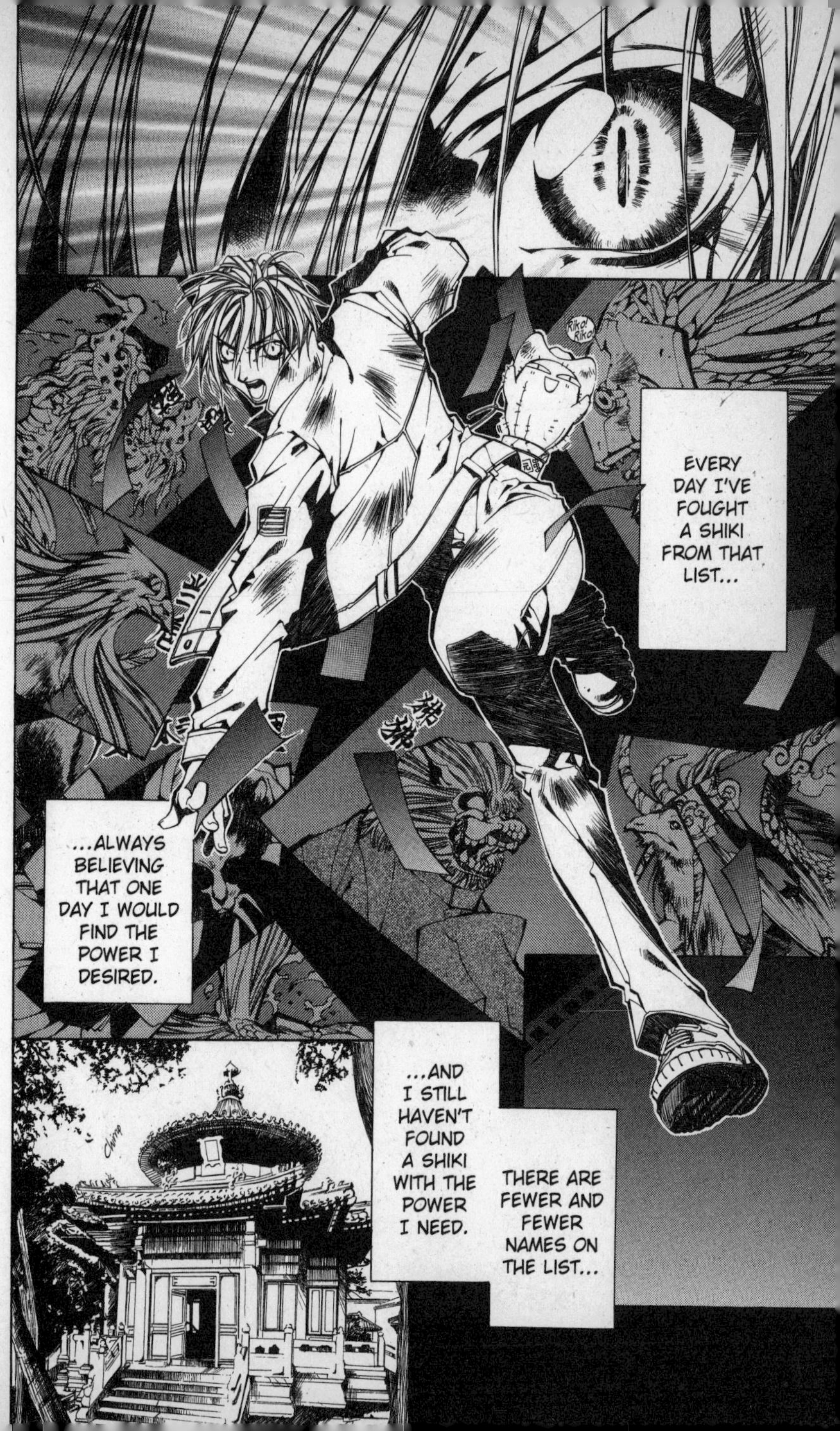
Riko! Riko!
EVERY DAY I'VE FOUGHT A SHIKI FROM THAT LIST...
...ALWAYS BELIEVING THAT ONE DAY I WOULD FIND THE POWER I DESIRED.
...AND I STILL HAVEN'T FOUND A SHIKI WITH THE POWER I NEED.
THERE ARE FEWER AND FEWER NAMES ON THE LIST...
Chirp

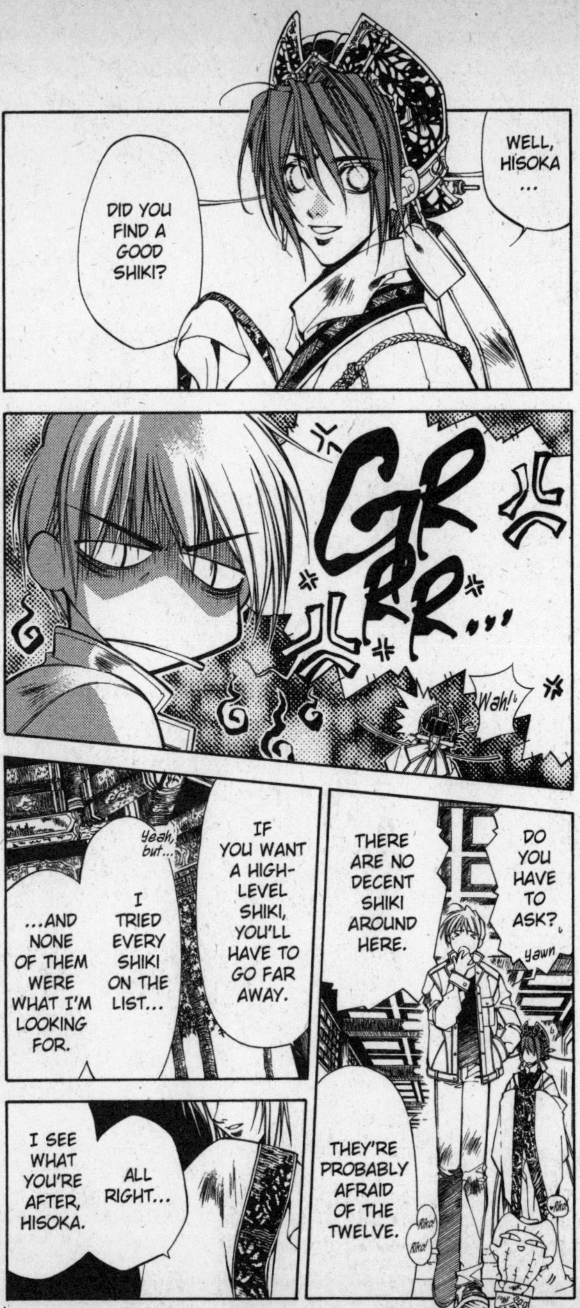
WELL, HISOKA ...
DID YOU FIND A GOOD SHIKI?
GRRR...
Wah!
DO YOU HAVE TO ASK?
yawn
THERE ARE NO DECENT SHIKI AROUND HERE.
THEY'RE PROBABLY AFRAID OF THE TWELVE.
IF YOU WANT A HIGH-LEVEL SHIKI, YOU'LL HAVE TO GO FAR AWAY.
Yeah, but...
I TRIED EVERY SHIKI ON THE LIST...
...AND NONE OF THEM WERE WHAT I'M LOOKING FOR.
ALL RIGHT...
I SEE WHAT YOU'RE AFTER, HISOKA.

Topic 2: Final Fantasy VII

I think Dragon Quest is my favorite game of the desktop computer era. Of the PlayStation games, my favorite has to be the Final Fantasy series. Actually, I started out playing FF VII. I'm still just a novice. I've played some of the later versions of FF, but I still like seven the best. The scenario, the characters, the music, and the whole feeling of it really appeal to me. I even bought the international version. There are a lot of things about the scenario that I don't understand, but it's fun to come up with my own interpretations. It makes it even more fun to play. I laugh, I cry, I meet new friends and sadly part with them right along with the characters. Just thinking about it makes me want to play. I was always asking people in the editorial department for tips on how to make Vincent open that box (laugh). I'm sorry for all the trouble I caused. I'd like to use this space to apologize. The best weapon for a man is a gun!

I love to see Vincent shoot.

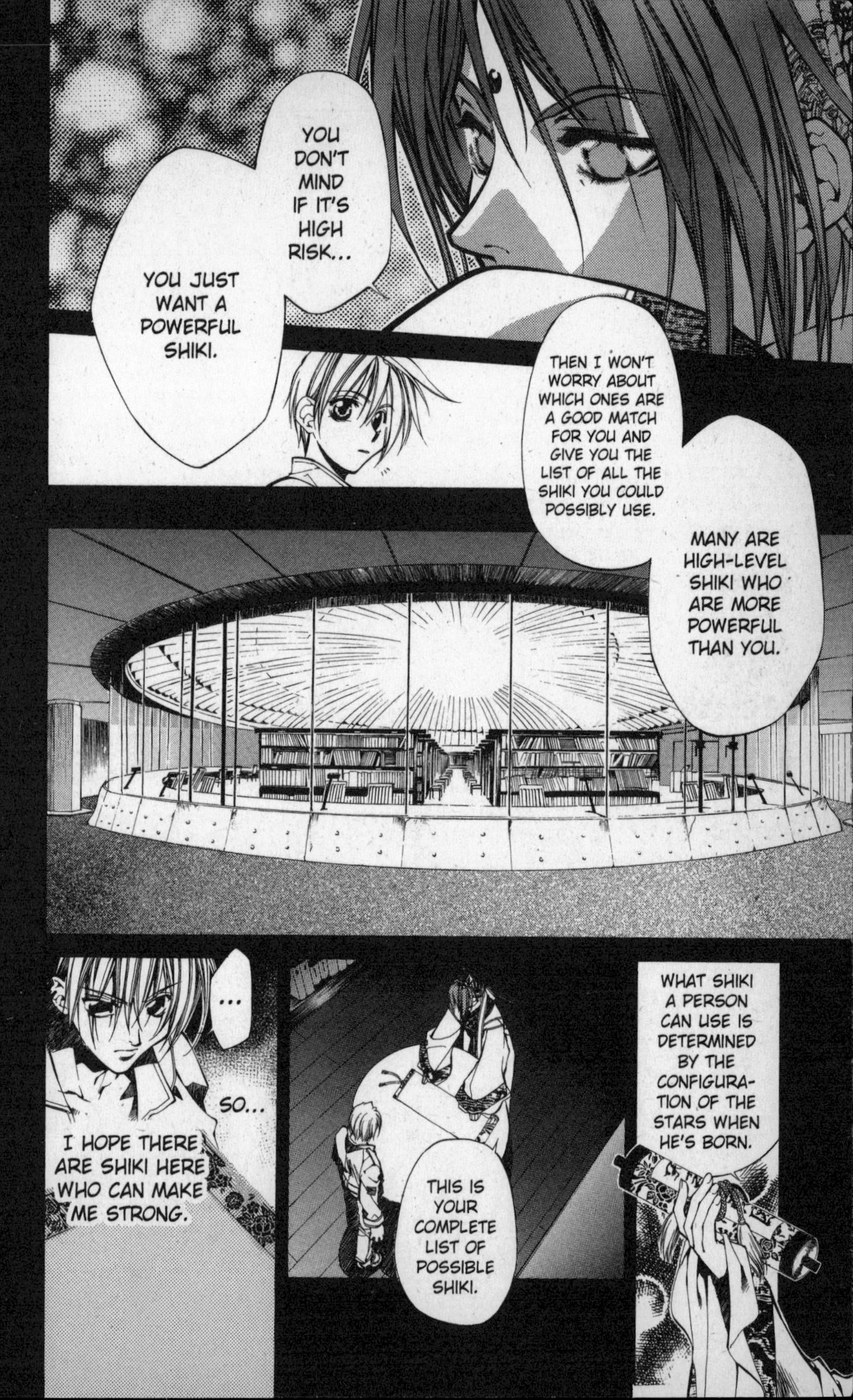
YOU DON'T MIND IF IT'S HIGH RISK...
YOU JUST WANT A POWERFUL SHIKI.
THEN I WON'T WORRY ABOUT WHICH ONES ARE A GOOD MATCH FOR YOU AND GIVE YOU THE LIST OF ALL THE SHIKI YOU COULD POSSIBLY USE.
MANY ARE HIGH-LEVEL SHIKI WHO ARE MORE POWERFUL THAN YOU.
WHAT SHIKI A PERSON CAN USE IS DETERMINED BY THE CONFIGURATION OF THE STARS WHEN HE'S BORN.
THIS IS YOUR COMPLETE LIST OF POSSIBLE SHIKI.
...
SO...
I HOPE THERE ARE SHIKI HERE WHO CAN MAKE ME STRONG.

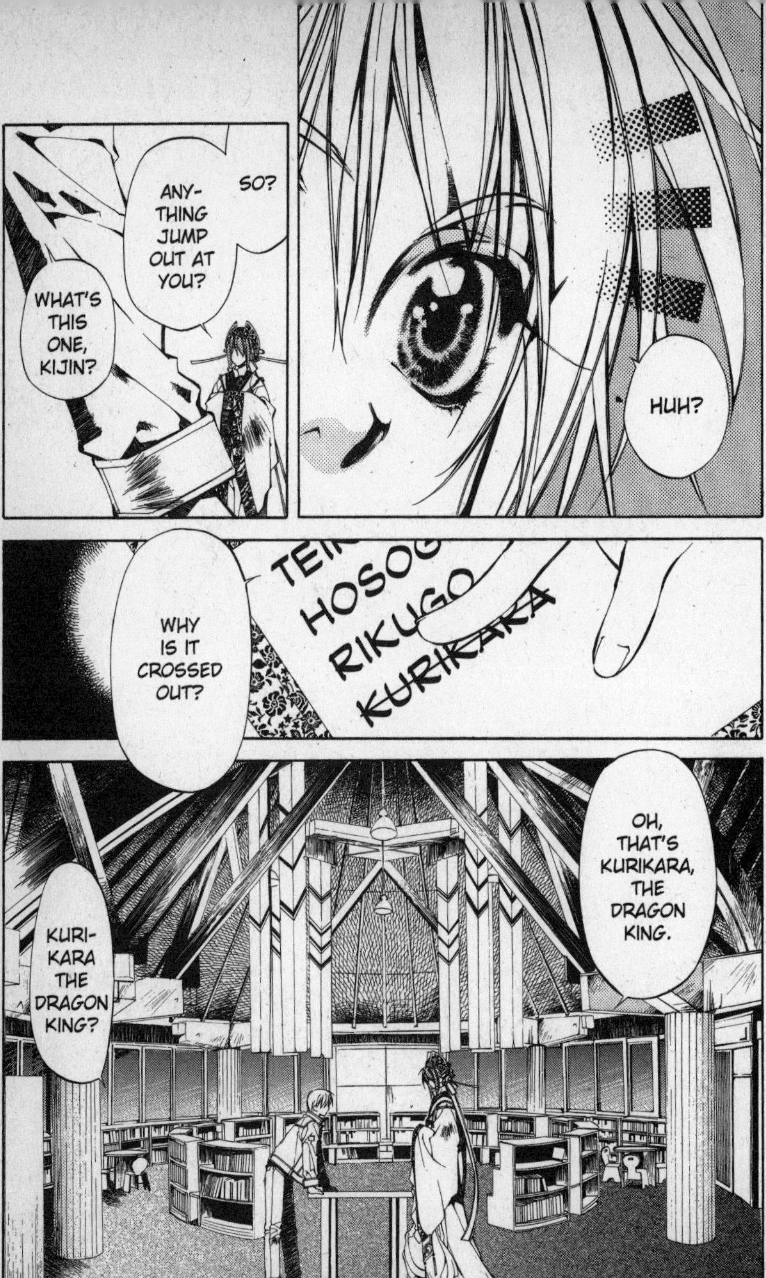
HUH?
SO?
ANY-THING JUMP OUT AT YOU?
WHAT'S THIS ONE, KIJIN?
RIKUGO
KURIKAKA
WHY IS IT CROSSED OUT?
OH, THAT'S KURIKARA, THE DRAGON KING.
KURI-KARA THE DRAGON KING?

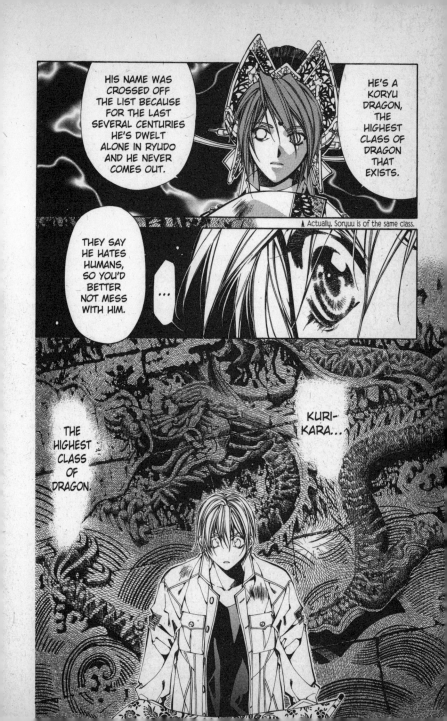

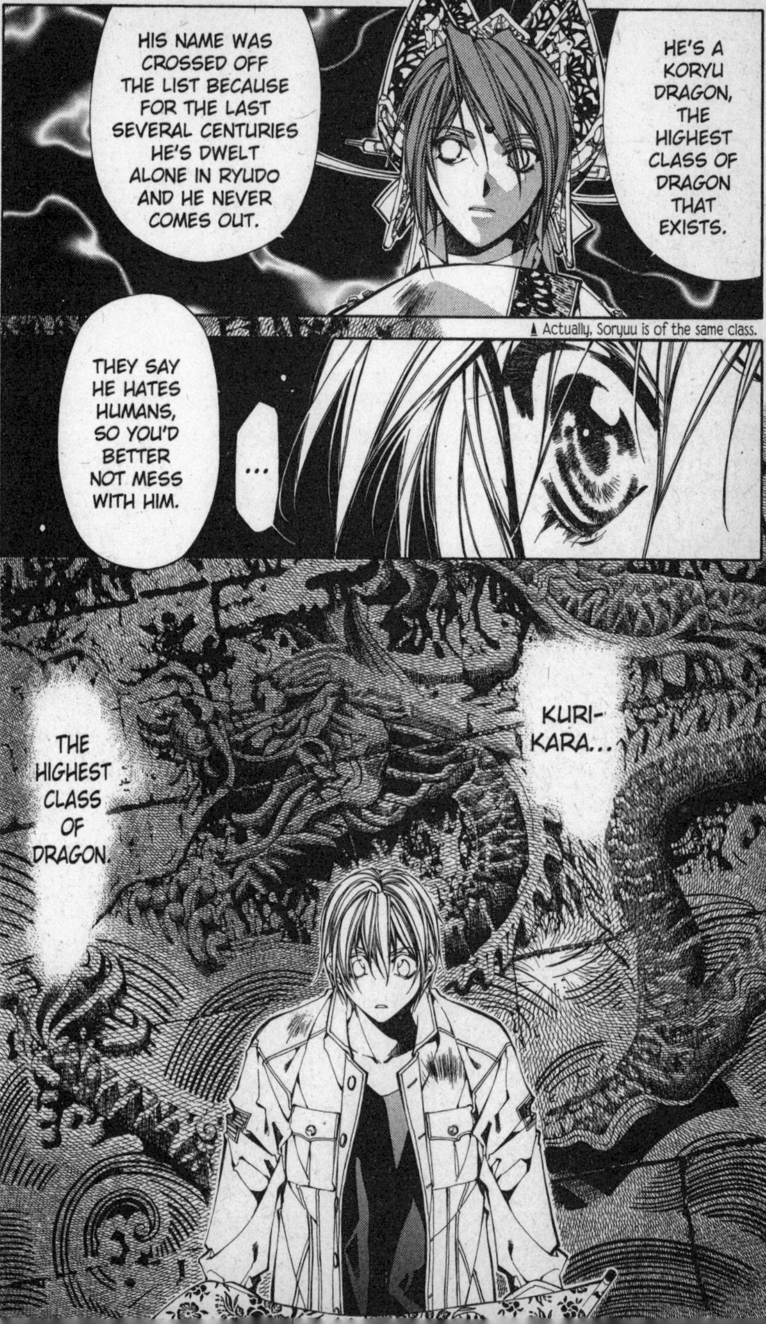
HE'S A KORYU DRAGON, THE HIGHEST CLASS OF DRAGON THAT EXISTS.
HIS NAME WAS CROSSED OFF THE LIST BECAUSE FOR THE LAST SEVERAL CENTURIES HE'S DWELT ALONE IN RYUDO AND HE NEVER COMES OUT.
▲ Actually, Soryuu is of the same class.
...
THEY SAY HE HATES HUMANS, SO YOU'D BETTER NOT MESS WITH HIM.
KURI-KARA...
THE HIGHEST CLASS OF DRAGON.

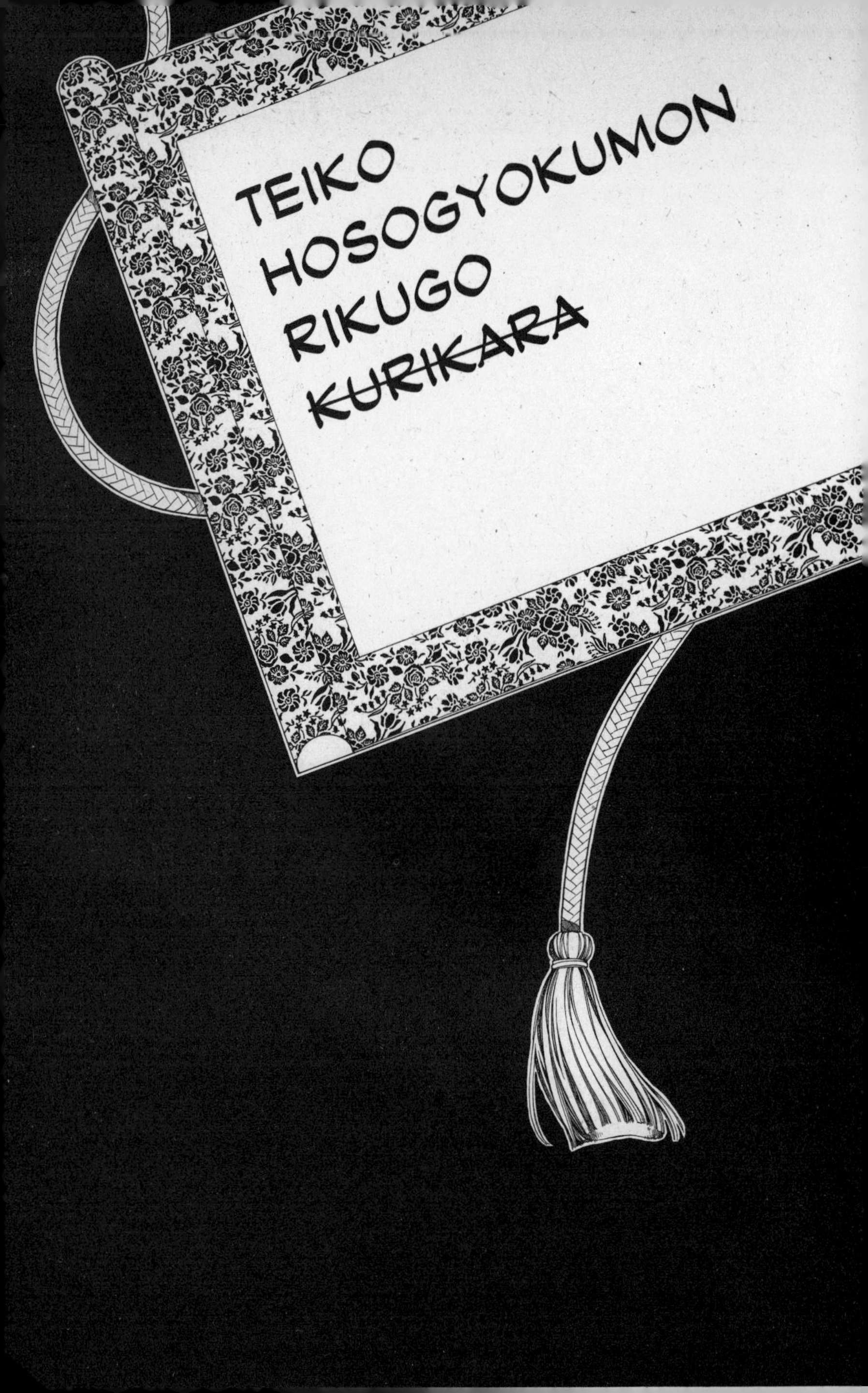
TEIKO
HOSOGYOKUMON
RIKUGO
KURIKARA

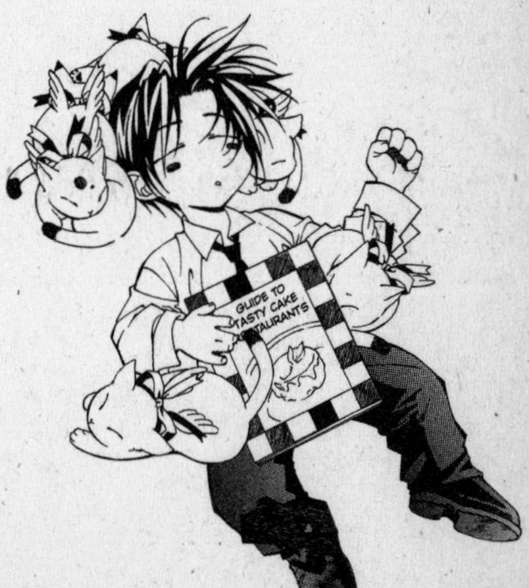
GUIDE TO
TASTY CAKE
RESTAURANTS

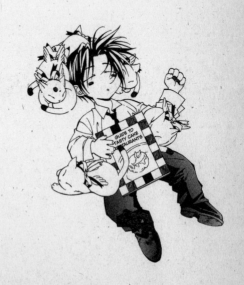

CHAPTER 40

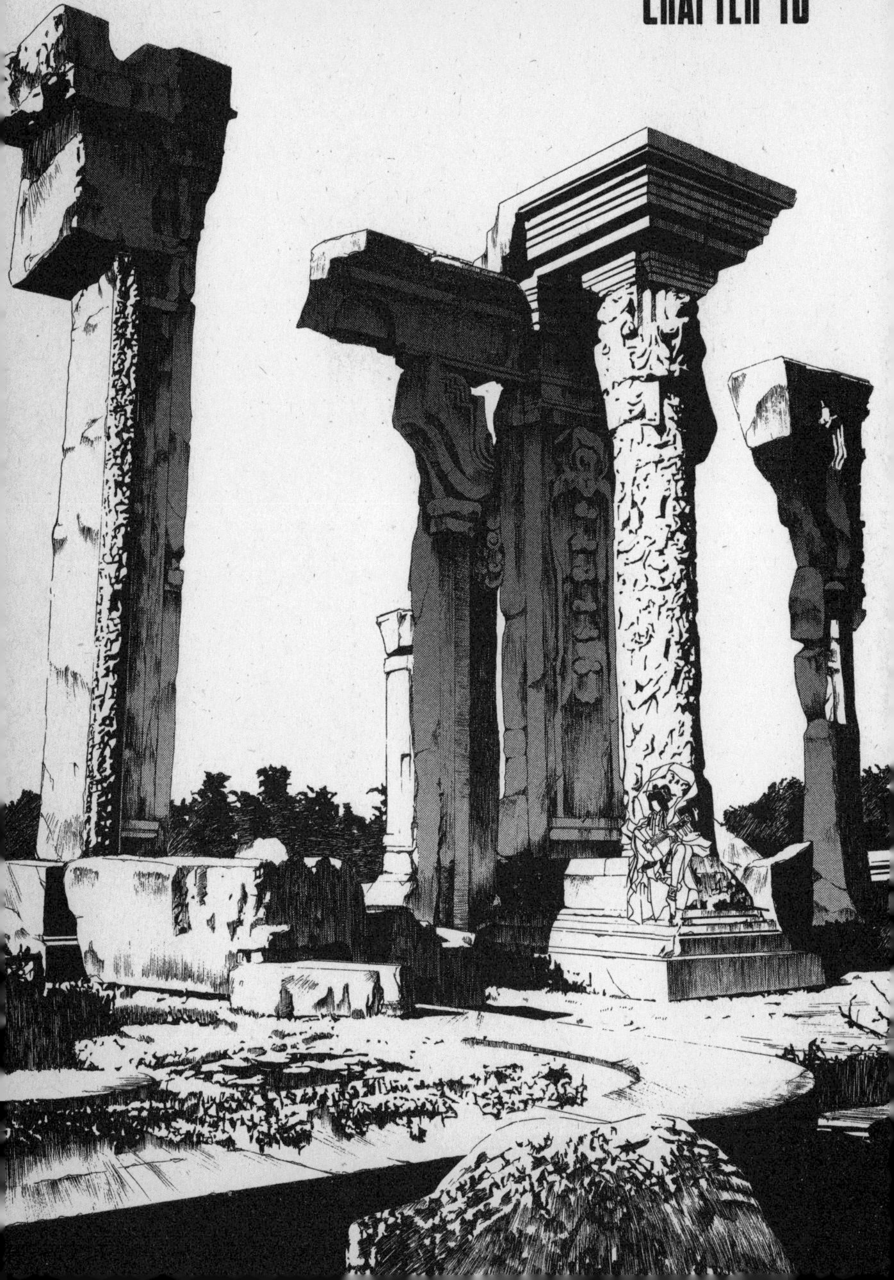

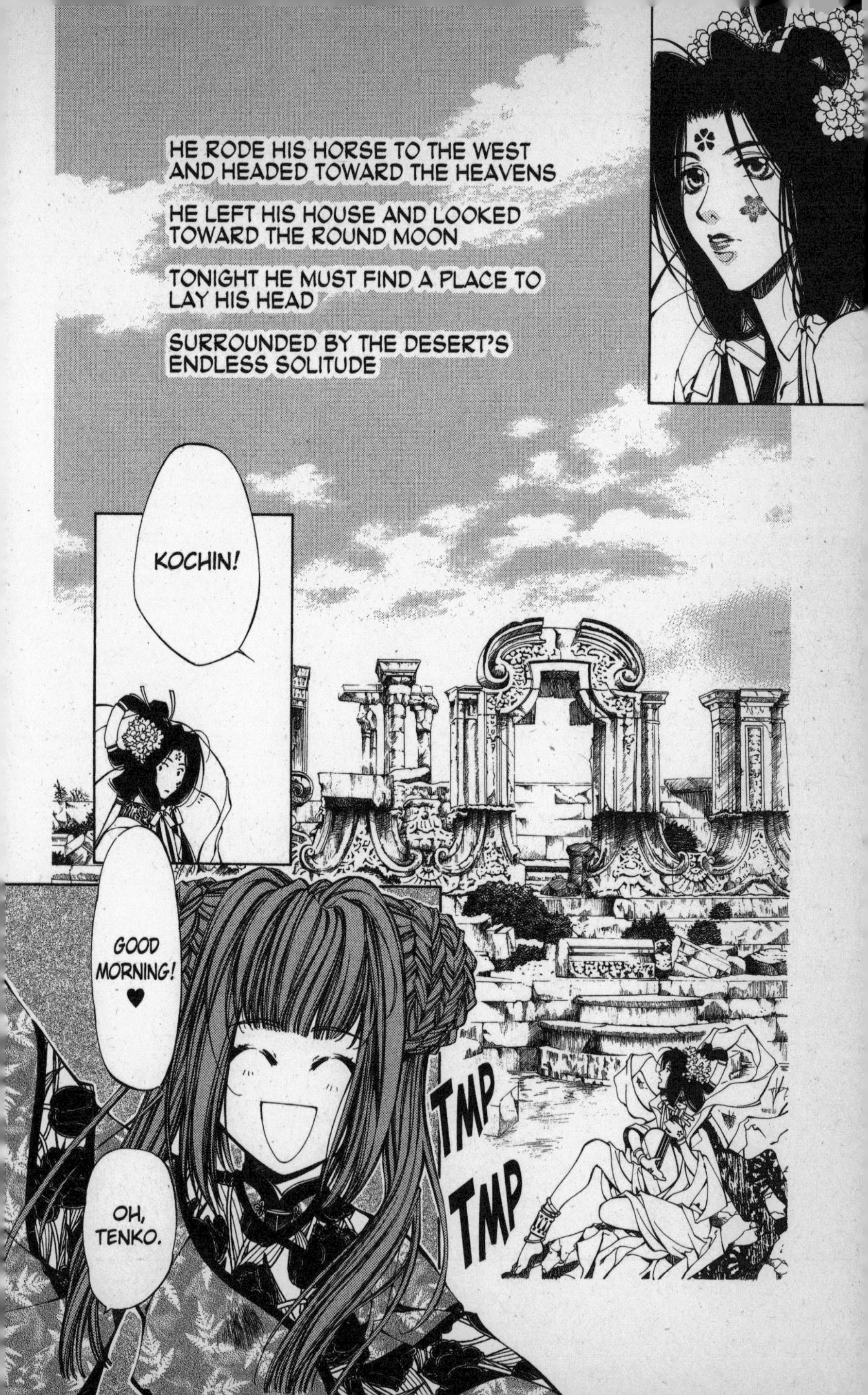
HE RODE HIS HORSE TO THE WEST AND HEADED TOWARD THE HEAVENS
HE LEFT HIS HOUSE AND LOOKED TOWARD THE ROUND MOON
TONIGHT HE MUST FIND A PLACE TO LAY HIS HEAD
SURROUNDED BY THE DESERT'S ENDLESS SOLITUDE
KOCHIN!
GOOD MORNING! ♥
TMP TMP
OH, TENKO.

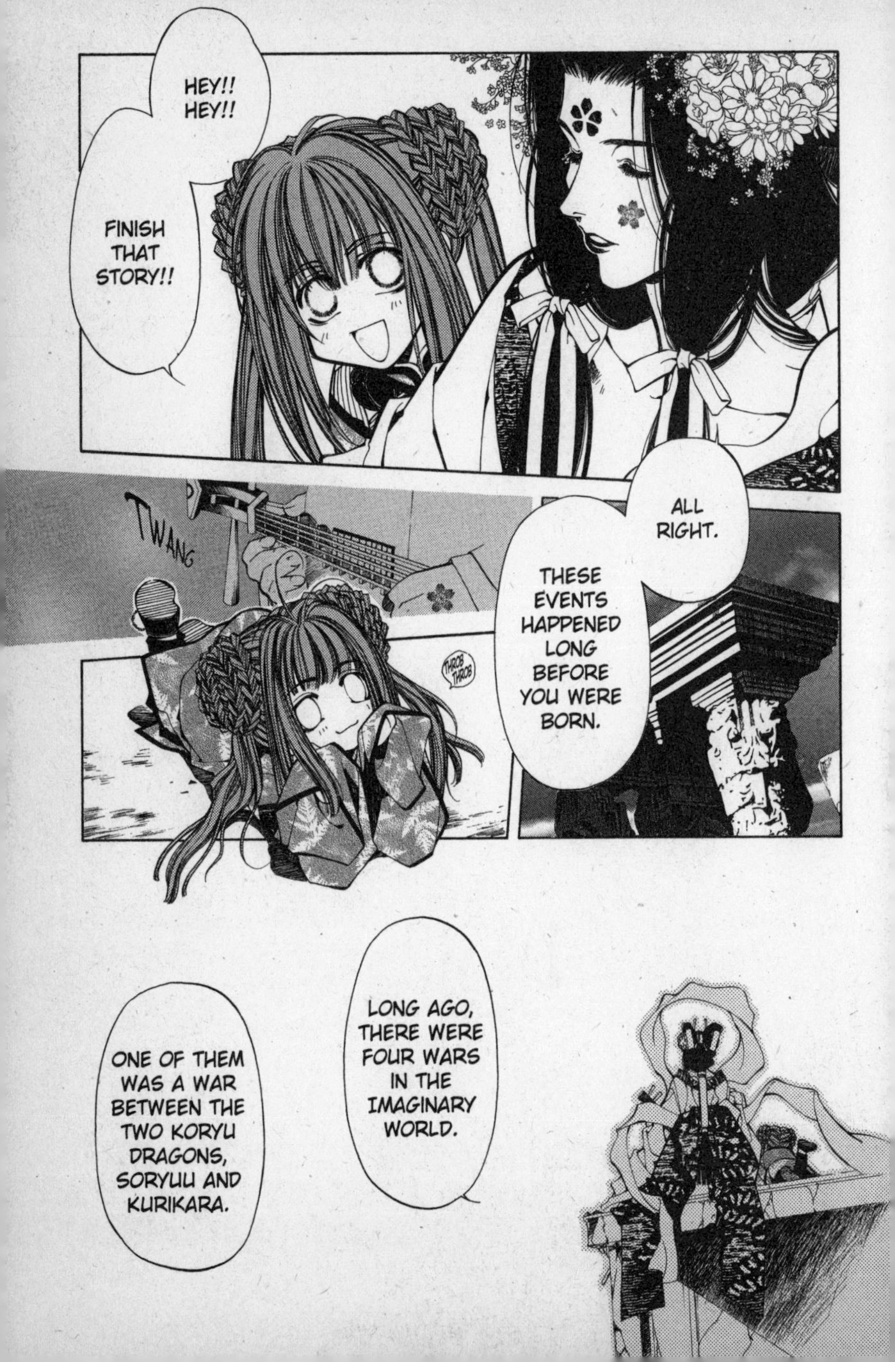
HEY!! HEY!!
FINISH THAT STORY!!
ALL RIGHT.
THESE EVENTS HAPPENED LONG BEFORE YOU WERE BORN.
TWANG
THROB THROB
LONG AGO, THERE WERE FOUR WARS IN THE IMAGINARY WORLD.
ONE OF THEM WAS A WAR BETWEEN THE TWO KORYU DRAGONS, SORYUU AND KURIKARA.

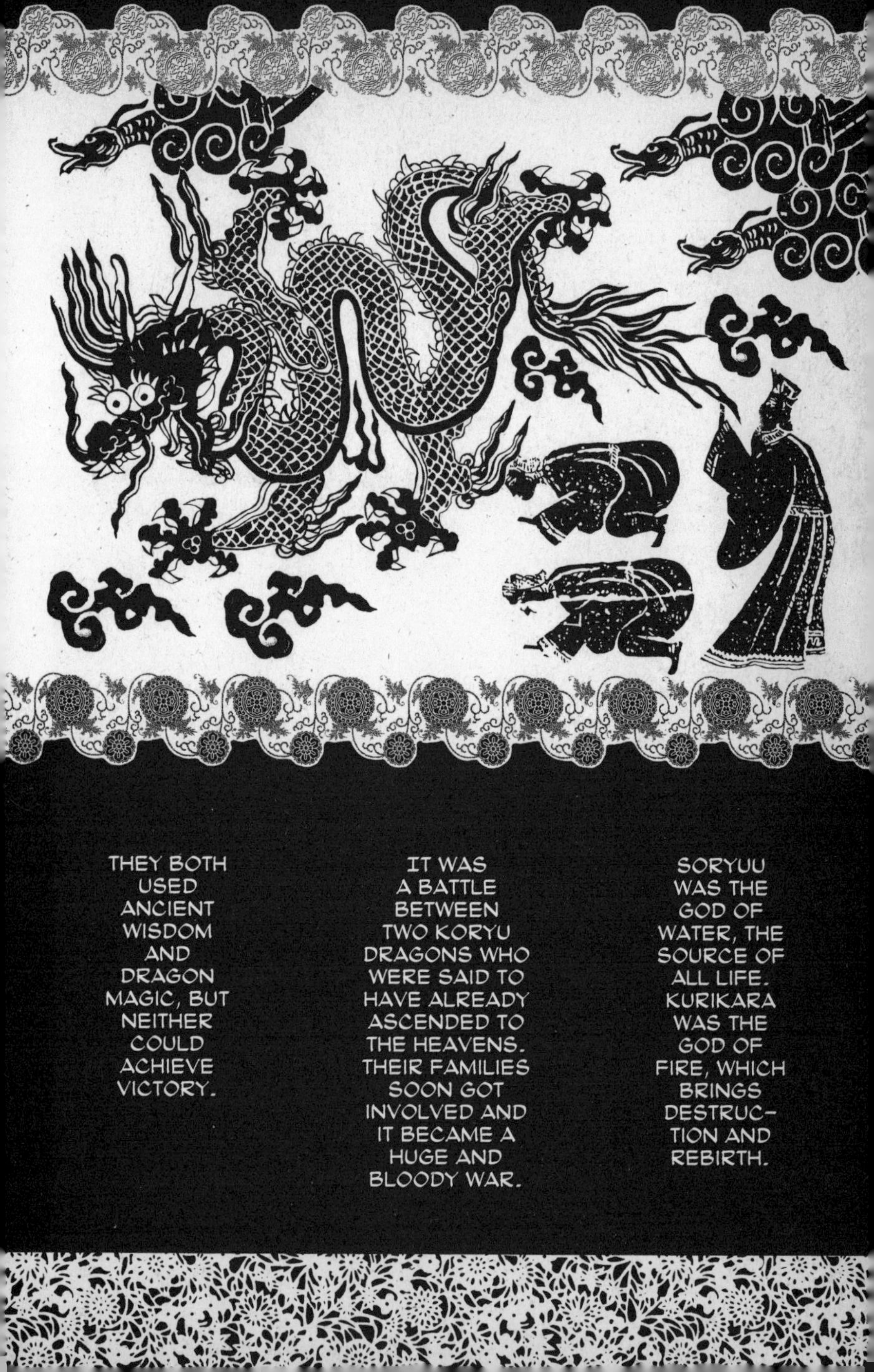
SORYUU WAS THE GOD OF WATER, THE SOURCE OF ALL LIFE. KURIKARA WAS THE GOD OF FIRE, WHICH BRINGS DESTRUCTION AND REBIRTH.
IT WAS A BATTLE BETWEEN TWO KORYU DRAGONS WHO WERE SAID TO HAVE ALREADY ASCENDED TO THE HEAVENS. THEIR FAMILIES SOON GOT INVOLVED AND IT BECAME A HUGE AND BLOODY WAR.
THEY BOTH USED ANCIENT WISDOM AND DRAGON MAGIC, BUT NEITHER COULD ACHIEVE VICTORY.

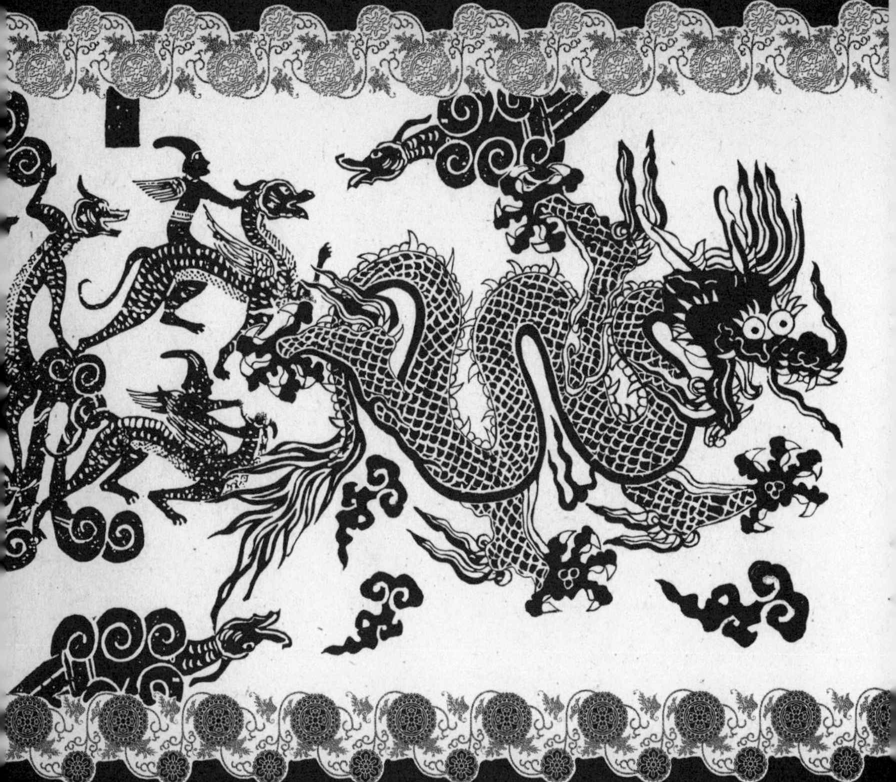

THE FLAMES OF KURIKARA, WITH HIS BODY OF BLACK STEEL, BURNED FOR SEVEN DAYS AND SEVEN NIGHTS. THEY SCORCHED THE EARTH AND DRIED UP THE SEVEN SEAS.

THE EMPEROR WAS SADDENED TO SEE THE DESTRUCTION OF THE WORLD, SO HE MARCHED FORTH WITH AN ARMY OF ONE MILLION SOLDIERS OF GOD TO AID SORYUU.

ON THE MORNING OF THE EIGHTH DAY, KURIKARA WAS DEFEATED.

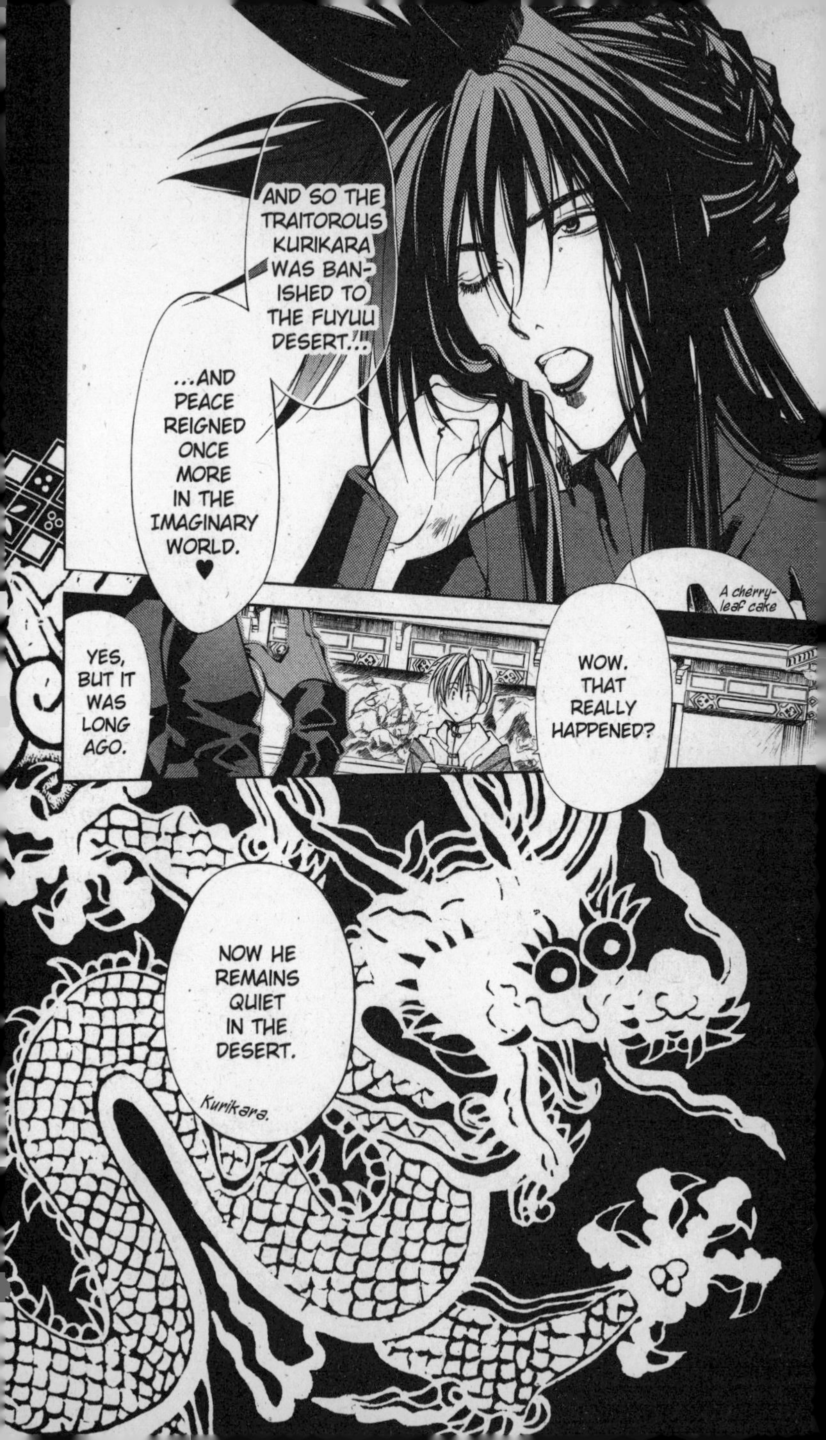
AND SO THE TRAITOROUS KURIKARA WAS BAN-ISHED TO THE FUYUU DESERT...
...AND PEACE REIGNED ONCE MORE IN THE IMAGINARY WORLD. ♥
A cherry-leaf cake
WOW. THAT REALLY HAPPENED?
YES, BUT IT WAS LONG AGO.
NOW HE REMAINS QUIET IN THE DESERT.
Kurikara.

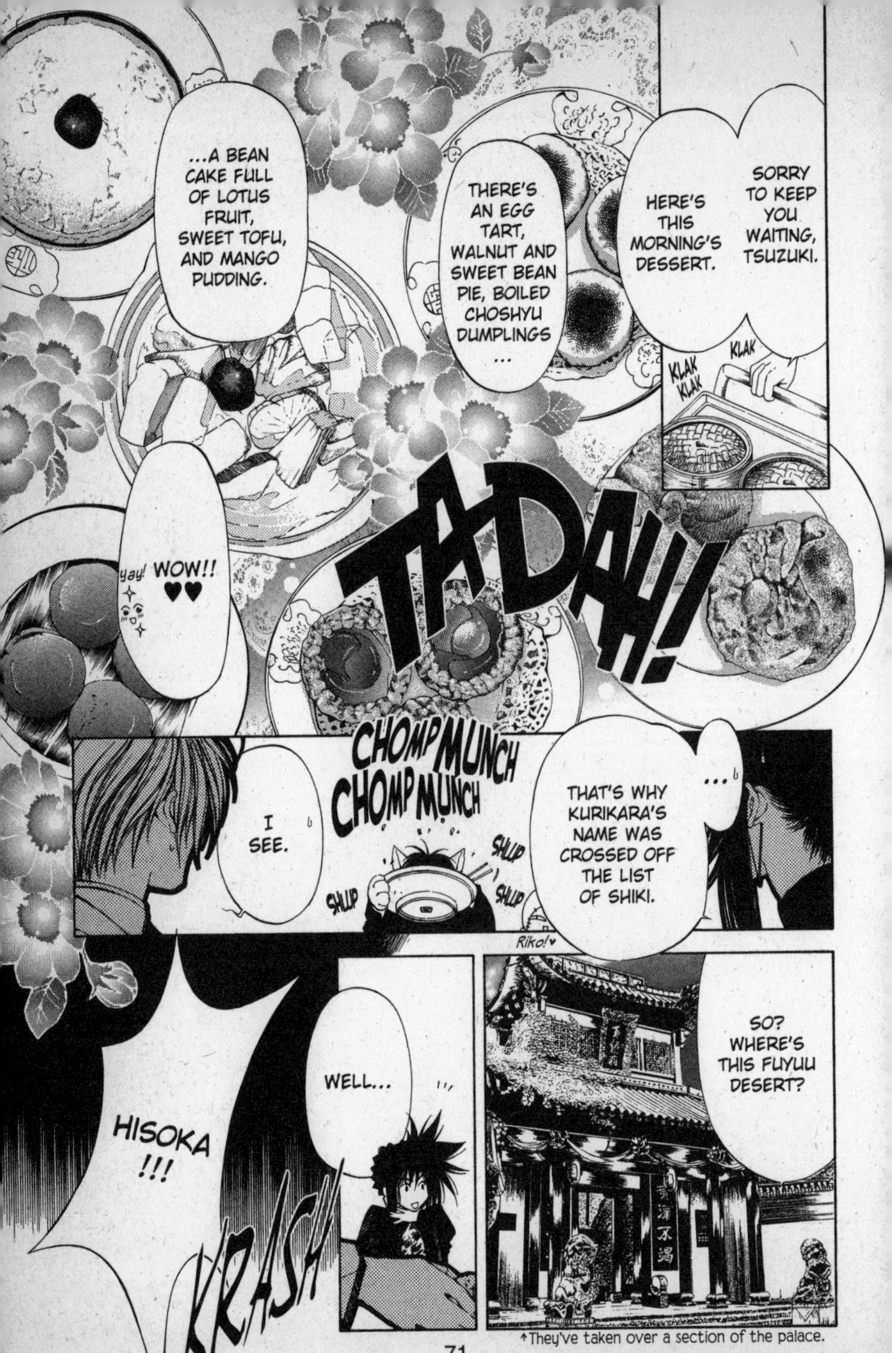
SORRY TO KEEP YOU WAITING, TSUZUKI.
HERE'S THIS MORNING'S DESSERT.
KLAK
KLAK KLAK
THERE'S AN EGG TART, WALNUT AND SWEET BEAN PIE, BOILED CHOSHYU DUMPLINGS ...
...A BEAN CAKE FULL OF LOTUS FRUIT, SWEET TOFU, AND MANGO PUDDING.
TADAH!!
yay! WOW!! ♥♥
...
THAT'S WHY KURIKARA'S NAME WAS CROSSED OFF THE LIST OF SHIKI.
CHOMP MUNCH CHOMP MUNCH
SHLUP SHLUP SHLUP
Riko!♥
I SEE.
SO? WHERE'S THIS FUYUU DESERT?
WELL...
HISOKA !!!
KRASH

↑They've taken over a section of the palace.

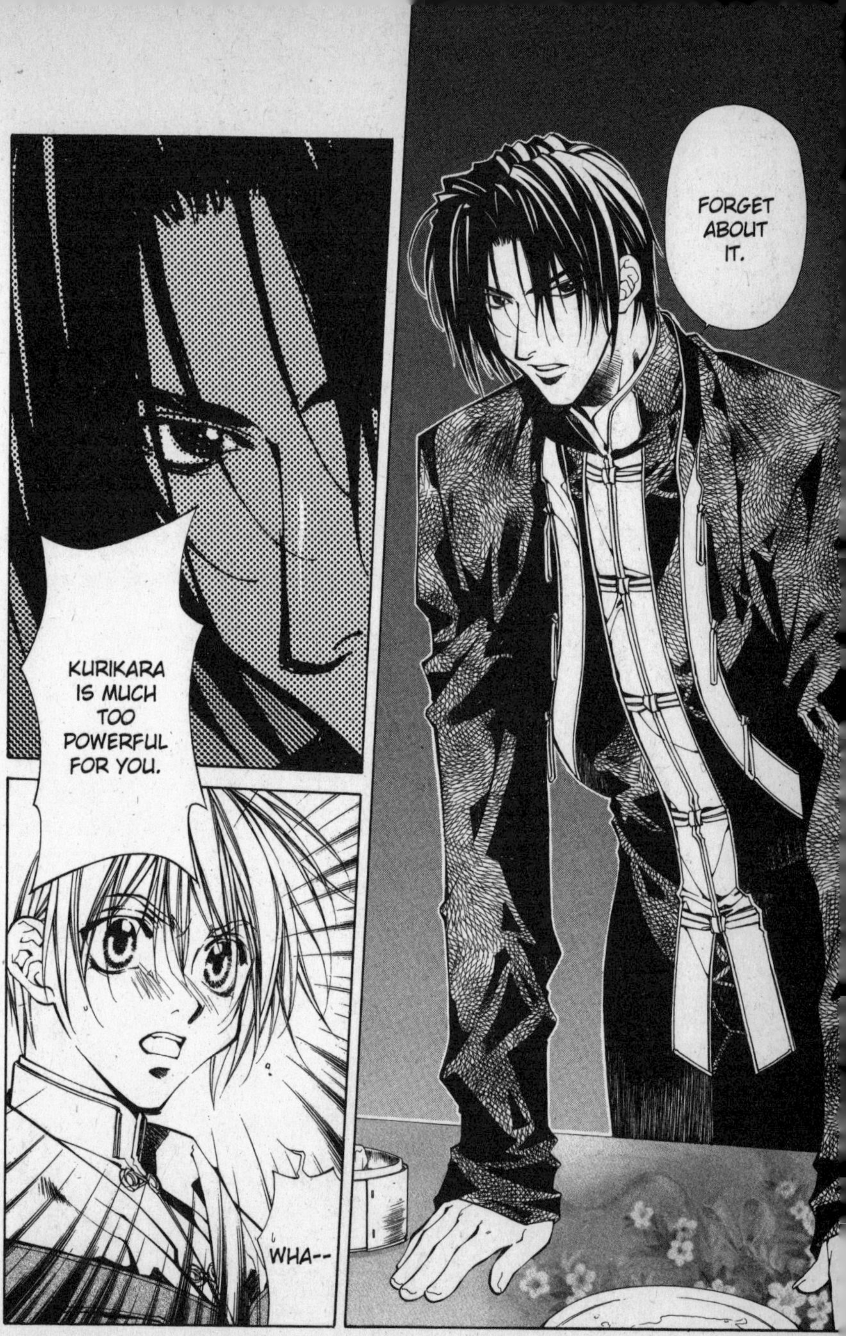
FORGET ABOUT IT.
KURIKARA IS MUCH TOO POWERFUL FOR YOU.
WHA--

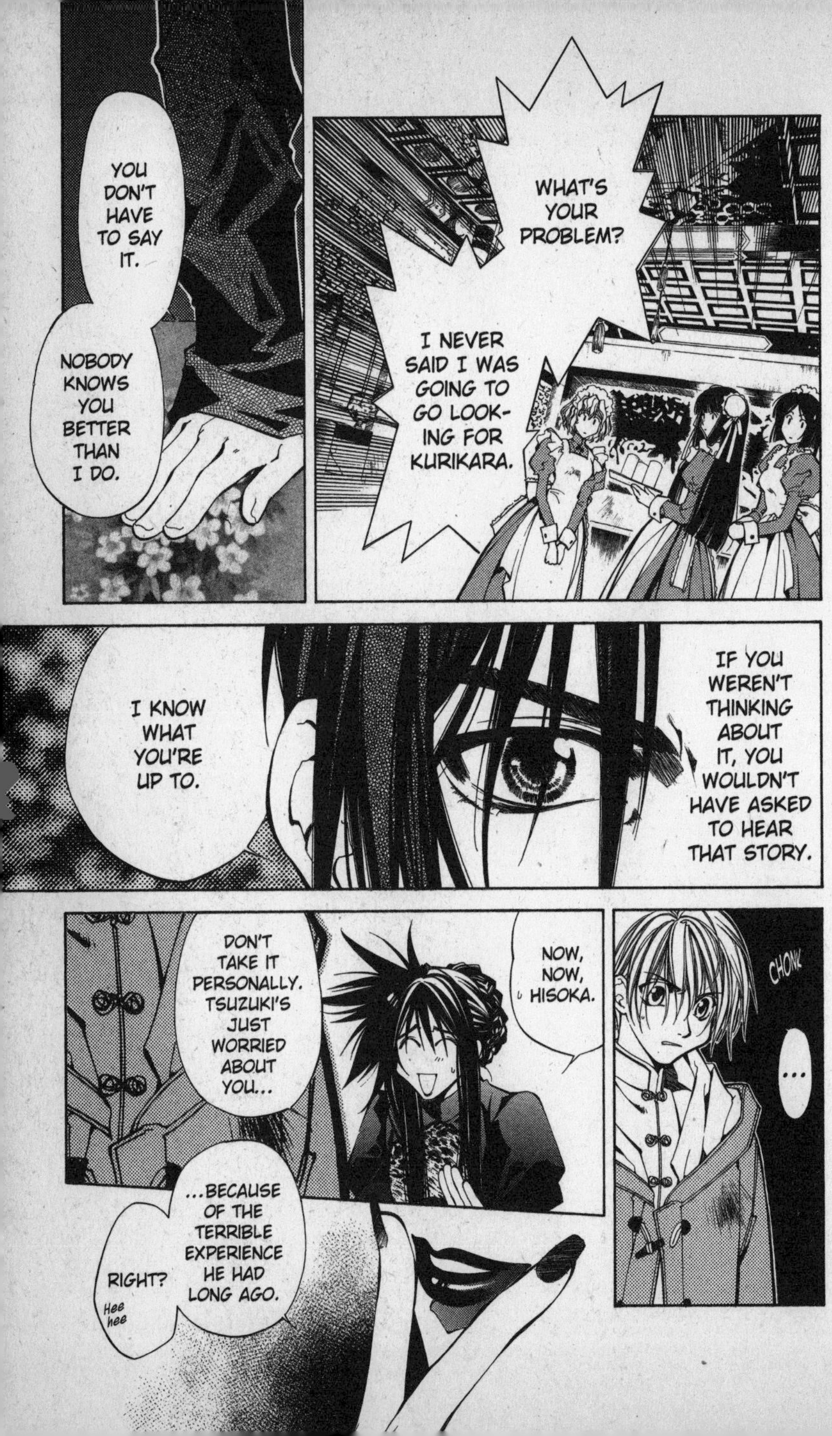
WHAT'S YOUR PROBLEM?
I NEVER SAID I WAS GOING TO GO LOOK-ING FOR KURIKARA.
YOU DON'T HAVE TO SAY IT.
NOBODY KNOWS YOU BETTER THAN I DO.
IF YOU WEREN'T THINKING ABOUT IT, YOU WOULDN'T HAVE ASKED TO HEAR THAT STORY.
I KNOW WHAT YOU'RE UP TO.
CHONK
...
NOW, NOW, HISOKA.
DON'T TAKE IT PERSONALLY. TSUZUKI'S JUST WORRIED ABOUT YOU...
...BECAUSE OF THE TERRIBLE EXPERIENCE HE HAD LONG AGO.
RIGHT?
Hee hee

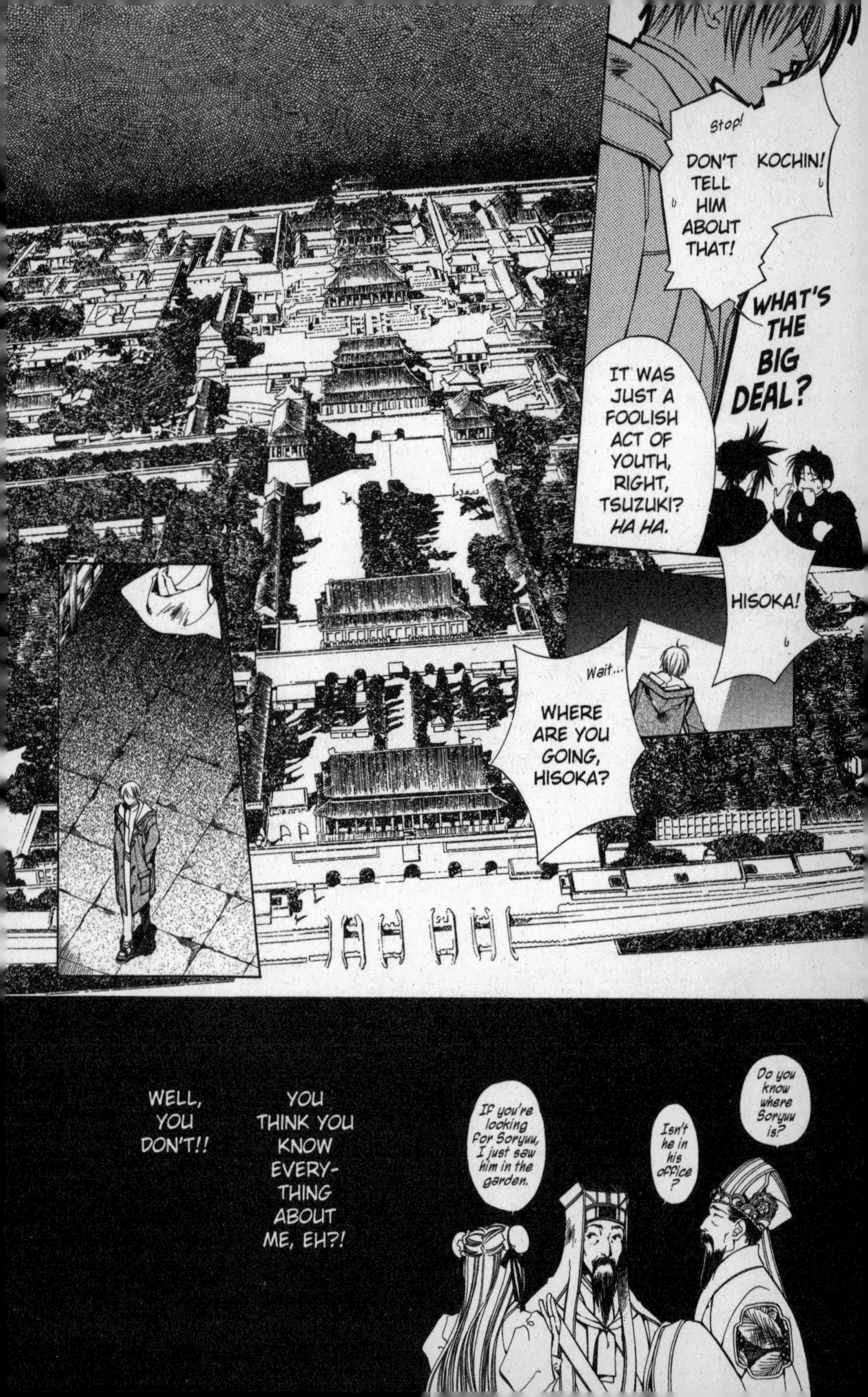

Stop! KOCHIN! DON'T TELL HIM ABOUT THAT!
WHAT'S THE BIG DEAL?
IT WAS JUST A FOOLISH ACT OF YOUTH, RIGHT, TSUZUKI? HA HA.
HISOKA!
Wait... WHERE ARE YOU GOING, HISOKA?
Do you know where Soryuu is?
Isn't he in his office?
If you're looking for Soryuu, I just saw him in the garden.
YOU THINK YOU KNOW EVERY-THING ABOUT ME, EH?!
WELL, YOU DON'T!!

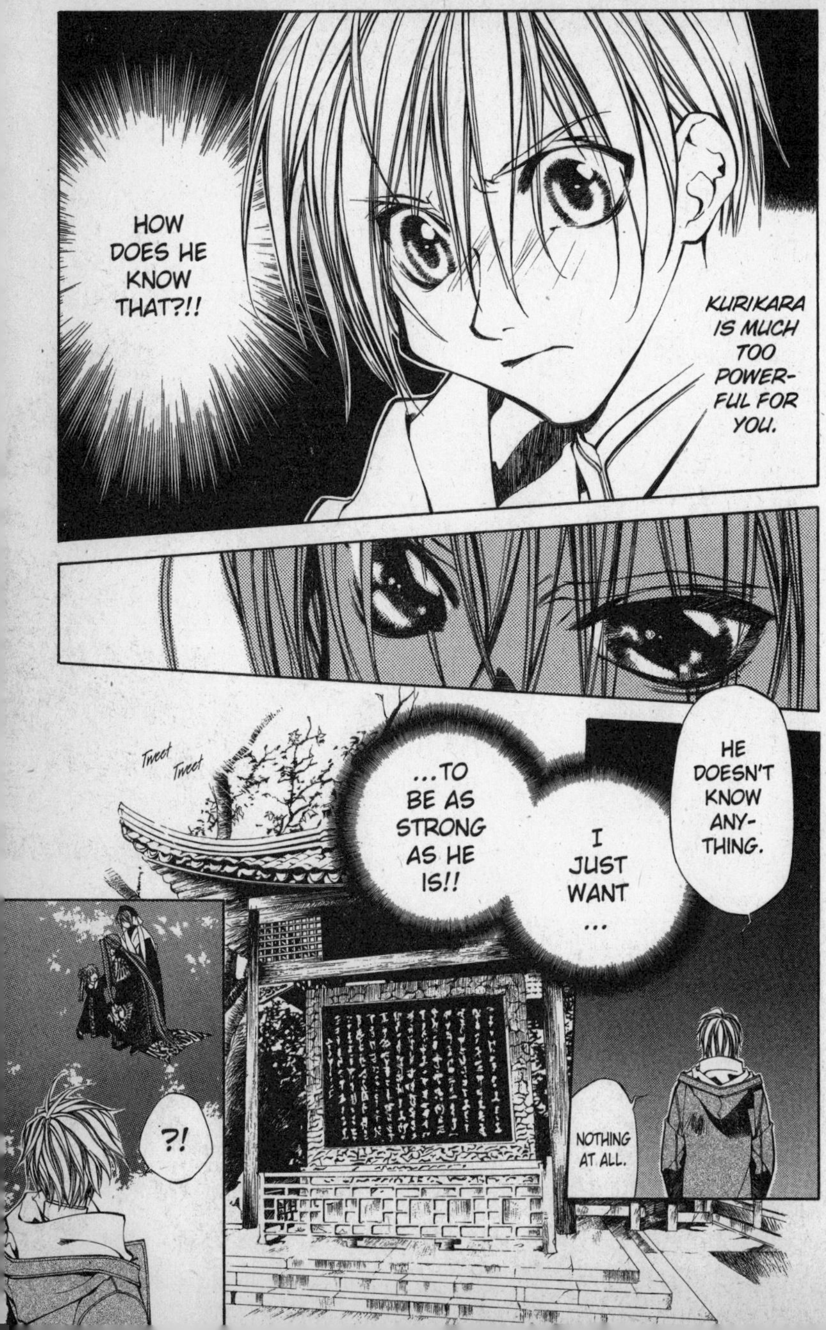
KURIKARA IS MUCH TOO POWERFUL FOR YOU.
HOW DOES HE KNOW THAT?!!
HE DOESN'T KNOW ANYTHING.
I JUST WANT ...
...TO BE AS STRONG AS HE IS!!
Tweet Tweet
NOTHING AT ALL.
?!

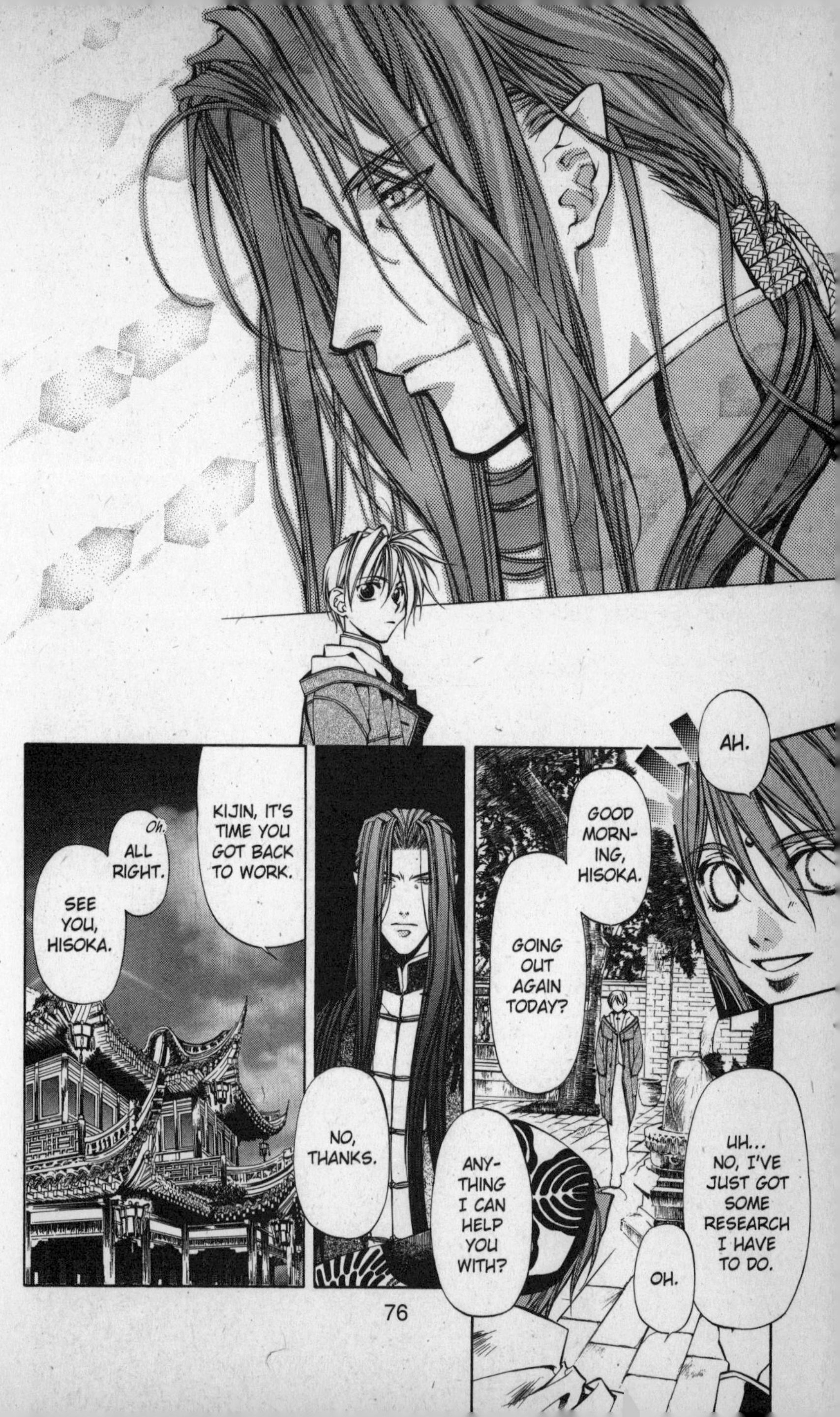
AH.
GOOD MORNING, HISOKA.
GOING OUT AGAIN TODAY?
UH... NO, I'VE JUST GOT SOME RESEARCH I HAVE TO DO.
OH.
ANYTHING I CAN HELP YOU WITH?
NO, THANKS.
KIJIN, IT'S TIME YOU GOT BACK TO WORK.
Oh. ALL RIGHT.
SEE YOU, HISOKA.

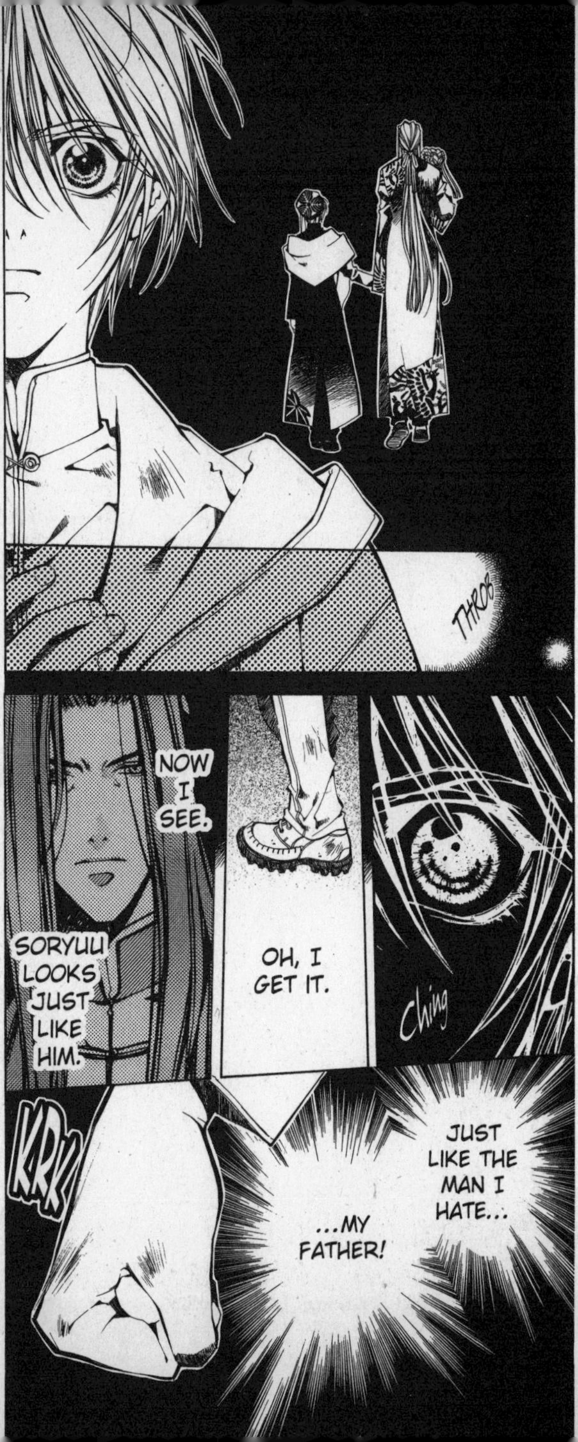
THROB
Ching
OH, I GET IT.
NOW I SEE.
SORYUU LOOKS JUST LIKE HIM.
JUST LIKE THE MAN I HATE...
...MY FATHER!
KRK

Topic 3: Wild Arms

To anybody out there who has a PlayStation and likes role playing games, check this one out! It's really, really fun! I'd almost put it on the same level as Dragon Quest and Final Fantasy. I really like the dramatic music too. It's a really wild game. And Rody really gets me.

HE'S COOL AND CUTE.

I usually don't like guys like that (laugh). Even though he's a male character, you see way more of him than the girls. And as the game goes on, we learn the secret of Rody's birth. I can't get enough of him. I'm a huge Rody fan! The fact that he was picked on as a child but grew up to be a good guy really gets to me. When I reach the end and the anime comes on, I always burst into tears. I can't watch it without crying. The anime is excellent. The whistling in the background makes me cry too. Michiko Naruke's music is the best. I want the whole soundtrack.

And there's a lot of extra stuff at the end.

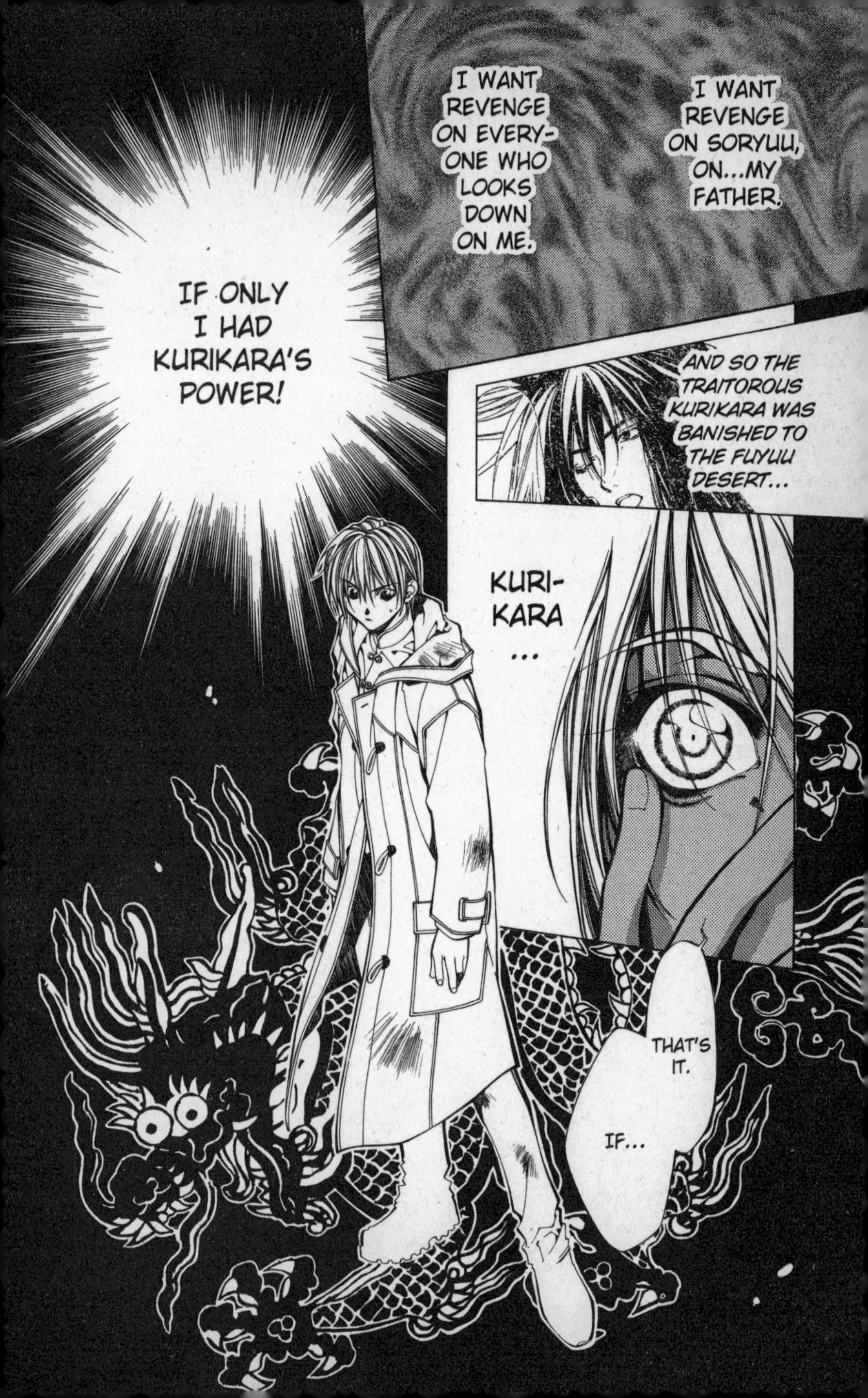
I WANT REVENGE ON SORYUU, ON...MY FATHER.
I WANT REVENGE ON EVERY-ONE WHO LOOKS DOWN ON ME.
AND SO THE TRAITOROUS KURIKARA WAS BANISHED TO THE FUYUU DESERT...
KURI-KARA ...
THAT'S IT.
IF...
IF ONLY I HAD KURIKARA'S POWER!

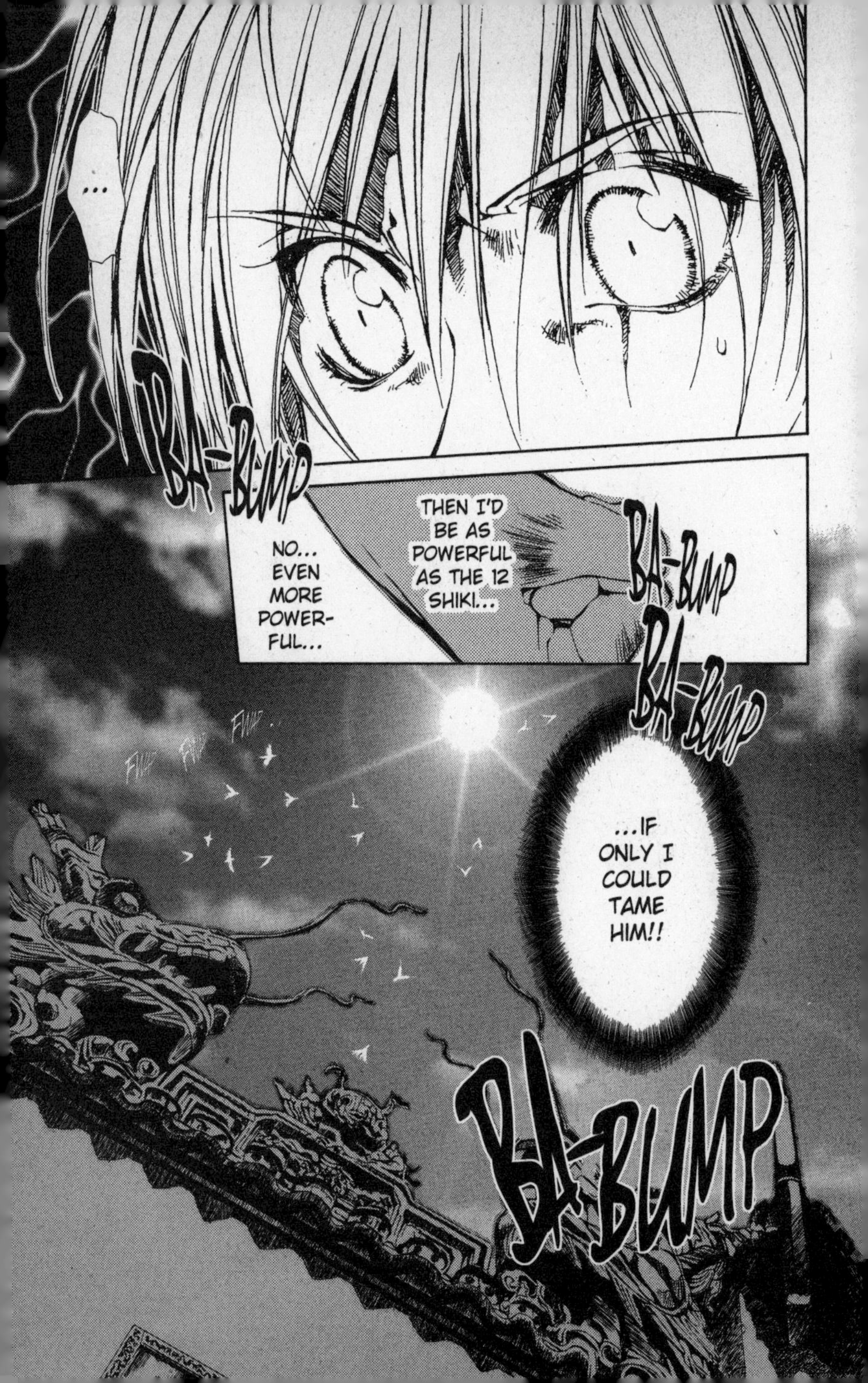
...
BA-BUMP
BA-BUMP
BA-BUMP
THEN I'D BE AS POWERFUL AS THE 12 SHIKI...
NO... EVEN MORE POWER-FUL...
...IF ONLY I COULD TAME HIM!!
BA-BUMP

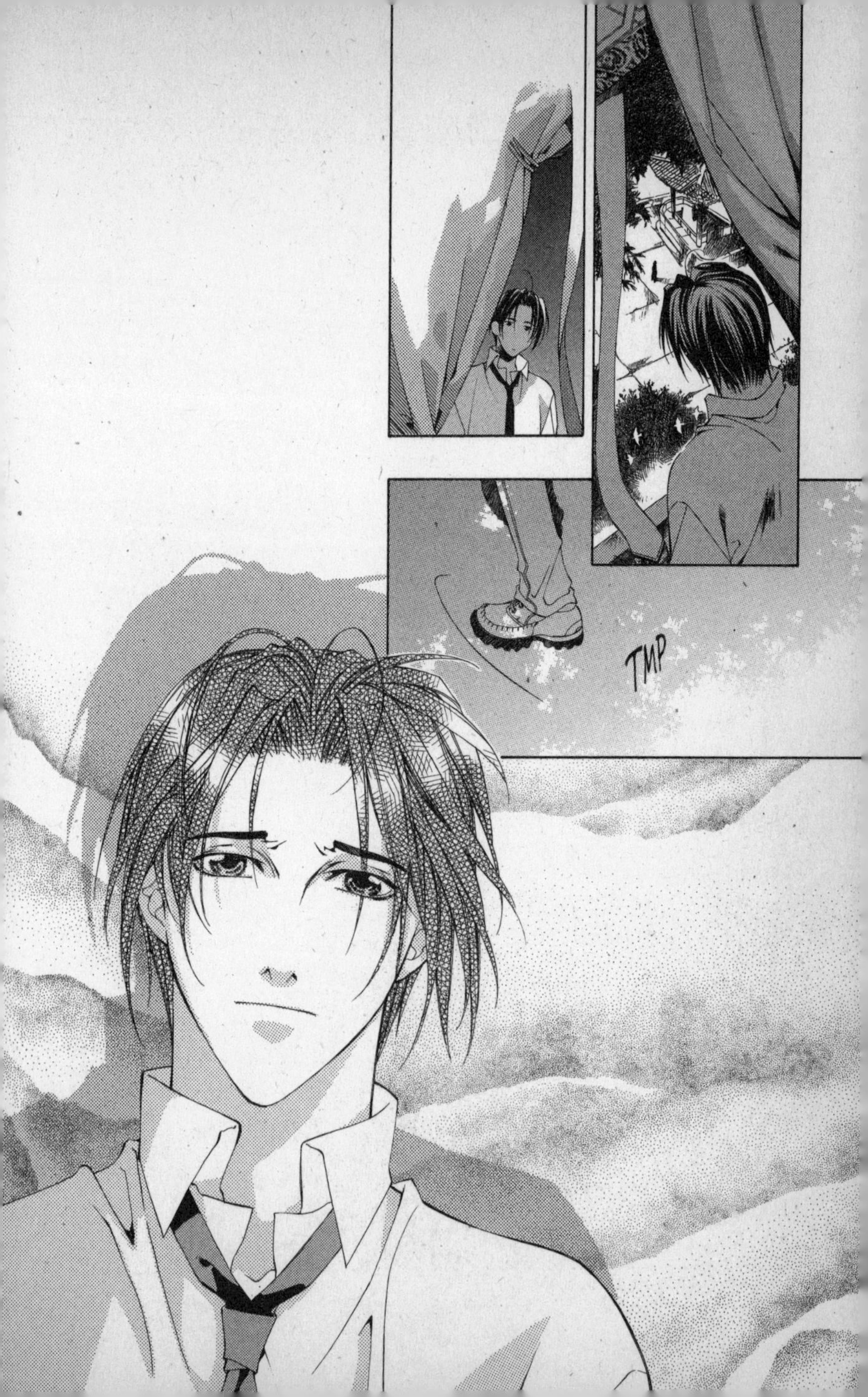
TMP

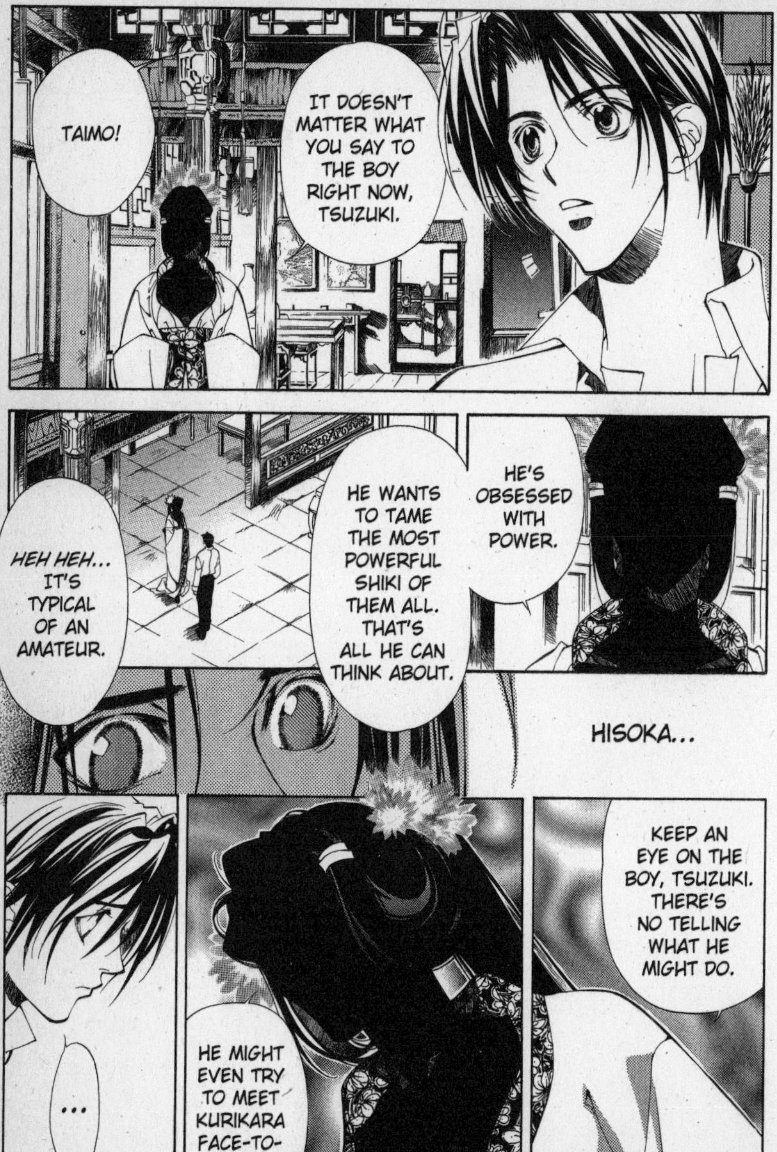
IT DOESN'T MATTER WHAT YOU SAY TO THE BOY RIGHT NOW, TSUZUKI.
TAIMO!
HE'S OBSESSED WITH POWER.
HE WANTS TO TAME THE MOST POWERFUL SHIKI OF THEM ALL. THAT'S ALL HE CAN THINK ABOUT.
HEH HEH... IT'S TYPICAL OF AN AMATEUR.
HISOKA...
KEEP AN EYE ON THE BOY, TSUZUKI. THERE'S NO TELLING WHAT HE MIGHT DO.
HE MIGHT EVEN TRY TO MEET KURIKARA FACE-TO-FACE.
...

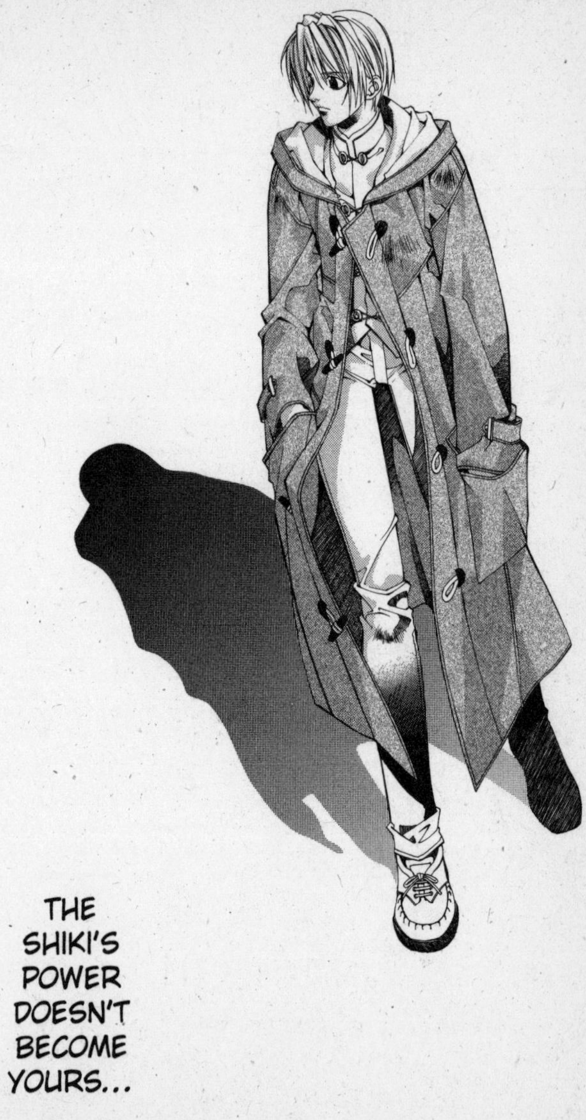
THE SHIKI'S POWER DOESN'T BECOME YOURS...

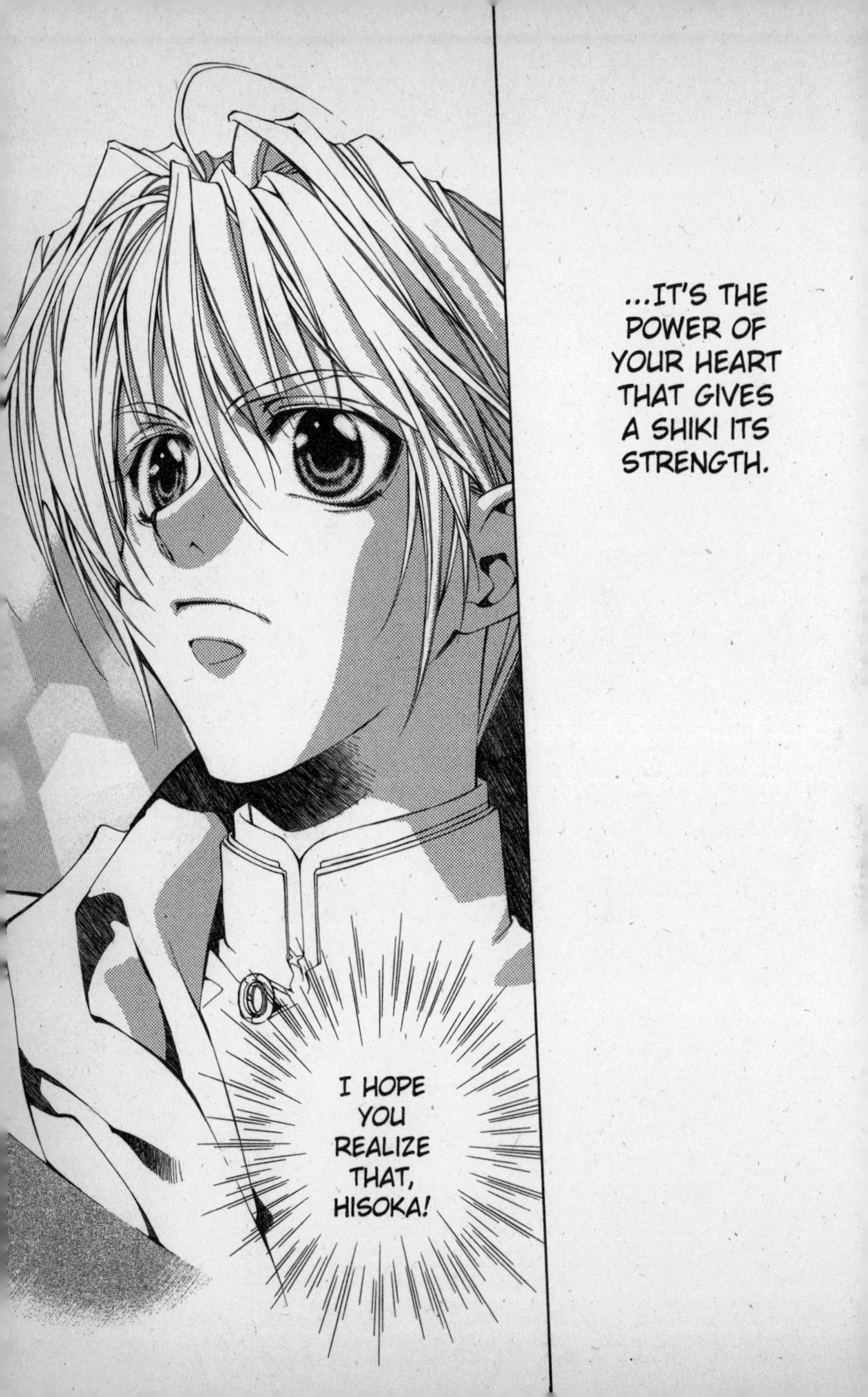
...IT'S THE POWER OF YOUR HEART THAT GIVES A SHIKI ITS STRENGTH.
I HOPE YOU REALIZE THAT, HISOKA!

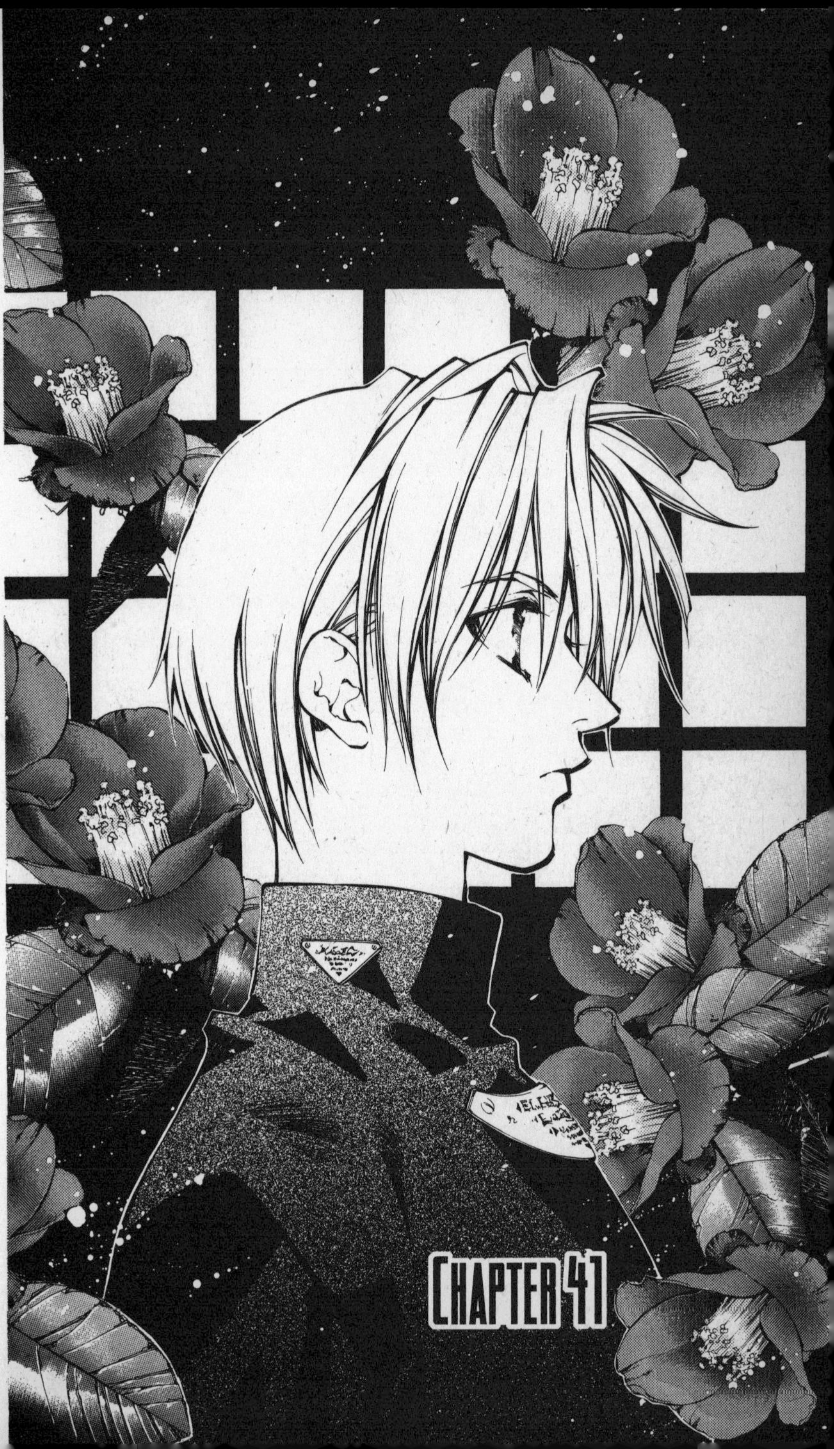
CHAPTER 41

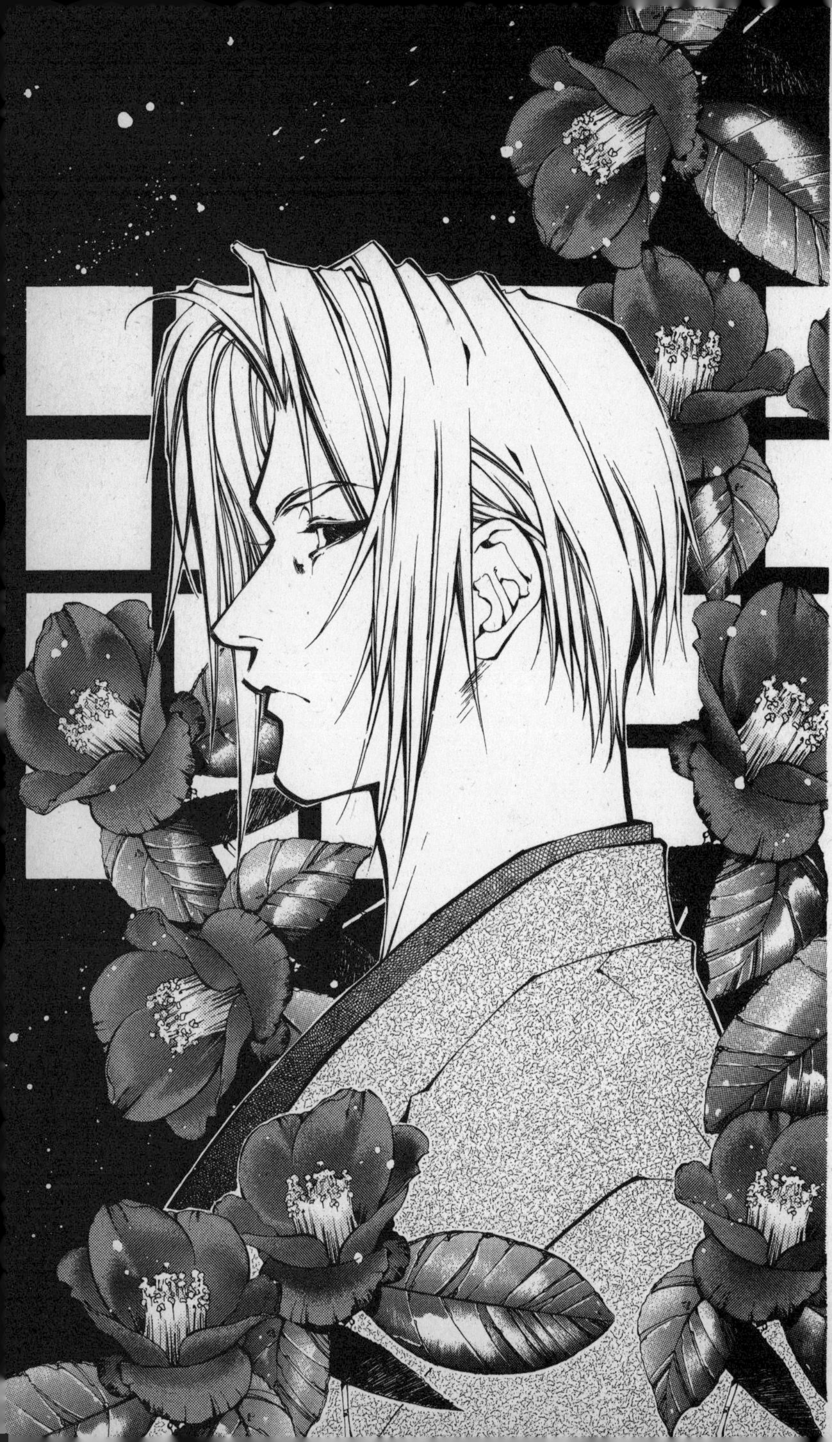

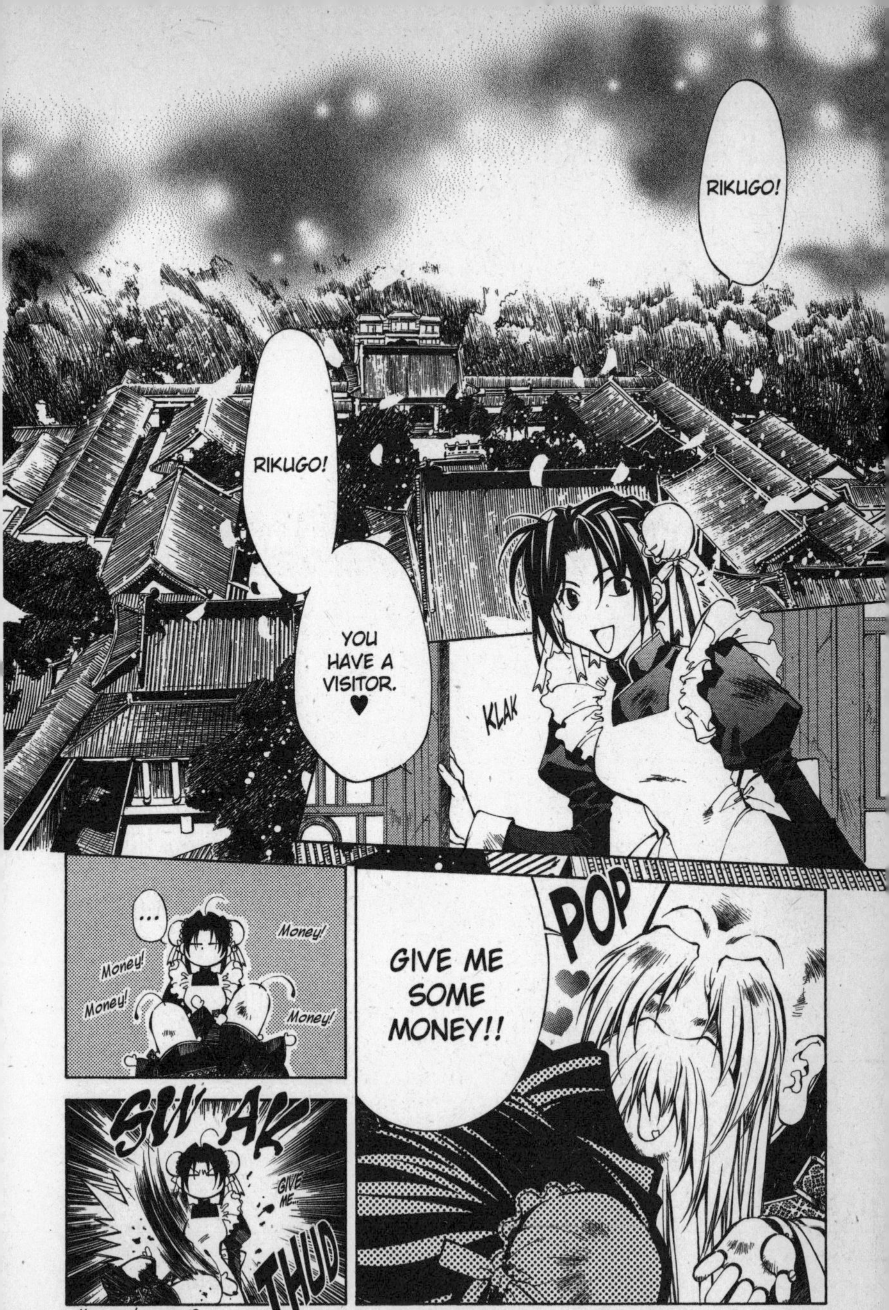
RIKUGO!
RIKUGO!
YOU HAVE A VISITOR. ♥
KLAK
POP
GIVE ME SOME MONEY!!
...
Money!
Money!
Money!
Money!
SWAK
GIVE ME...
THUD

Hey, you're one of the four great kings.

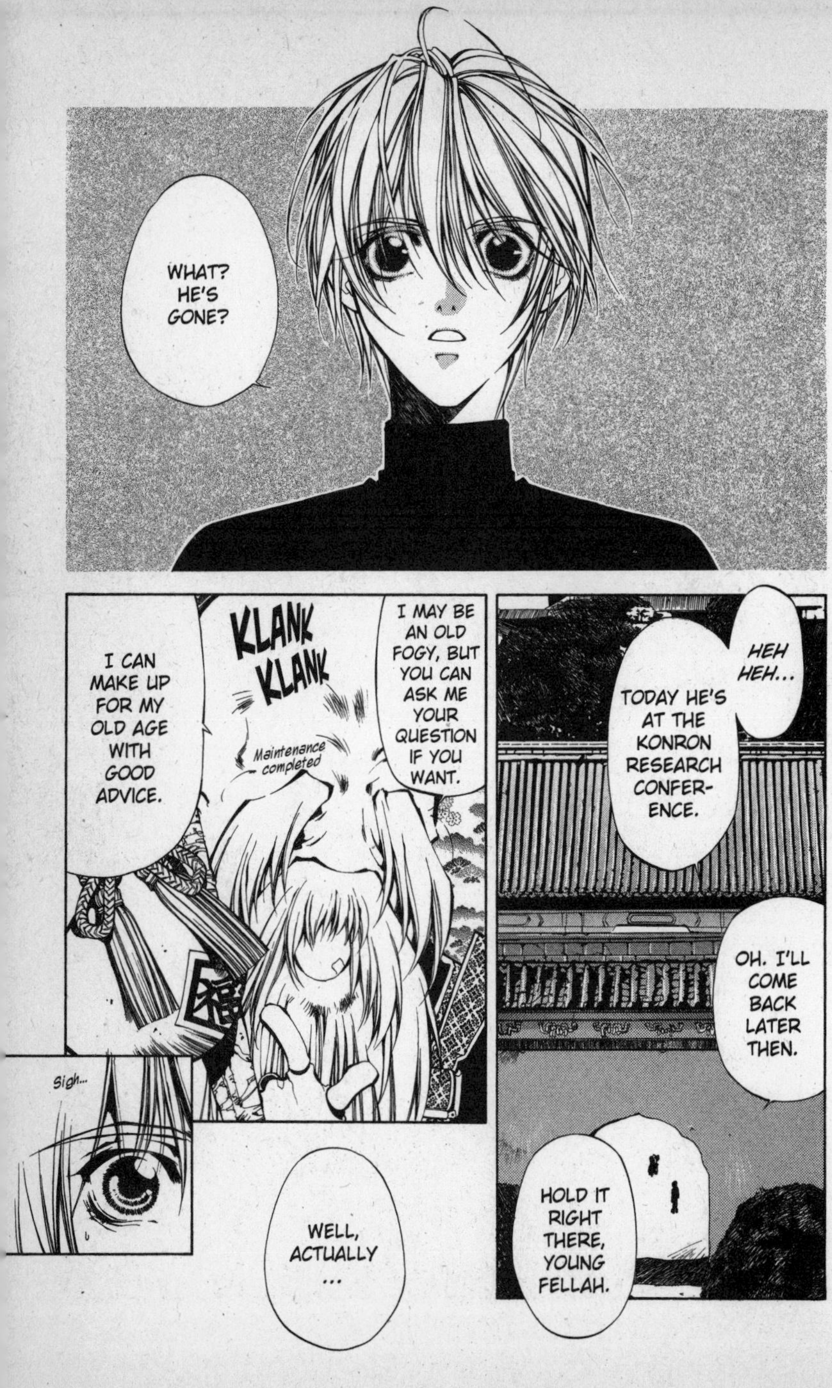
WHAT? HE'S GONE?
HEH HEH...
TODAY HE'S AT THE KONRON RESEARCH CONFERENCE.
OH. I'LL COME BACK LATER THEN.
HOLD IT RIGHT THERE, YOUNG FELLAH.
I MAY BE AN OLD FOGY, BUT YOU CAN ASK ME YOUR QUESTION IF YOU WANT.
KLANK KLANK
Maintenance completed
I CAN MAKE UP FOR MY OLD AGE WITH GOOD ADVICE.
WELL, ACTUALLY...
Sigh...

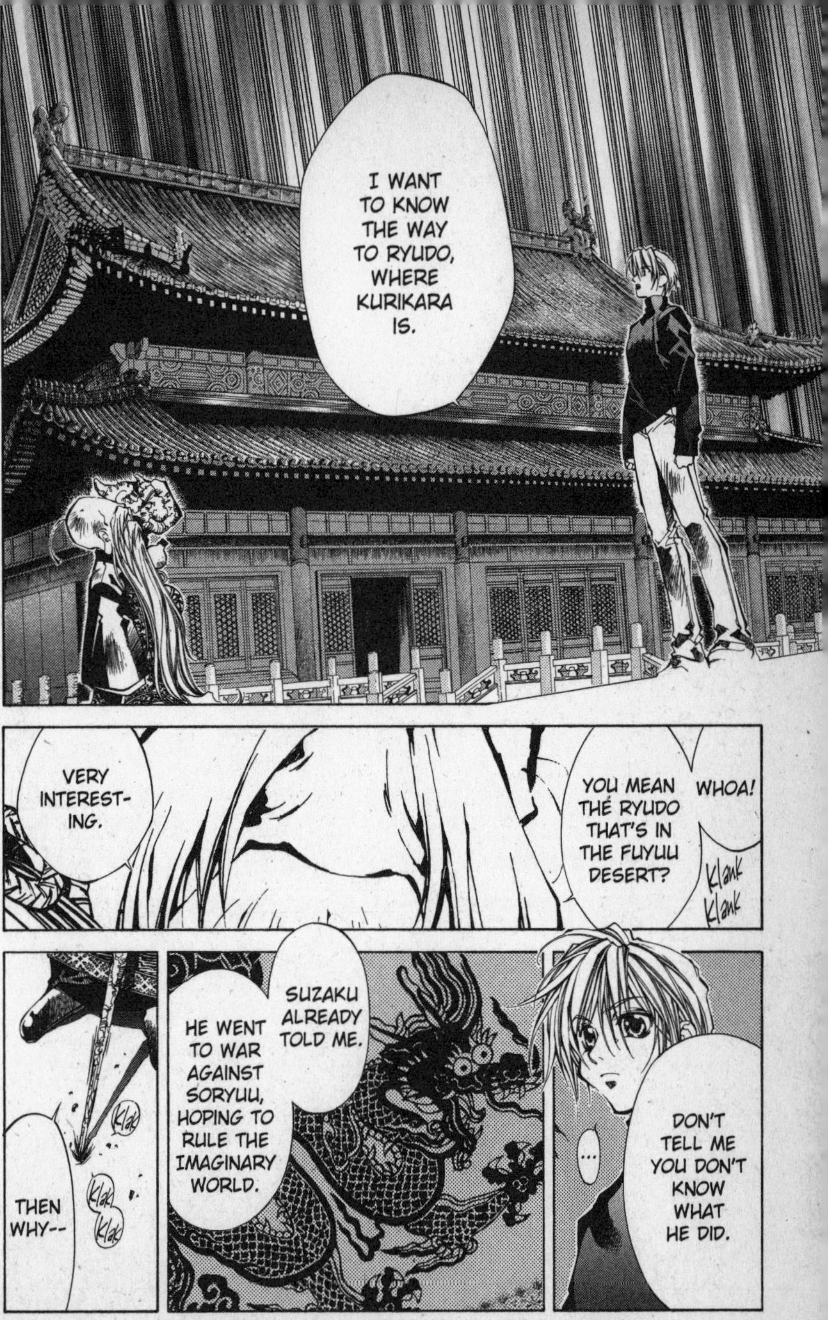
I WANT TO KNOW THE WAY TO RYUDO, WHERE KURIKARA IS.
WHOA!
YOU MEAN THE RYUDO THAT'S IN THE FUYUU DESERT?
Klank Klank
VERY INTEREST-ING.
DON'T TELL ME YOU DON'T KNOW WHAT HE DID.
...
SUZAKU ALREADY TOLD ME.
HE WENT TO WAR AGAINST SORYUU, HOPING TO RULE THE IMAGINARY WORLD.
Klak
Klak Klak
THEN WHY--

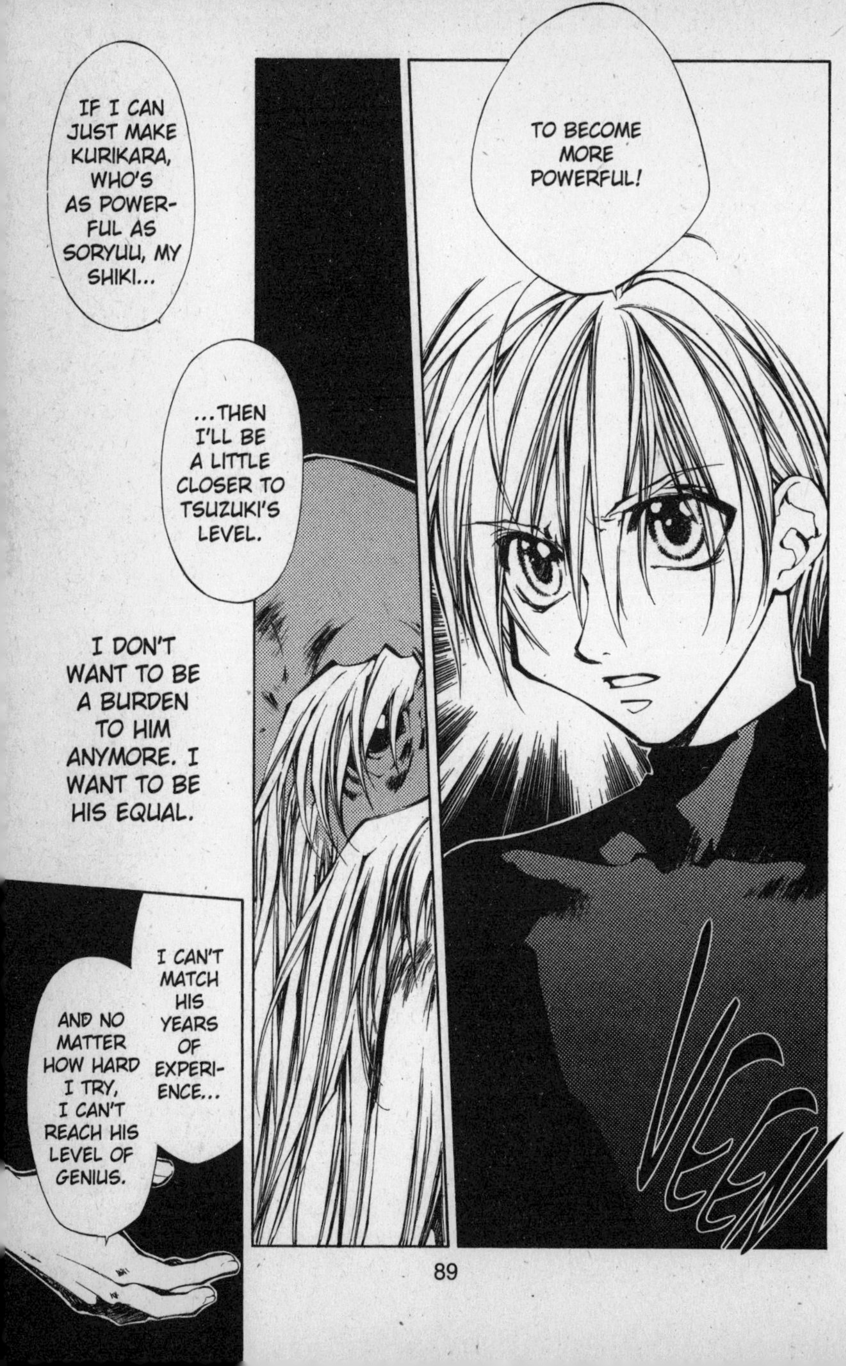

TO BECOME MORE POWERFUL!
VEEEN
IF I CAN JUST MAKE KURIKARA, WHO'S AS POWERFUL AS SORYUU, MY SHIKI...
...THEN I'LL BE A LITTLE CLOSER TO TSUZUKI'S LEVEL.
I DON'T WANT TO BE A BURDEN TO HIM ANYMORE. I WANT TO BE HIS EQUAL.
I CAN'T MATCH HIS YEARS OF EXPERIENCE...
AND NO MATTER HOW HARD I TRY, I CAN'T REACH HIS LEVEL OF GENIUS.

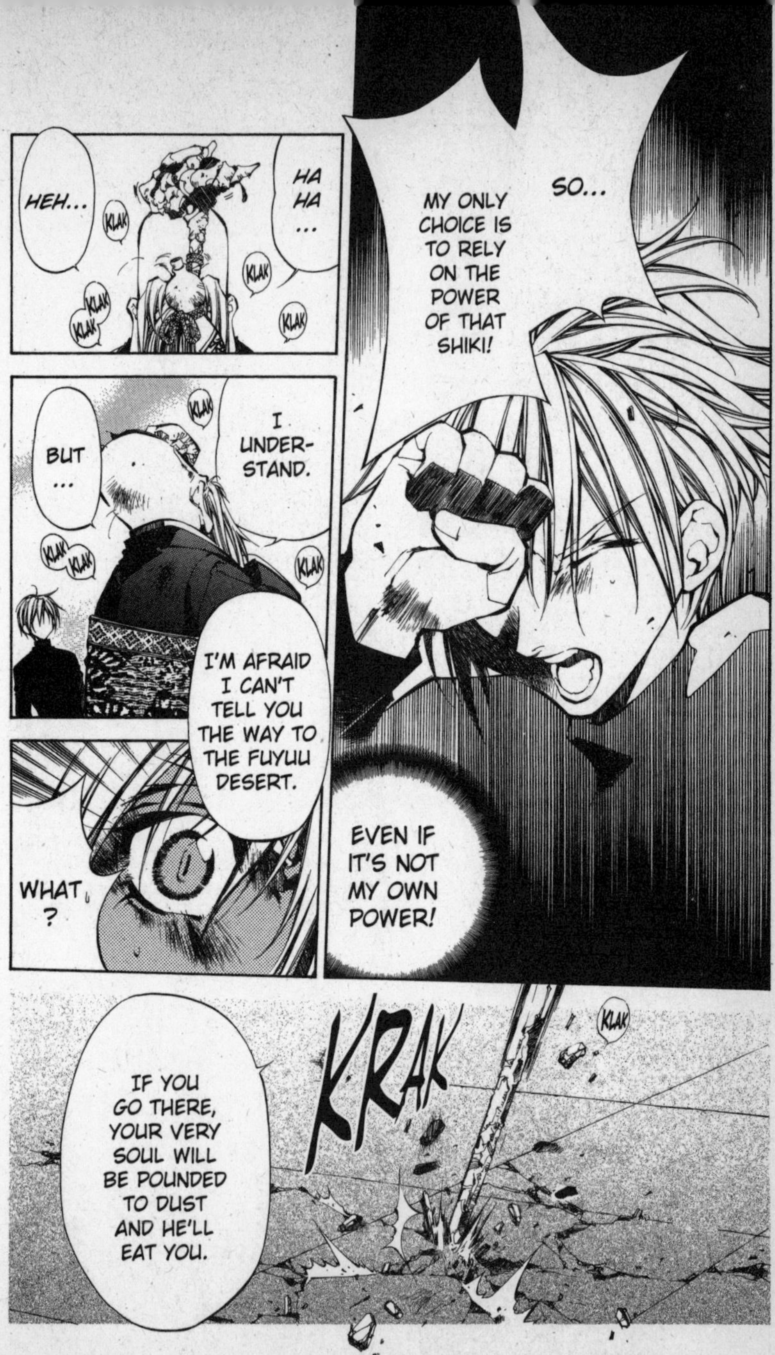
SO...
MY ONLY CHOICE IS TO RELY ON THE POWER OF THAT SHIKI!
EVEN IF IT'S NOT MY OWN POWER!
HA HA ...
KLAK
KLAK
KLAK
KLAK
KLAK
HEH...
KLAK
I UNDER-STAND.
KLAK
BUT ...
KLAK
KLAK
I'M AFRAID I CAN'T TELL YOU THE WAY TO THE FUYUU DESERT.
WHAT ?
KLAK
KRAK
IF YOU GO THERE, YOUR VERY SOUL WILL BE POUNDED TO DUST AND HE'LL EAT YOU.

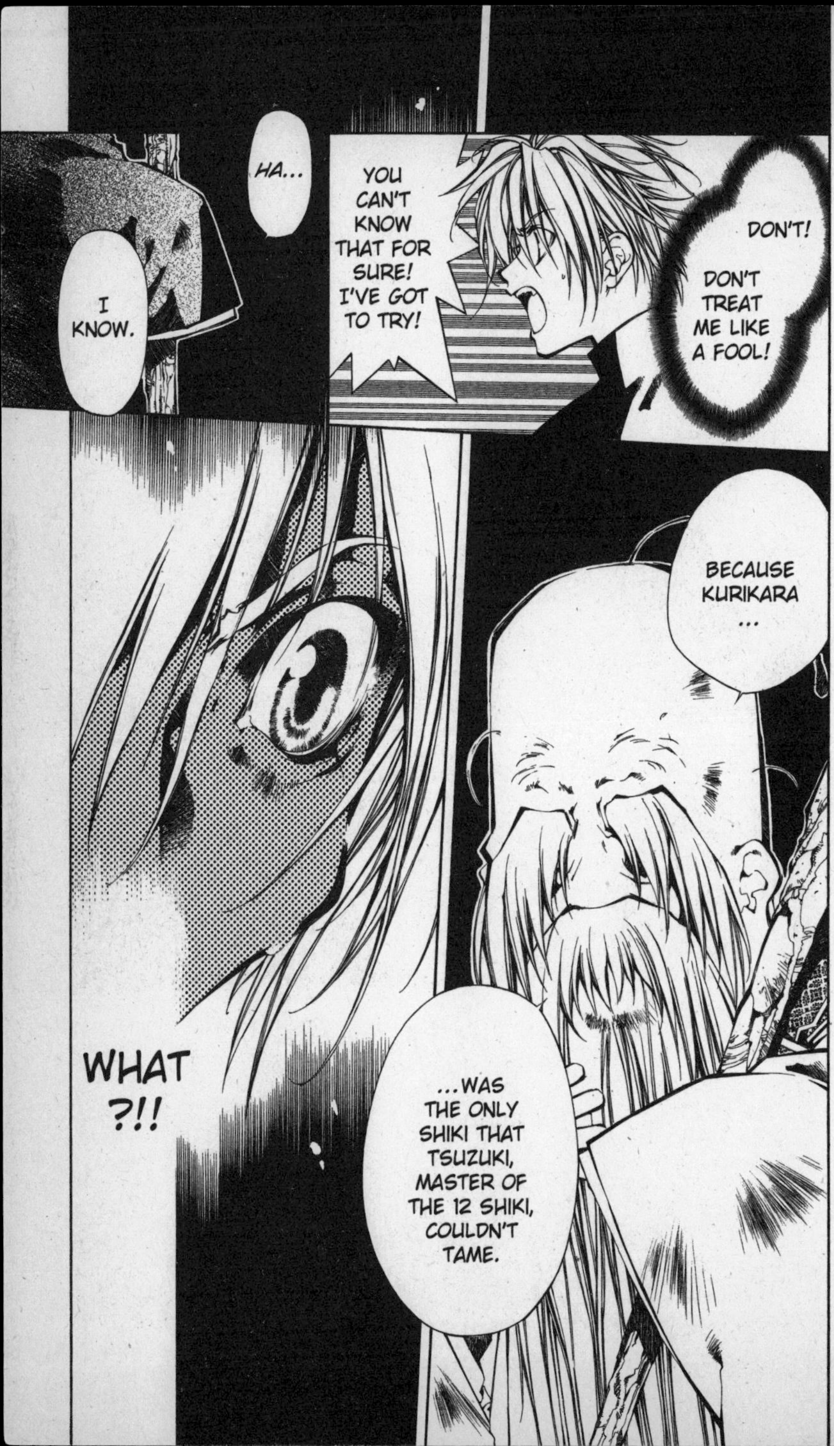
DON'T!
DON'T TREAT ME LIKE A FOOL!
YOU CAN'T KNOW THAT FOR SURE! I'VE GOT TO TRY!
HA...
I KNOW.
BECAUSE KURIKARA...
...WAS THE ONLY SHIKI THAT TSUZUKI, MASTER OF THE 12 SHIKI, COULDN'T TAME.
WHAT?!!

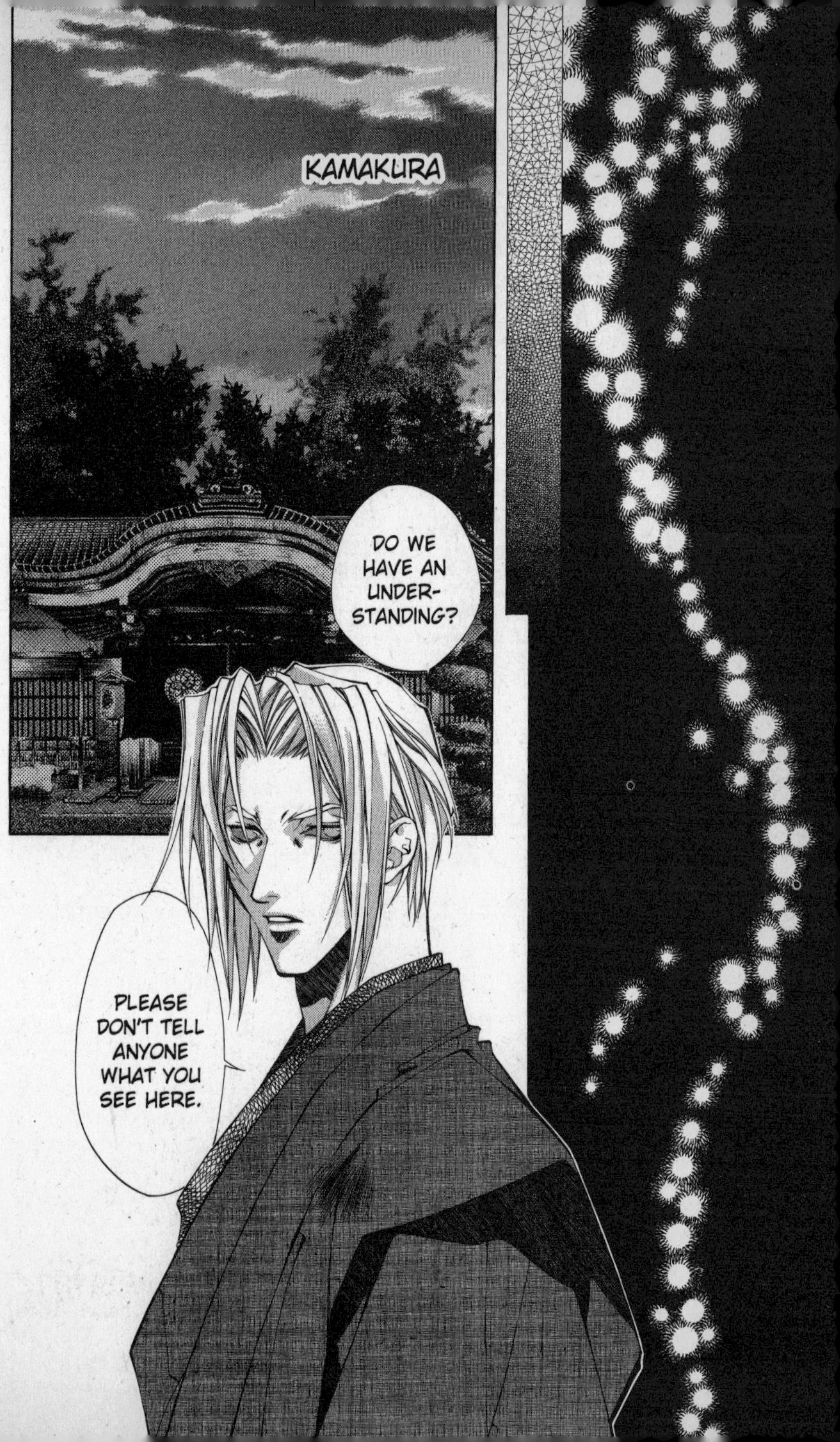
KAMAKURA
DO WE HAVE AN UNDER-STANDING?
PLEASE DON'T TELL ANYONE WHAT YOU SEE HERE.

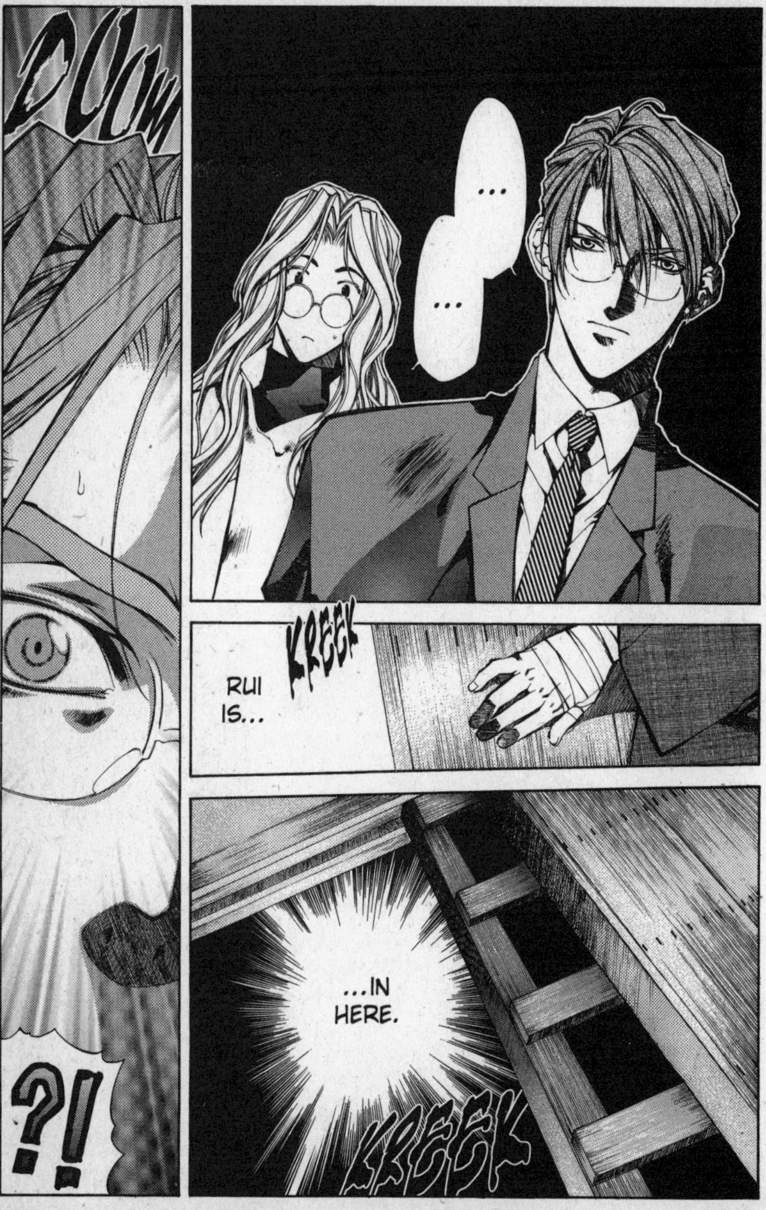
...
...
RUI IS...
KREEK
...IN HERE.
KREEK
DUUM
?!

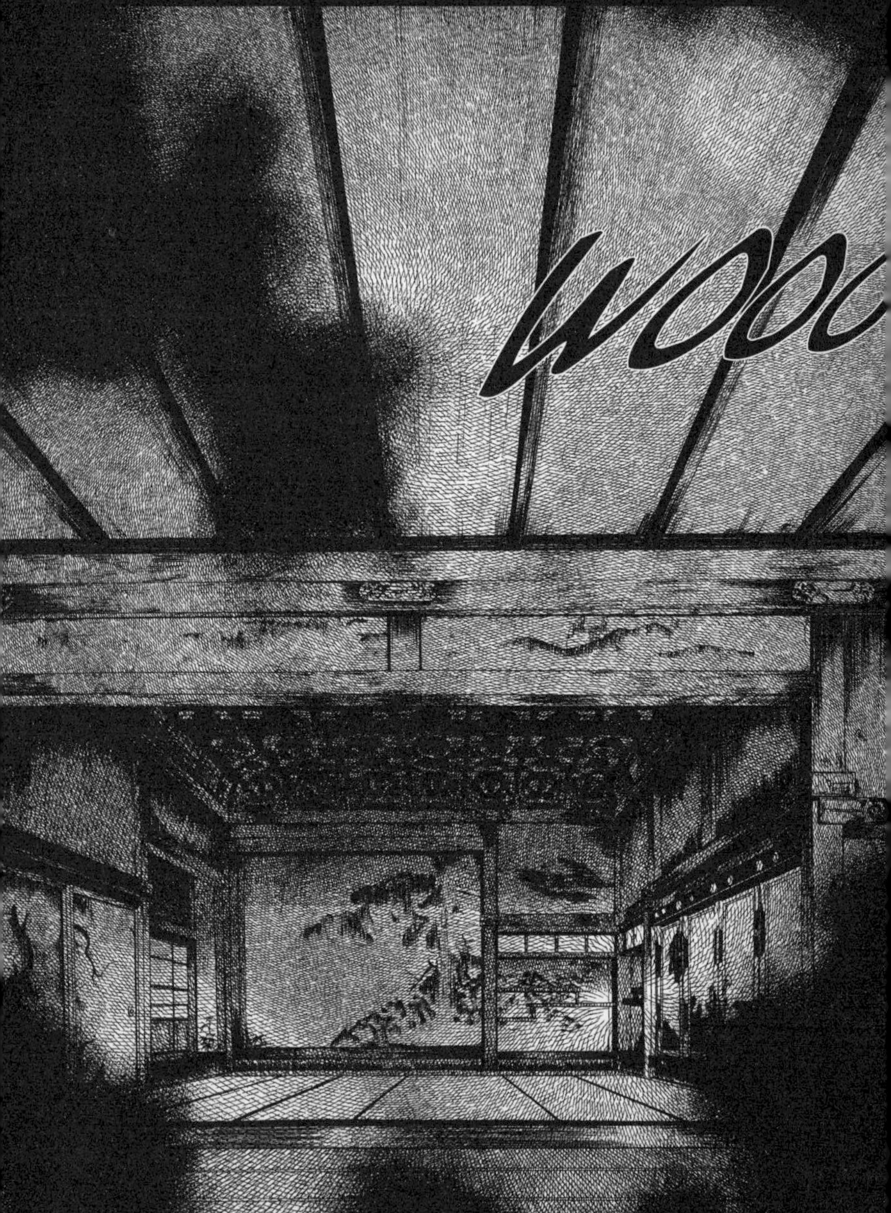
WOOO

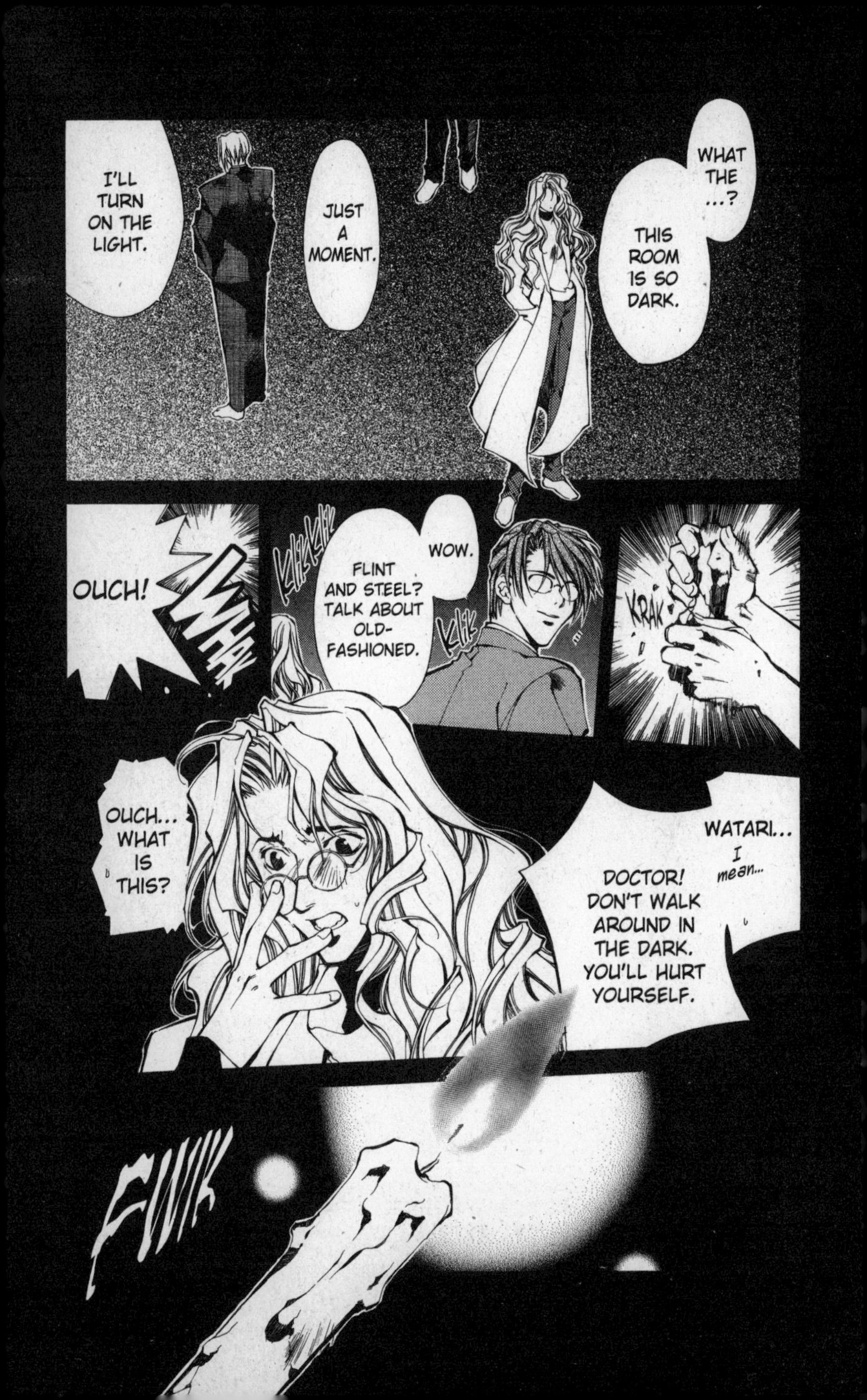
WHAT THE ...?
THIS ROOM IS SO DARK.
JUST A MOMENT.
I'LL TURN ON THE LIGHT.
KRAK
KLIK
WOW.
FLINT AND STEEL? TALK ABOUT OLD-FASHIONED.
KLIKKLIK
WHAK
OUCH!
WATARI... I mean...
DOCTOR! DON'T WALK AROUND IN THE DARK. YOU'LL HURT YOURSELF.
OUCH... WHAT IS THIS?
FWIK

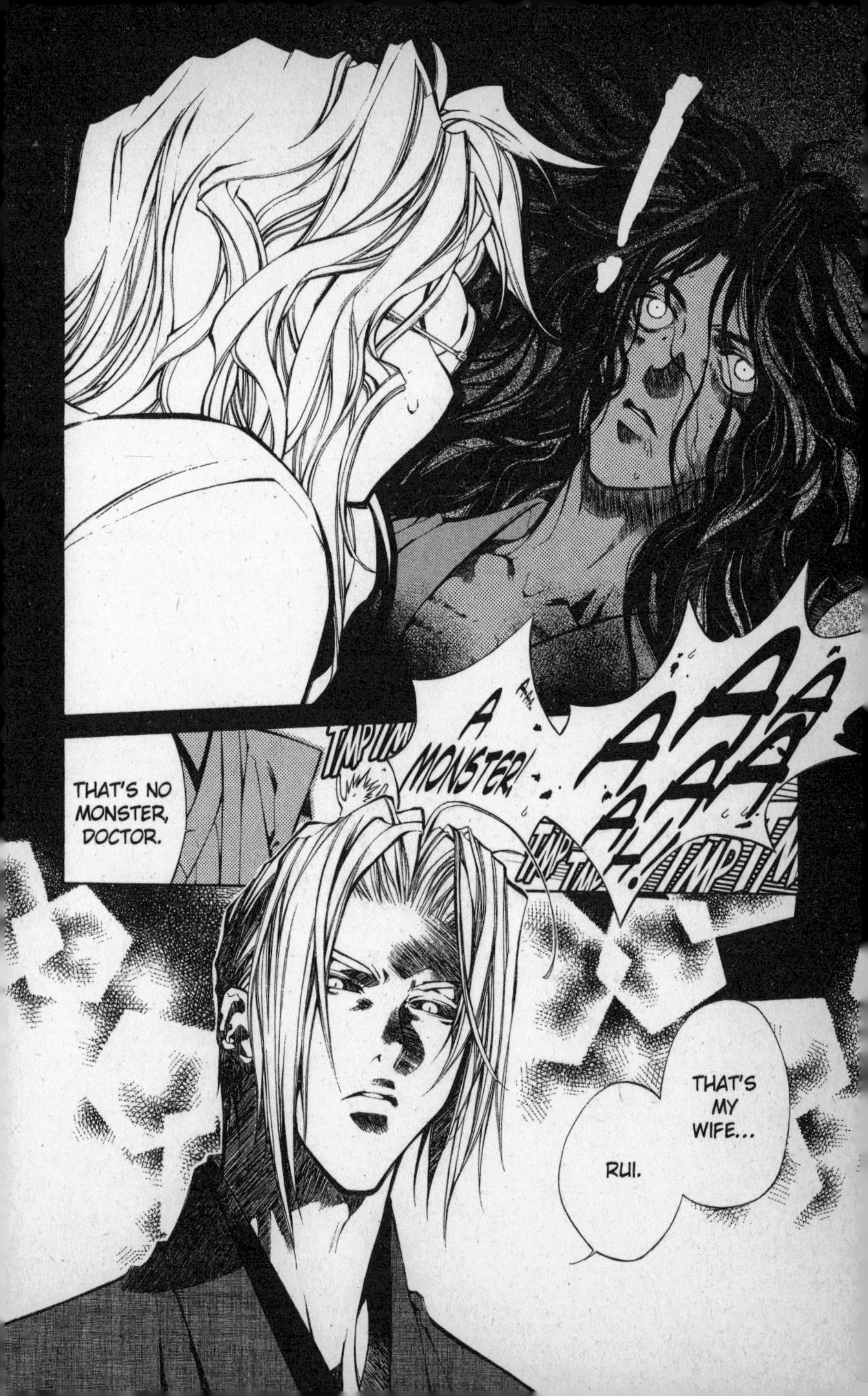

A MONSTER!
AAAAAH!
TMP TMP TMP TMP
TMP TMP
THAT'S NO MONSTER, DOCTOR.
THAT'S MY WIFE... RUI.

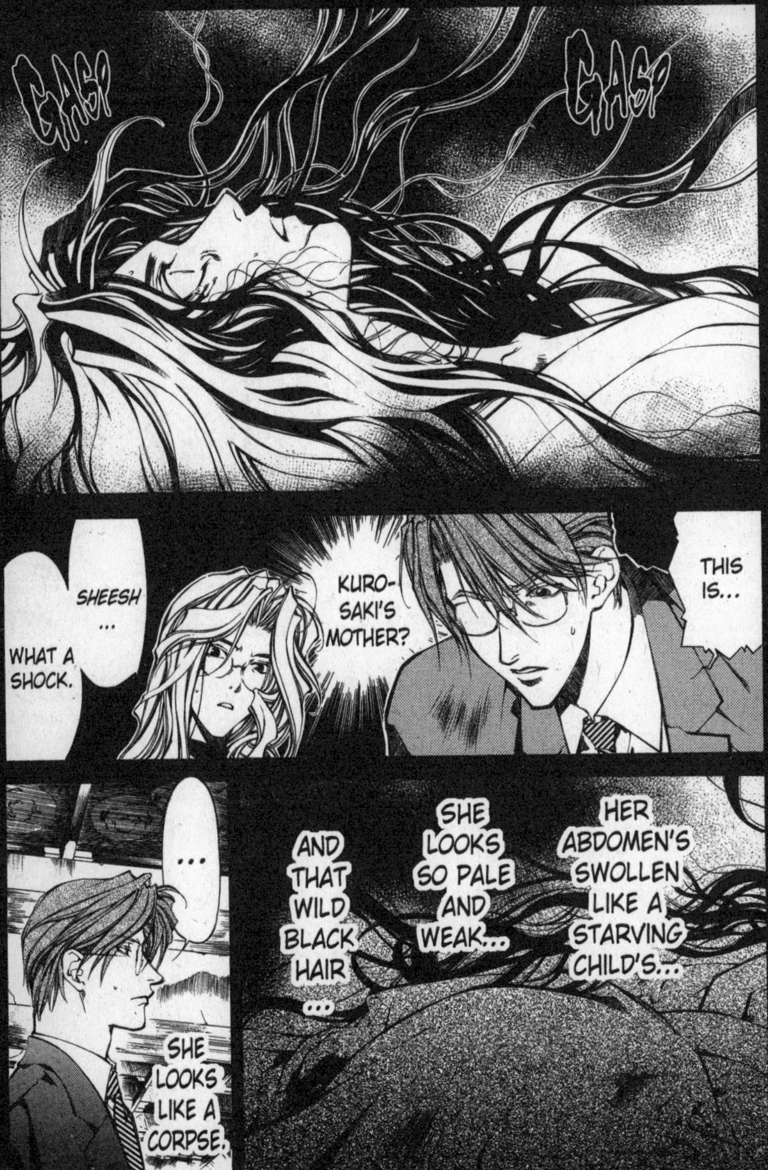
GASP
GASP
THIS IS...
KURO-SAKI'S MOTHER?
SHEESH...
WHAT A SHOCK.
HER ABDOMEN'S SWOLLEN LIKE A STARVING CHILD'S...
SHE LOOKS SO PALE AND WEAK...
AND THAT WILD BLACK HAIR...
...
SHE LOOKS LIKE A CORPSE.

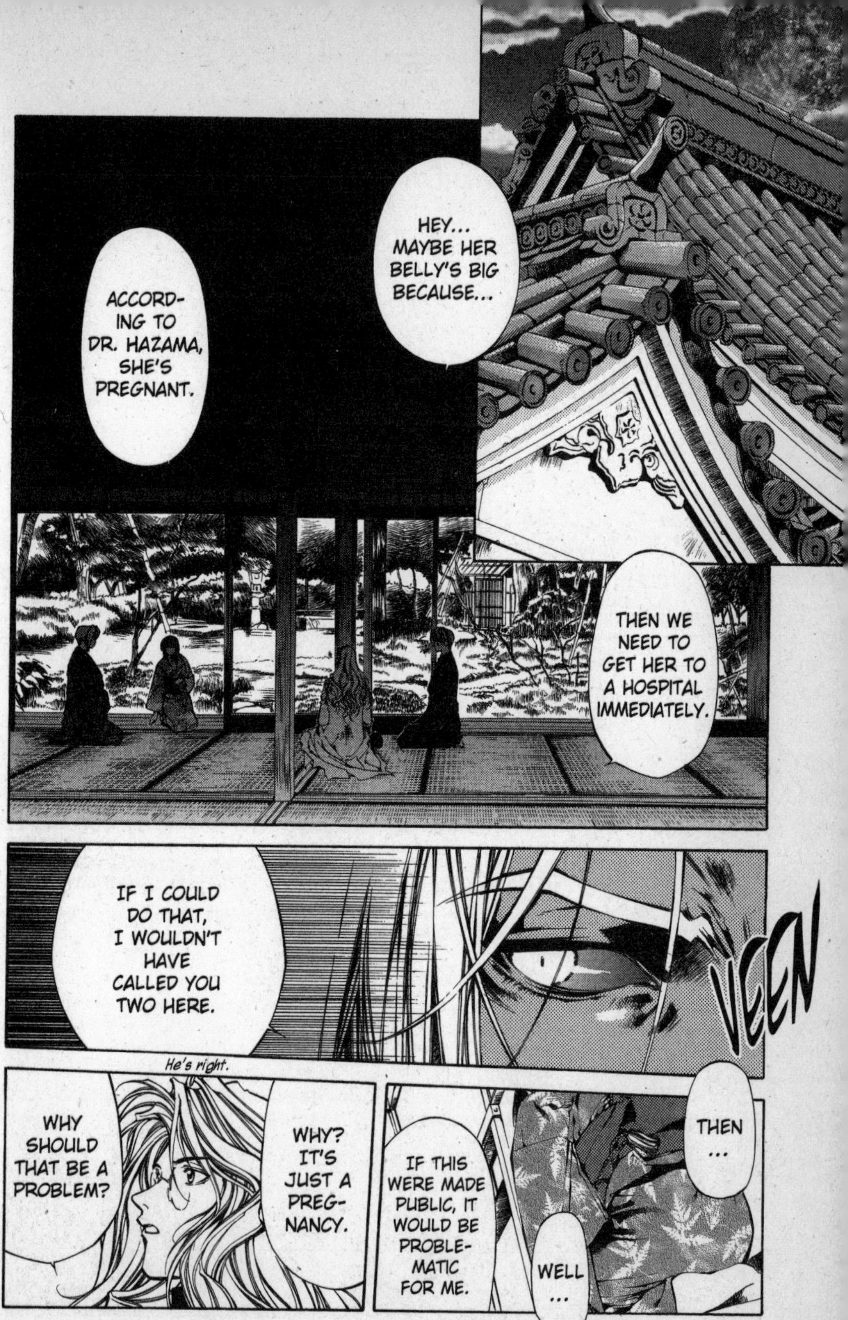
HEY... MAYBE HER BELLY'S BIG BECAUSE...
ACCORD-ING TO DR. HAZAMA, SHE'S PREGNANT.
THEN WE NEED TO GET HER TO A HOSPITAL IMMEDIATELY.
IF I COULD DO THAT, I WOULDN'T HAVE CALLED YOU TWO HERE.
VEEN
He's right.
THEN...
WELL...
IF THIS WERE MADE PUBLIC, IT WOULD BE PROBLE-MATIC FOR ME.
WHY? IT'S JUST A PREG-NANCY.
WHY SHOULD THAT BE A PROBLEM?

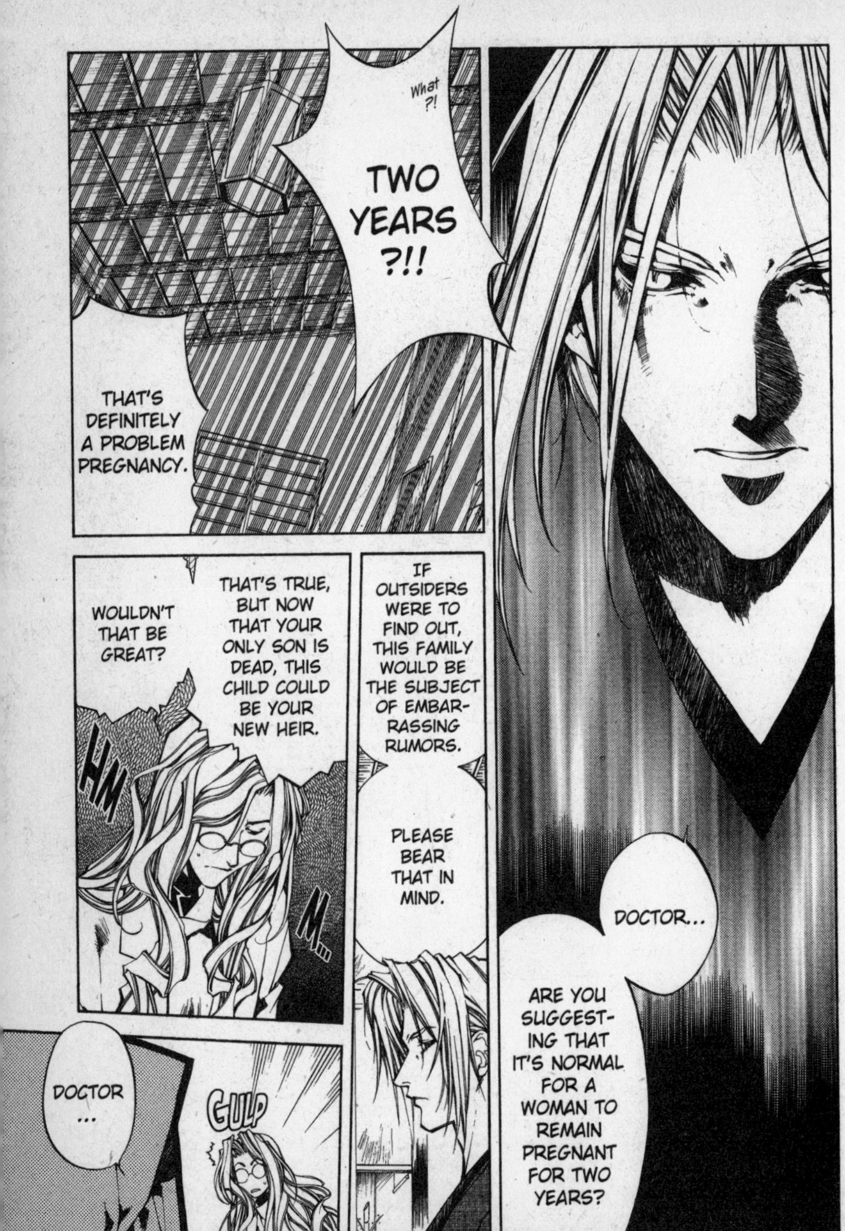
DOCTOR...
ARE YOU SUGGEST-ING THAT IT'S NORMAL FOR A WOMAN TO REMAIN PREGNANT FOR TWO YEARS?
What ?!
TWO YEARS ?!!
THAT'S DEFINITELY A PROBLEM PREGNANCY.
IF OUTSIDERS WERE TO FIND OUT, THIS FAMILY WOULD BE THE SUBJECT OF EMBAR-RASSING RUMORS.
PLEASE BEAR THAT IN MIND.
THAT'S TRUE, BUT NOW THAT YOUR ONLY SON IS DEAD, THIS CHILD COULD BE YOUR NEW HEIR.
WOULDN'T THAT BE GREAT?
HM
M...
DOCTOR ...
GULP

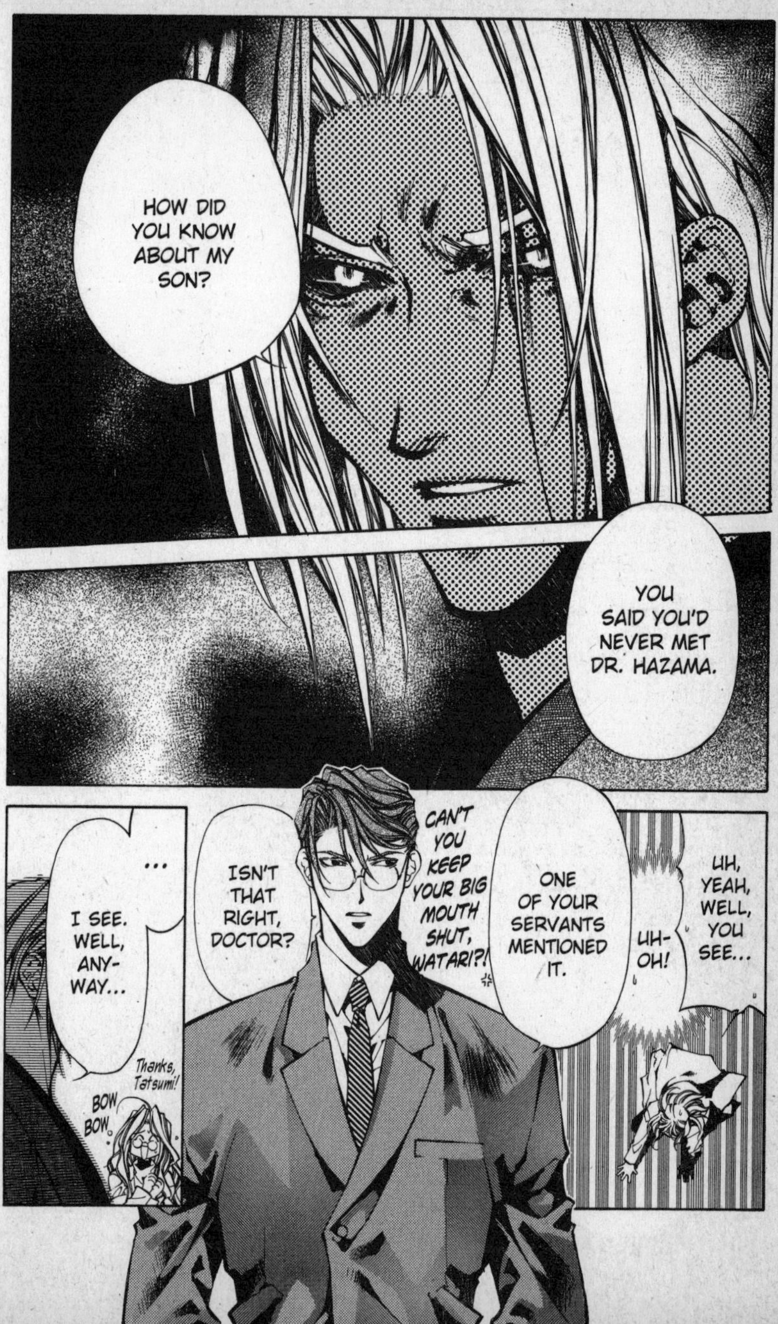
HOW DID YOU KNOW ABOUT MY SON?
YOU SAID YOU'D NEVER MET DR. HAZAMA.
UH, YEAH, WELL, YOU SEE...
UH-OH!
ONE OF YOUR SERVANTS MENTIONED IT.
CAN'T YOU KEEP YOUR BIG MOUTH SHUT, WATARI?!
ISN'T THAT RIGHT, DOCTOR?
...
I SEE. WELL, ANY-WAY...
Thanks, Tatsumi!
BOW BOW

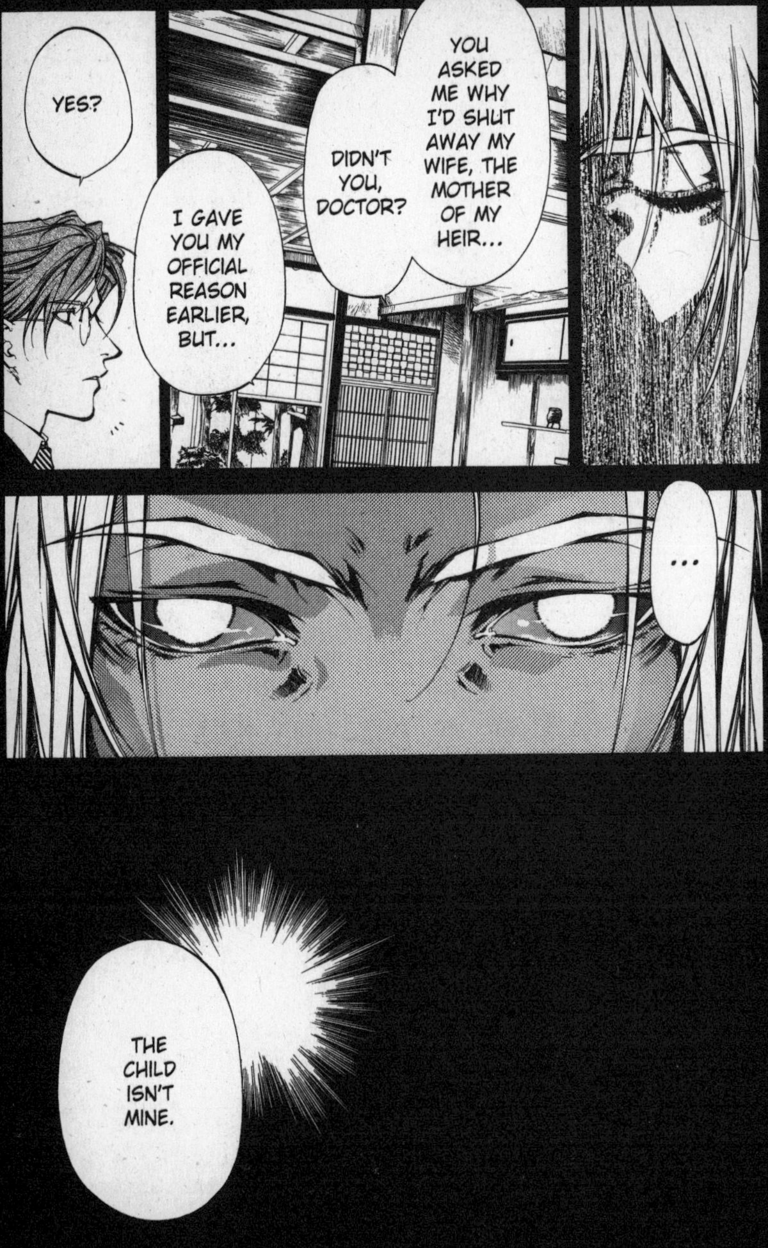
YOU ASKED ME WHY I'D SHUT AWAY MY WIFE, THE MOTHER OF MY HEIR...
DIDN'T YOU, DOCTOR?
I GAVE YOU MY OFFICIAL REASON EARLIER, BUT...
YES?
...
THE CHILD ISN'T MINE.

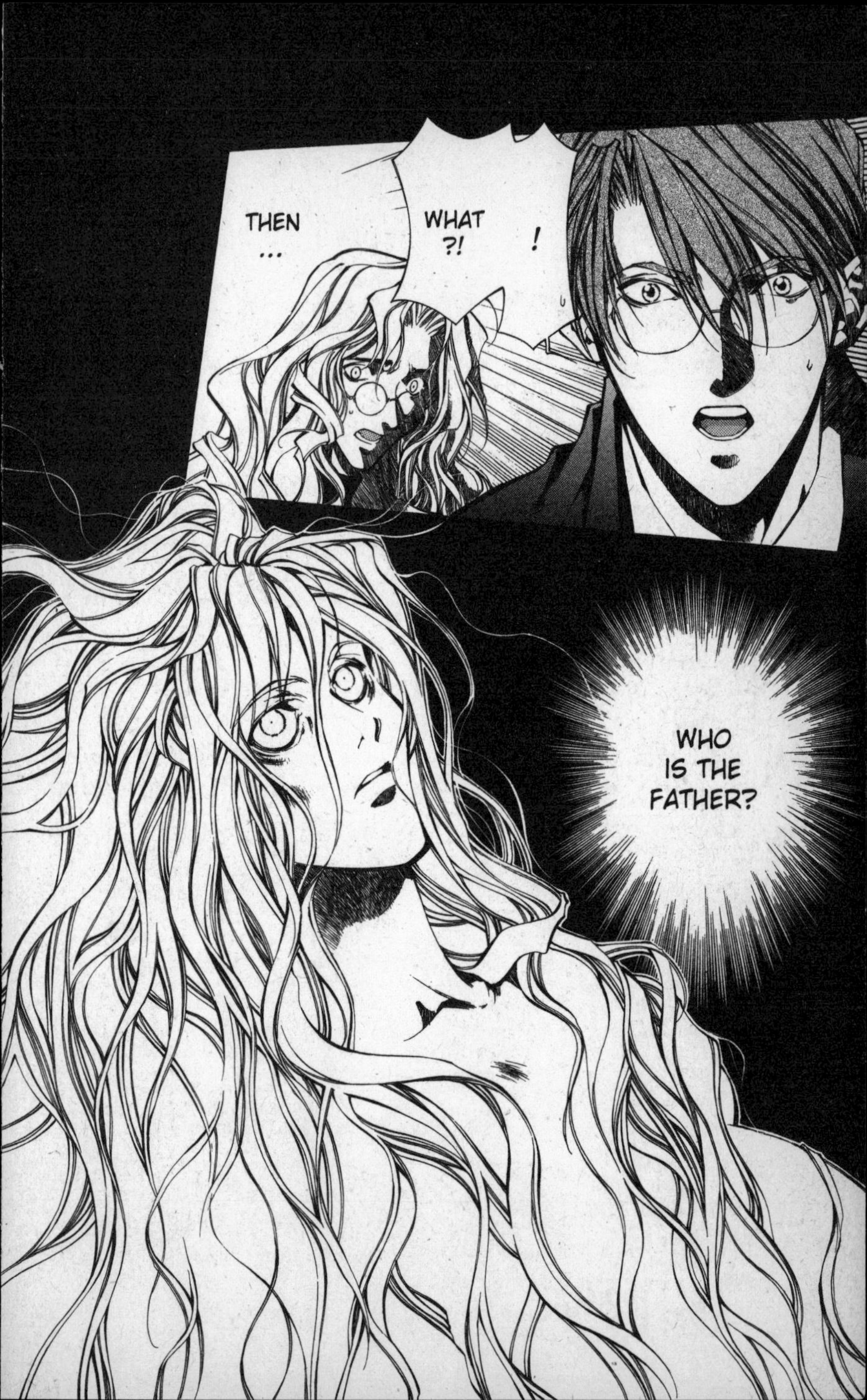
!
WHAT ?!
THEN ...
WHO IS THE FATHER?

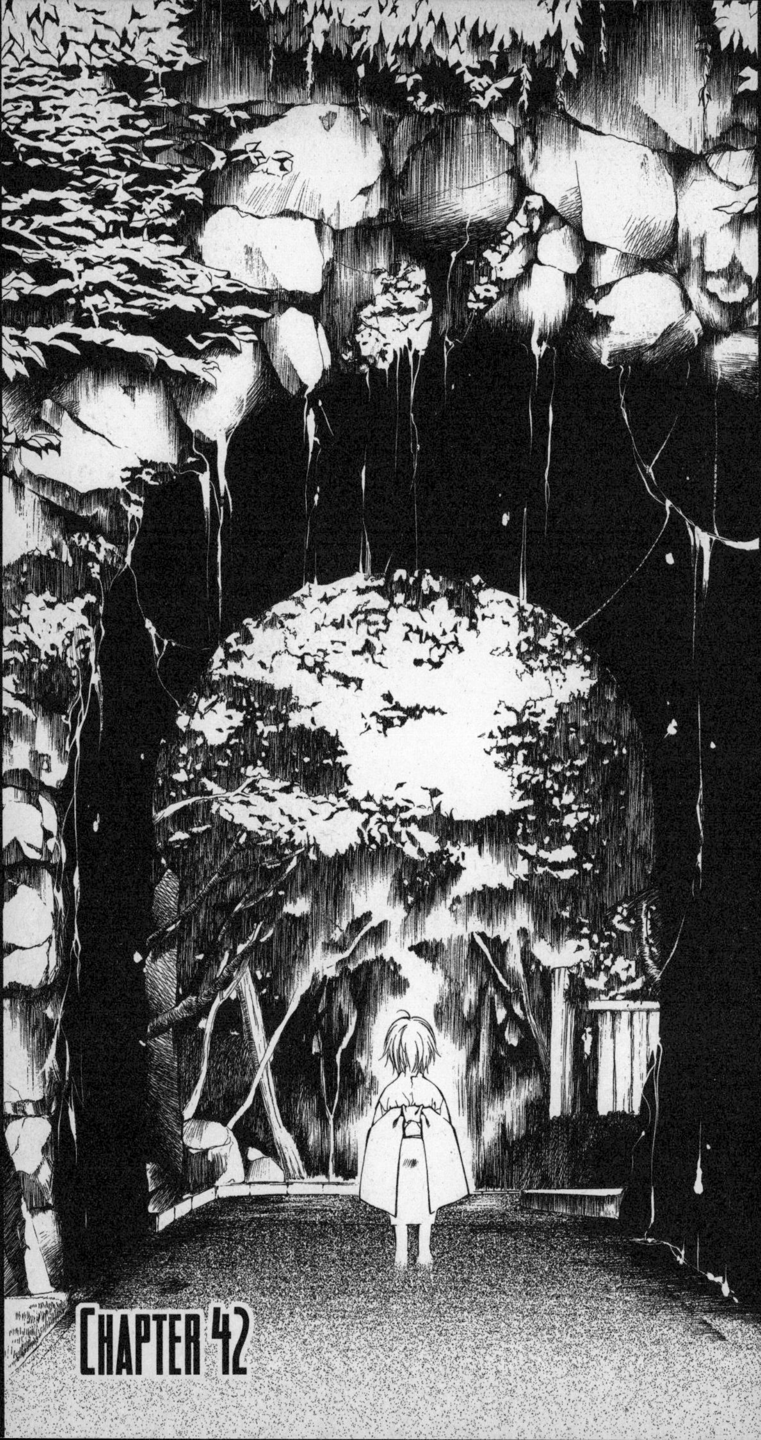
CHAPTER 42

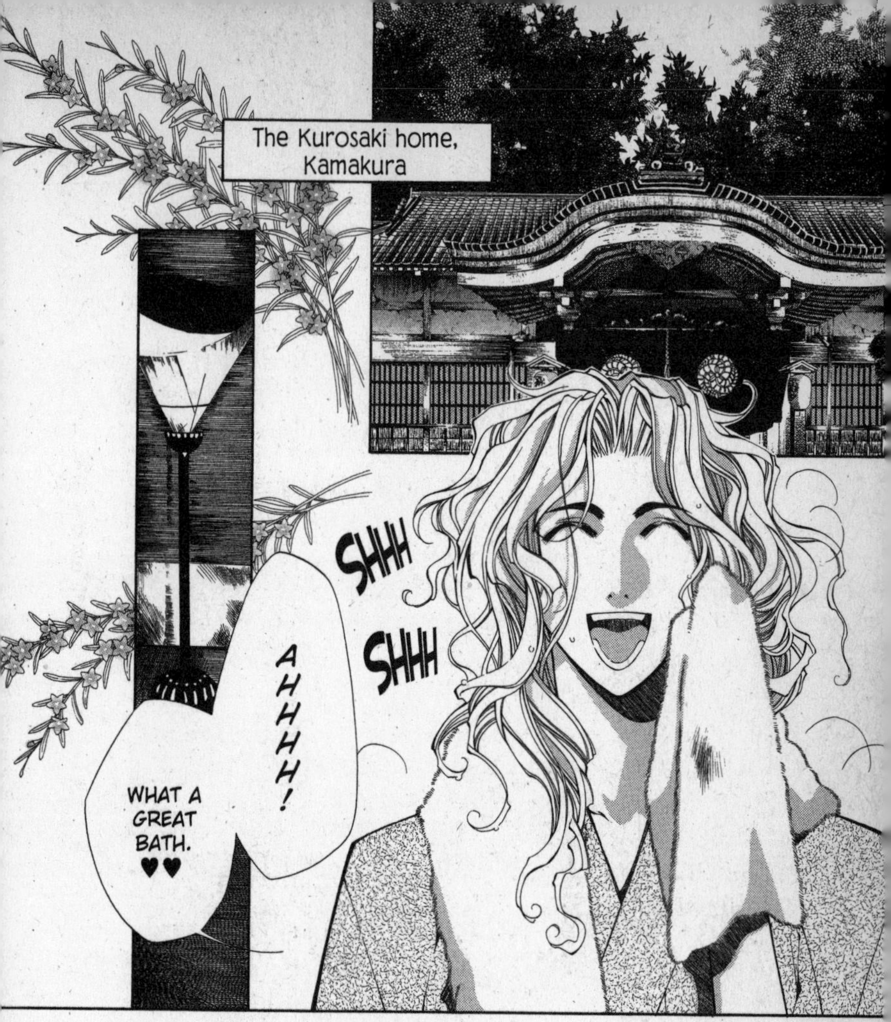
The Kurosaki home, Kamakura
SHHH
SHHH
AHHHHH!
WHAT A GREAT BATH. ♥♥

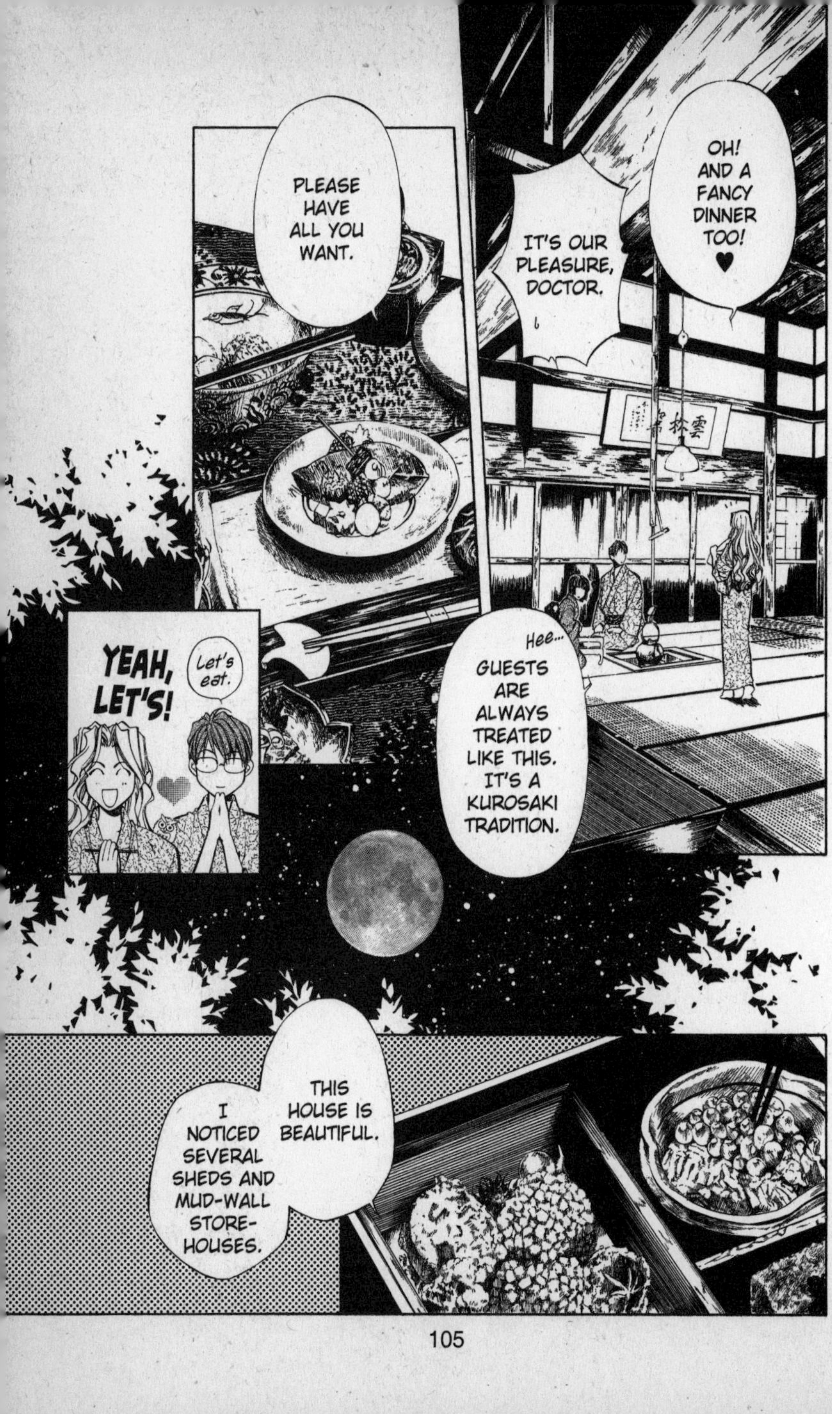
OH! AND A FANCY DINNER TOO! ♥
IT'S OUR PLEASURE, DOCTOR.
Hee...
GUESTS ARE ALWAYS TREATED LIKE THIS. IT'S A KUROSAKI TRADITION.
PLEASE HAVE ALL YOU WANT.
Let's eat.
YEAH, LET'S!
THIS HOUSE IS BEAUTIFUL.
I NOTICED SEVERAL SHEDS AND MUD-WALL STORE-HOUSES.

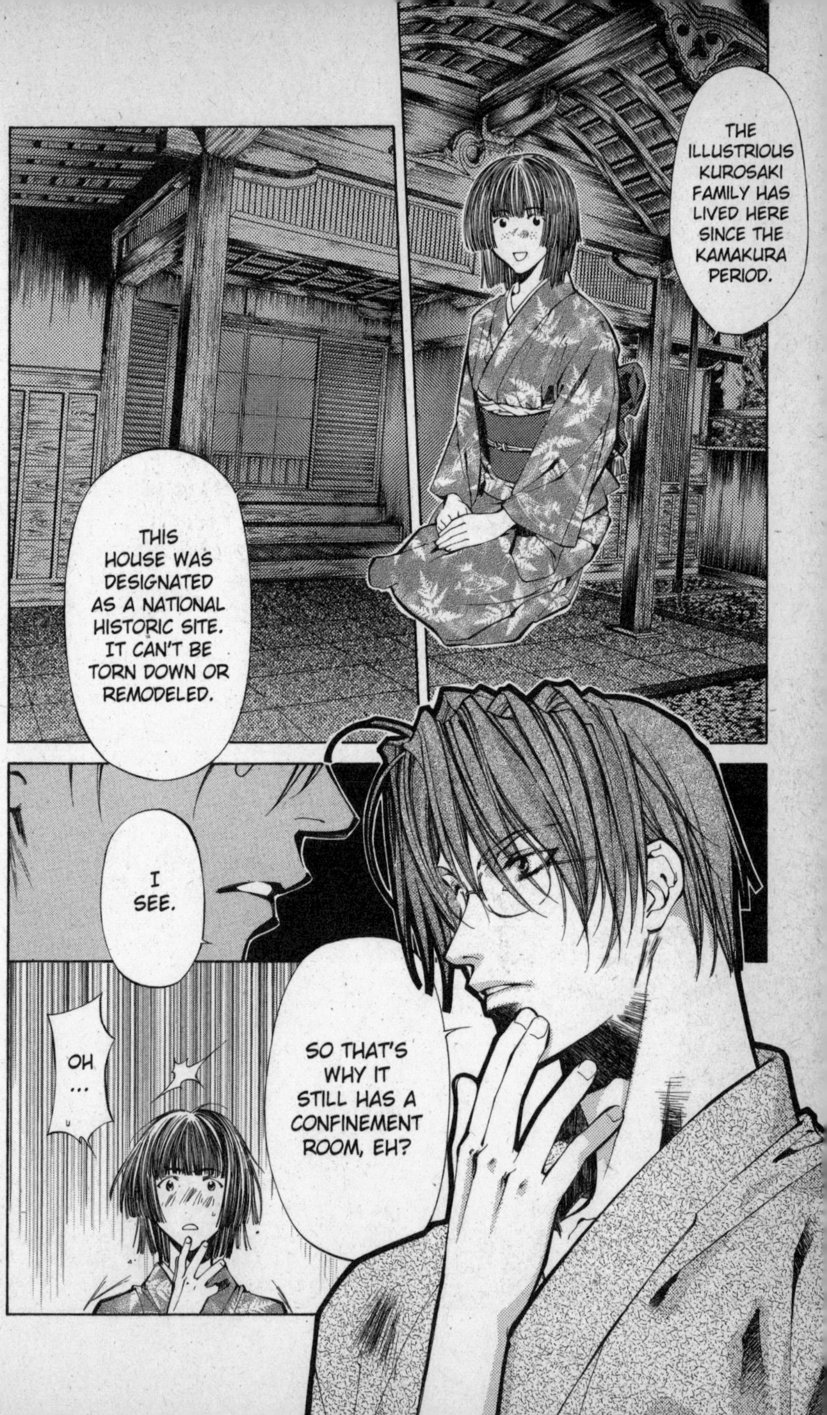
THE ILLUSTRIOUS KUROSAKI FAMILY HAS LIVED HERE SINCE THE KAMAKURA PERIOD.
THIS HOUSE WAS DESIGNATED AS A NATIONAL HISTORIC SITE. IT CAN'T BE TORN DOWN OR REMODELED.
I SEE.
SO THAT'S WHY IT STILL HAS A CONFINEMENT ROOM, EH?
OH ...

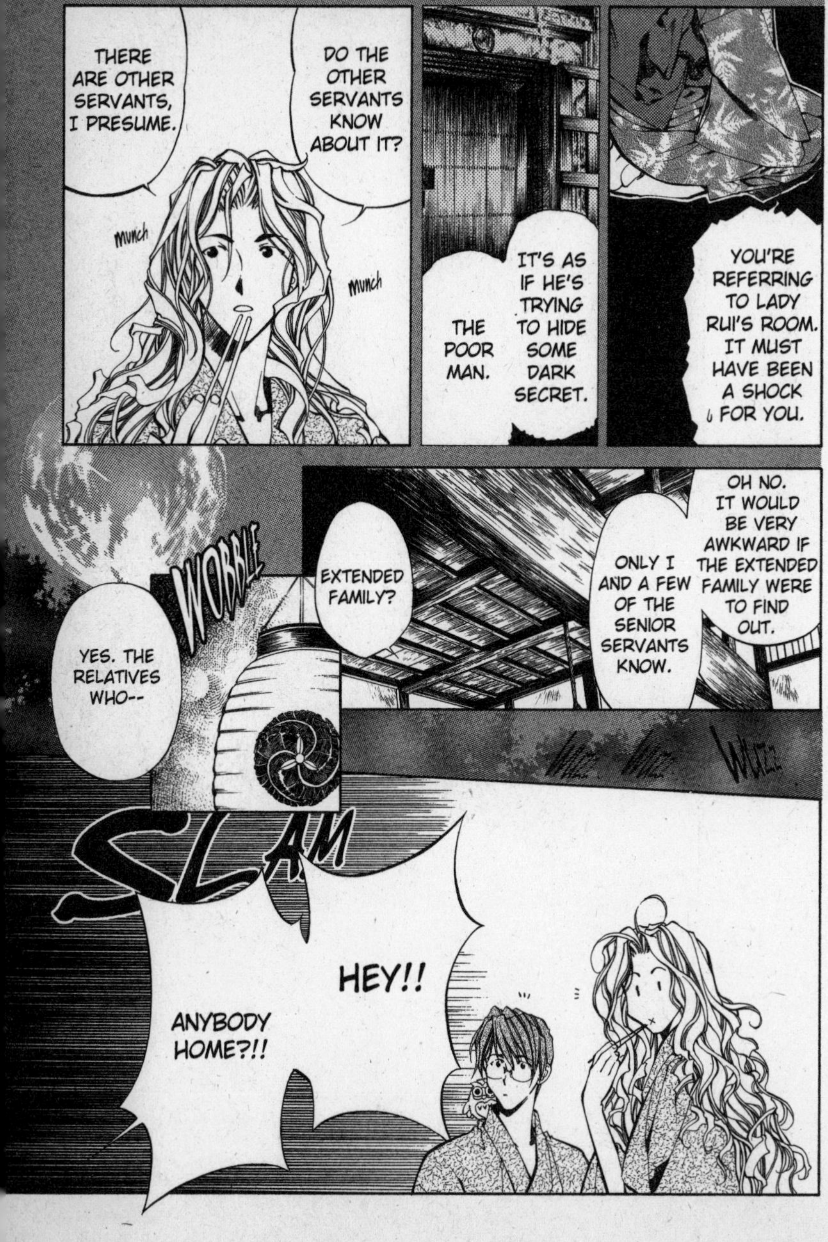
YOU'RE REFERRING TO LADY RUI'S ROOM. IT MUST HAVE BEEN A SHOCK FOR YOU.
IT'S AS IF HE'S TRYING TO HIDE SOME DARK SECRET.
THE POOR MAN.
DO THE OTHER SERVANTS KNOW ABOUT IT?
THERE ARE OTHER SERVANTS, I PRESUME.
munch
munch
OH NO. IT WOULD BE VERY AWKWARD IF THE EXTENDED FAMILY WERE TO FIND OUT.
ONLY I AND A FEW OF THE SENIOR SERVANTS KNOW.
EXTENDED FAMILY?
WOBBLE
YES. THE RELATIVES WHO--
SLAM
HEY!!
ANYBODY HOME?!!

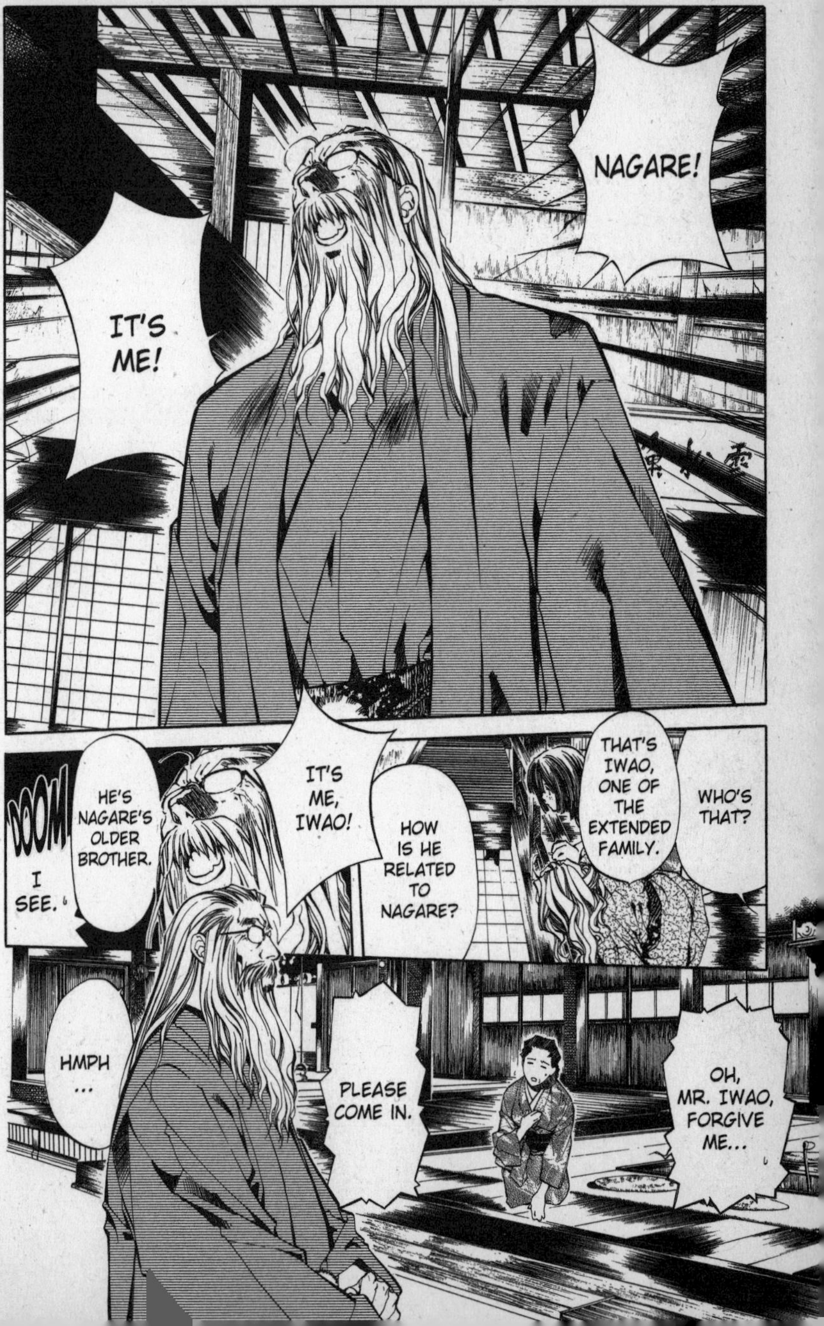
NAGARE!
IT'S ME!
WHO'S THAT?
THAT'S IWAO, ONE OF THE EXTENDED FAMILY.
HOW IS HE RELATED TO NAGARE?
IT'S ME, IWAO!
HE'S NAGARE'S OLDER BROTHER.
DOOM
I SEE.
OH, MR. IWAO, FORGIVE ME...
PLEASE COME IN.
HMPH ...

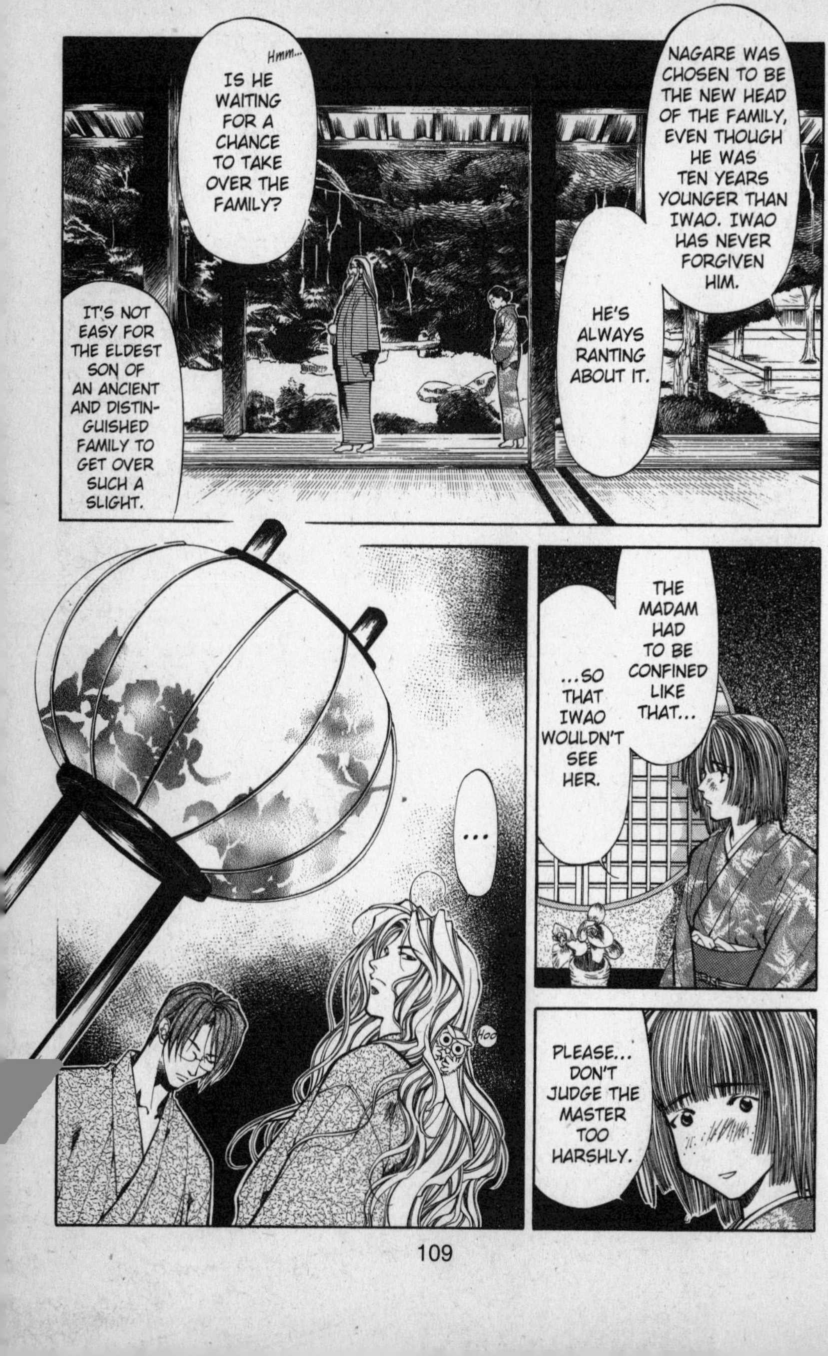
NAGARE WAS CHOSEN TO BE THE NEW HEAD OF THE FAMILY, EVEN THOUGH HE WAS TEN YEARS YOUNGER THAN IWAO. IWAO HAS NEVER FORGIVEN HIM.
HE'S ALWAYS RANTING ABOUT IT.
Hmm...
IS HE WAITING FOR A CHANCE TO TAKE OVER THE FAMILY?
IT'S NOT EASY FOR THE ELDEST SON OF AN ANCIENT AND DISTIN-GUISHED FAMILY TO GET OVER SUCH A SLIGHT.
THE MADAM HAD TO BE CONFINED LIKE THAT...
...SO THAT IWAO WOULDN'T SEE HER.
PLEASE... DON'T JUDGE THE MASTER TOO HARSHLY.
...
Hoo

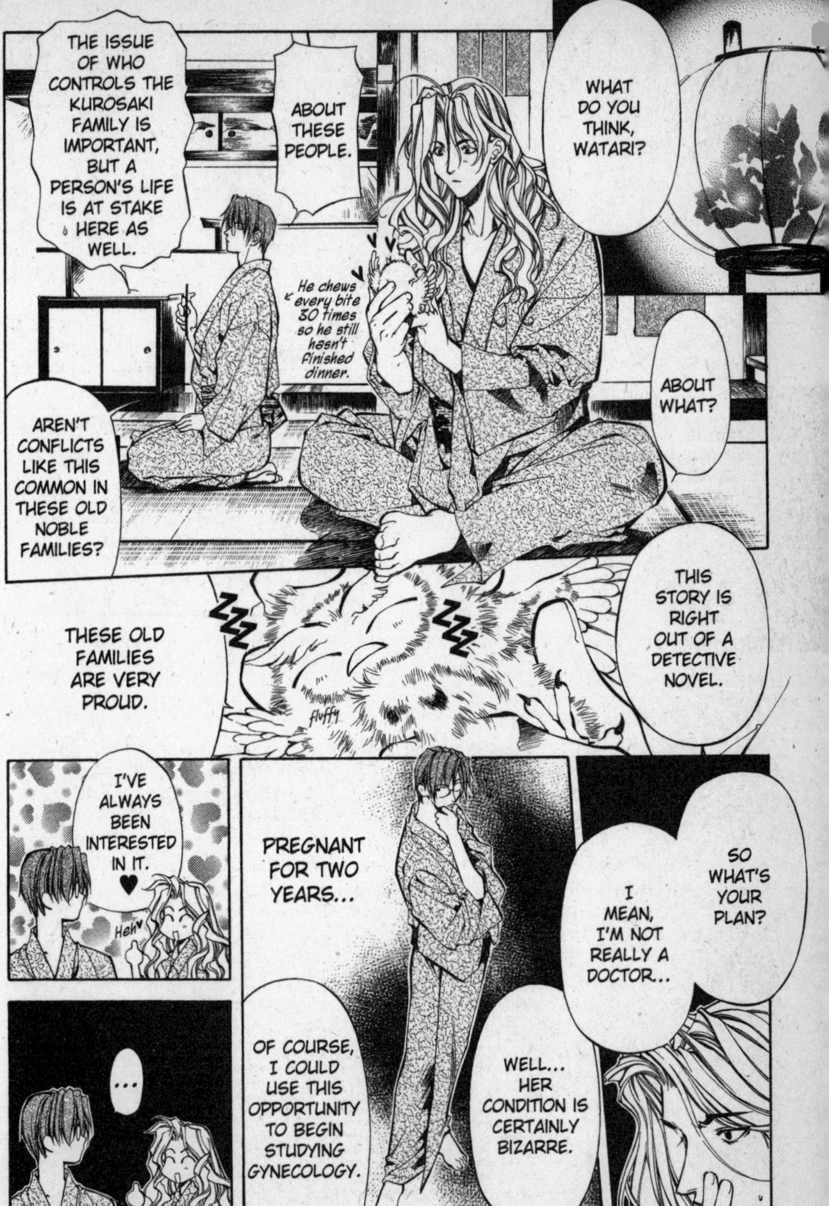
WHAT DO YOU THINK, WATARI?
ABOUT WHAT?
ABOUT THESE PEOPLE.
THE ISSUE OF WHO CONTROLS THE KUROSAKI FAMILY IS IMPORTANT, BUT A PERSON'S LIFE IS AT STAKE HERE AS WELL.
He chews every bite 30 times so he still hasn't finished dinner.
AREN'T CONFLICTS LIKE THIS COMMON IN THESE OLD NOBLE FAMILIES?
THIS STORY IS RIGHT OUT OF A DETECTIVE NOVEL.
ZZZ
ZZZ
fluffy
THESE OLD FAMILIES ARE VERY PROUD.
SO WHAT'S YOUR PLAN?
I MEAN, I'M NOT REALLY A DOCTOR...
WELL... HER CONDITION IS CERTAINLY BIZARRE.
PREGNANT FOR TWO YEARS...
OF COURSE, I COULD USE THIS OPPORTUNITY TO BEGIN STUDYING GYNECOLOGY.
I'VE ALWAYS BEEN INTERESTED IN IT. ♥
Heh♥
...

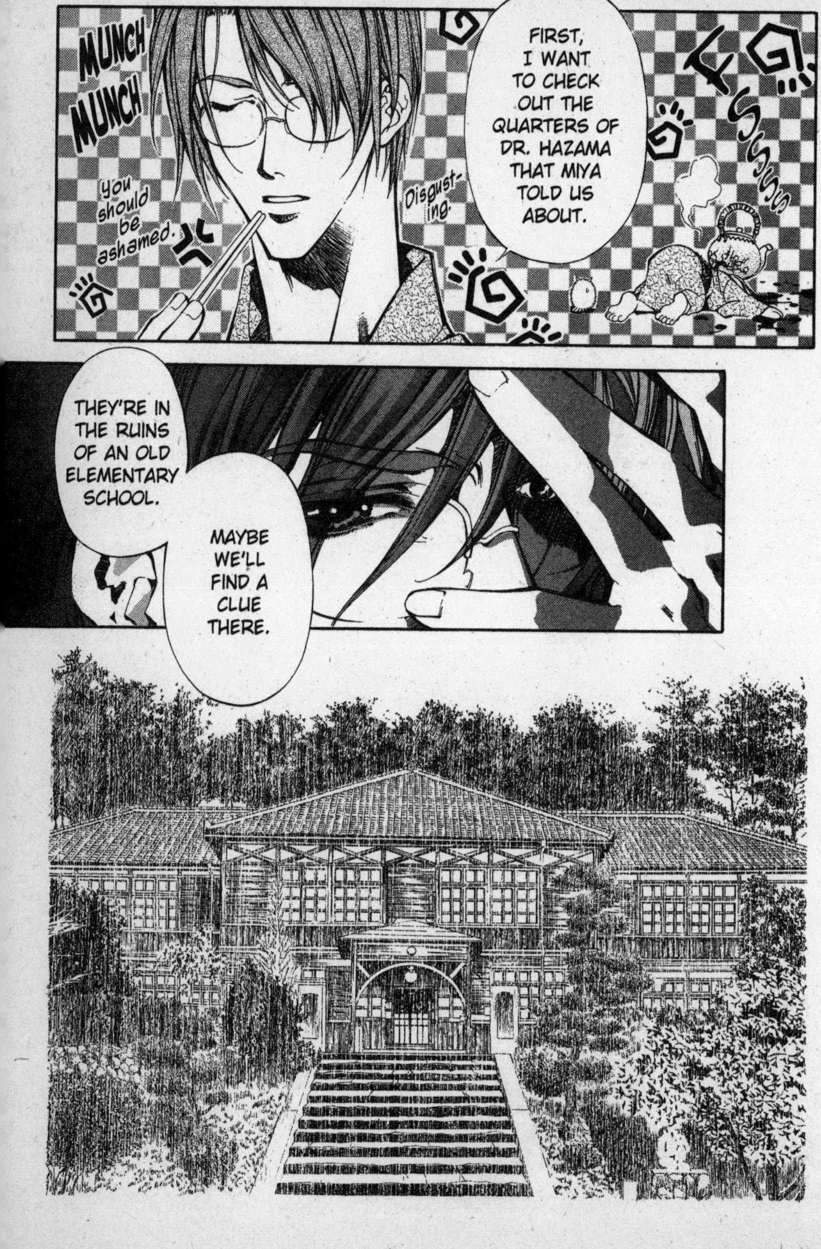
FIRST, I WANT TO CHECK OUT THE QUARTERS OF DR. HAZAMA THAT MIYA TOLD US ABOUT.
MUNCH MUNCH
Disgust-ing.
you should be ashamed.
THEY'RE IN THE RUINS OF AN OLD ELEMENTARY SCHOOL.
MAYBE WE'LL FIND A CLUE THERE.

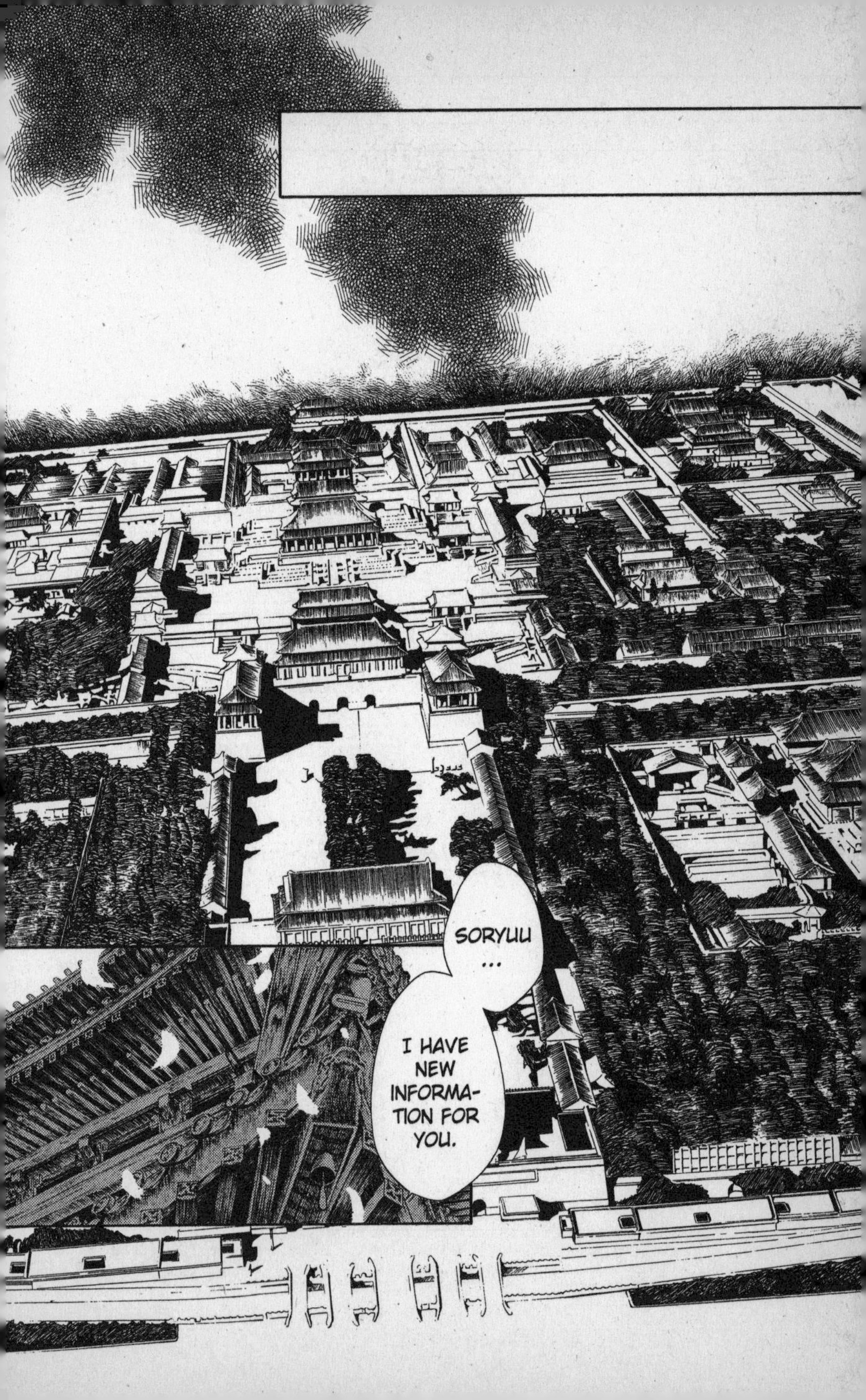
SORYUU ...
I HAVE NEW INFORMATION FOR YOU.

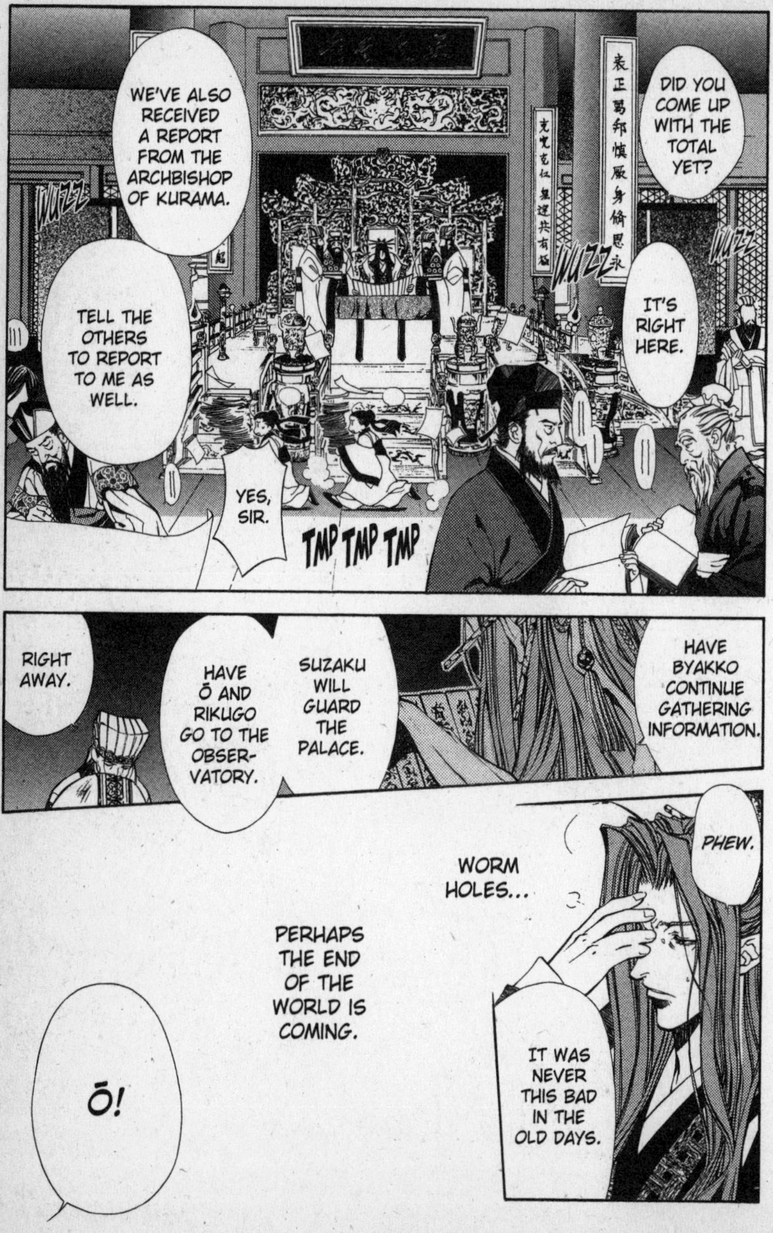
DID YOU COME UP WITH THE TOTAL YET?
WUZZ
IT'S RIGHT HERE.
WE'VE ALSO RECEIVED A REPORT FROM THE ARCHBISHOP OF KURAMA.
WUZZ
WUZZ
TELL THE OTHERS TO REPORT TO ME AS WELL.
YES, SIR.
TMP TMP TMP
HAVE BYAKKO CONTINUE GATHERING INFORMATION.
SUZAKU WILL GUARD THE PALACE.
HAVE Ō AND RIKUGO GO TO THE OBSERVATORY.
RIGHT AWAY.
PHEW.
WORM HOLES...
PERHAPS THE END OF THE WORLD IS COMING.
IT WAS NEVER THIS BAD IN THE OLD DAYS.
Ō!

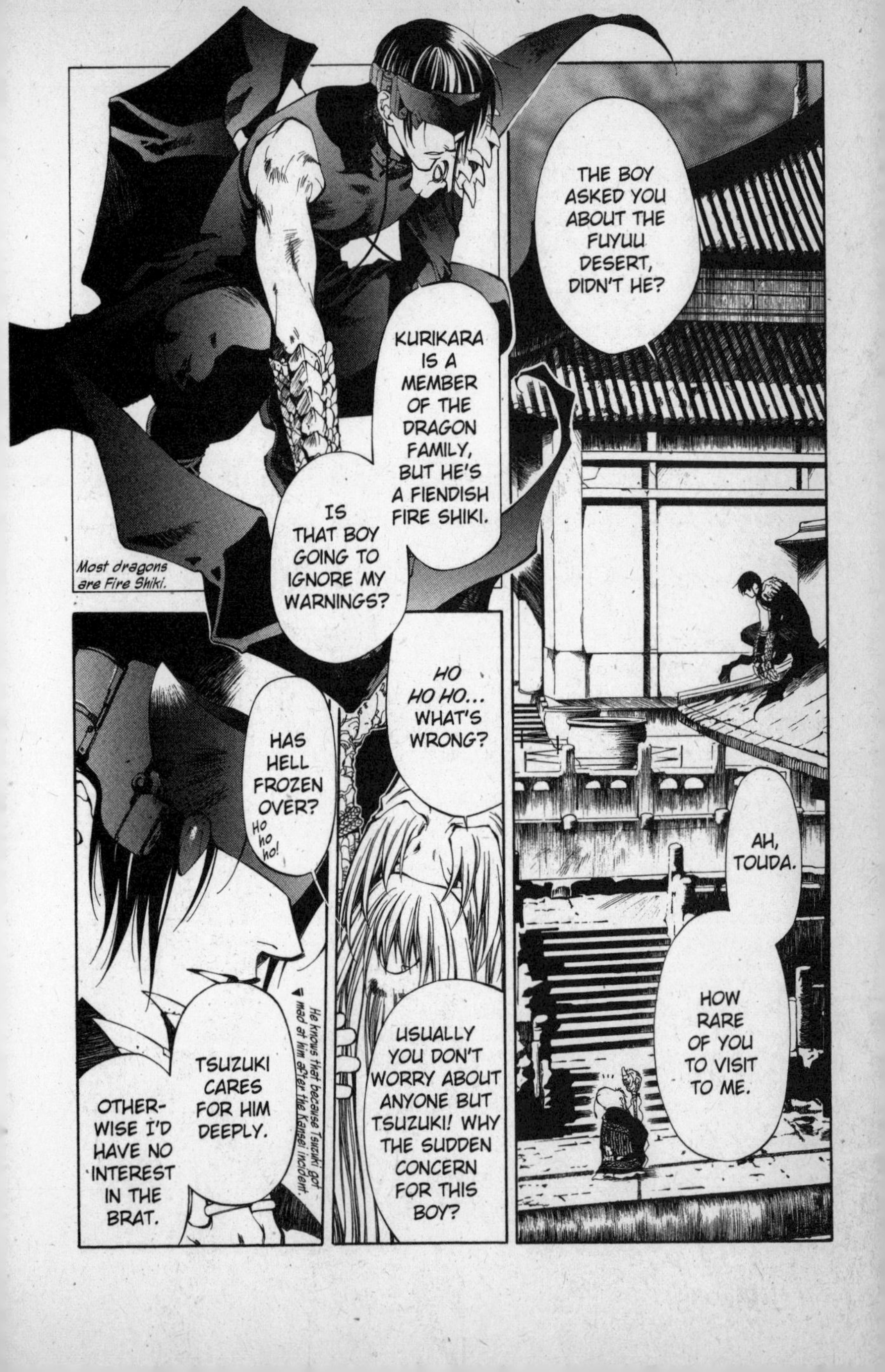
THE BOY ASKED YOU ABOUT THE FUYUU DESERT, DIDN'T HE?
AH, TOUDA.
HOW RARE OF YOU TO VISIT TO ME.
KURIKARA IS A MEMBER OF THE DRAGON FAMILY, BUT HE'S A FIENDISH FIRE SHIKI.
IS THAT BOY GOING TO IGNORE MY WARNINGS?
Most dragons are Fire Shiki.
HO HO HO... WHAT'S WRONG?
USUALLY YOU DON'T WORRY ABOUT ANYONE BUT TSUZUKI! WHY THE SUDDEN CONCERN FOR THIS BOY?
He knows that because Tsuzuki got mad at him after the Kansei incident.
HAS HELL FROZEN OVER?
Ho ho ho!
TSUZUKI CARES FOR HIM DEEPLY.
OTHER-WISE I'D HAVE NO INTEREST IN THE BRAT.

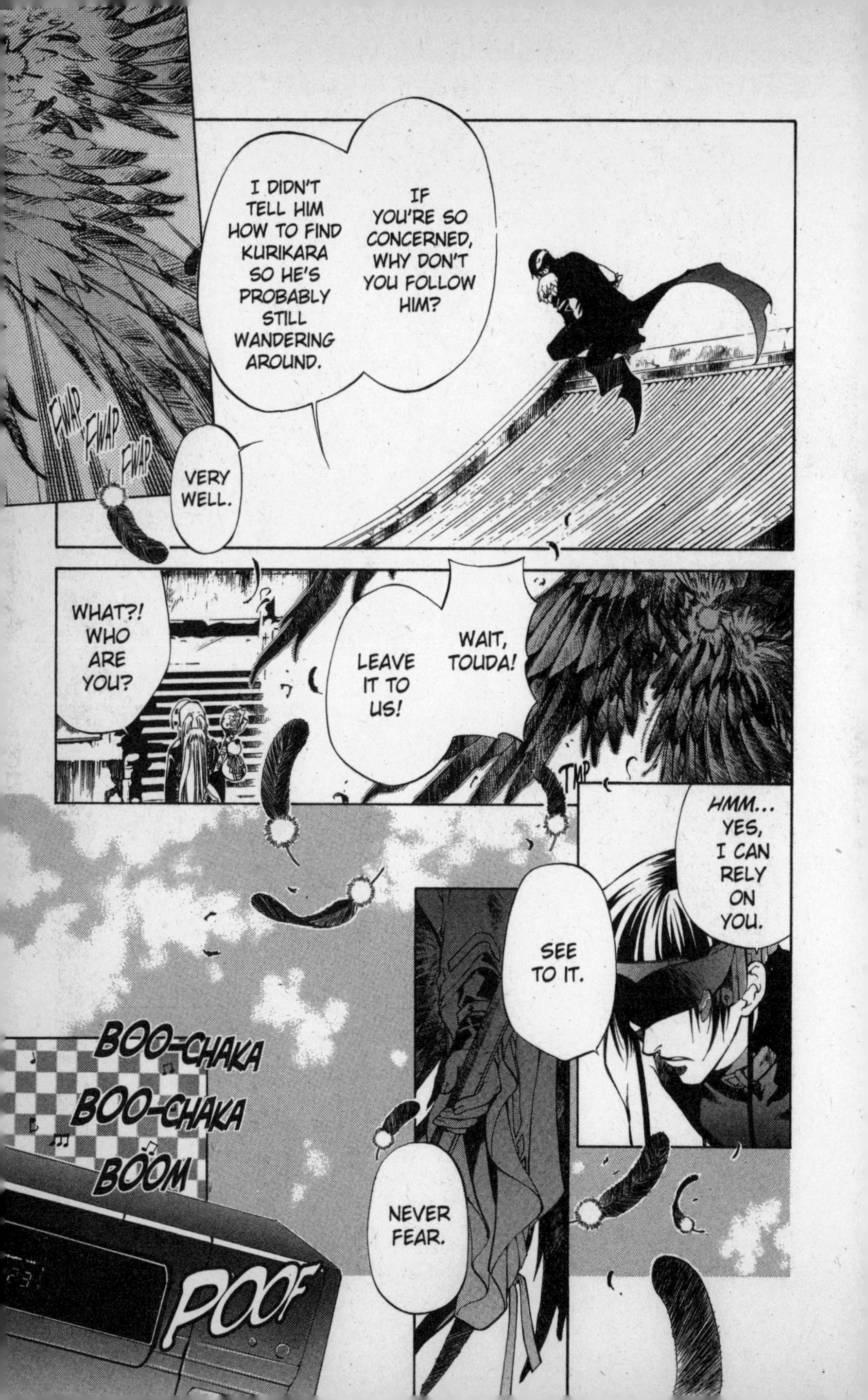
IF YOU'RE SO CONCERNED, WHY DON'T YOU FOLLOW HIM?
I DIDN'T TELL HIM HOW TO FIND KURIKARA SO HE'S PROBABLY STILL WANDERING AROUND.
VERY WELL.
FWAP FWAP FWAP
WAIT, TOUDA!
LEAVE IT TO US!
WHAT?! WHO ARE YOU?
TMP
HMM... YES, I CAN RELY ON YOU.
SEE TO IT.
NEVER FEAR.
BOO-CHAKA
BOO-CHAKA
BOOM
POOF

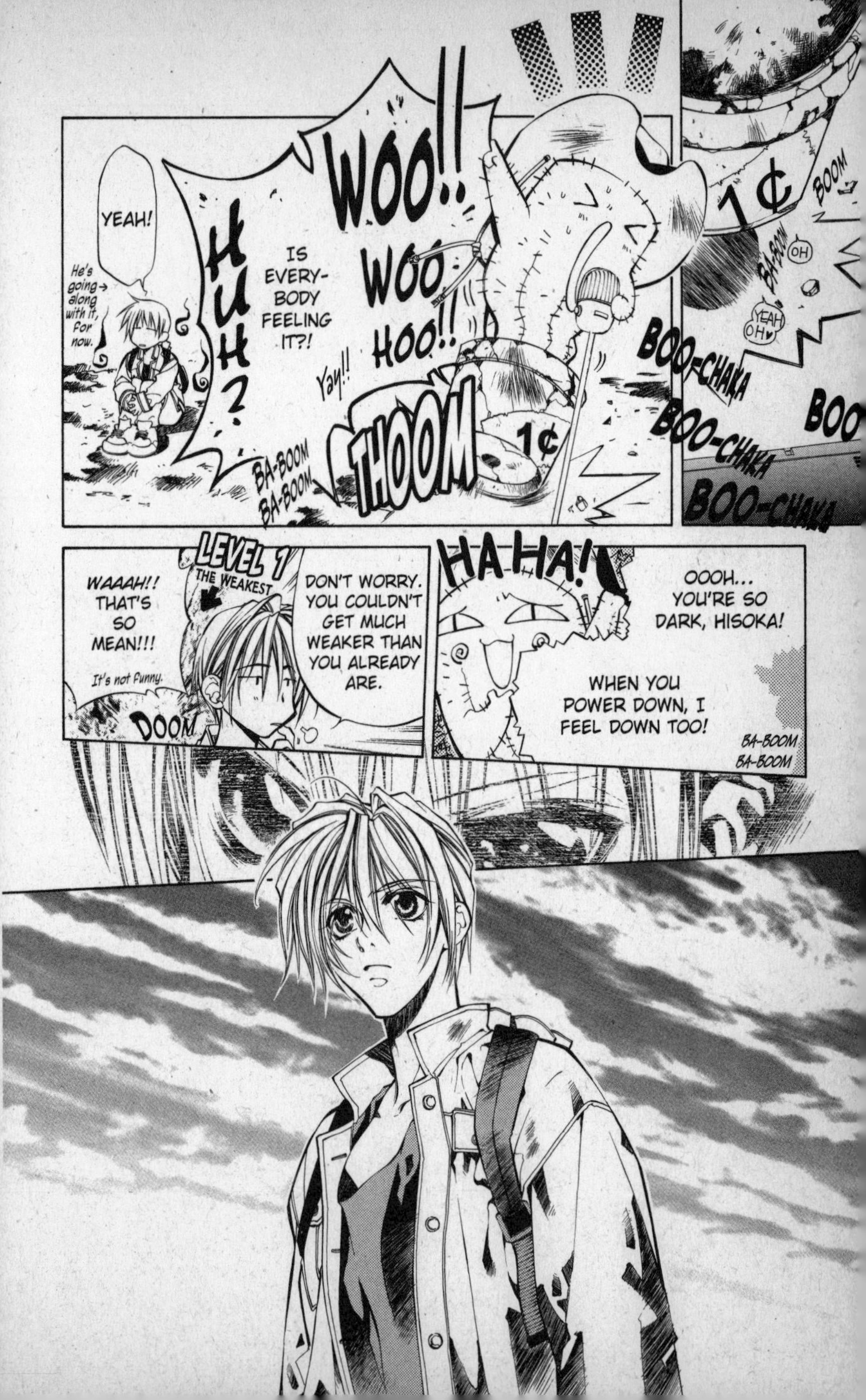
1¢
BOOM
BA-BOOM
OH
YEAH OH♥
BOO-CHAKA
BOO-CHAKA
BOO-CHAKA
BOO
WOO!!
WOO HOO!!
IS EVERY-BODY FEELING IT?!
Yay!!
THOOM
1¢
BA-BOOM BA-BOOM
HUH?
YEAH!
He's going along with it, for now.
HA HA!
OOOH... YOU'RE SO DARK, HISOKA!
WHEN YOU POWER DOWN, I FEEL DOWN TOO!
BA-BOOM BA-BOOM
DON'T WORRY. YOU COULDN'T GET MUCH WEAKER THAN YOU ALREADY ARE.
LEVEL 1
THE WEAKEST
WAAAH!! THAT'S SO MEAN!!!
It's not funny.
DOOM

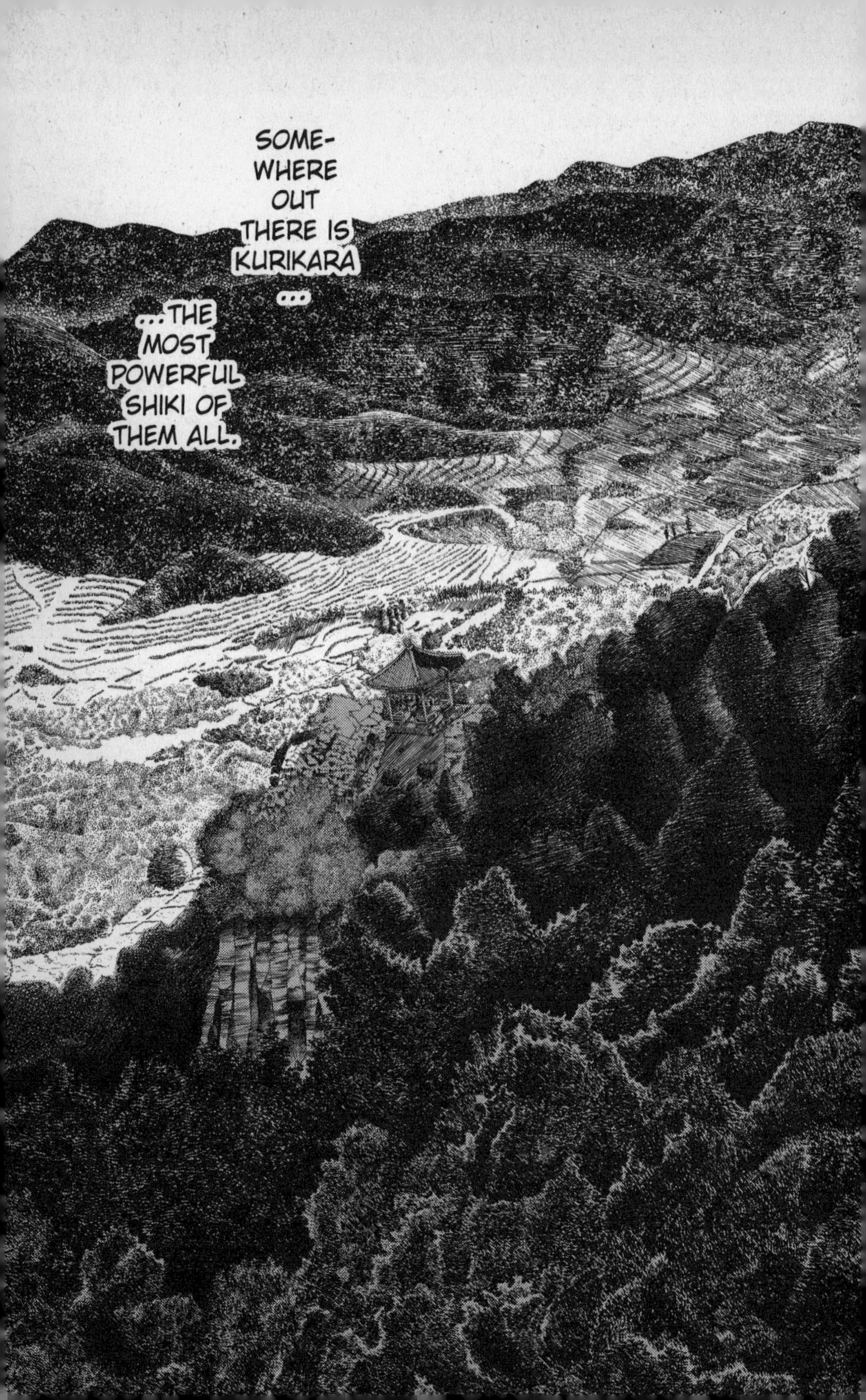
SOME-WHERE OUT THERE IS KURIKARA ...
...THE MOST POWERFUL SHIKI OF THEM ALL.

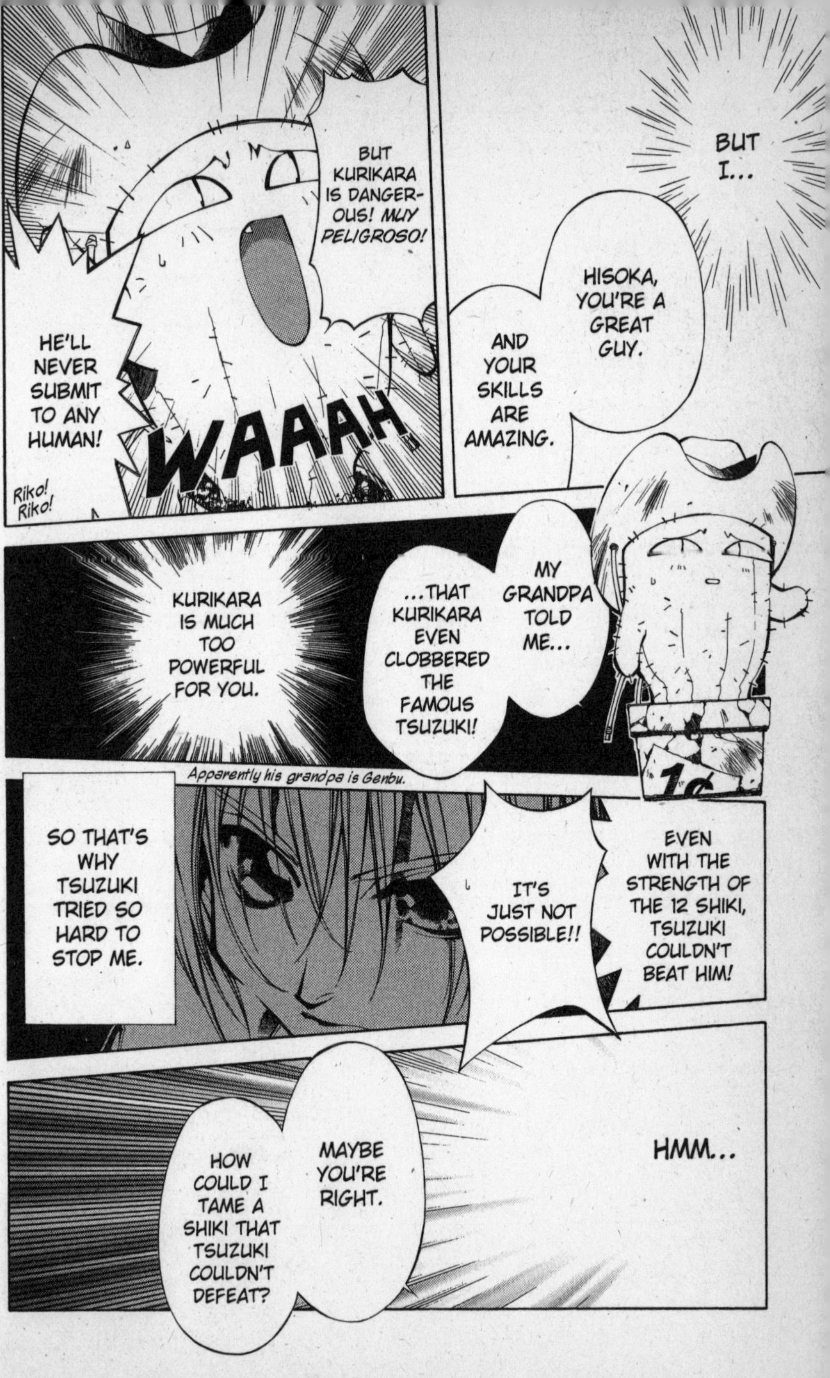
BUT I...
HISOKA, YOU'RE A GREAT GUY.
AND YOUR SKILLS ARE AMAZING.
BUT KURIKARA IS DANGER-OUS! *MUY PELIGROSO!*
HE'LL NEVER SUBMIT TO ANY HUMAN!
WAAAH
Riko! Riko!
MY GRANDPA TOLD ME...
...THAT KURIKARA EVEN CLOBBERED THE FAMOUS TSUZUKI!
KURIKARA IS MUCH TOO POWERFUL FOR YOU.
1¢
Apparently his grandpa is Genbu.
EVEN WITH THE STRENGTH OF THE 12 SHIKI, TSUZUKI COULDN'T BEAT HIM!
IT'S JUST NOT POSSIBLE!!
SO THAT'S WHY TSUZUKI TRIED SO HARD TO STOP ME.
HMM...
MAYBE YOU'RE RIGHT.
HOW COULD I TAME A SHIKI THAT TSUZUKI COULDN'T DEFEAT?

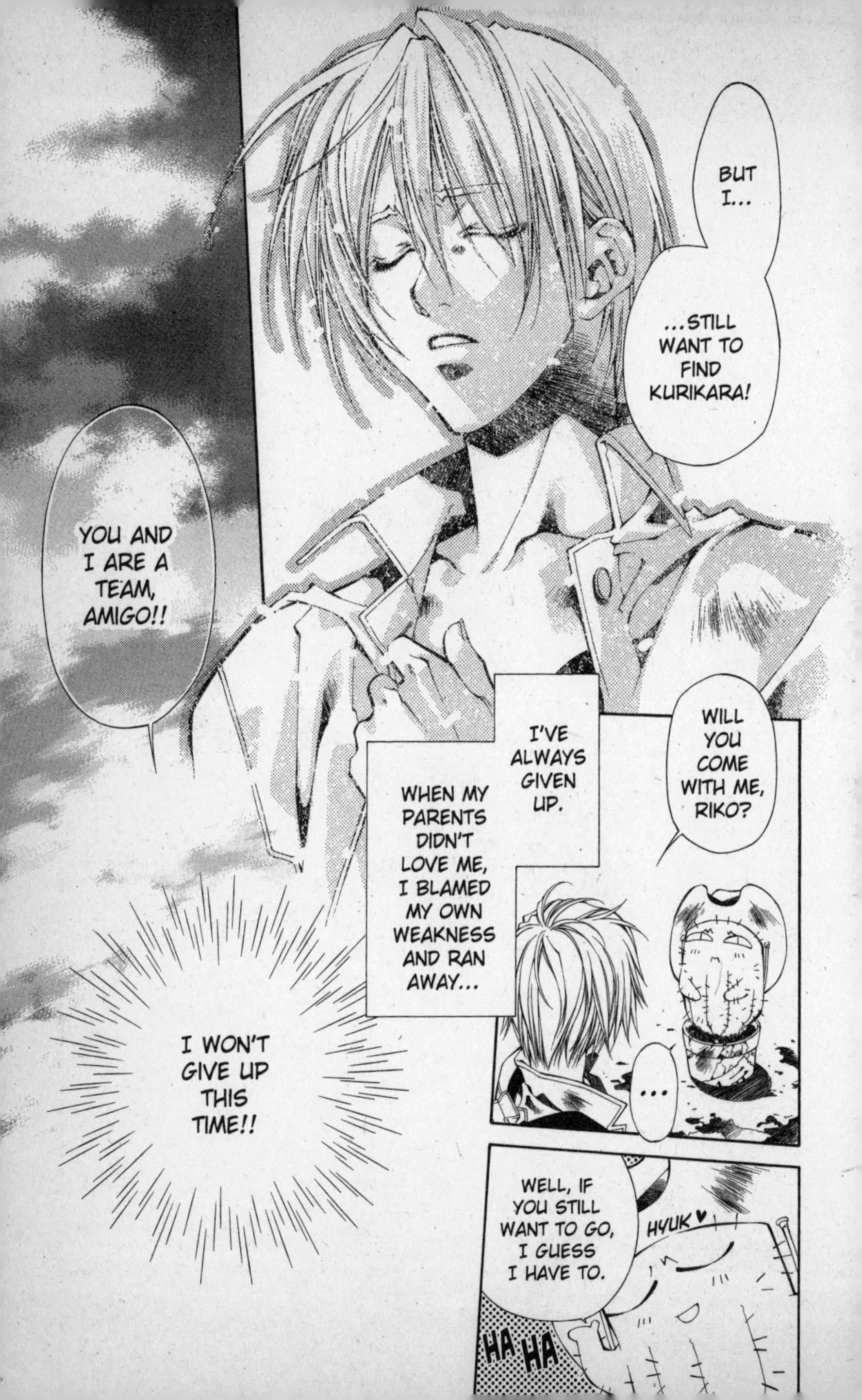
BUT I...
...STILL WANT TO FIND KURIKARA!
WILL YOU COME WITH ME, RIKO?
I'VE ALWAYS GIVEN UP.
WHEN MY PARENTS DIDN'T LOVE ME, I BLAMED MY OWN WEAKNESS AND RAN AWAY...
...
WELL, IF YOU STILL WANT TO GO, I GUESS I HAVE TO.
HYUK♥
HA HA
YOU AND I ARE A TEAM, AMIGO!!
I WON'T GIVE UP THIS TIME!!

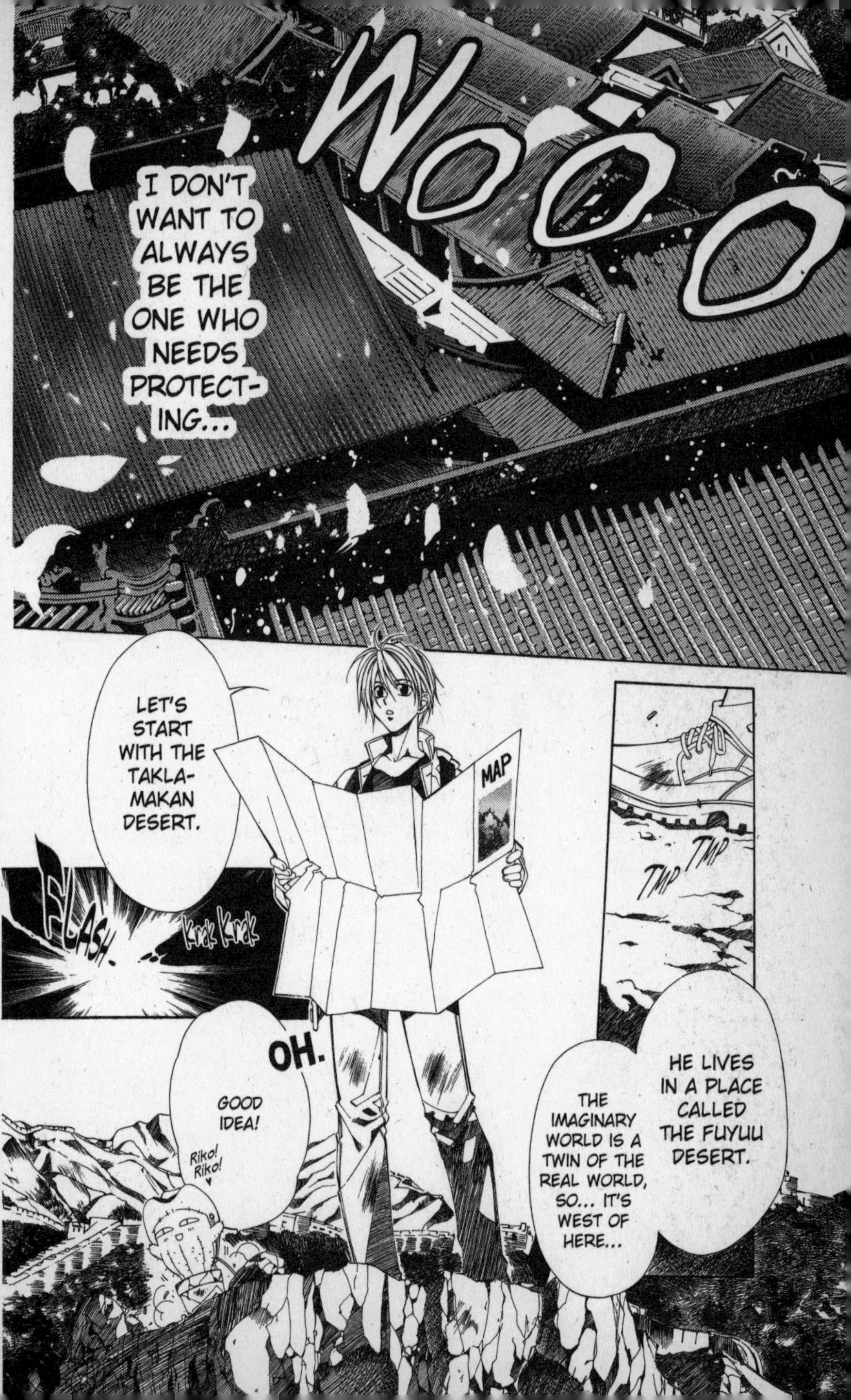
WOOOO
I DON'T WANT TO ALWAYS BE THE ONE WHO NEEDS PROTECTING...
TMP TMP
LET'S START WITH THE TAKLA-MAKAN DESERT.
FLASH
Krak Krak
HE LIVES IN A PLACE CALLED THE FUYUU DESERT.
THE IMAGINARY WORLD IS A TWIN OF THE REAL WORLD, SO... IT'S WEST OF HERE...
OH.
GOOD IDEA!
Riko! Riko!

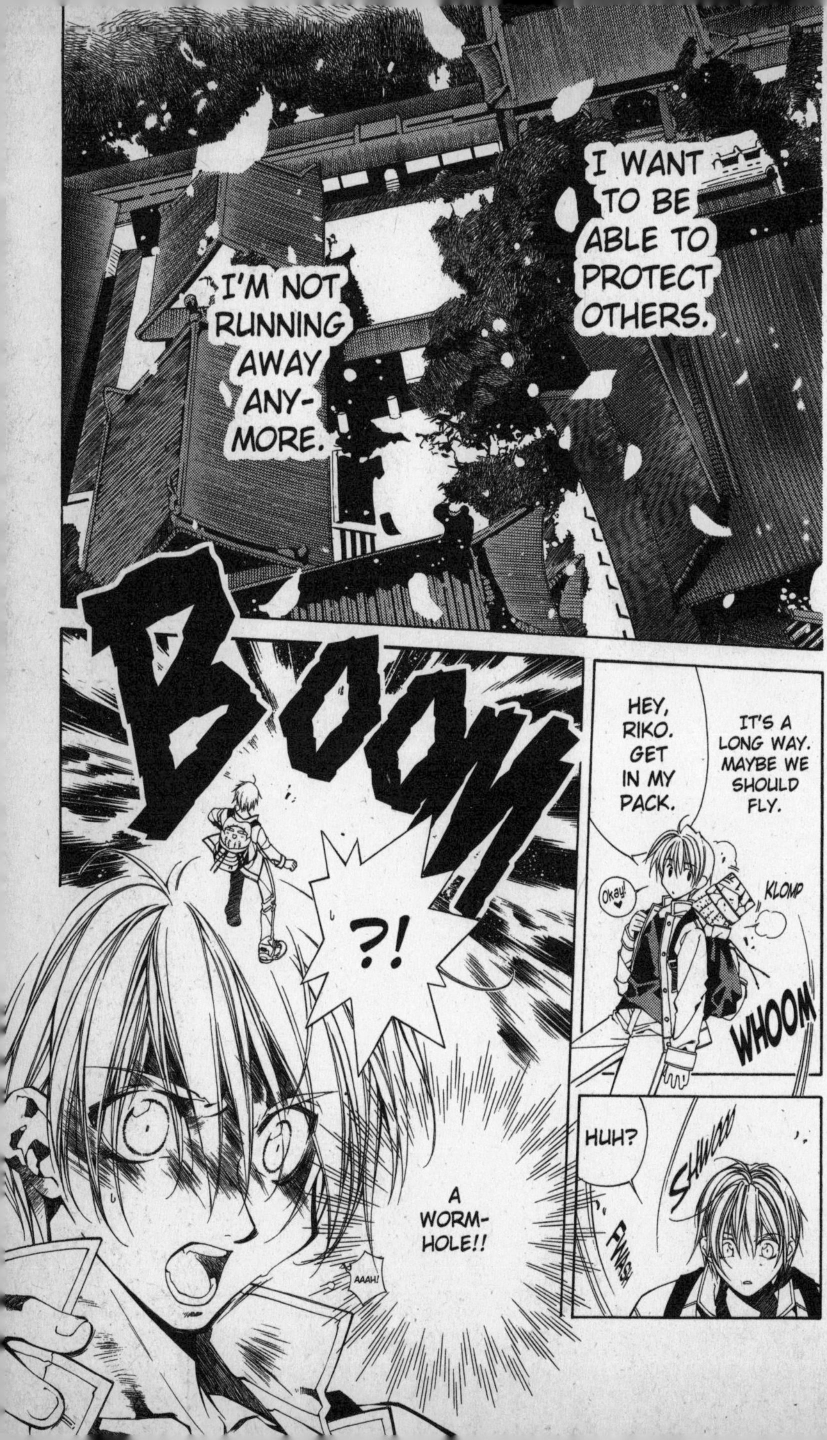
I WANT TO BE ABLE TO PROTECT OTHERS.
I'M NOT RUNNING AWAY ANYMORE.
IT'S A LONG WAY. MAYBE WE SHOULD FLY.
HEY, RIKO. GET IN MY PACK.
Okay!
KLOMP
WHOOM
HUH?
SHWOO
FWASH
BOOM
?!
A WORM-HOLE!!
AAAH!

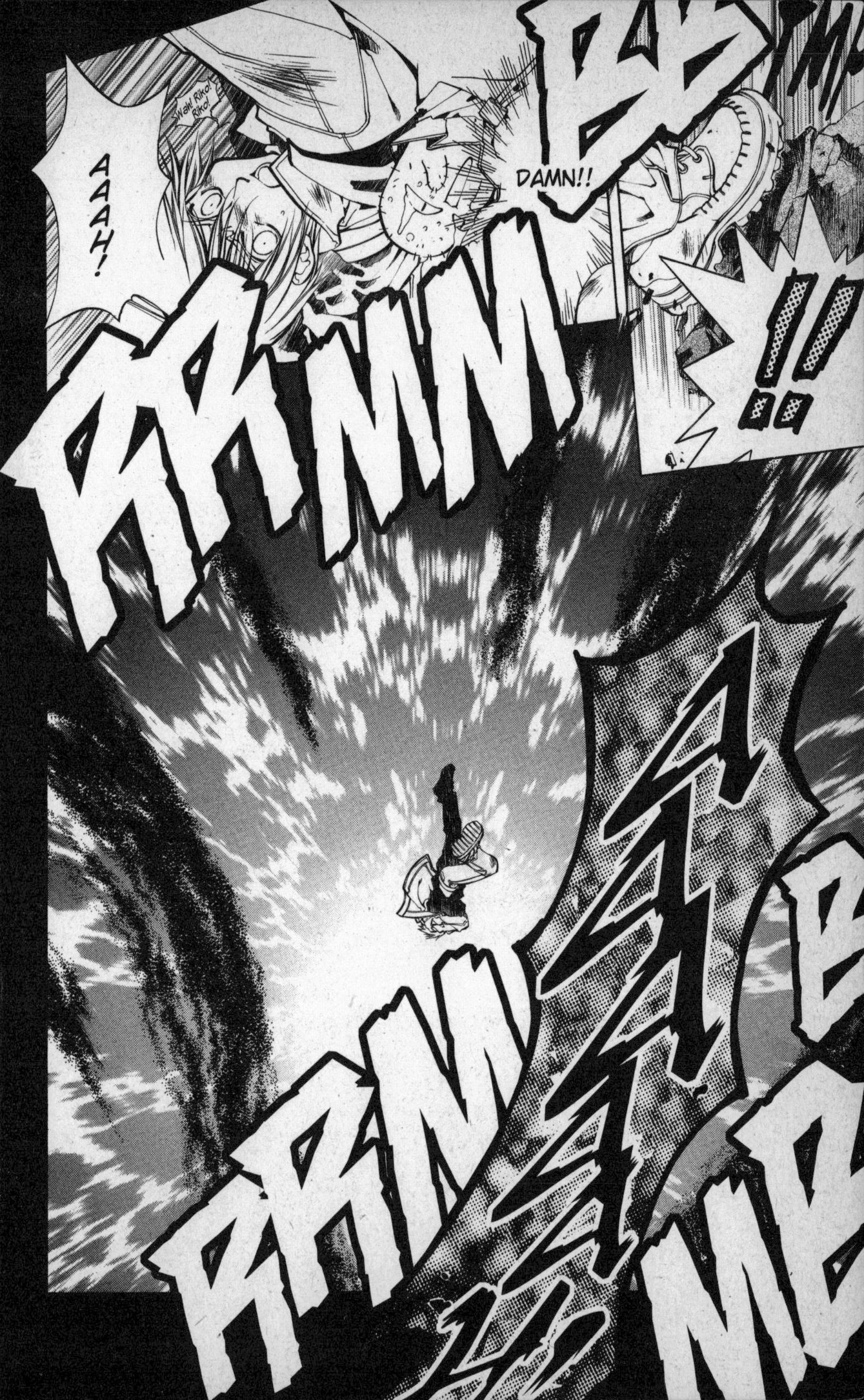
DAMN!!
Wah! Riko! Riko!
AAAAH!

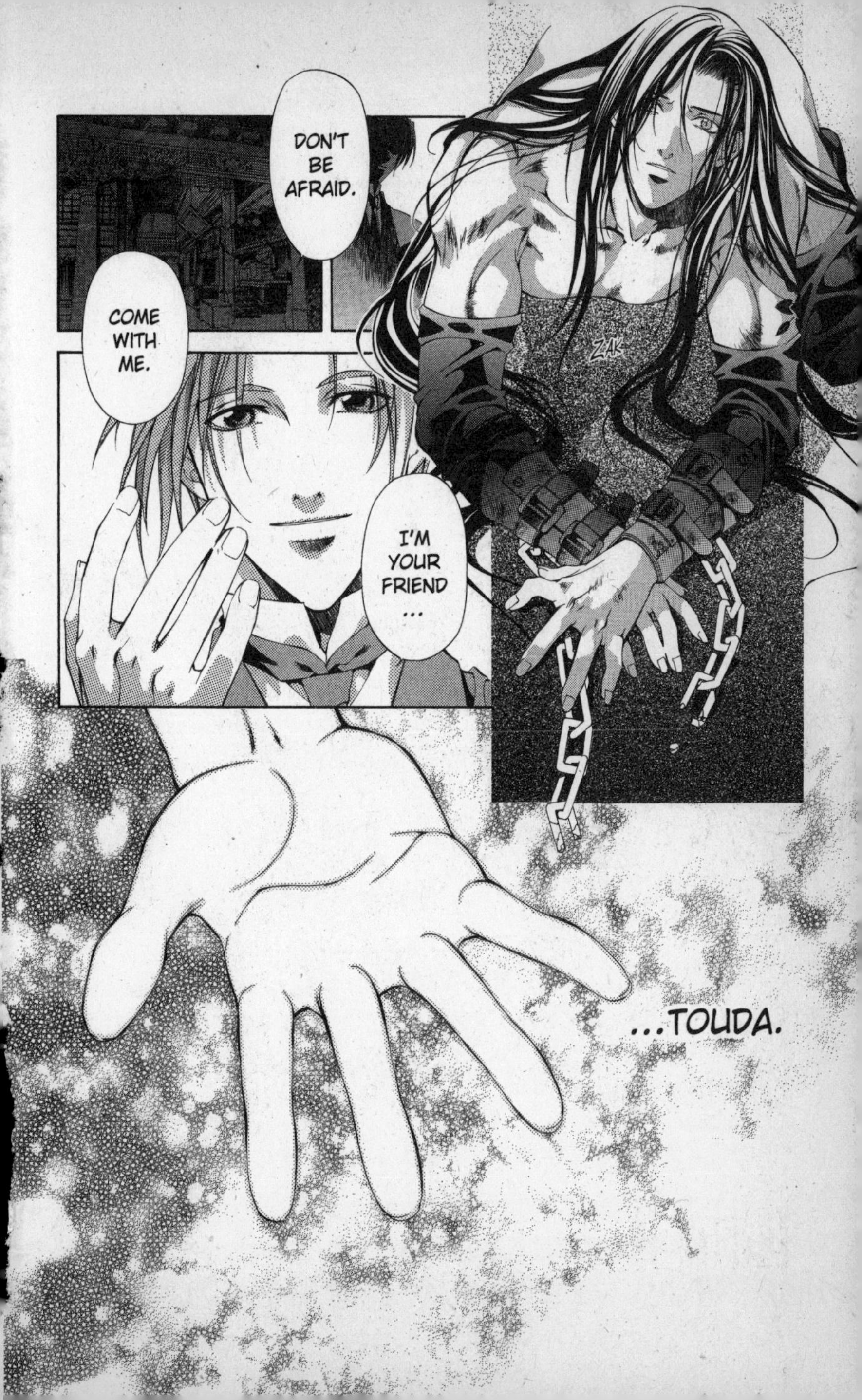
ZAK
DON'T BE AFRAID.
COME WITH ME.
I'M YOUR FRIEND...
...TOUDA.

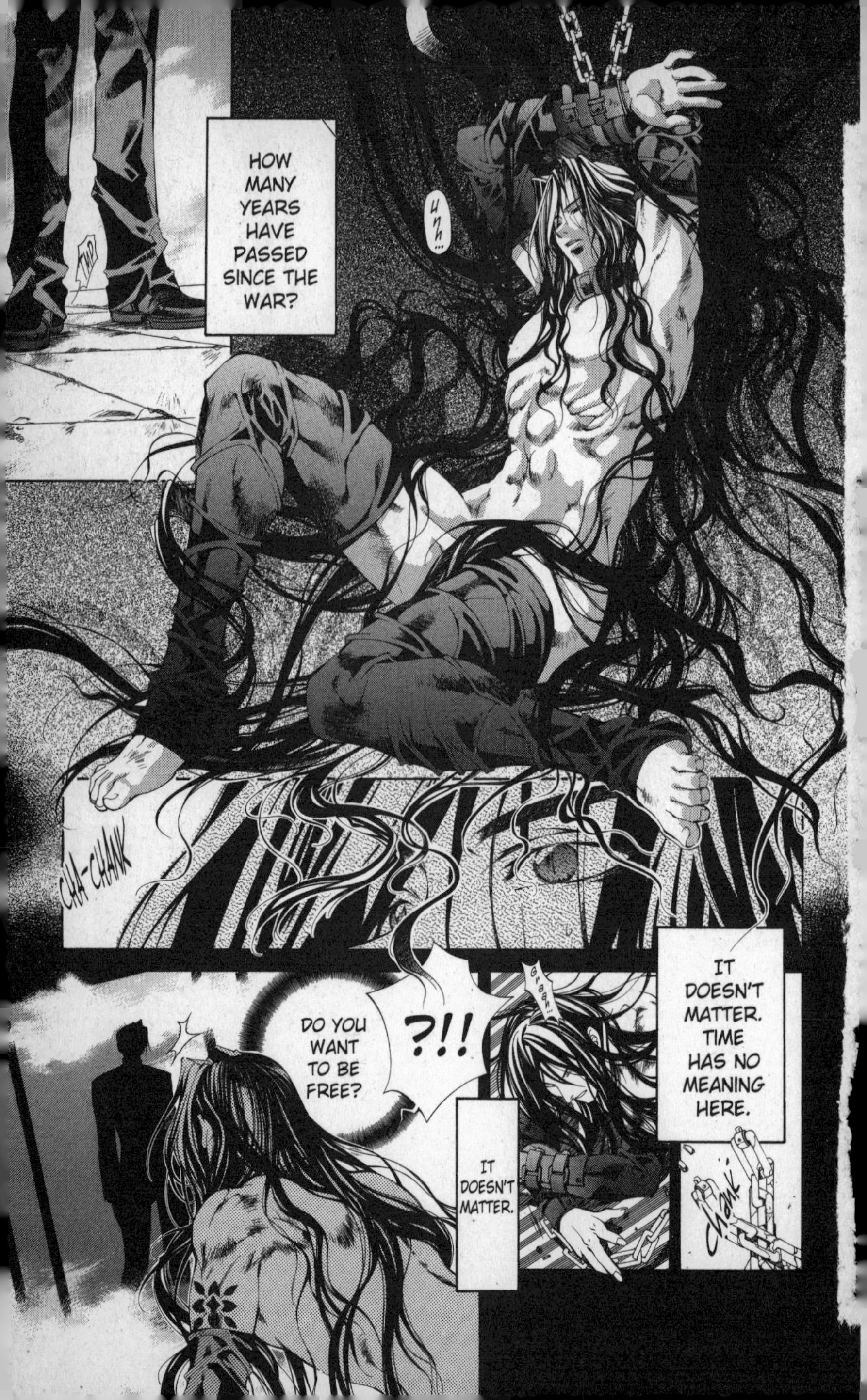
unh...
HOW MANY YEARS HAVE PASSED SINCE THE WAR?
TMP
CHA-CHANK
IT DOESN'T MATTER. TIME HAS NO MEANING HERE.
CHANK
IT DOESN'T MATTER.
?!!
DO YOU WANT TO BE FREE?

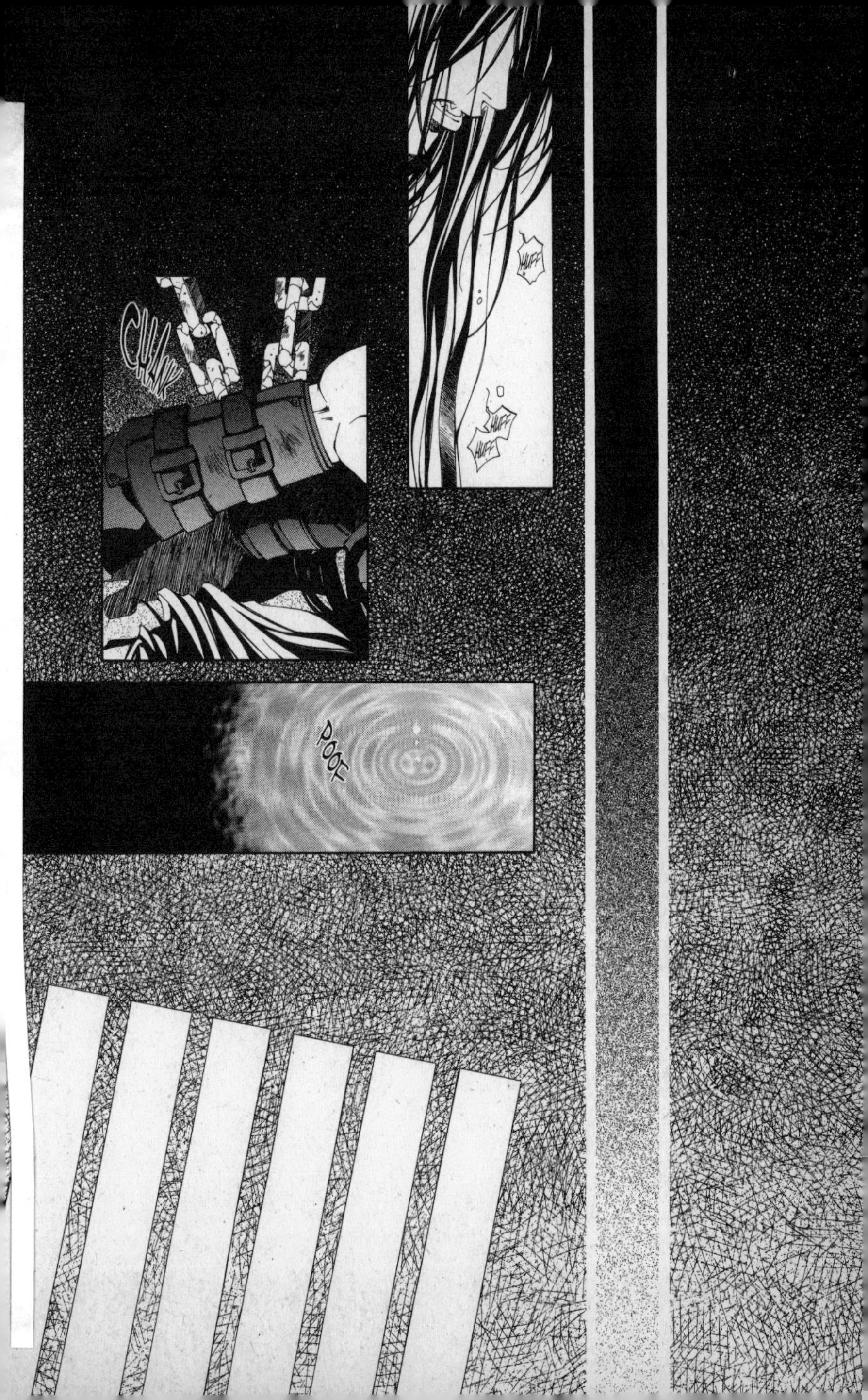
HUFF
HUFF
HUFF
POOF

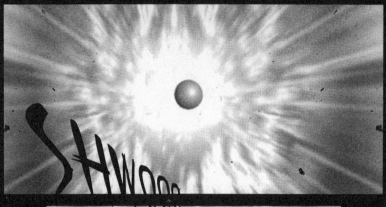

SHwooo

POOF

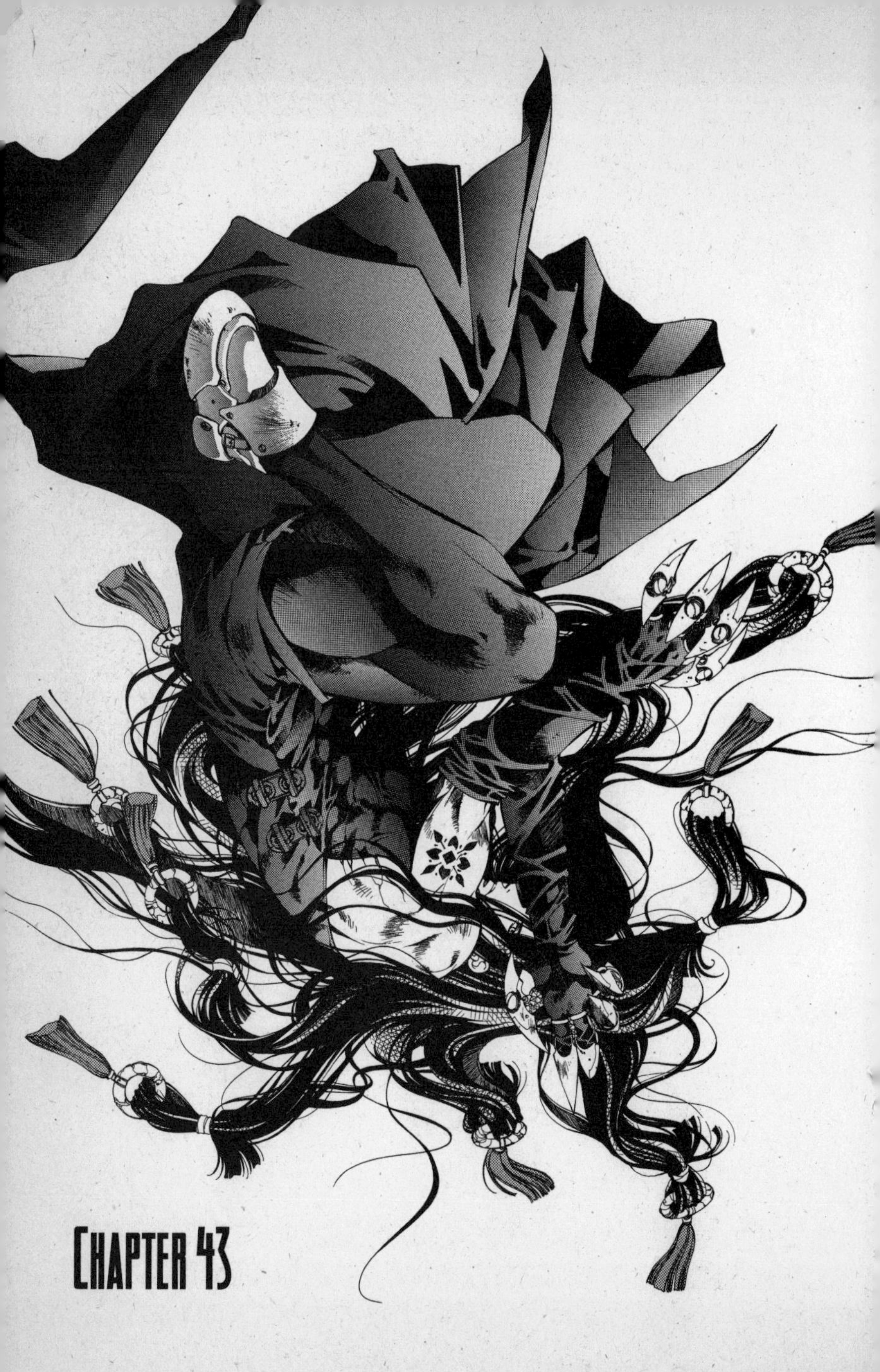

CHAPTER 43

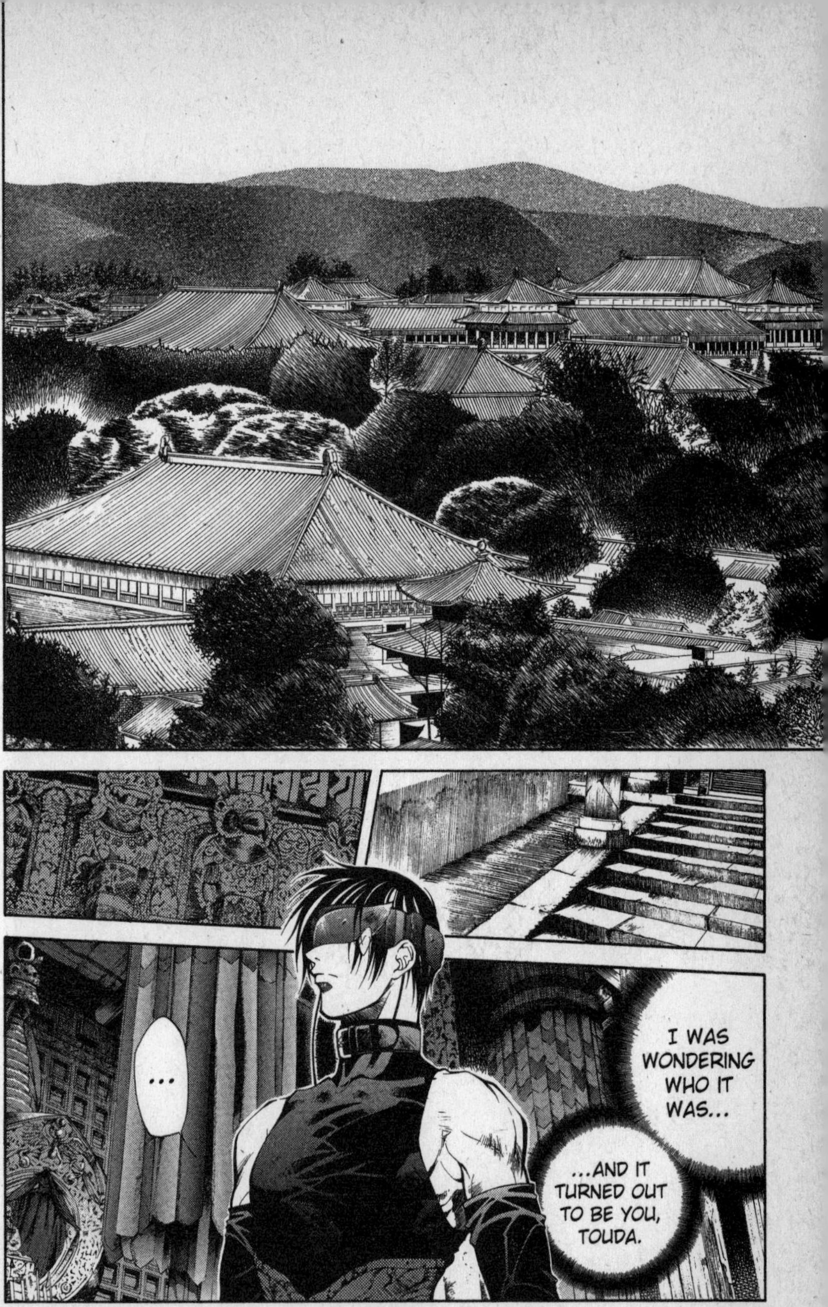
I WAS WONDERING WHO IT WAS...
...AND IT TURNED OUT TO BE YOU, TOUDA.
...

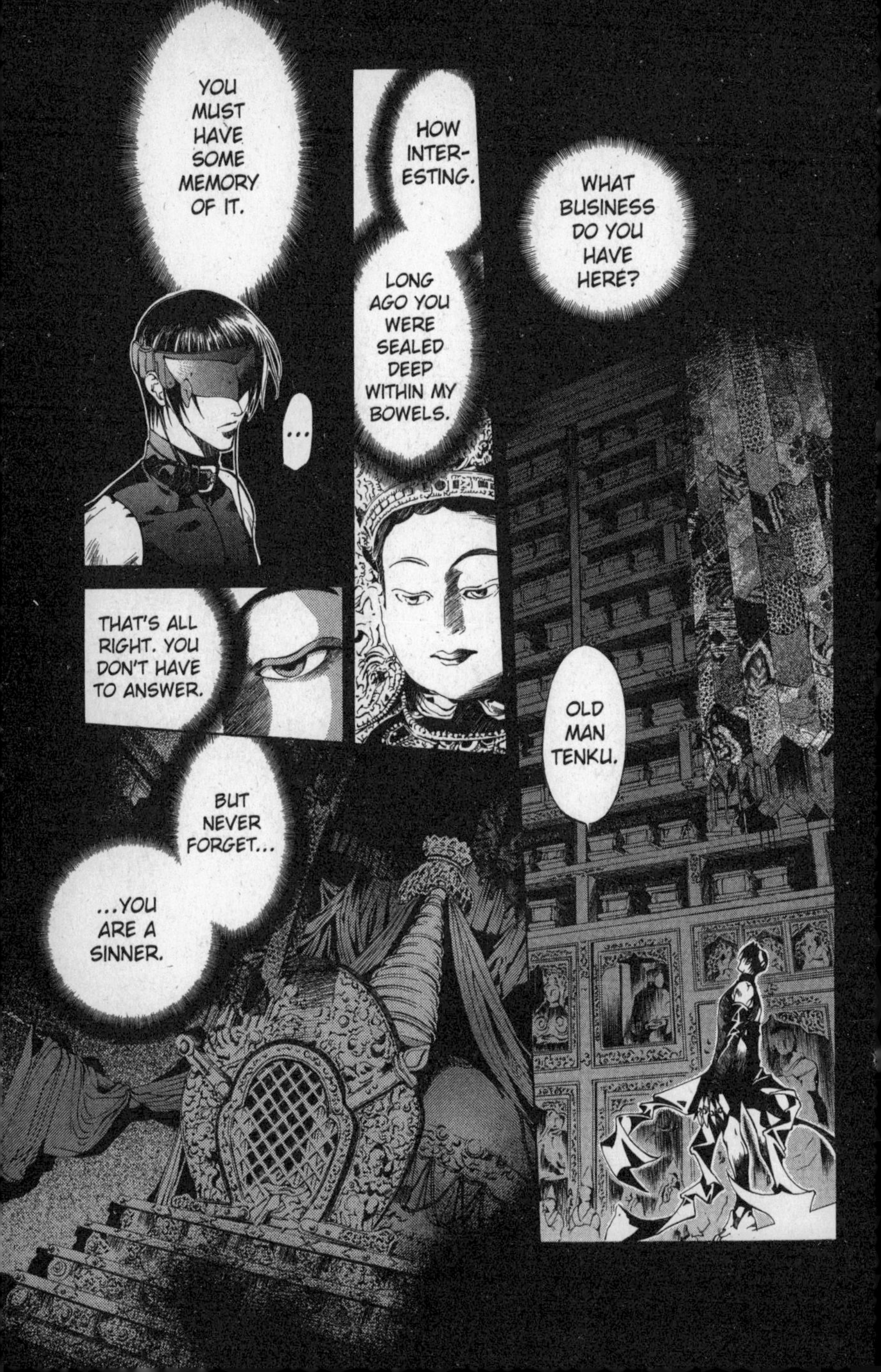
WHAT BUSINESS DO YOU HAVE HERE?
OLD MAN TENKU.
HOW INTER-ESTING.
LONG AGO YOU WERE SEALED DEEP WITHIN MY BOWELS.
YOU MUST HAVE SOME MEMORY OF IT.
...
THAT'S ALL RIGHT. YOU DON'T HAVE TO ANSWER.
BUT NEVER FORGET...
...YOU ARE A SINNER.

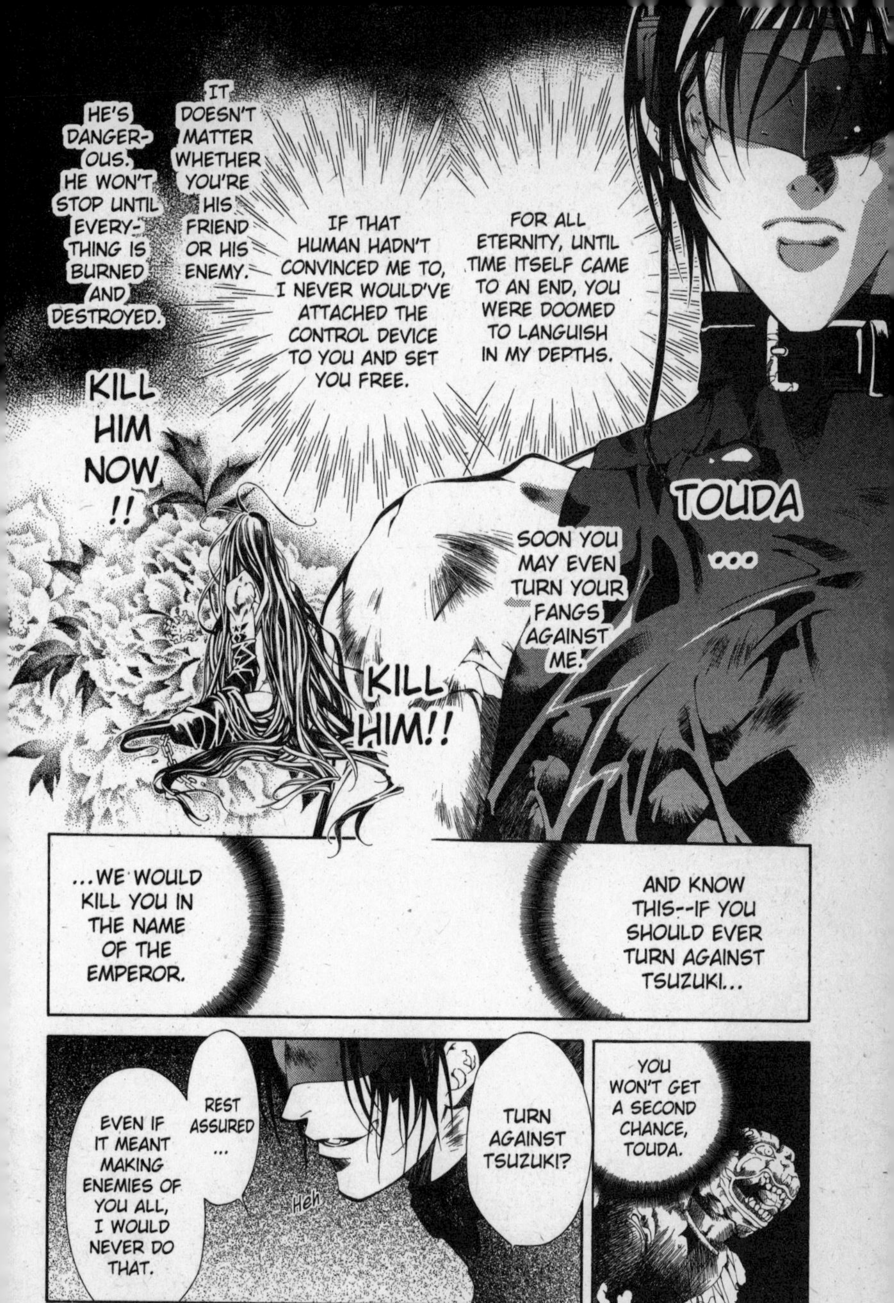
FOR ALL ETERNITY, UNTIL TIME ITSELF CAME TO AN END, YOU WERE DOOMED TO LANGUISH IN MY DEPTHS.
IF THAT HUMAN HADN'T CONVINCED ME TO, I NEVER WOULD'VE ATTACHED THE CONTROL DEVICE TO YOU AND SET YOU FREE.
IT DOESN'T MATTER WHETHER YOU'RE HIS FRIEND OR HIS ENEMY.
HE'S DANGEROUS. HE WON'T STOP UNTIL EVERYTHING IS BURNED AND DESTROYED.
TOUDA...
SOON YOU MAY EVEN TURN YOUR FANGS AGAINST ME.
KILL HIM NOW!!
KILL HIM!!
AND KNOW THIS--IF YOU SHOULD EVER TURN AGAINST TSUZUKI...
...WE WOULD KILL YOU IN THE NAME OF THE EMPEROR.
YOU WON'T GET A SECOND CHANCE, TOUDA.
TURN AGAINST TSUZUKI?
REST ASSURED...
Heh
EVEN IF IT MEANT MAKING ENEMIES OF YOU ALL, I WOULD NEVER DO THAT.

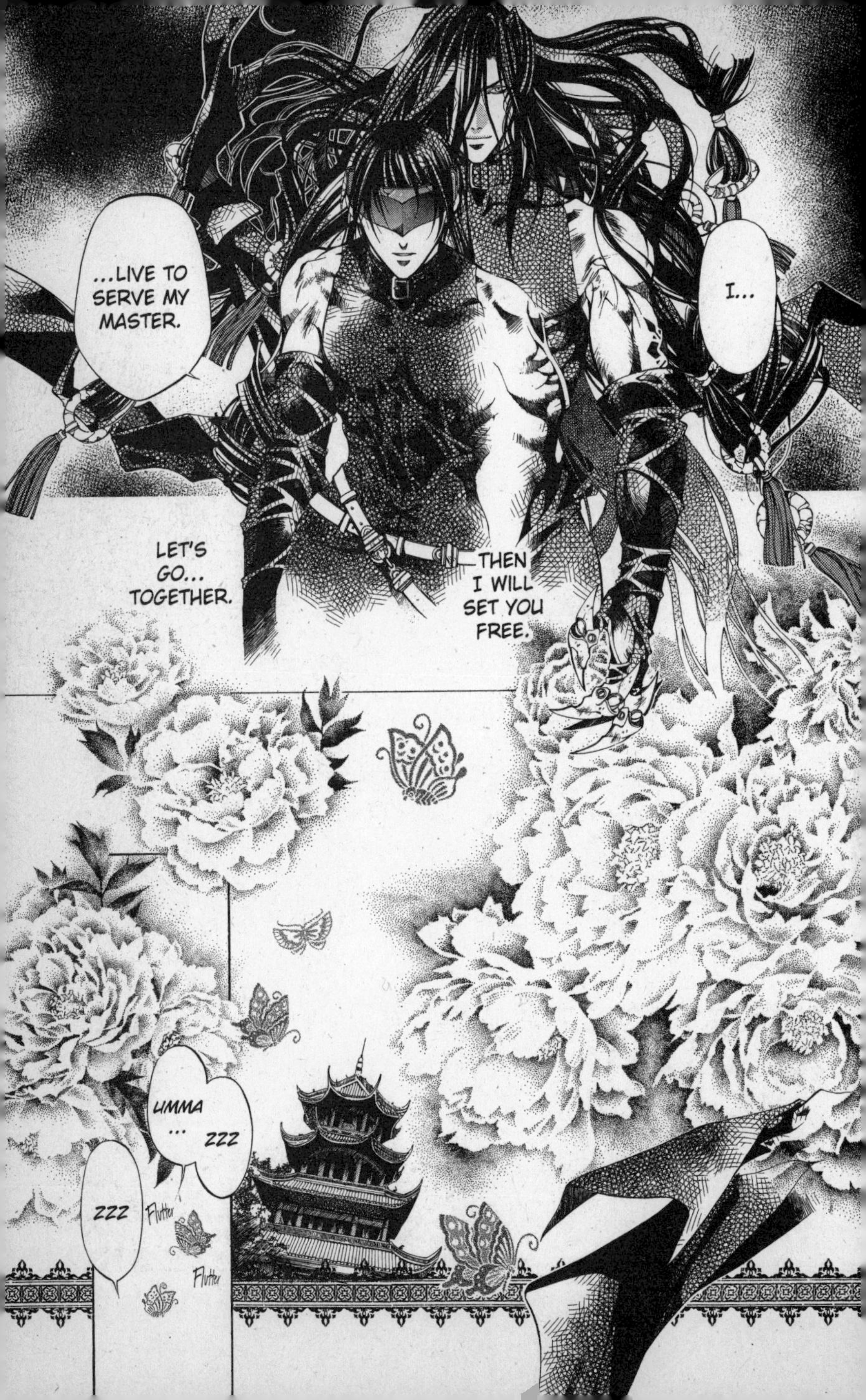
I...
...LIVE TO SERVE MY MASTER.
THEN I WILL SET YOU FREE.
LET'S GO... TOGETHER.
UMMA ... ZZZ
ZZZ
Flutter
Flutter

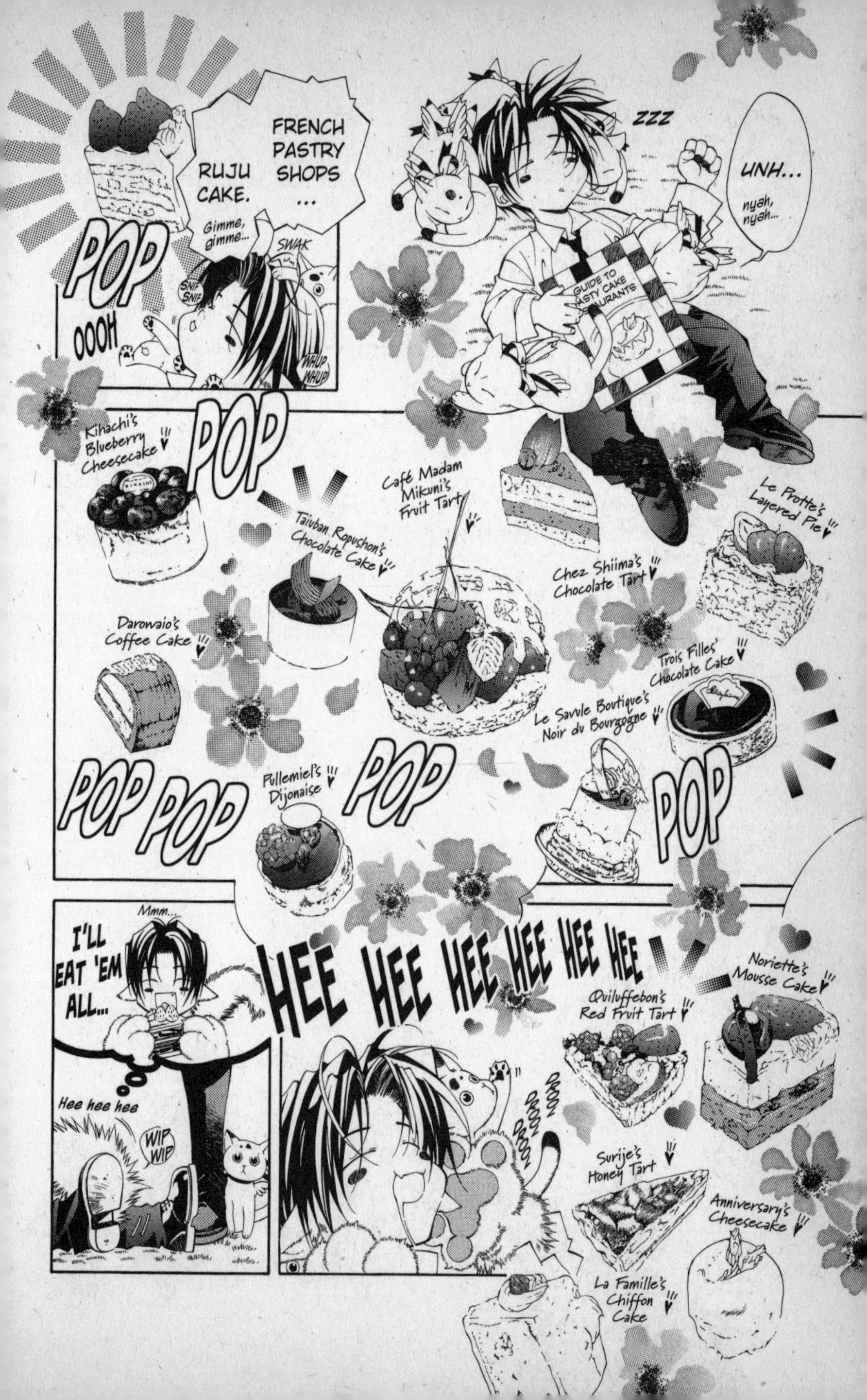
ZZZ
UNH...
nyah, nyah...
GUIDE TO
ASTY CAKE
FRENCH PASTRY SHOPS ...
RUJU CAKE.
Gimme, gimme...
SWAK
POP
SNIF SNIF
OOOH
WHUP WHUP
Le Protte's Layered Pie
Café Madam Mikuni's Fruit Tart
POP
Kihachi's Blueberry Cheesecake
Chez Shiima's Chocolate Tart
Taiuban Ropushon's Chocolate Cake
Darowaio's Coffee Cake
Trois Filles' Chocolate Cake
Le Savule Boutique's Noir du Bourgogne
POP
Pullemiel's Dijonaise
POP
POP
POP
HEE HEE HEE HEE HEE HEE
Noriette's Mousse Cake
Quiluffebon's Red Fruit Tart
DROOL DROOL DROOL
Surije's Honey Tart
Anniversary's Cheesecake
La Famille's Chiffon Cake
Mmm...
I'LL EAT 'EM ALL...
Hee hee hee
WIP WIP

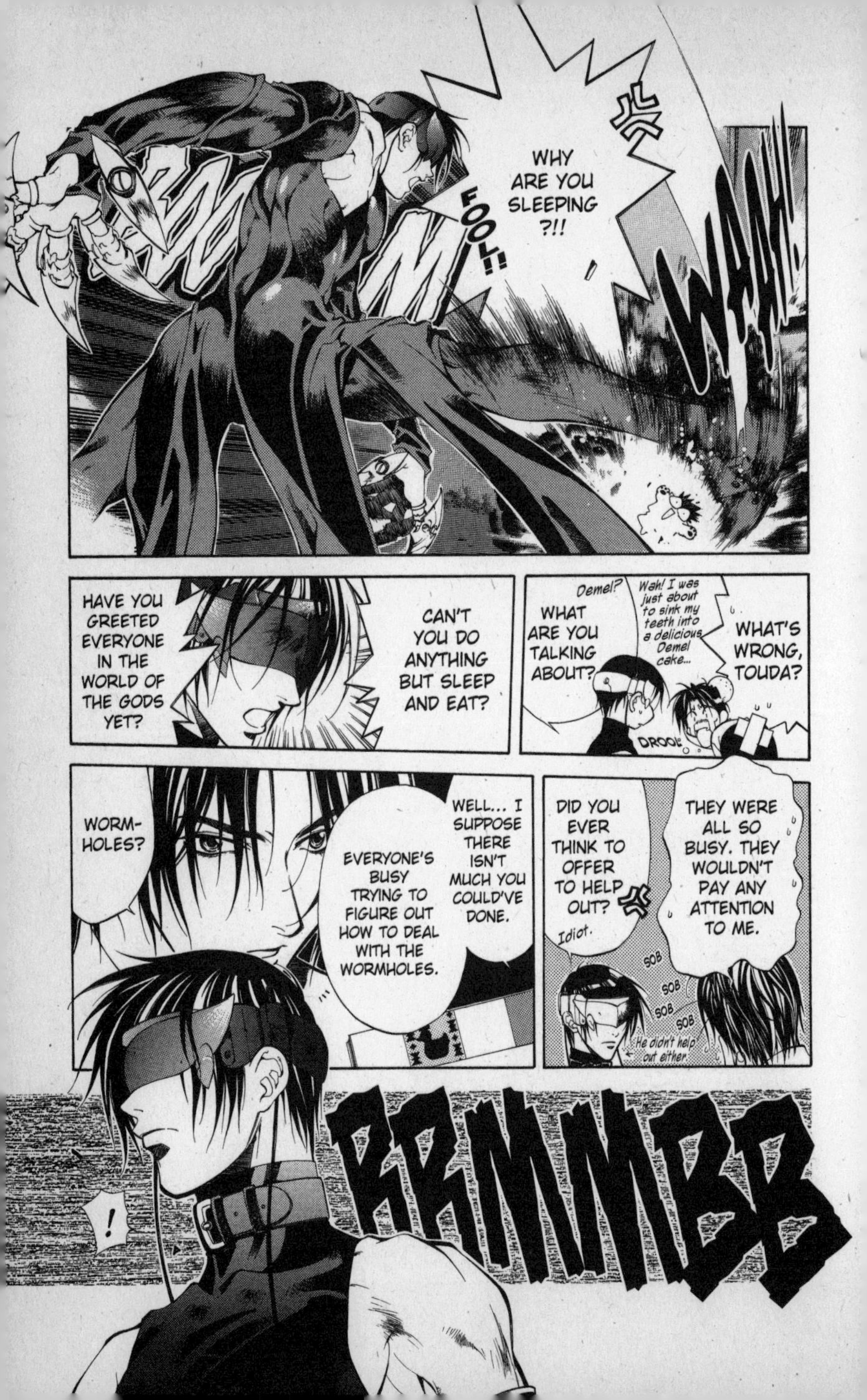
WHY ARE YOU SLEEPING ?!!
FOOL!!
WHAT'S WRONG, TOUDA?
Wah! I was just about to sink my teeth into a delicious Demel cake...
Demel?
WHAT ARE YOU TALKING ABOUT?
DROOL
CAN'T YOU DO ANYTHING BUT SLEEP AND EAT?
HAVE YOU GREETED EVERYONE IN THE WORLD OF THE GODS YET?
THEY WERE ALL SO BUSY. THEY WOULDN'T PAY ANY ATTENTION TO ME.
DID YOU EVER THINK TO OFFER TO HELP OUT?
Idiot.
SOB SOB SOB SOB
He didn't help out either.
WELL... I SUPPOSE THERE ISN'T MUCH YOU COULD'VE DONE.
EVERYONE'S BUSY TRYING TO FIGURE OUT HOW TO DEAL WITH THE WORMHOLES.
WORM-HOLES?
BRMMBB
!

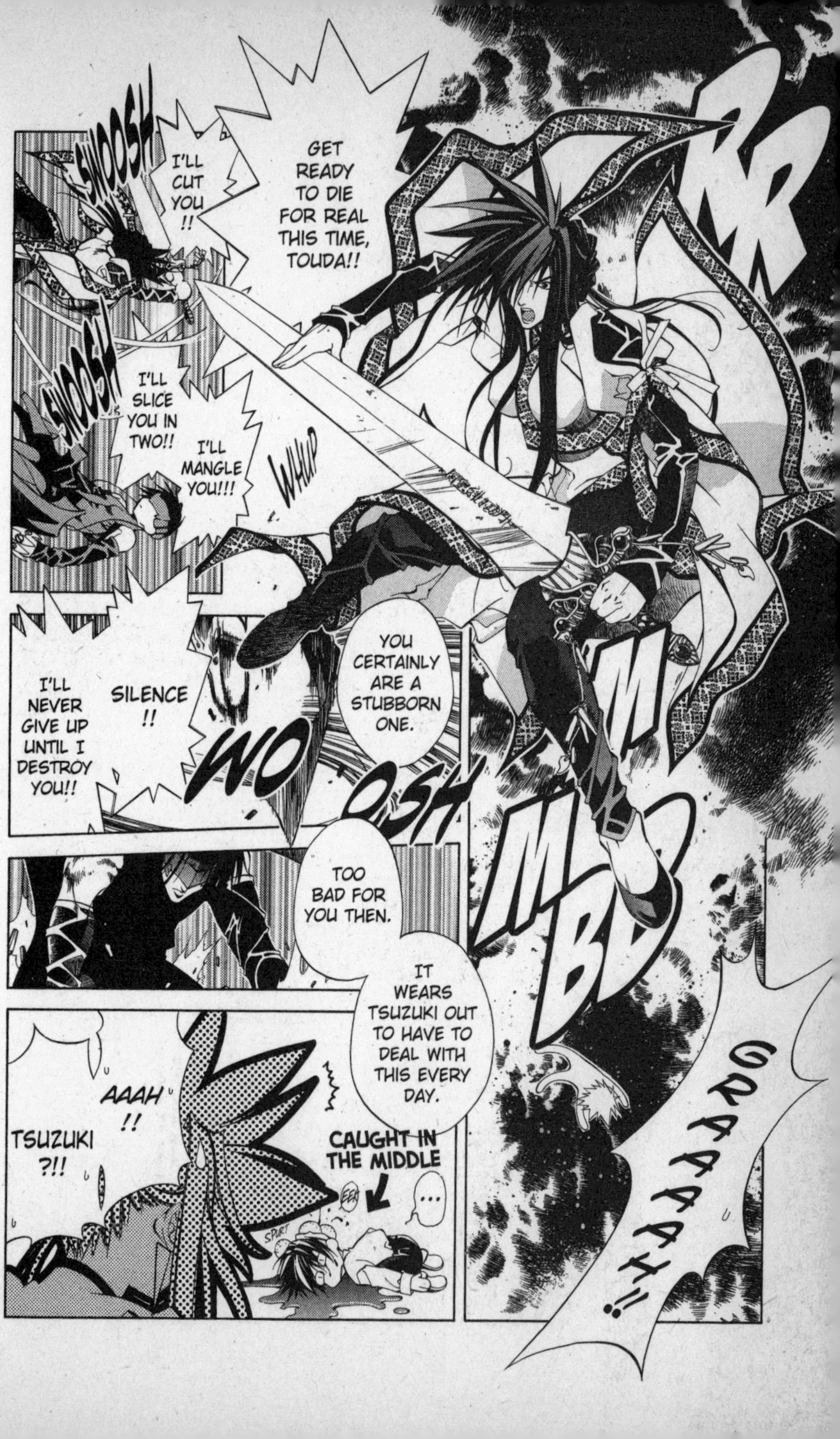
RR
GET READY TO DIE FOR REAL THIS TIME, TOUDA!!
SWOOSH
I'LL CUT YOU!!
SWOOSH
I'LL SLICE YOU IN TWO!!
I'LL MANGLE YOU!!
WHUP
M
M
YOU CERTAINLY ARE A STUBBORN ONE.
SILENCE!!
I'LL NEVER GIVE UP UNTIL I DESTROY YOU!!
WO
OSH
TOO BAD FOR YOU THEN.
BD
GRAAAAAH!!
IT WEARS TSUZUKI OUT TO HAVE TO DEAL WITH THIS EVERY DAY.
CAUGHT IN THE MIDDLE
...
EEK
SPURT
AAAH!!
TSUZUKI?!!

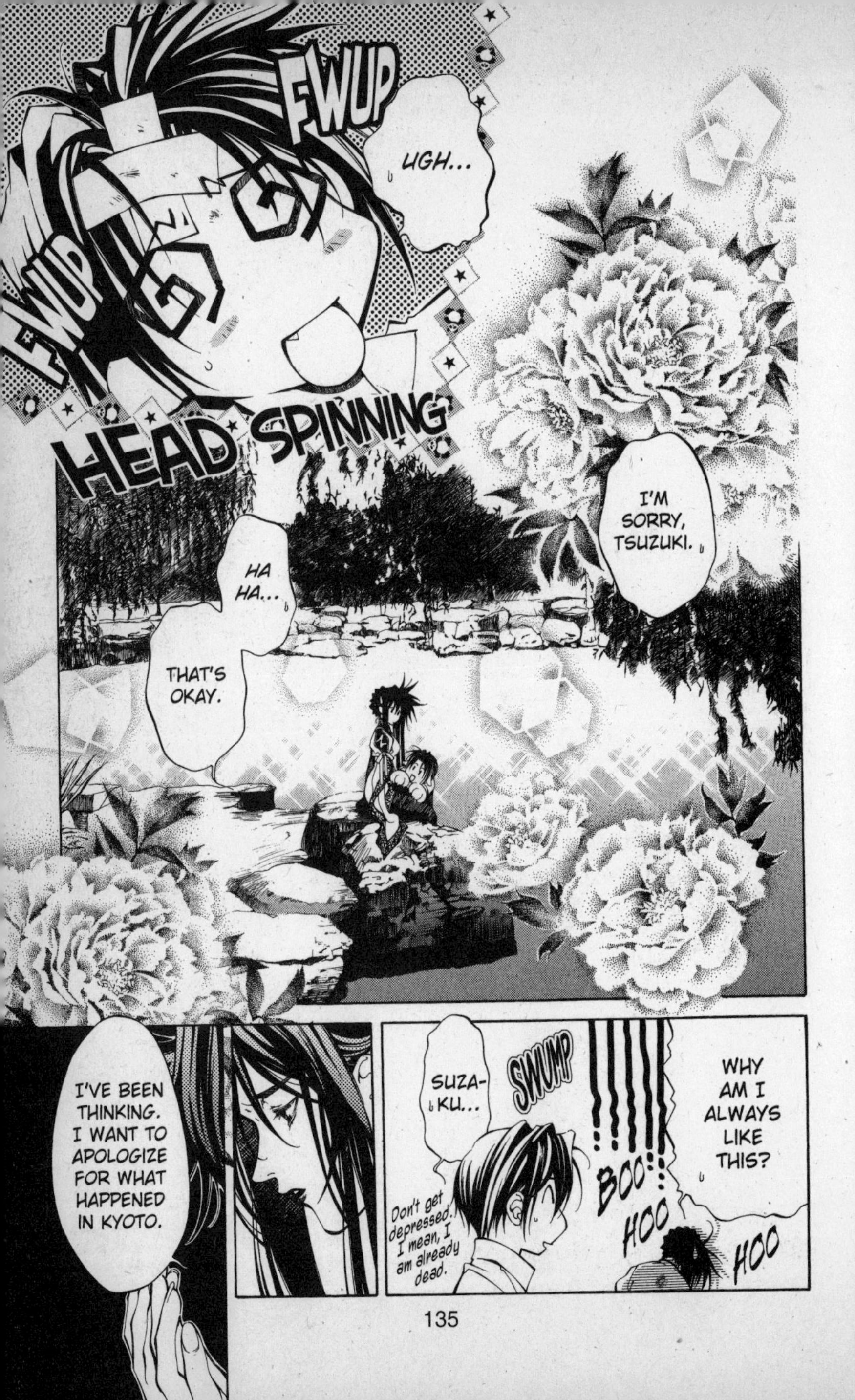
F-WUP
UGH...
F-WUP
HEAD SPINNING
I'M SORRY, TSUZUKI.
HA HA...
THAT'S OKAY.
WHY AM I ALWAYS LIKE THIS?
BOO HOO
HOO
SWUMP
SUZA-KU...
Don't get depressed. I mean, I am already dead.
I'VE BEEN THINKING. I WANT TO APOLOGIZE FOR WHAT HAPPENED IN KYOTO.

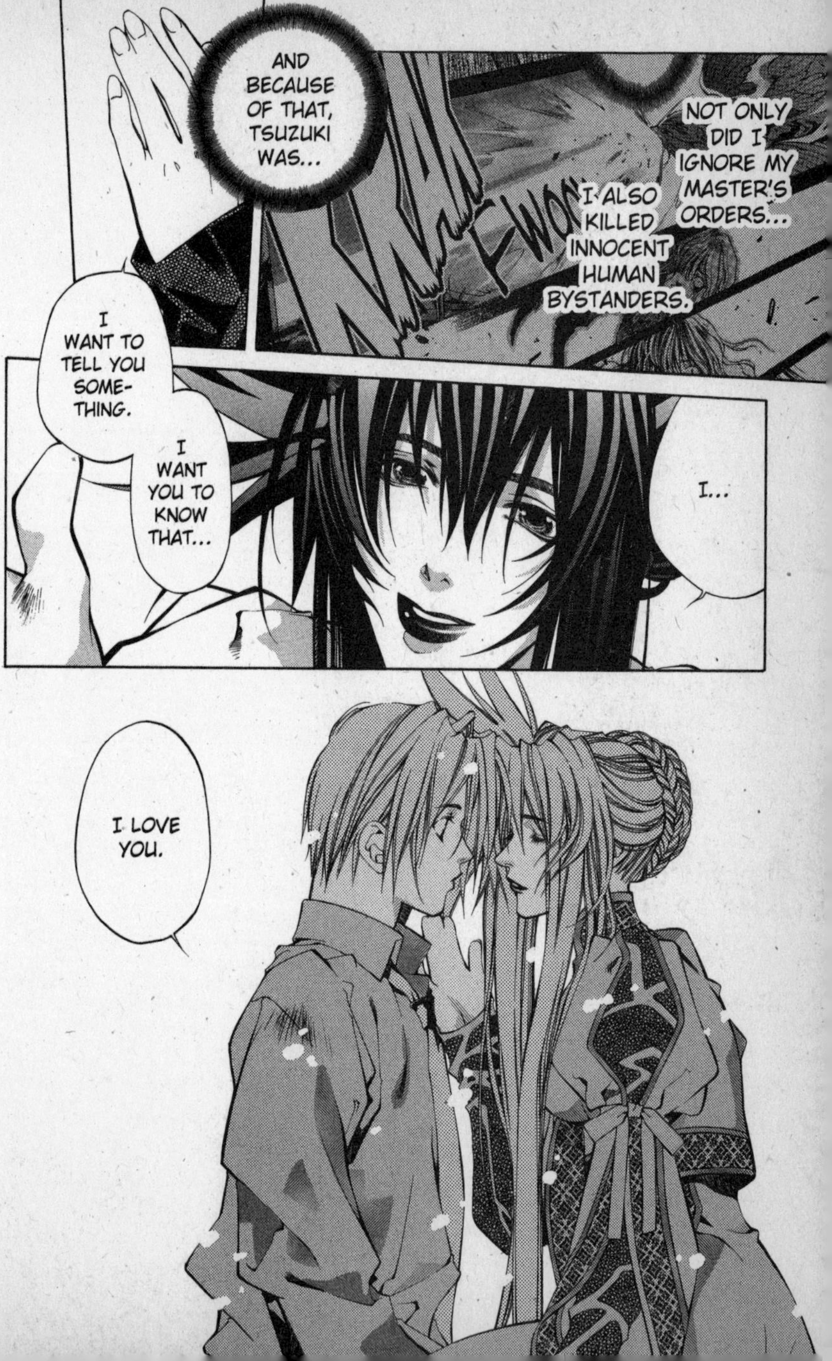
NOT ONLY DID I IGNORE MY MASTER'S ORDERS...
I ALSO KILLED INNOCENT HUMAN BYSTANDERS.
AND BECAUSE OF THAT, TSUZUKI WAS...
I...
I WANT TO TELL YOU SOMETHING.
I WANT YOU TO KNOW THAT...
I LOVE YOU.

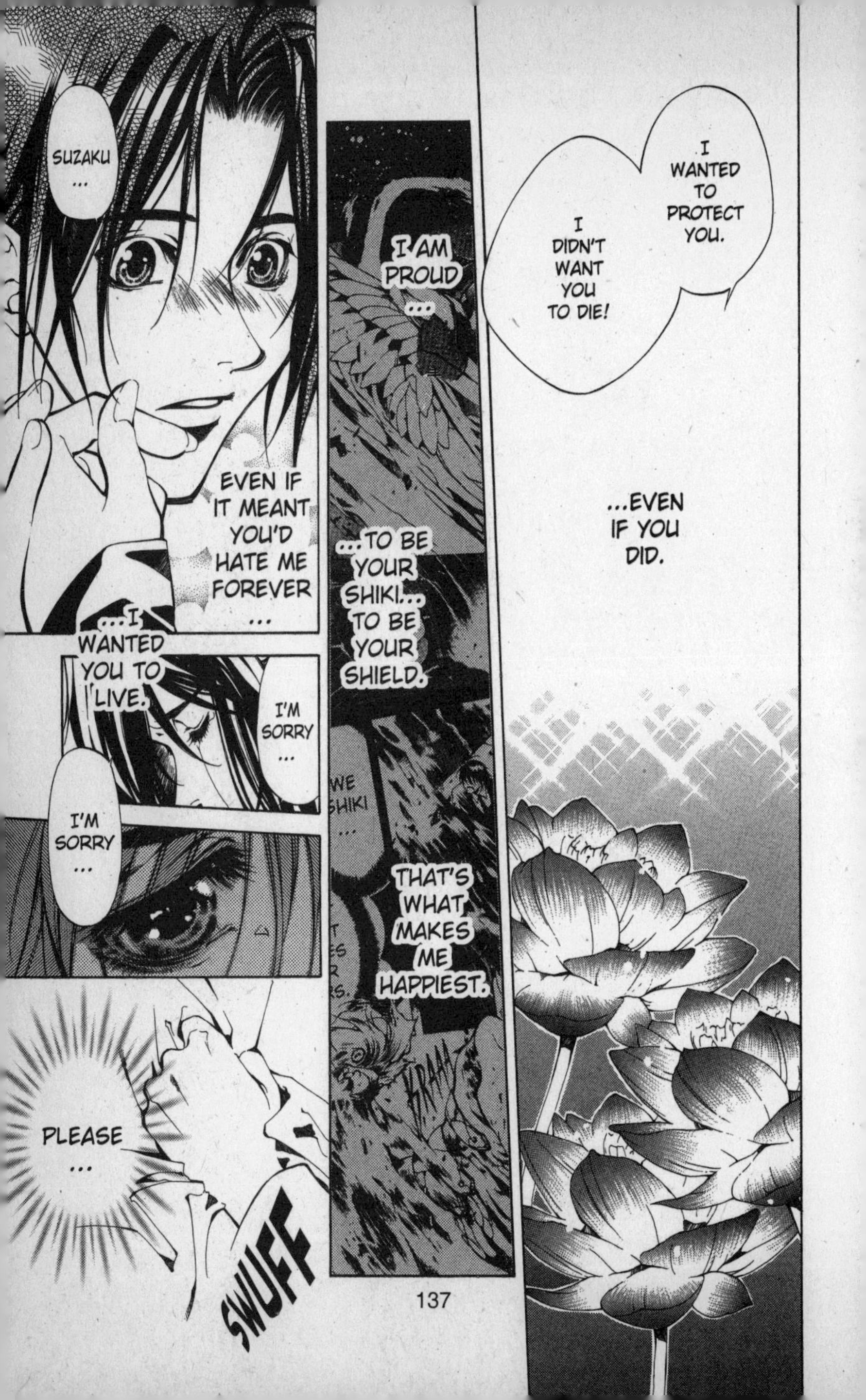
I WANTED TO PROTECT YOU.
I DIDN'T WANT YOU TO DIE!
...EVEN IF YOU DID.
I AM PROUD...
...TO BE YOUR SHIKI... TO BE YOUR SHIELD.
THAT'S WHAT MAKES ME HAPPIEST.
SUZAKU...
EVEN IF IT MEANT YOU'D HATE ME FOREVER...
...I WANTED YOU TO LIVE.
I'M SORRY...
I'M SORRY...
PLEASE...
SWUFF

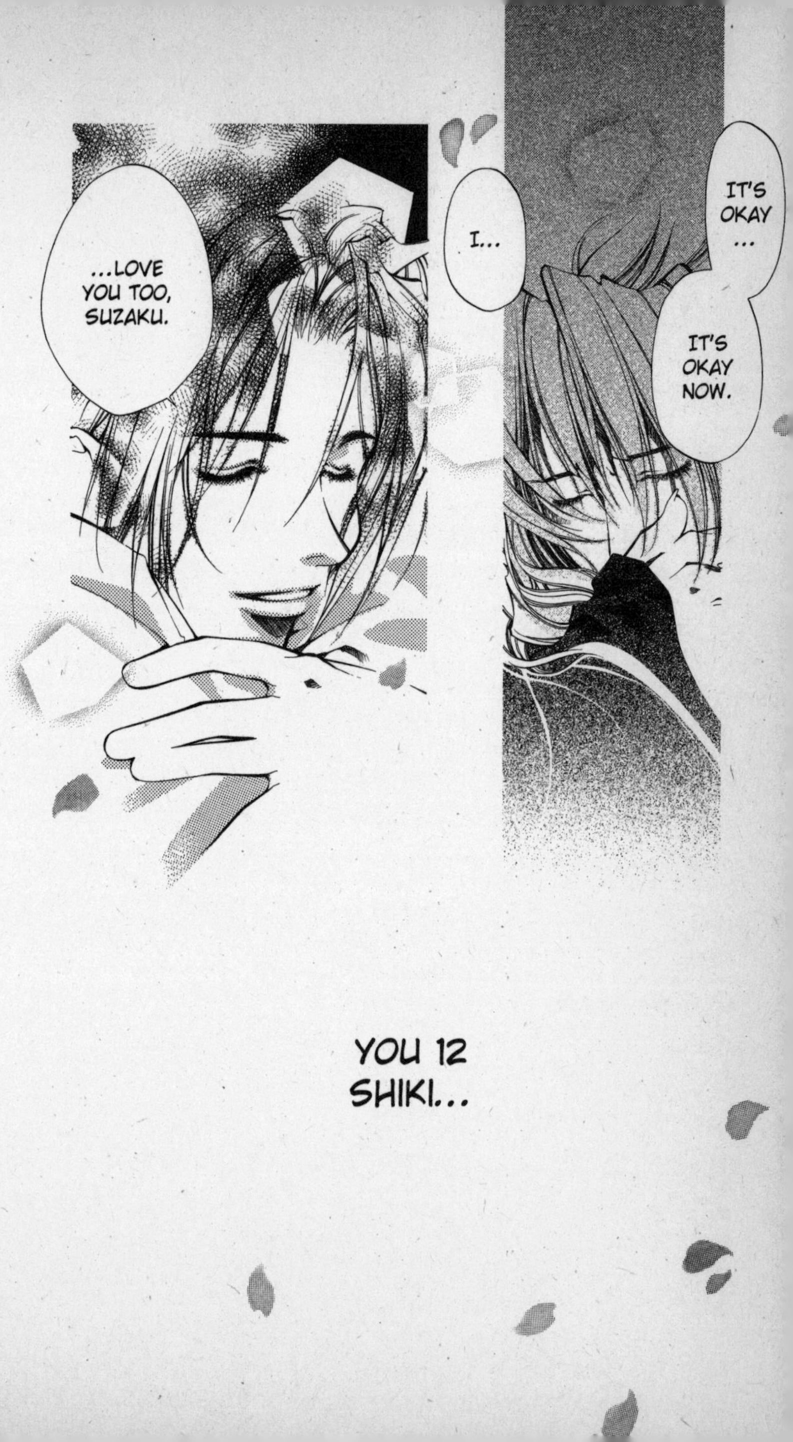
IT'S OKAY ...
I...
IT'S OKAY NOW.
...LOVE YOU TOO, SUZAKU.
YOU 12 SHIKI...

...ARE
MY
PRIDE
AND
JOY.

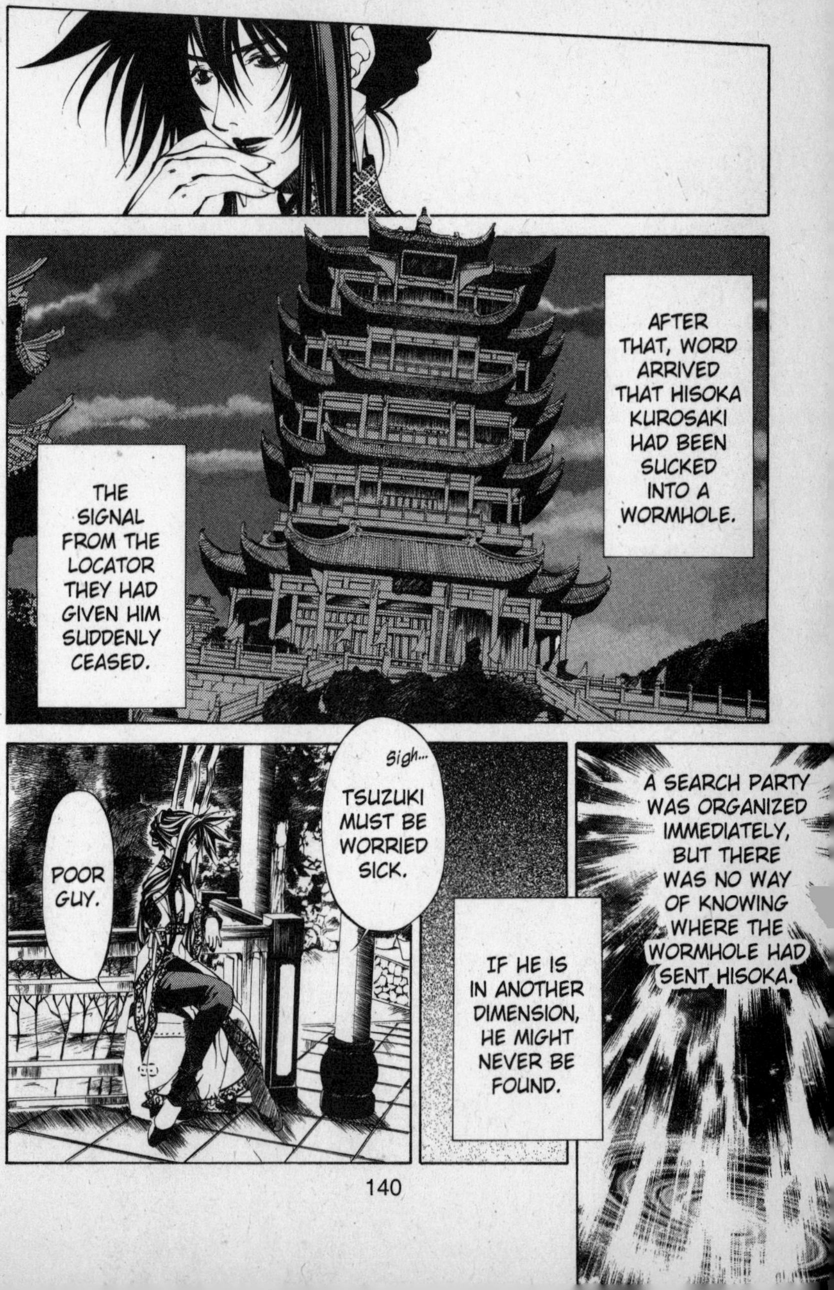

AFTER THAT, WORD ARRIVED THAT HISOKA KUROSAKI HAD BEEN SUCKED INTO A WORMHOLE.
THE SIGNAL FROM THE LOCATOR THEY HAD GIVEN HIM SUDDENLY CEASED.
A SEARCH PARTY WAS ORGANIZED IMMEDIATELY, BUT THERE WAS NO WAY OF KNOWING WHERE THE WORMHOLE HAD SENT HISOKA.
IF HE IS IN ANOTHER DIMENSION, HE MIGHT NEVER BE FOUND.
Sigh...
TSUZUKI MUST BE WORRIED SICK.
POOR GUY.

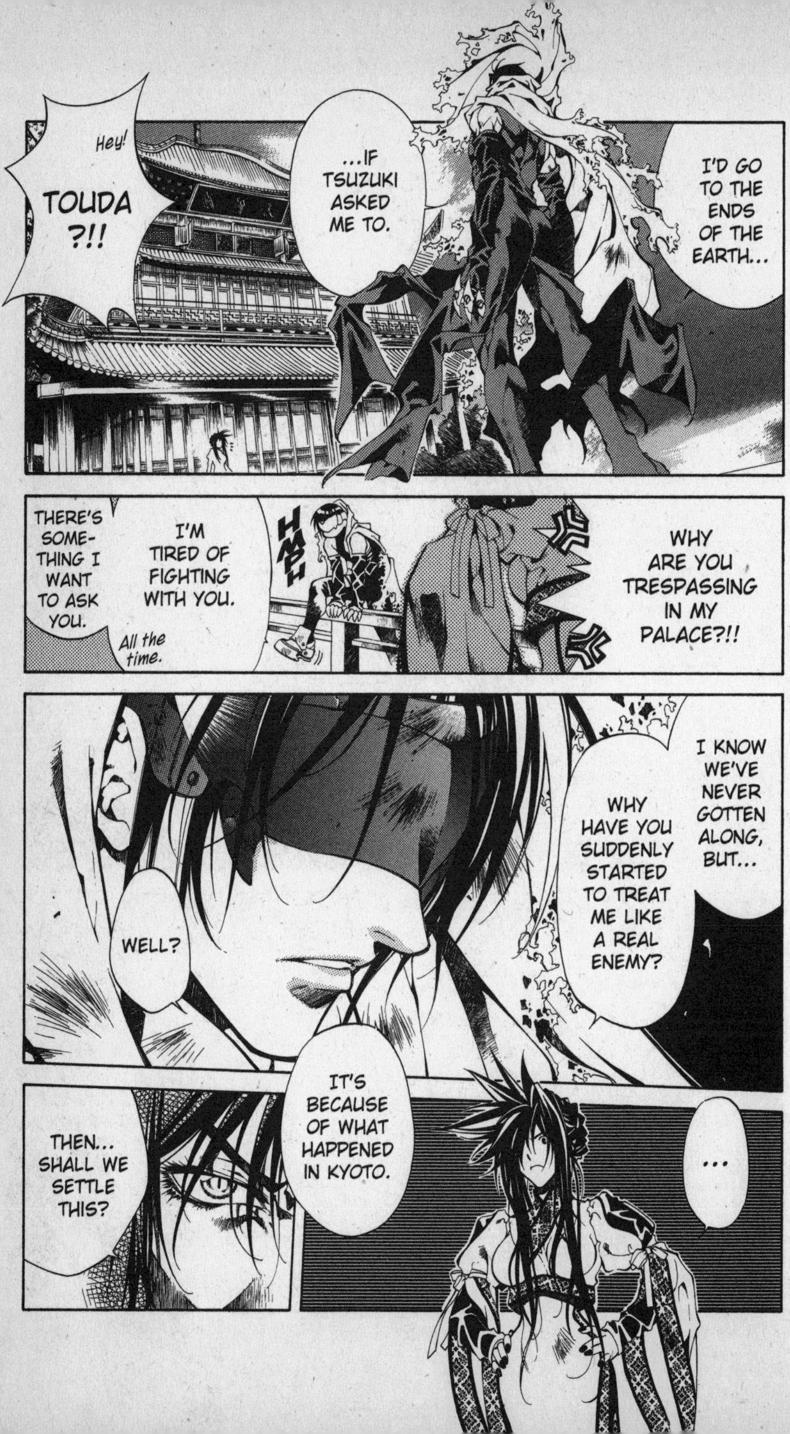
I'D GO TO THE ENDS OF THE EARTH...
...IF TSUZUKI ASKED ME TO.
Hey!
TOUDA ?!!
WHY ARE YOU TRESPASSING IN MY PALACE?!!
HMPH
I'M TIRED OF FIGHTING WITH YOU.
All the time.
THERE'S SOME-THING I WANT TO ASK YOU.
I KNOW WE'VE NEVER GOTTEN ALONG, BUT...
WHY HAVE YOU SUDDENLY STARTED TO TREAT ME LIKE A REAL ENEMY?
WELL?
...
IT'S BECAUSE OF WHAT HAPPENED IN KYOTO.
THEN... SHALL WE SETTLE THIS?

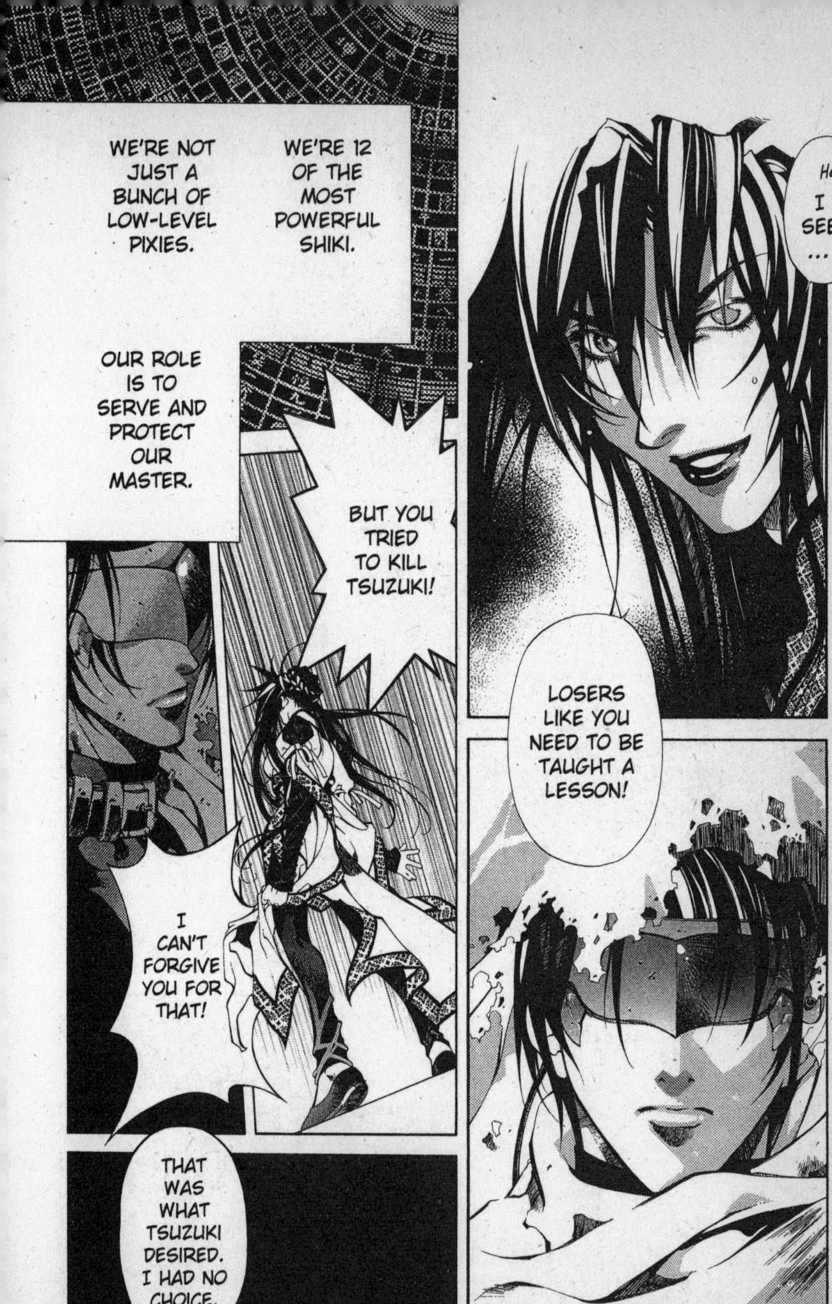
Heh. I SEE ...
LOSERS LIKE YOU NEED TO BE TAUGHT A LESSON!
WE'RE 12 OF THE MOST POWERFUL SHIKI.
WE'RE NOT JUST A BUNCH OF LOW-LEVEL PIXIES.
OUR ROLE IS TO SERVE AND PROTECT OUR MASTER.
BUT YOU TRIED TO KILL TSUZUKI!
I CAN'T FORGIVE YOU FOR THAT!
THAT WAS WHAT TSUZUKI DESIRED. I HAD NO CHOICE.

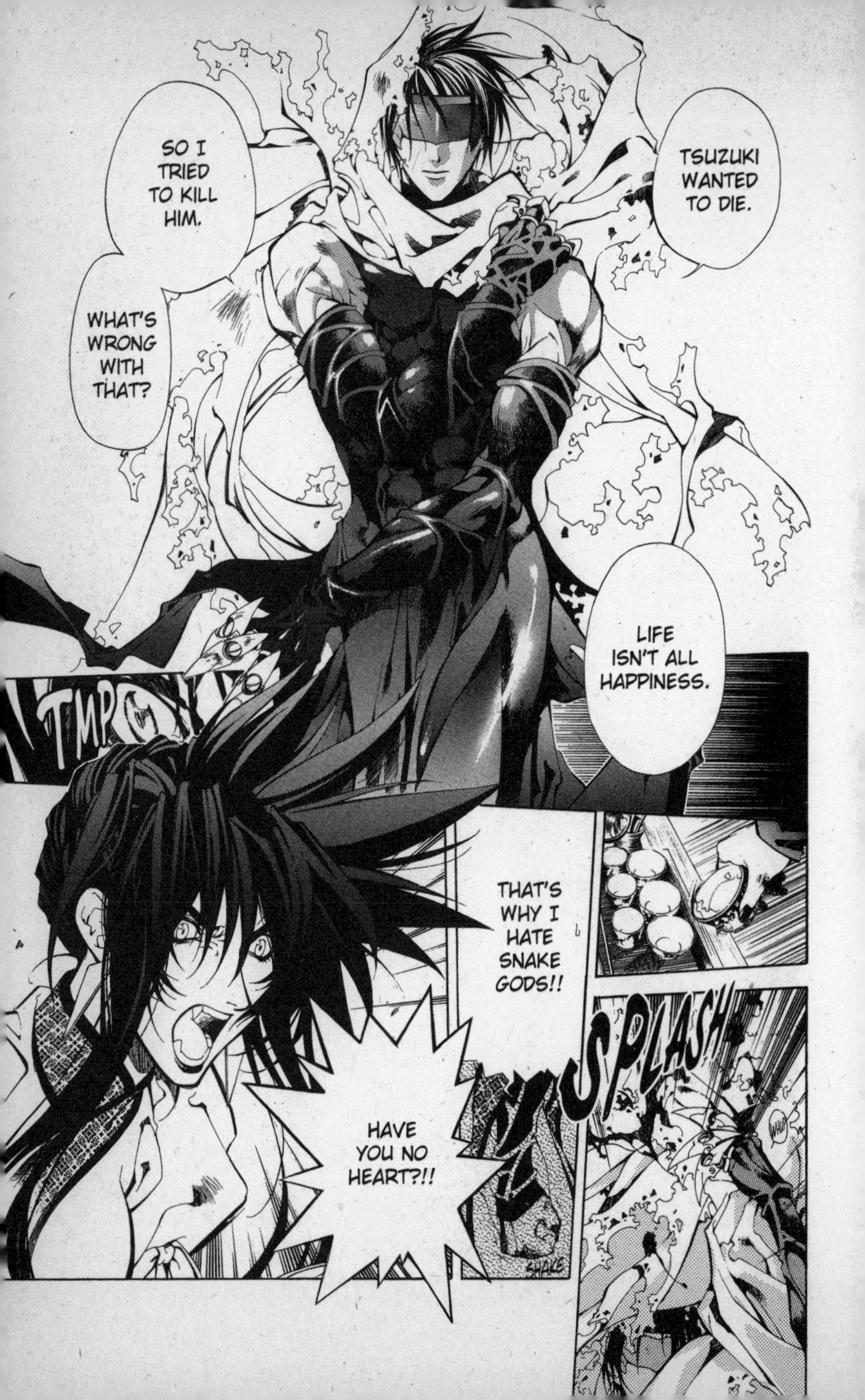
TSUZUKI WANTED TO DIE.
SO I TRIED TO KILL HIM.
WHAT'S WRONG WITH THAT?
LIFE ISN'T ALL HAPPINESS.
SPLASH
TMP
THAT'S WHY I HATE SNAKE GODS!!
HAVE YOU NO HEART?!!
SHAKE

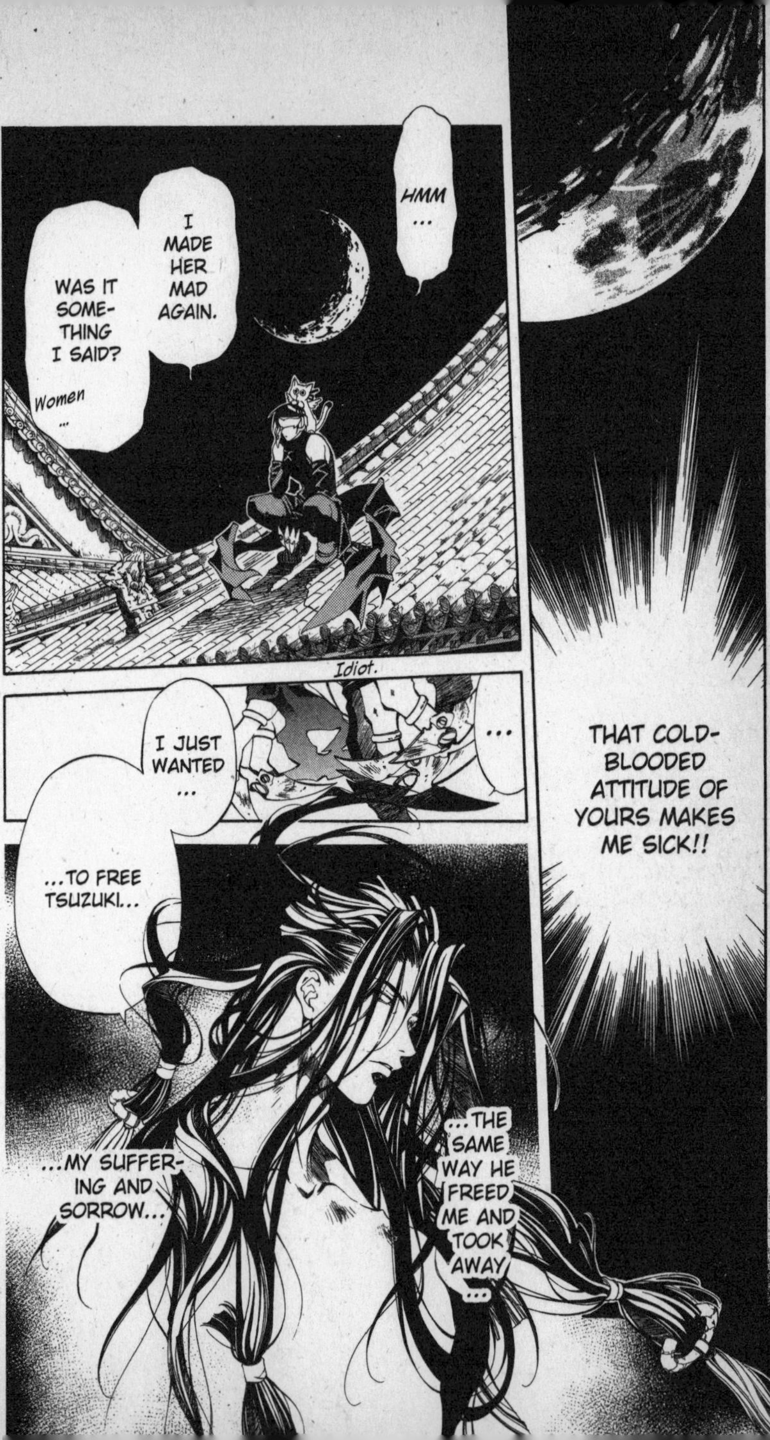
THAT COLD-BLOODED ATTITUDE OF YOURS MAKES ME SICK!!
HMM...
I MADE HER MAD AGAIN.
WAS IT SOMETHING I SAID?
Women...
Idiot.
...
I JUST WANTED...
...TO FREE TSUZUKI...
...THE SAME WAY HE FREED ME AND TOOK AWAY...
...MY SUFFERING AND SORROW...

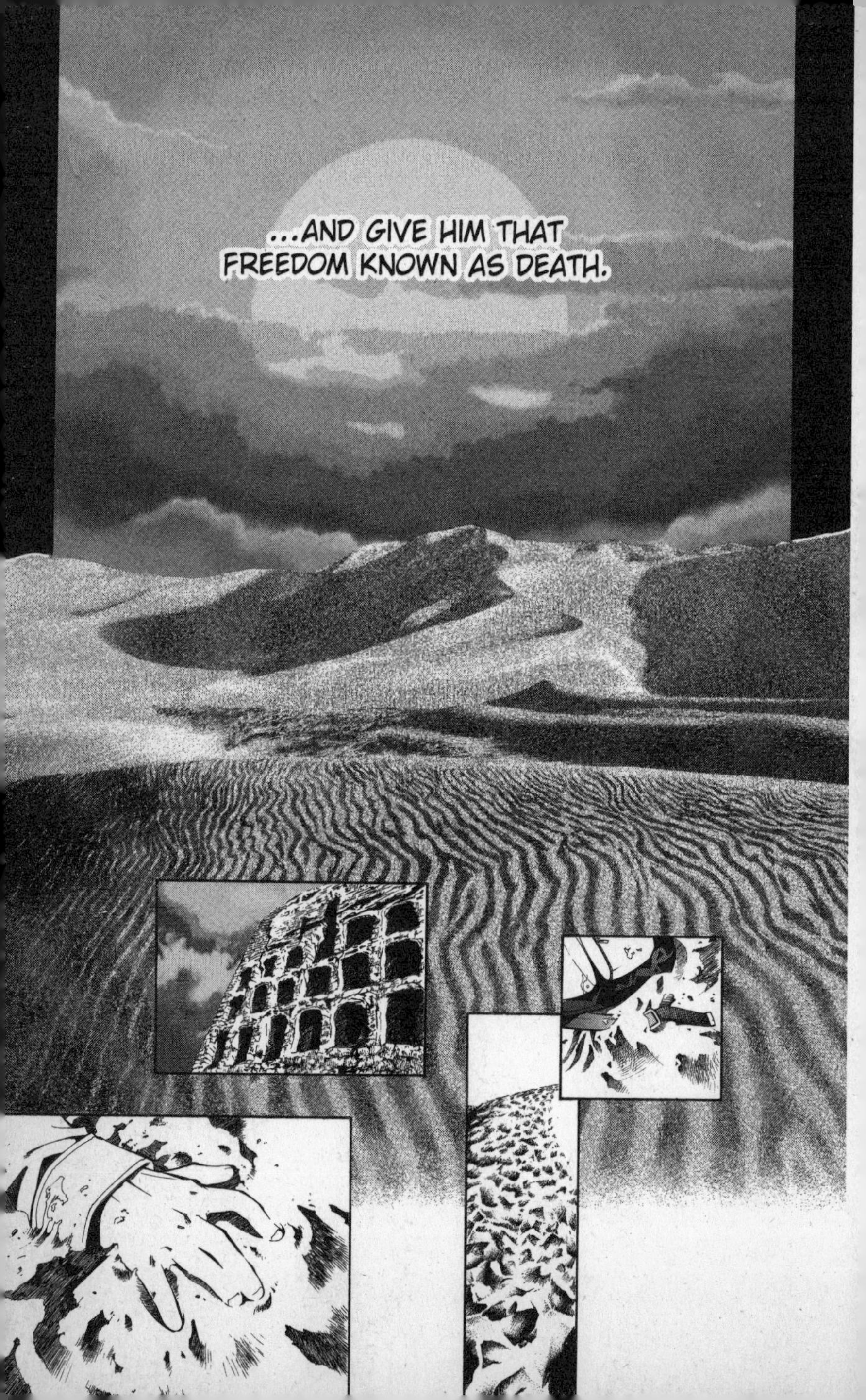
...AND GIVE HIM THAT FREEDOM KNOWN AS DEATH.

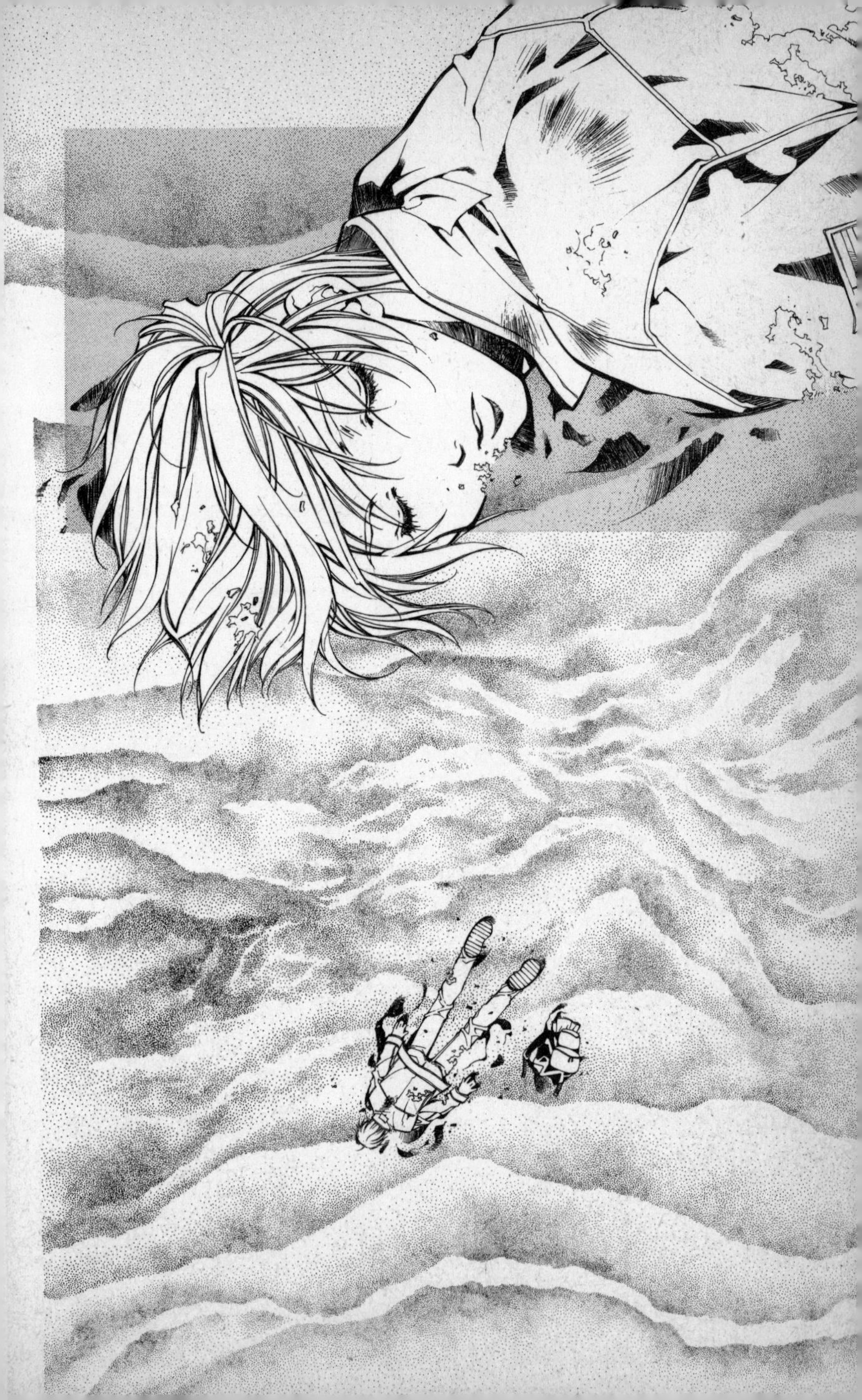

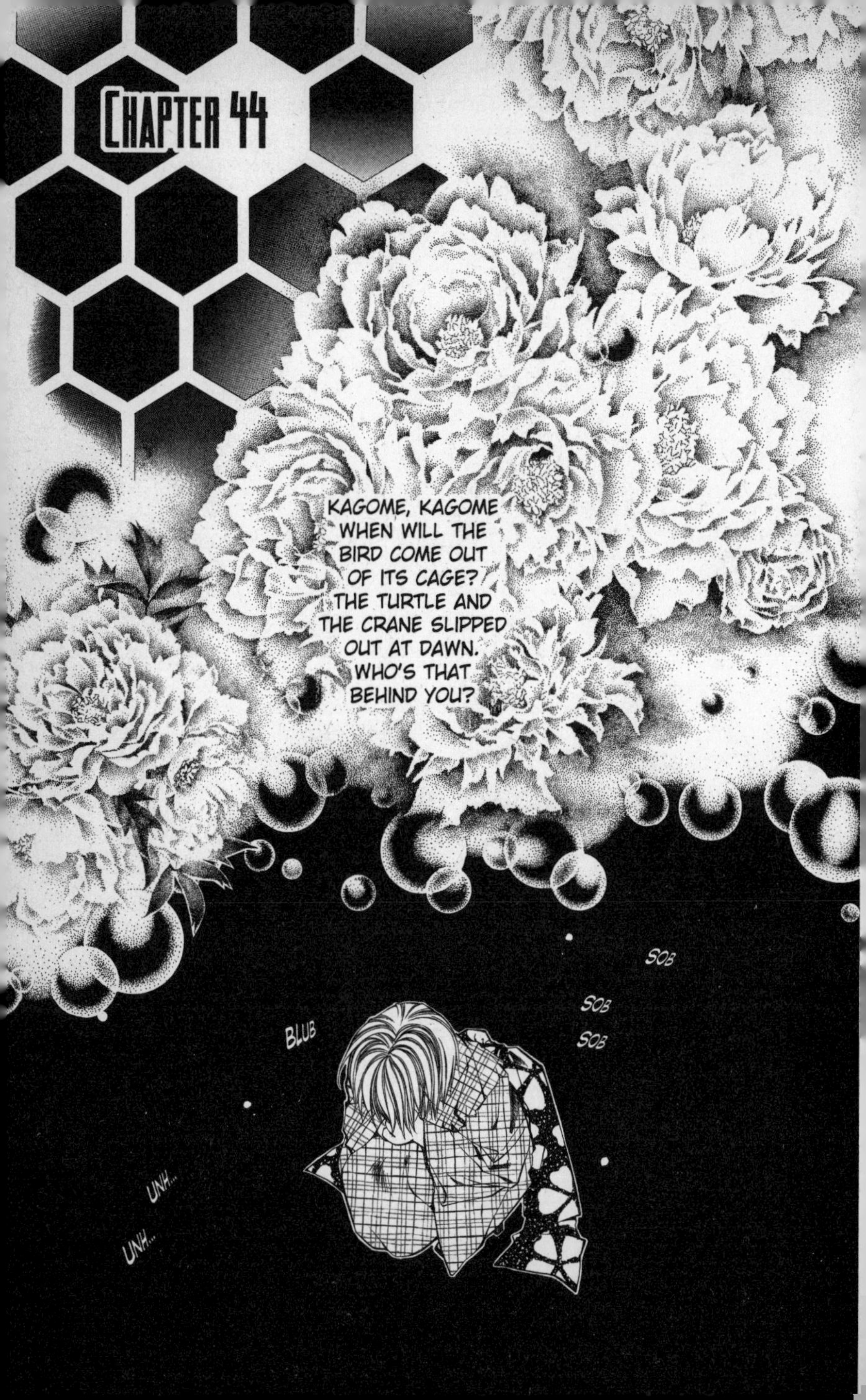
CHAPTER 44
KAGOME, KAGOME WHEN WILL THE BIRD COME OUT OF ITS CAGE? THE TURTLE AND THE CRANE SLIPPED OUT AT DAWN. WHO'S THAT BEHIND YOU?
SOB
SOB
SOB
BLUB
UNH...
UNH...

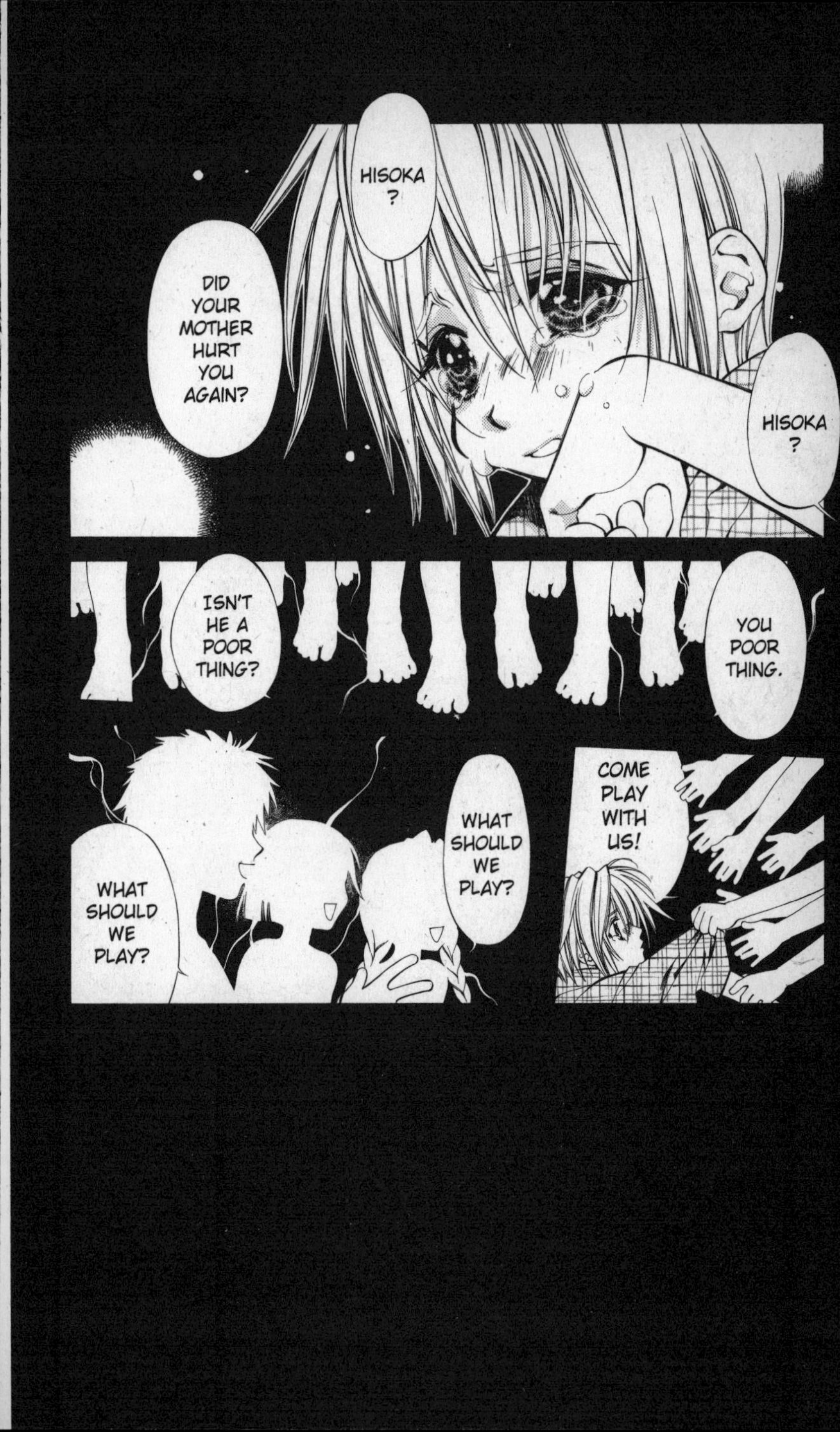
HISOKA?
HISOKA?
DID YOUR MOTHER HURT YOU AGAIN?
YOU POOR THING.
ISN'T HE A POOR THING?
COME PLAY WITH US!
WHAT SHOULD WE PLAY?
WHAT SHOULD WE PLAY?

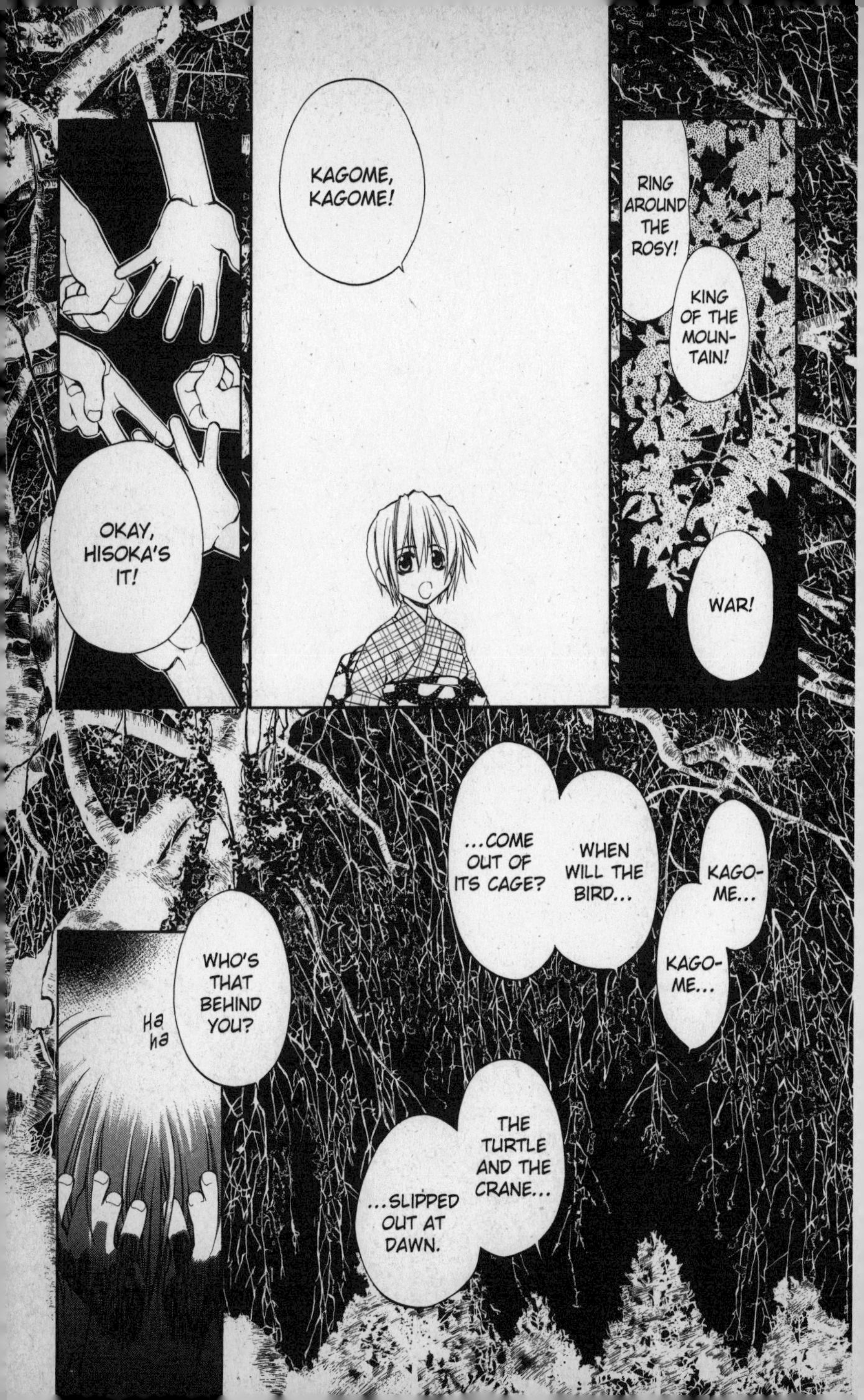
RING AROUND THE ROSY!
KING OF THE MOUNTAIN!
WAR!
KAGOME, KAGOME!
OKAY, HISOKA'S IT!
KAGO-ME...
KAGO-ME...
WHEN WILL THE BIRD...
...COME OUT OF ITS CAGE?
THE TURTLE AND THE CRANE...
...SLIPPED OUT AT DAWN.
WHO'S THAT BEHIND YOU?
Ha ha

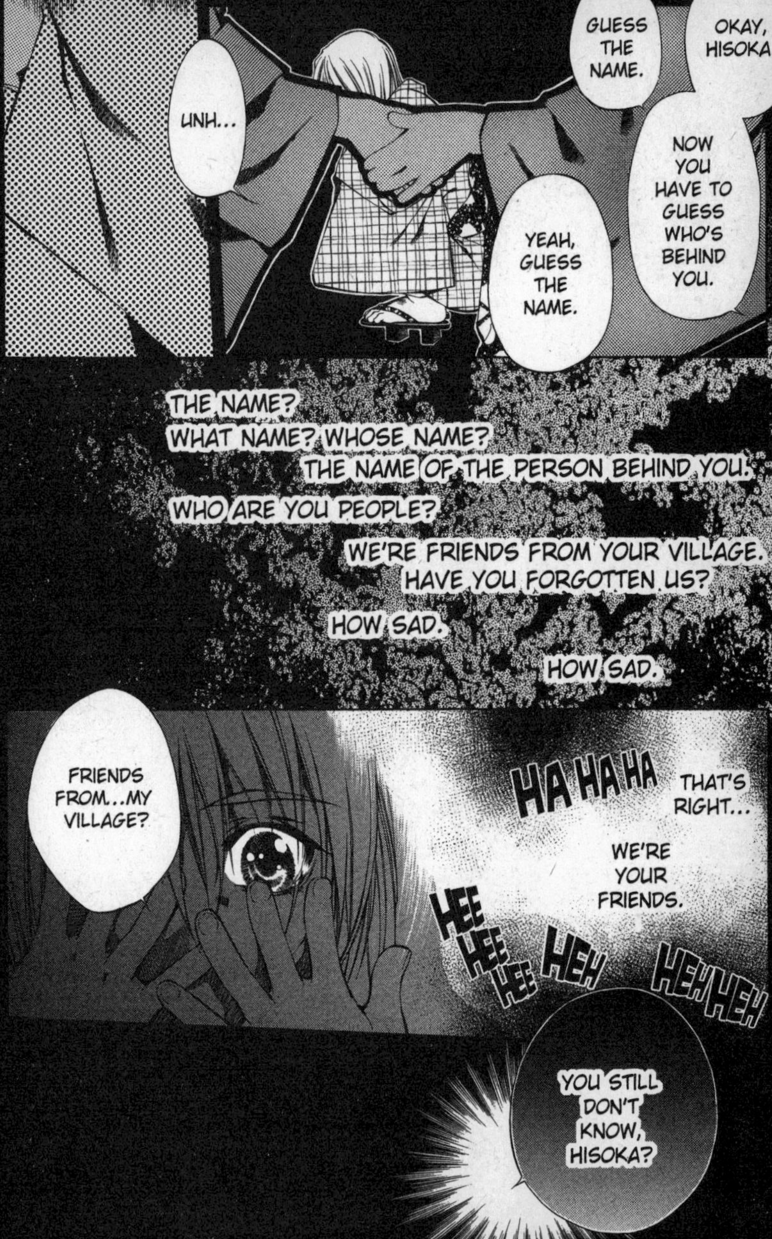
OKAY, HISOKA.
GUESS THE NAME.
NOW YOU HAVE TO GUESS WHO'S BEHIND YOU.
YEAH, GUESS THE NAME.
UNH...
THE NAME?
WHAT NAME? WHOSE NAME?
THE NAME OF THE PERSON BEHIND YOU.
WHO ARE YOU PEOPLE?
WE'RE FRIENDS FROM YOUR VILLAGE. HAVE YOU FORGOTTEN US?
HOW SAD.
HOW SAD.
THAT'S RIGHT...
HA HA HA
WE'RE YOUR FRIENDS.
HEH HEH
HEH
HEE HEE HEE
FRIENDS FROM...MY VILLAGE?
YOU STILL DON'T KNOW, HISOKA?

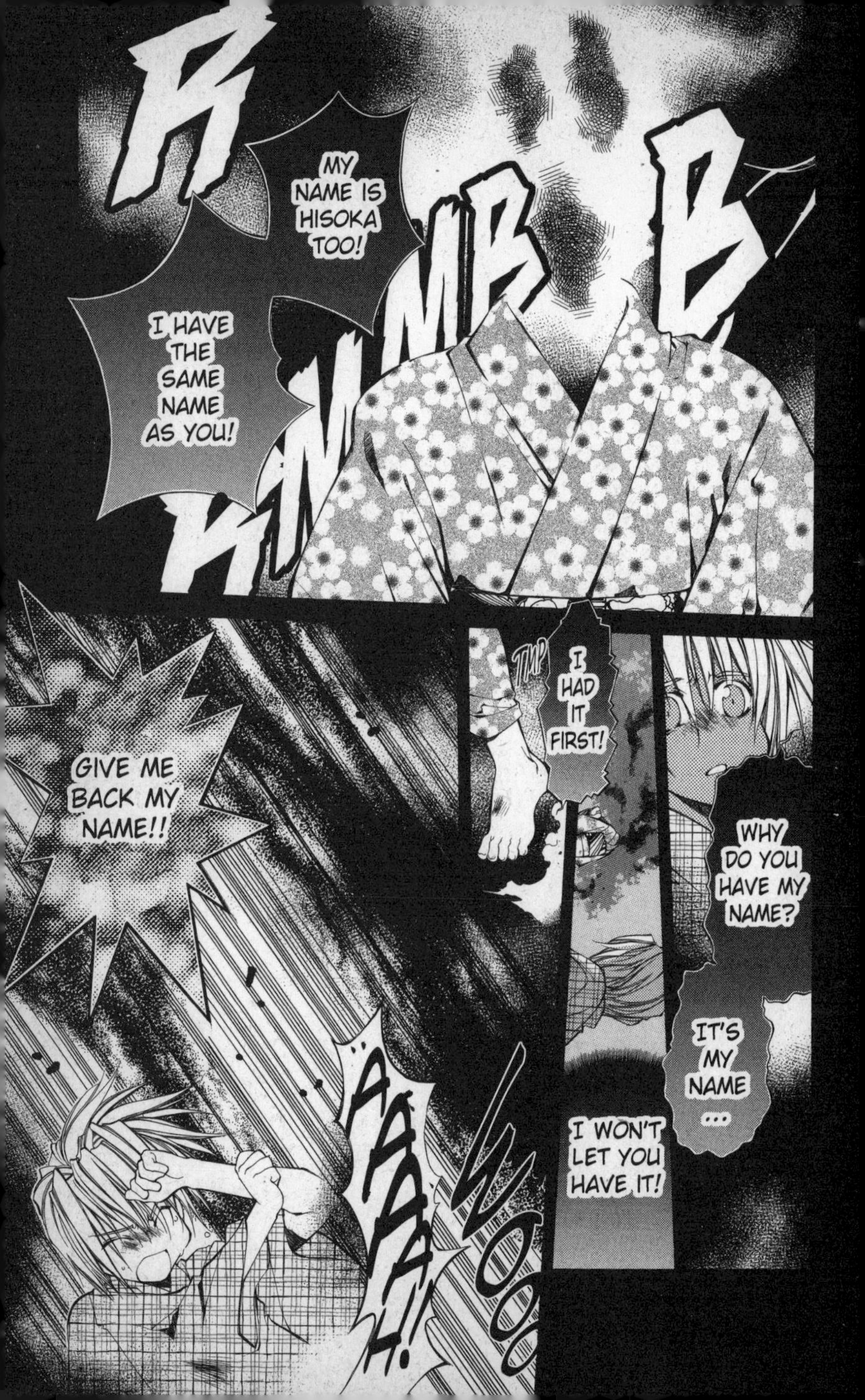
MY NAME IS HISOKA TOO!
I HAVE THE SAME NAME AS YOU!
I HAD IT FIRST!
WHY DO YOU HAVE MY NAME?
IT'S MY NAME ...
I WON'T LET YOU HAVE IT!
GIVE ME BACK MY NAME!!

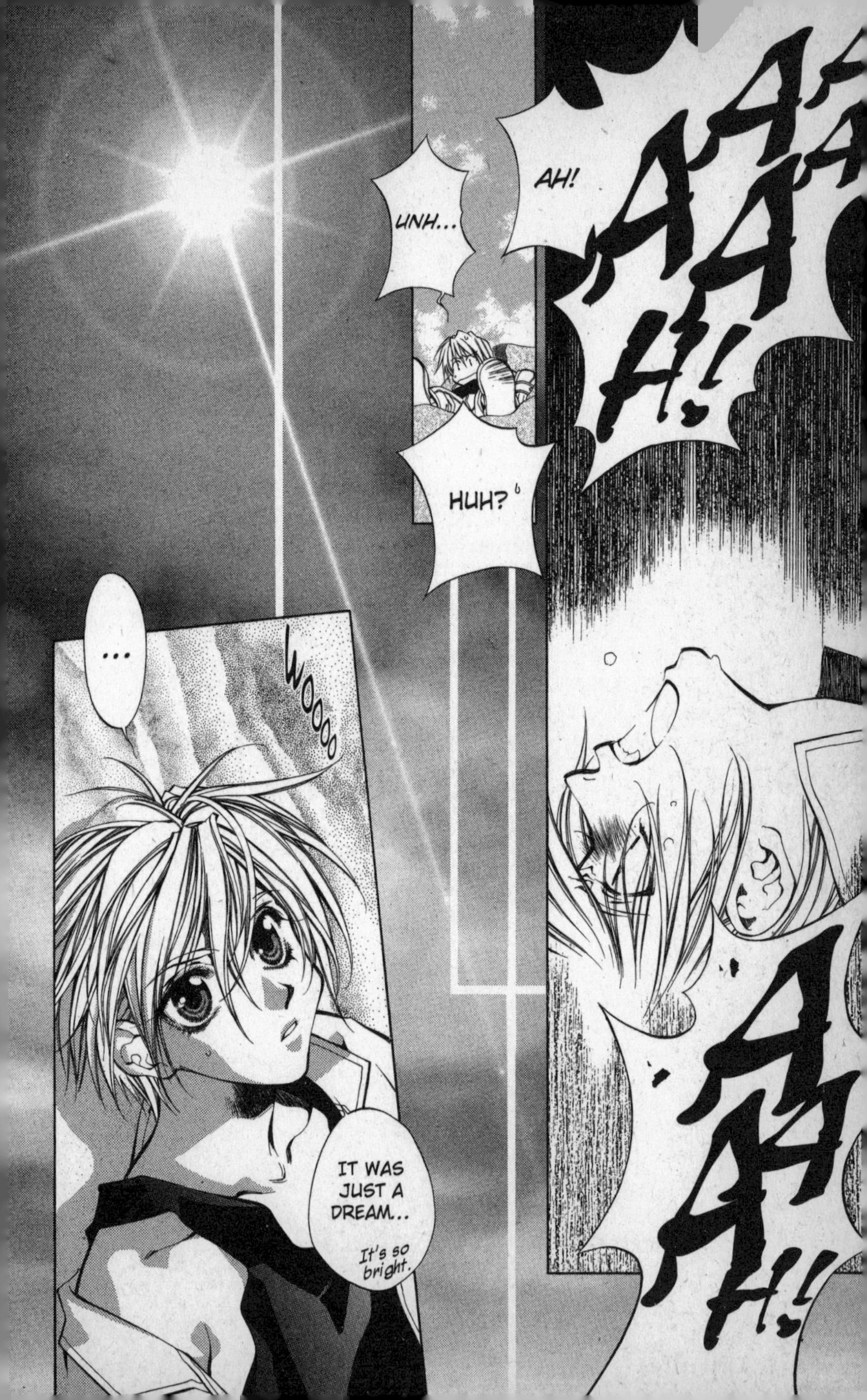
AAAAH!
AAAH!
AH!
UNH...
HUH?
...
WOOOO
IT WAS JUST A DREAM..
It's so bright.

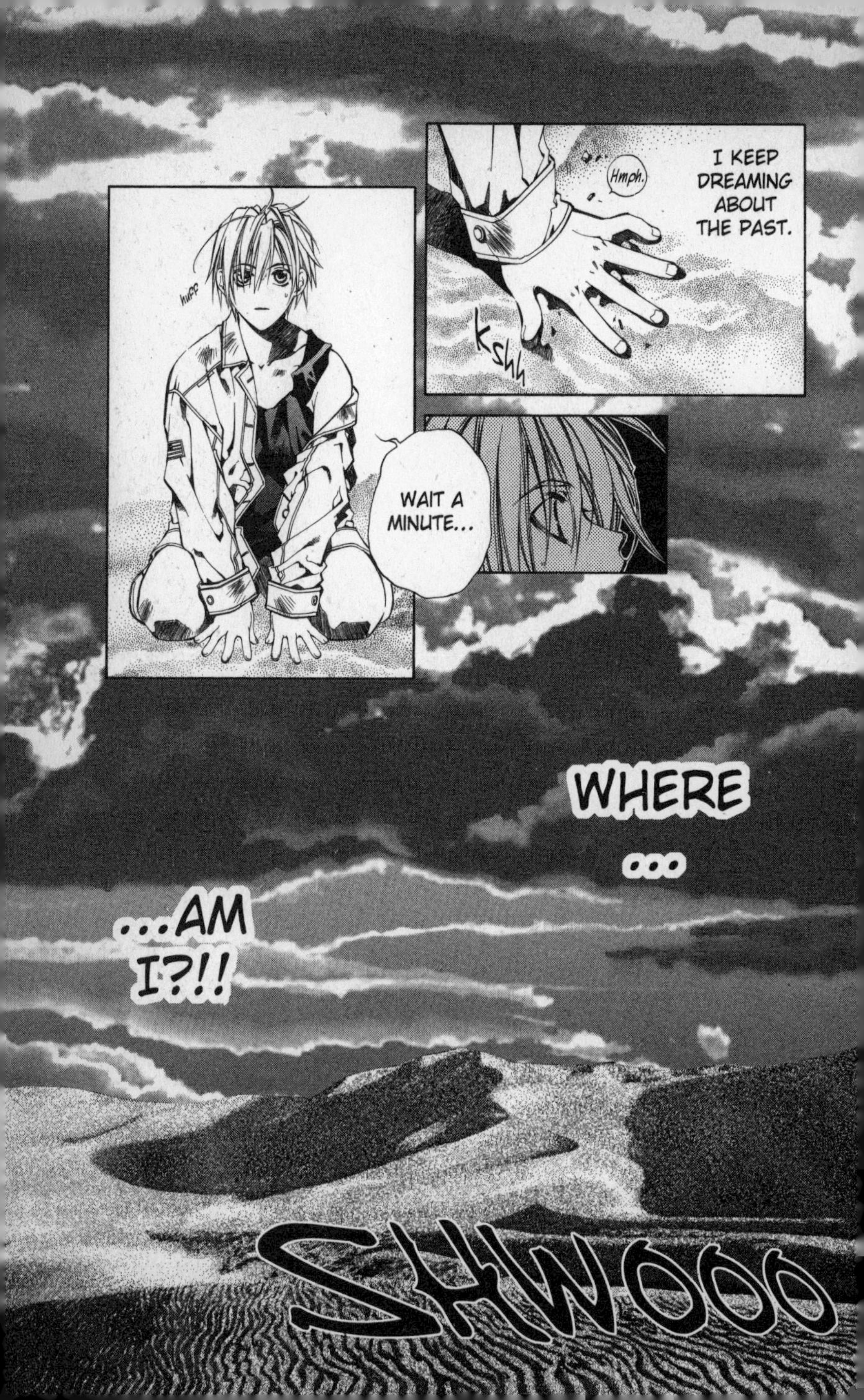

I KEEP DREAMING ABOUT THE PAST.
Hmph.
kshh
WAIT A MINUTE...
huff
WHERE...
...AM I?!!
SHWOOO

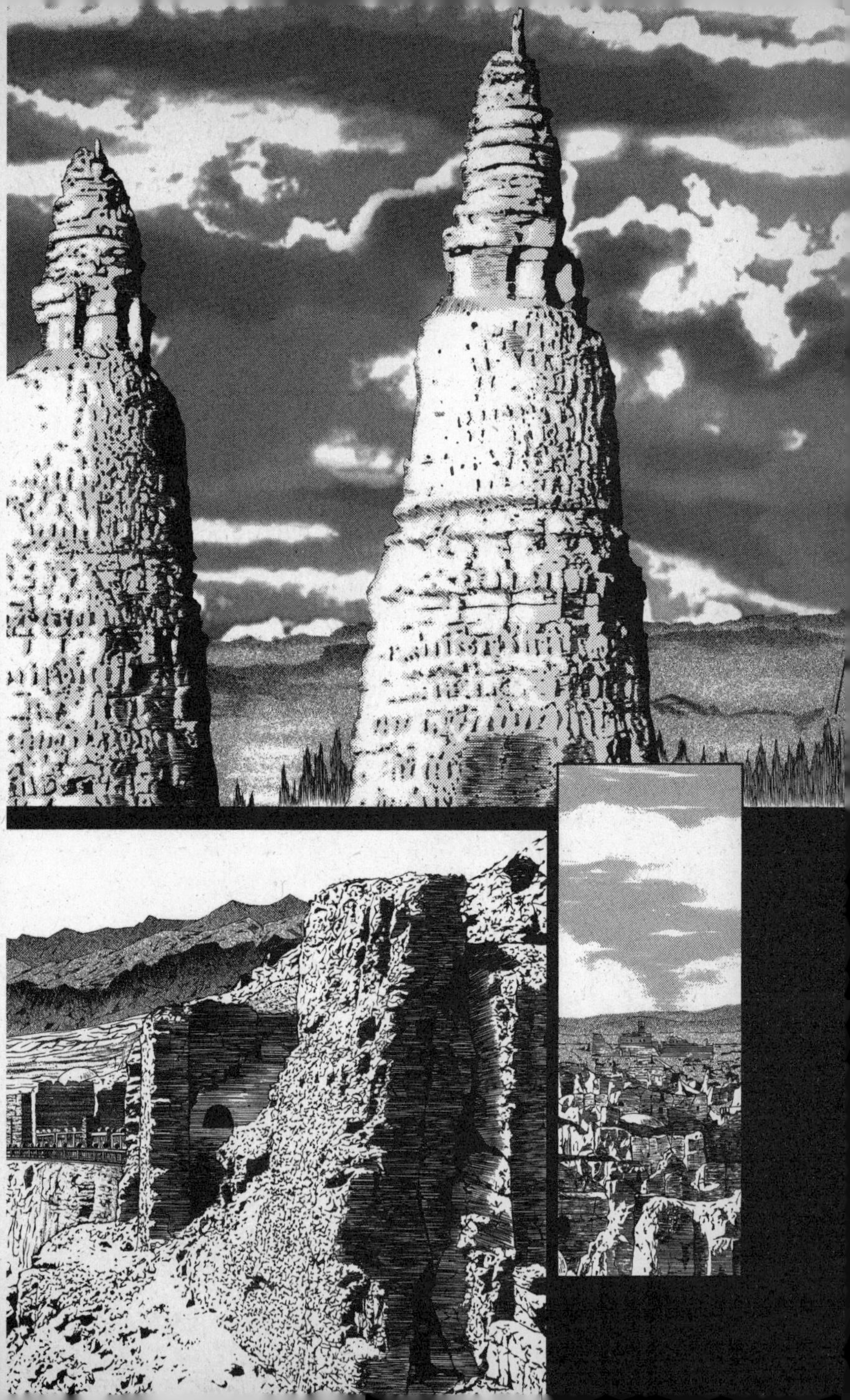

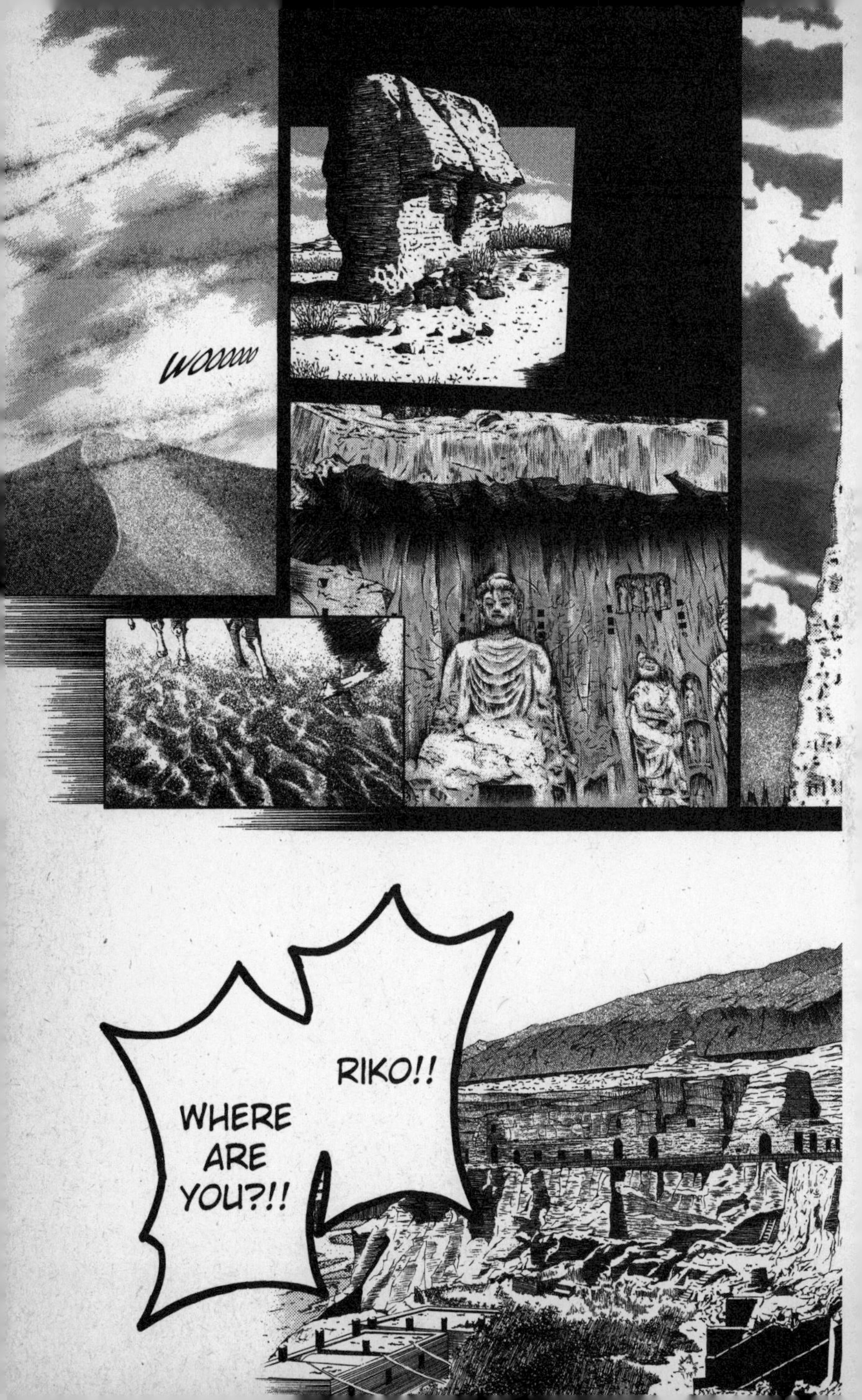
WOOOOO
RIKO!!
WHERE ARE YOU?!!

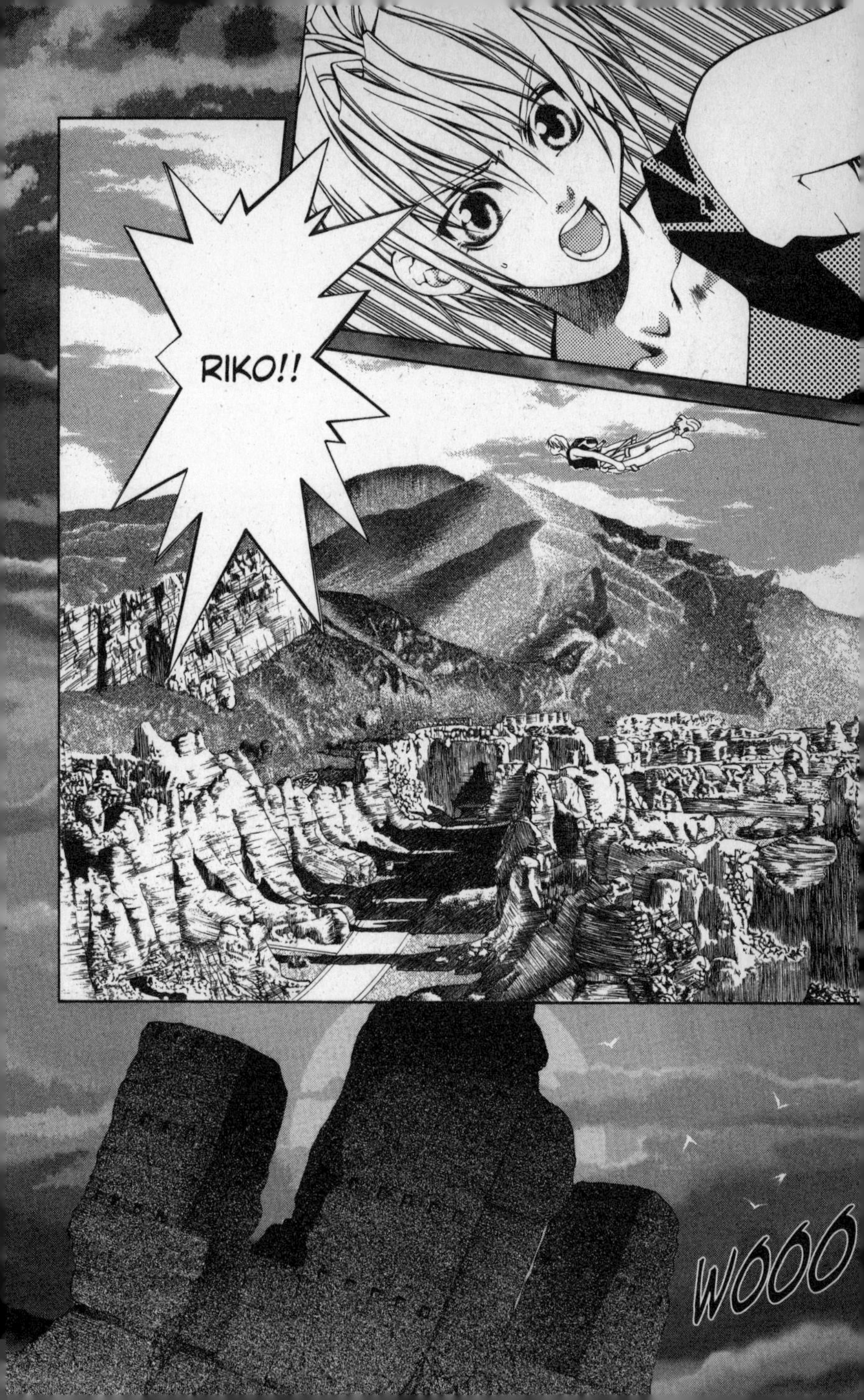
RIKO!!
WOOO

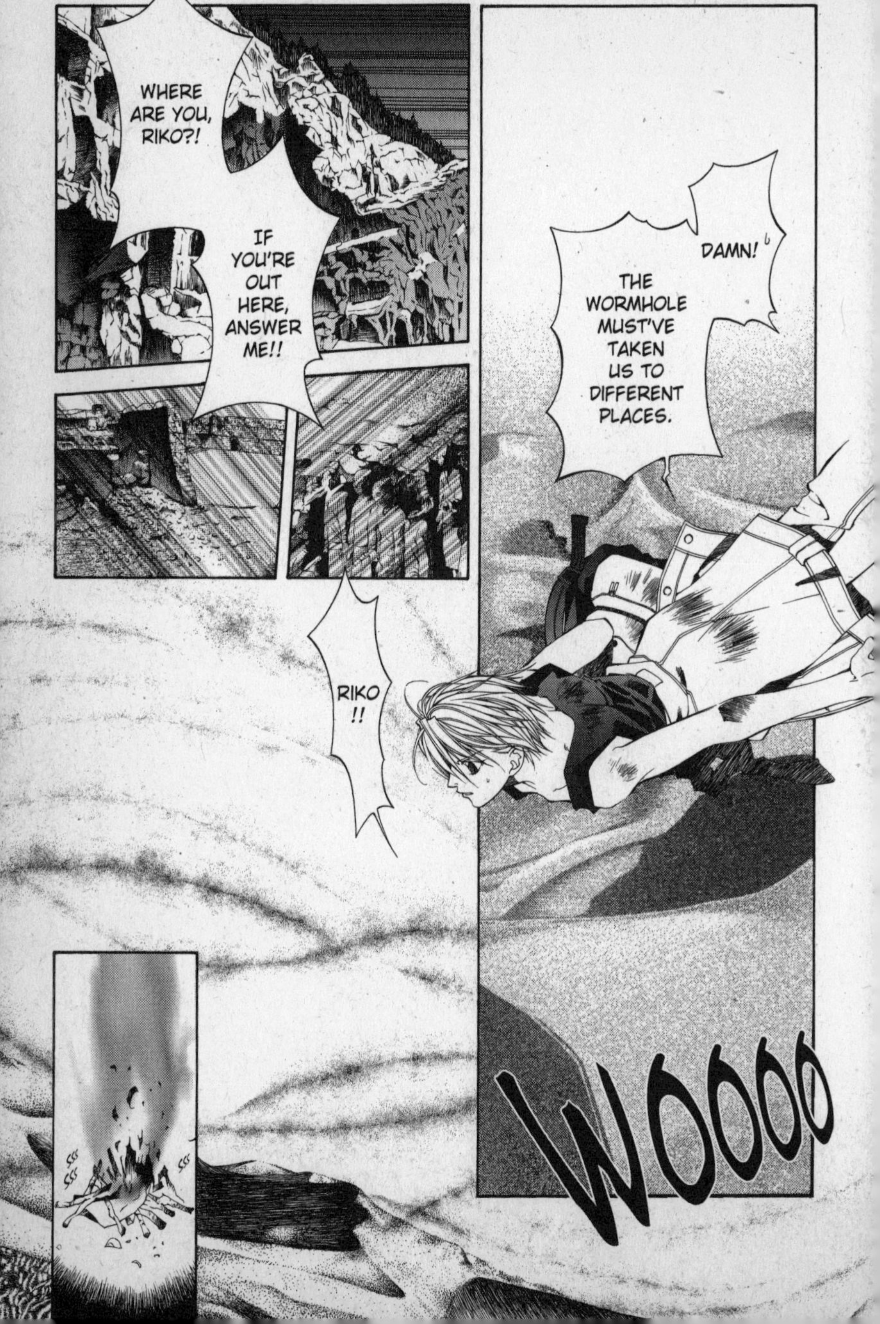
DAMN!
THE WORMHOLE MUST'VE TAKEN US TO DIFFERENT PLACES.
WOOOO
WHERE ARE YOU, RIKO?!
IF YOU'RE OUT HERE, ANSWER ME!!
RIKO!!
SSS SSS
SSS

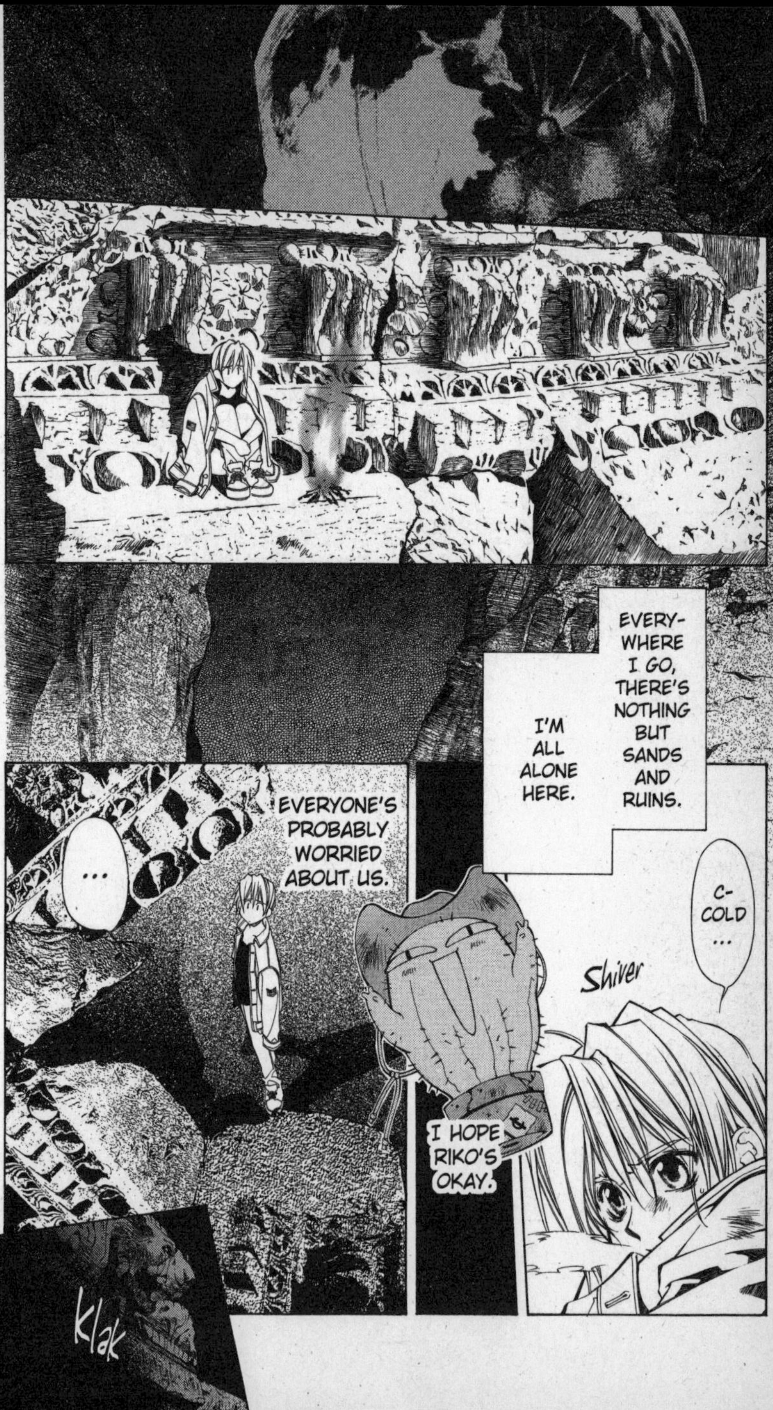
EVERYWHERE I GO, THERE'S NOTHING BUT SANDS AND RUINS.
I'M ALL ALONE HERE.
C-COLD...
Shiver
I HOPE RIKO'S OKAY.
EVERYONE'S PROBABLY WORRIED ABOUT US.
...
Klak

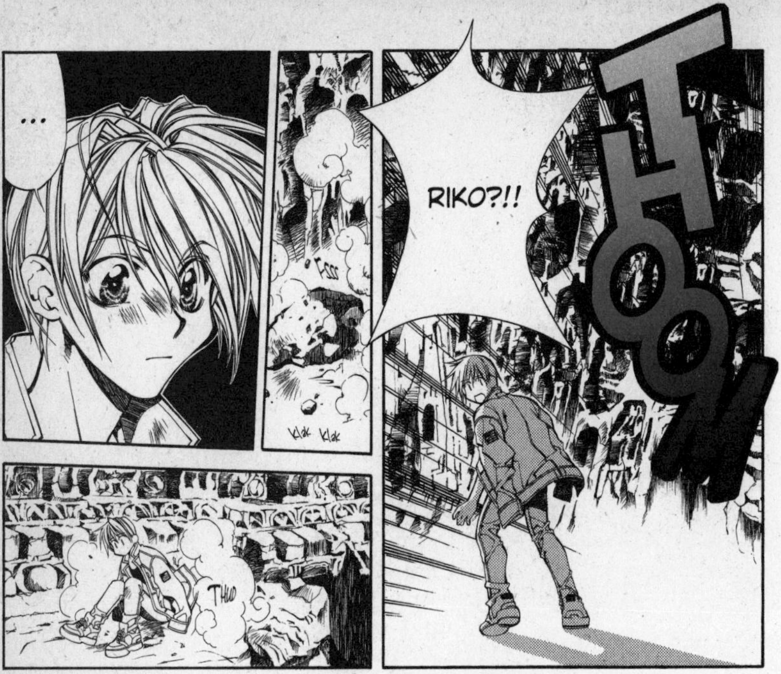
RIKO?!!
THOOM!
FSSS
KLAK KLAK
...
THUD

IT NEVER USED TO BOTHER ME...

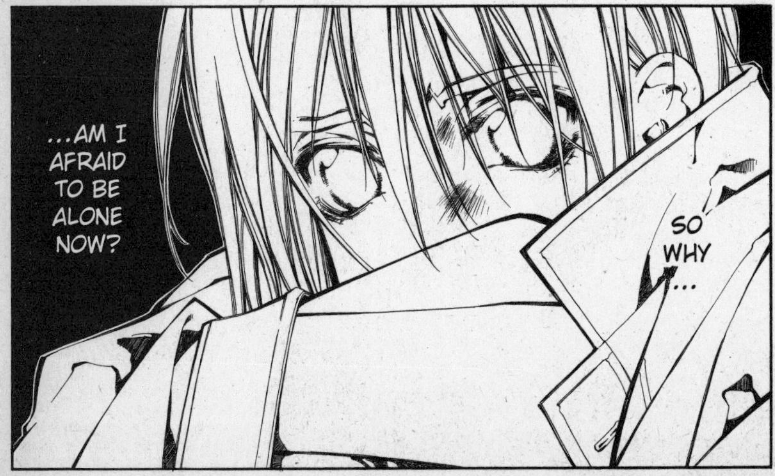
SO WHY...
...AM I AFRAID TO BE ALONE NOW?

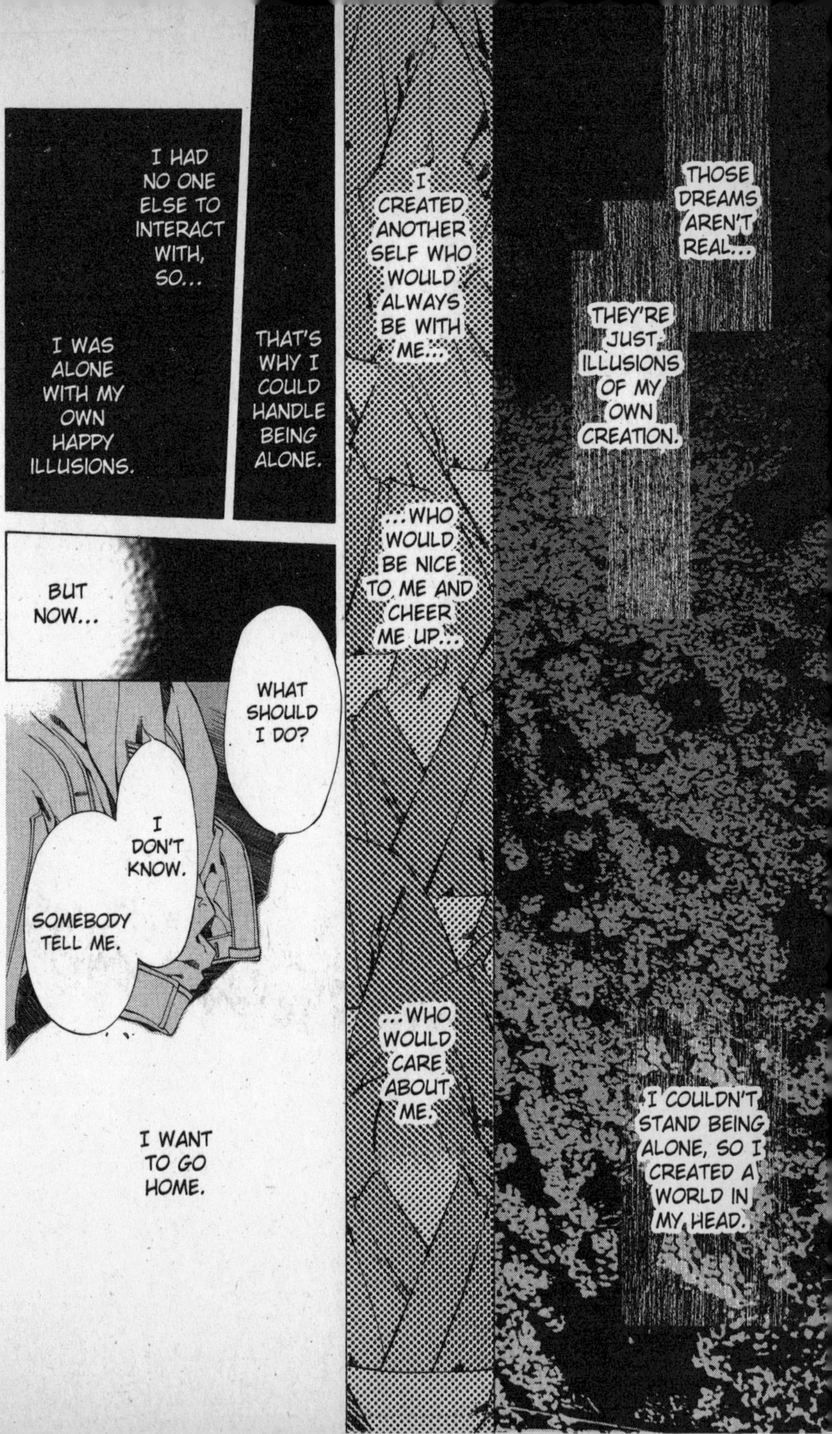
THOSE DREAMS AREN'T REAL...
THEY'RE JUST ILLUSIONS OF MY OWN CREATION.
I COULDN'T STAND BEING ALONE, SO I CREATED A WORLD IN MY HEAD.
I CREATED ANOTHER SELF WHO WOULD ALWAYS BE WITH ME...
...WHO WOULD BE NICE TO ME AND CHEER ME UP...
...WHO WOULD CARE ABOUT ME.
THAT'S WHY I COULD HANDLE BEING ALONE.
I HAD NO ONE ELSE TO INTERACT WITH, SO...
I WAS ALONE WITH MY OWN HAPPY ILLUSIONS.
BUT NOW...
WHAT SHOULD I DO?
I DON'T KNOW.
SOMEBODY TELL ME.
I WANT TO GO HOME.

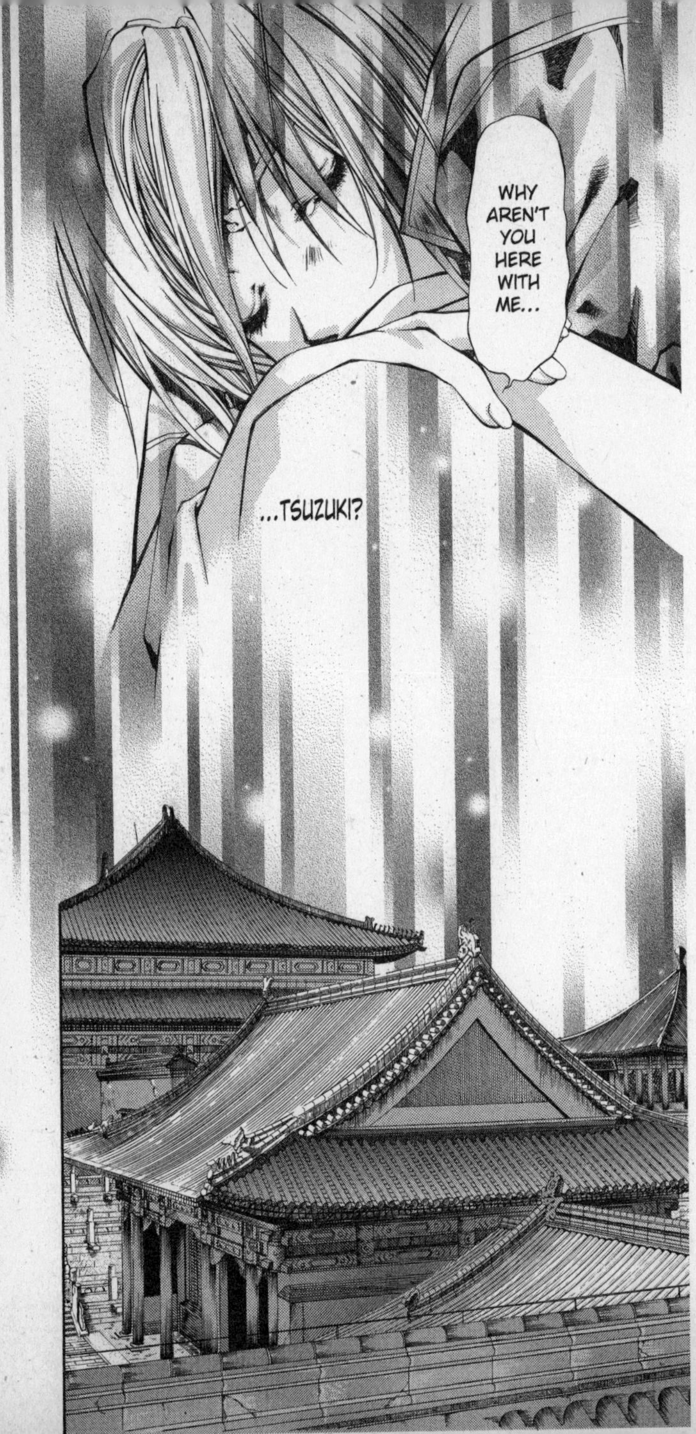
WHY AREN'T YOU HERE WITH ME...
...TSUZUKI?

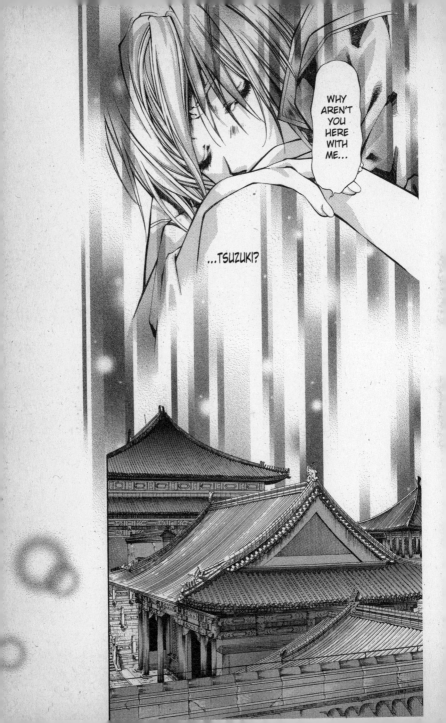

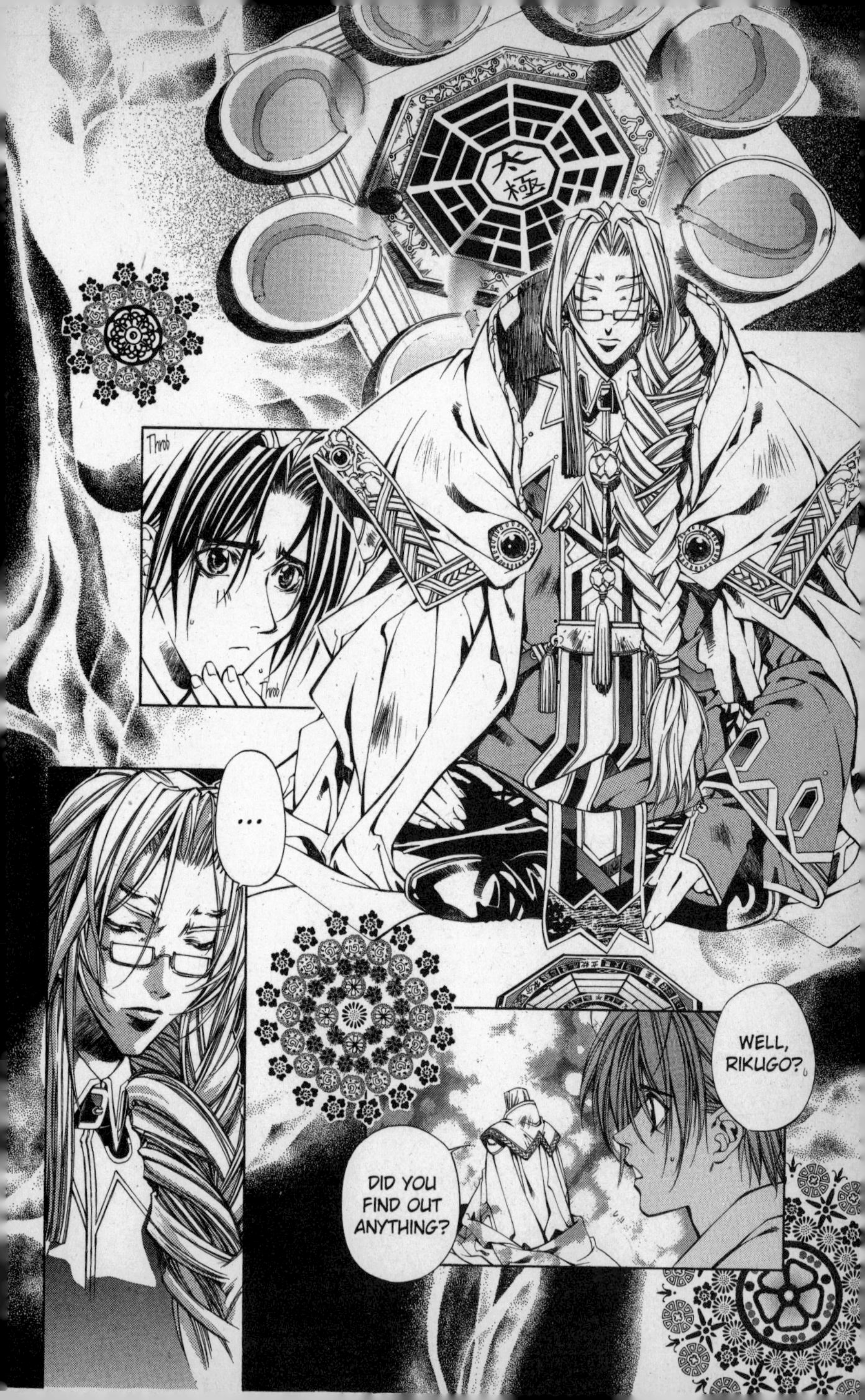
太極
Throb
Throb
WELL, RIKUGO?
DID YOU FIND OUT ANYTHING?
...

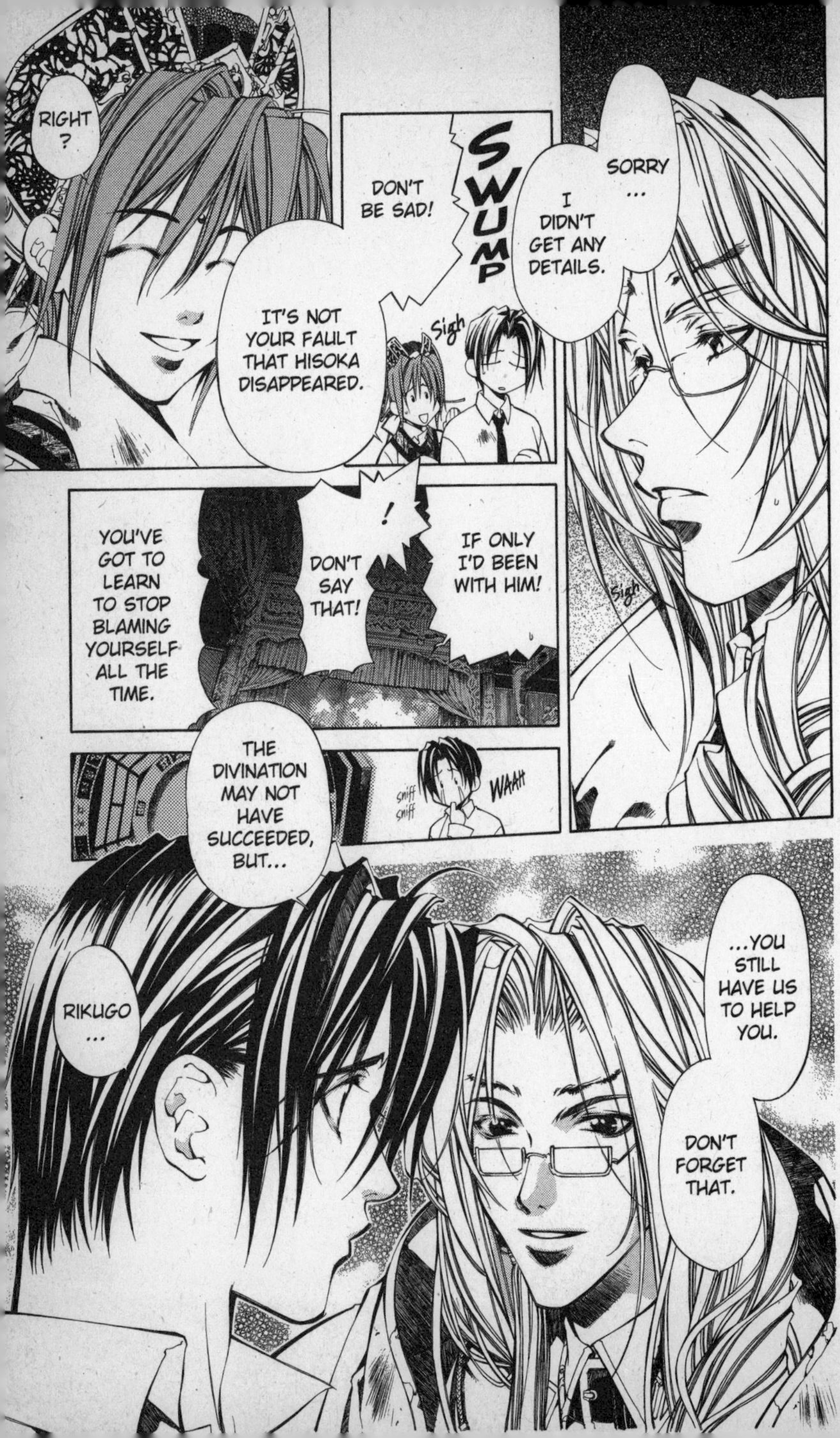
SORRY ...
I DIDN'T GET ANY DETAILS.
Sigh
DON'T BE SAD!
SWUMP
IT'S NOT YOUR FAULT THAT HISOKA DISAPPEARED.
Sigh
RIGHT ?
IF ONLY I'D BEEN WITH HIM!
!
DON'T SAY THAT!
YOU'VE GOT TO LEARN TO STOP BLAMING YOURSELF ALL THE TIME.
WAAH
sniff sniff
THE DIVINATION MAY NOT HAVE SUCCEEDED, BUT...
...YOU STILL HAVE US TO HELP YOU.
DON'T FORGET THAT.
RIKUGO ...

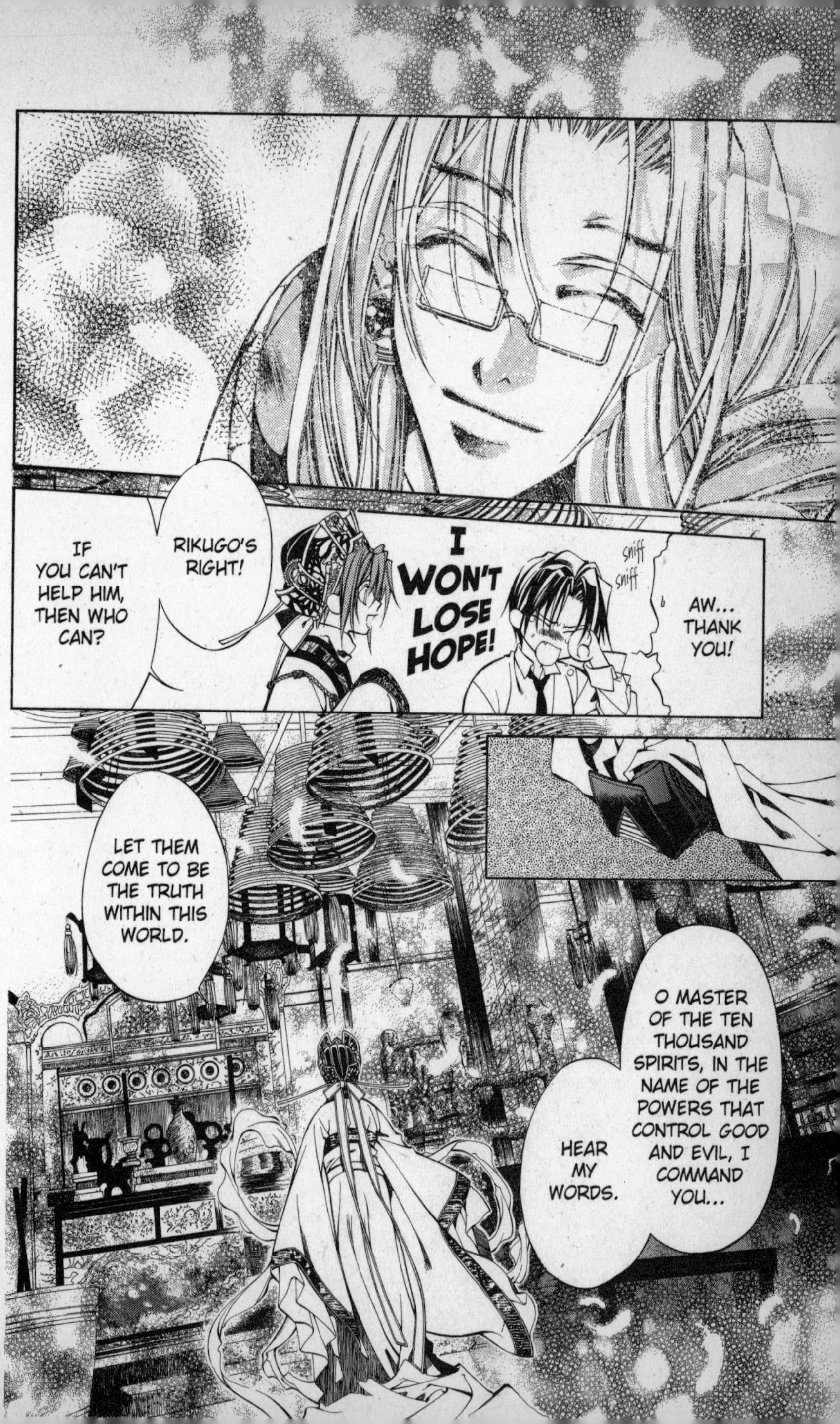
AW... THANK YOU!
sniff sniff
I WON'T LOSE HOPE!
RIKUGO'S RIGHT!
IF YOU CAN'T HELP HIM, THEN WHO CAN?
O MASTER OF THE TEN THOUSAND SPIRITS, IN THE NAME OF THE POWERS THAT CONTROL GOOD AND EVIL, I COMMAND YOU...
HEAR MY WORDS.
LET THEM COME TO BE THE TRUTH WITHIN THIS WORLD.

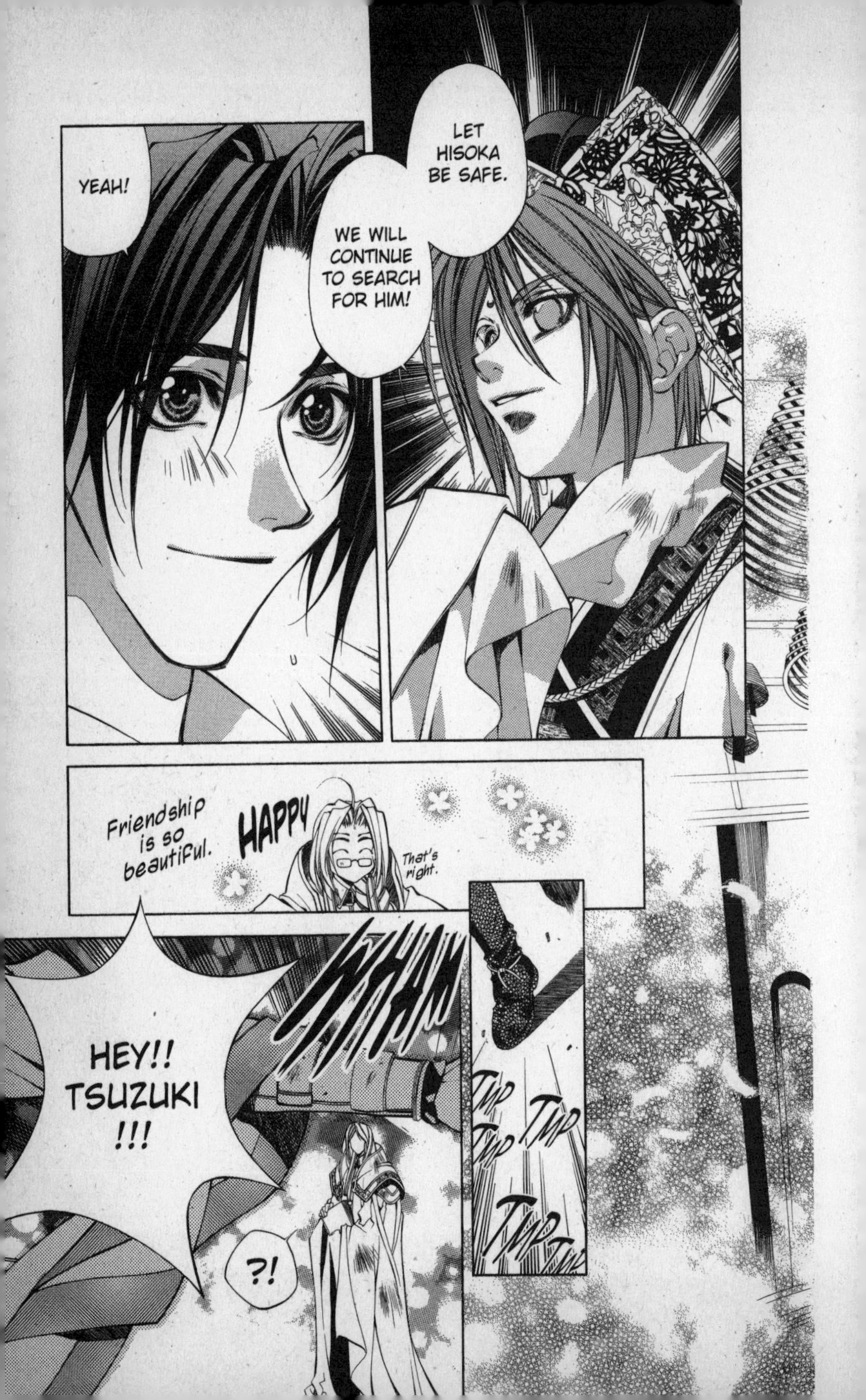

LET HISOKA BE SAFE.
WE WILL CONTINUE TO SEARCH FOR HIM!
YEAH!
Friendship is so beautiful.
HAPPY
That's right.
TMP TMP TMP TMP TMP TMP
WHAM
HEY!! TSUZUKI !!!
?!

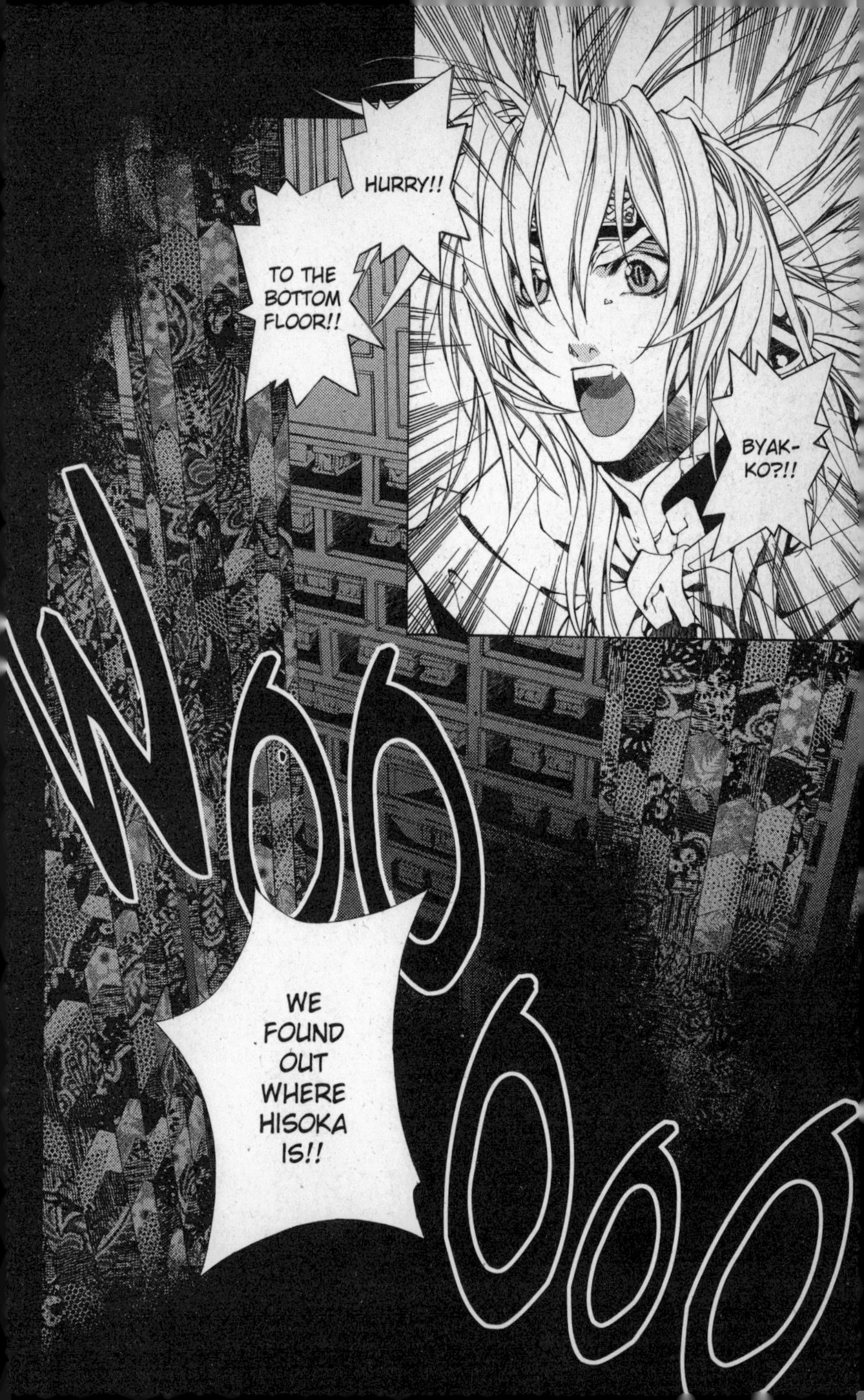
HURRY!!
TO THE BOTTOM FLOOR!!
BYAK-KO?!!
WOOOOOO
WE FOUND OUT WHERE HISOKA IS!!

CHAPTER 45

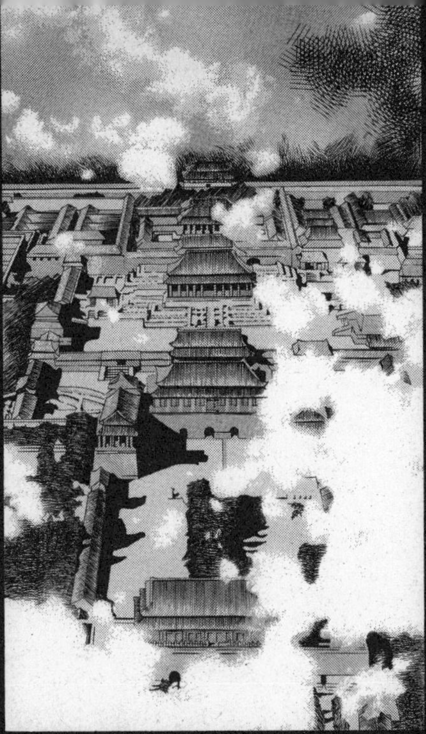

THE IMAGINARY WORLD CONTINUED SLOWLY DOWN THE PATH TOWARD DESTRUCTION.

MEANWHILE...

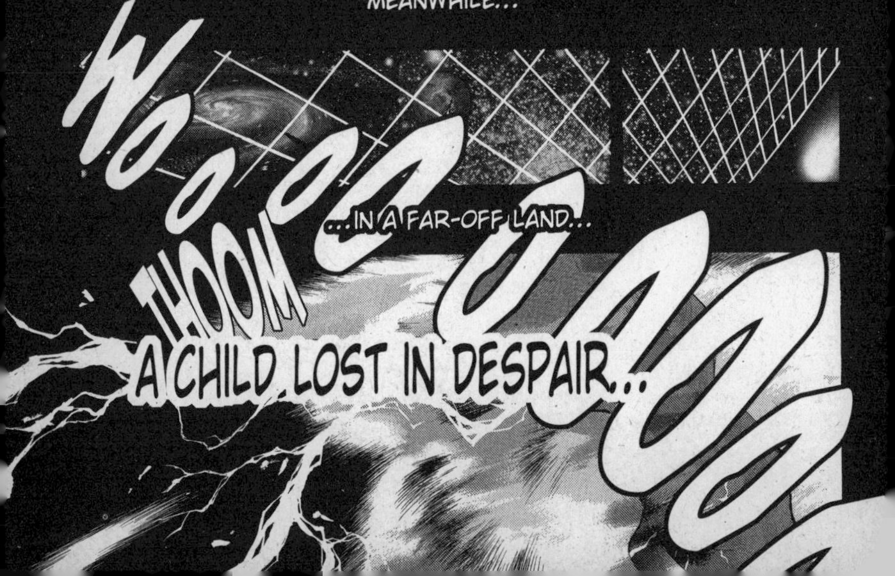
...IN A FAR-OFF LAND...
THOOM
A CHILD LOST IN DESPAIR...

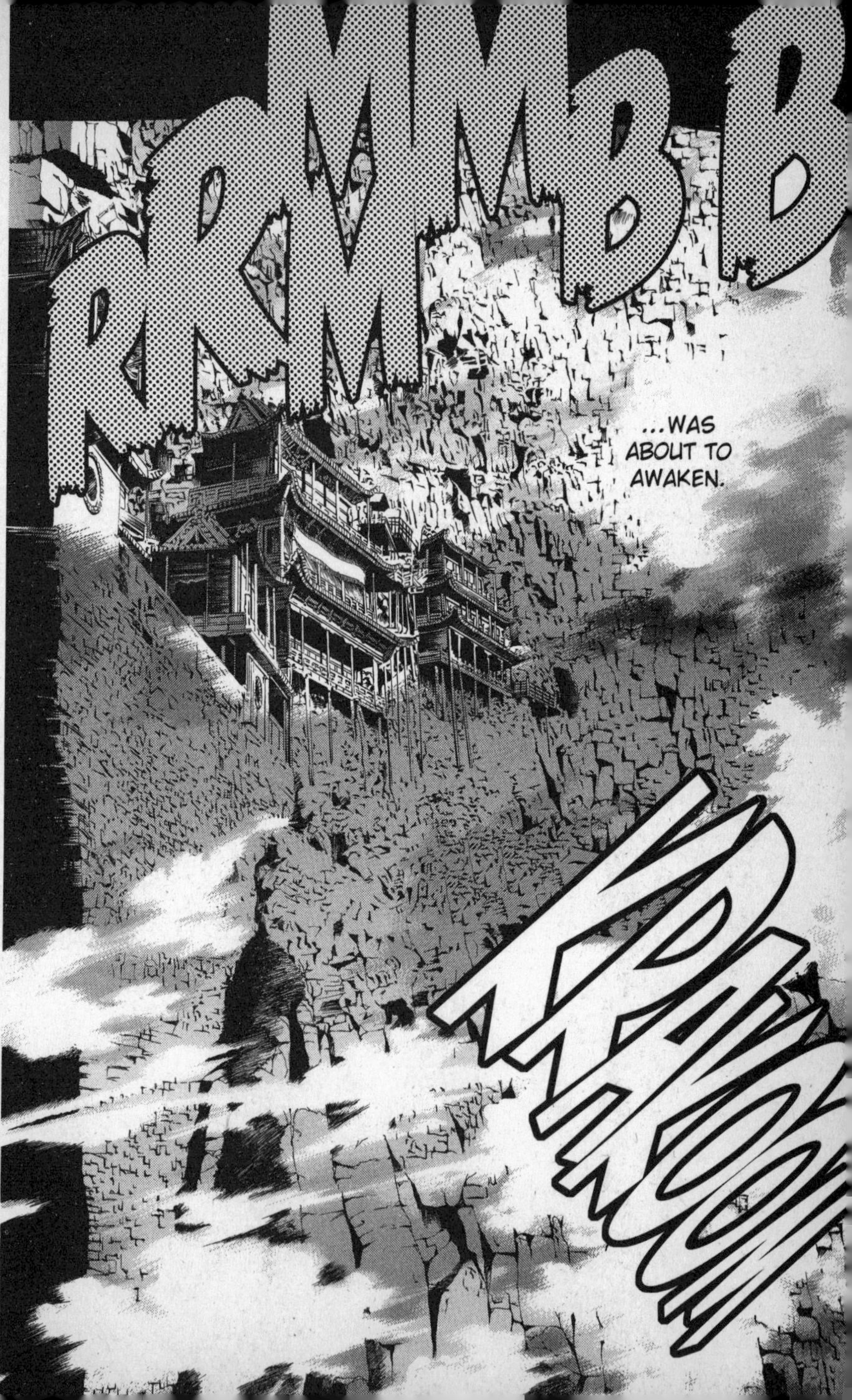
...WAS ABOUT TO AWAKEN.

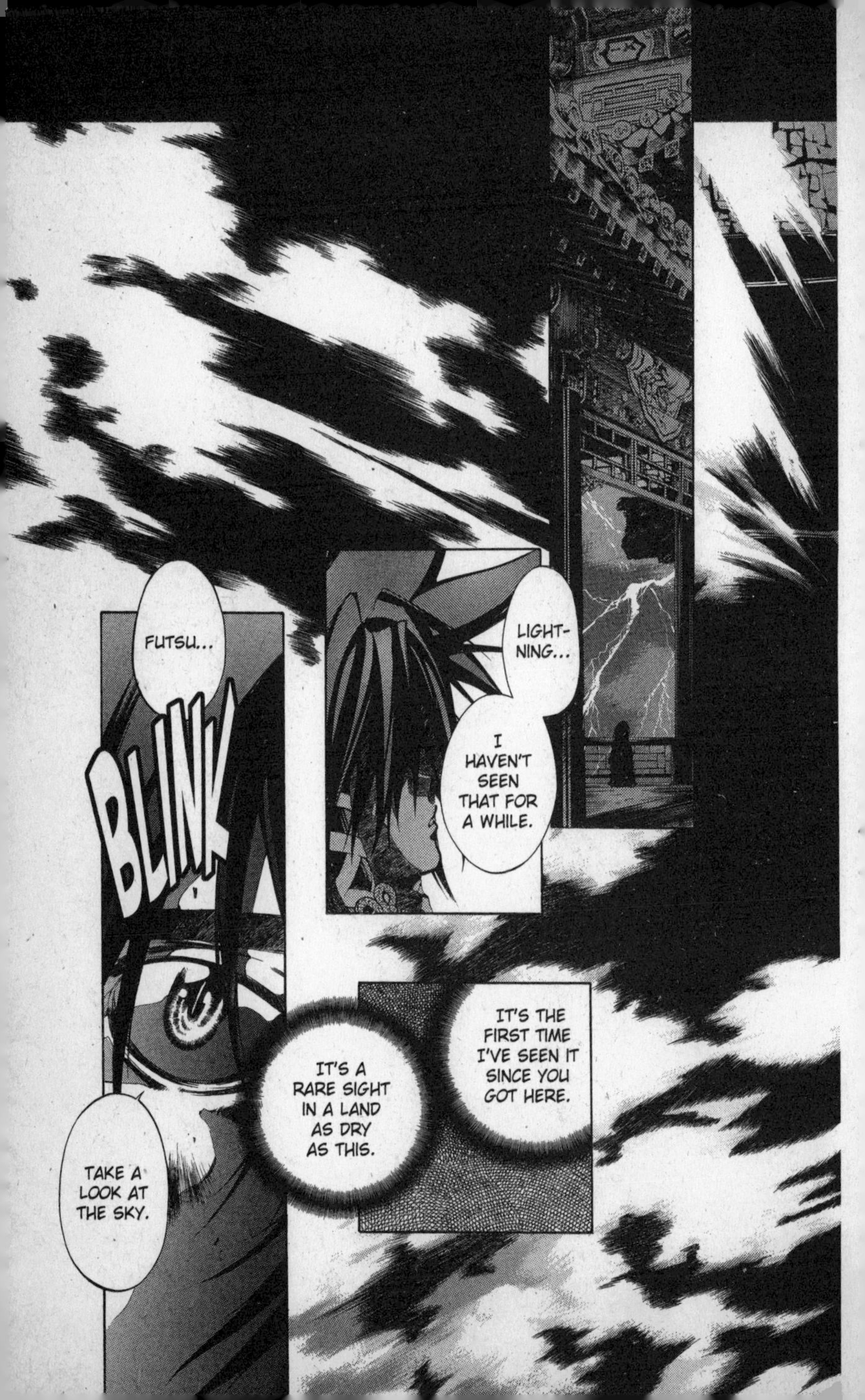
LIGHT-NING...
I HAVEN'T SEEN THAT FOR A WHILE.
IT'S THE FIRST TIME I'VE SEEN IT SINCE YOU GOT HERE.
IT'S A RARE SIGHT IN A LAND AS DRY AS THIS.
FUTSU...
BLINK
TAKE A LOOK AT THE SKY.

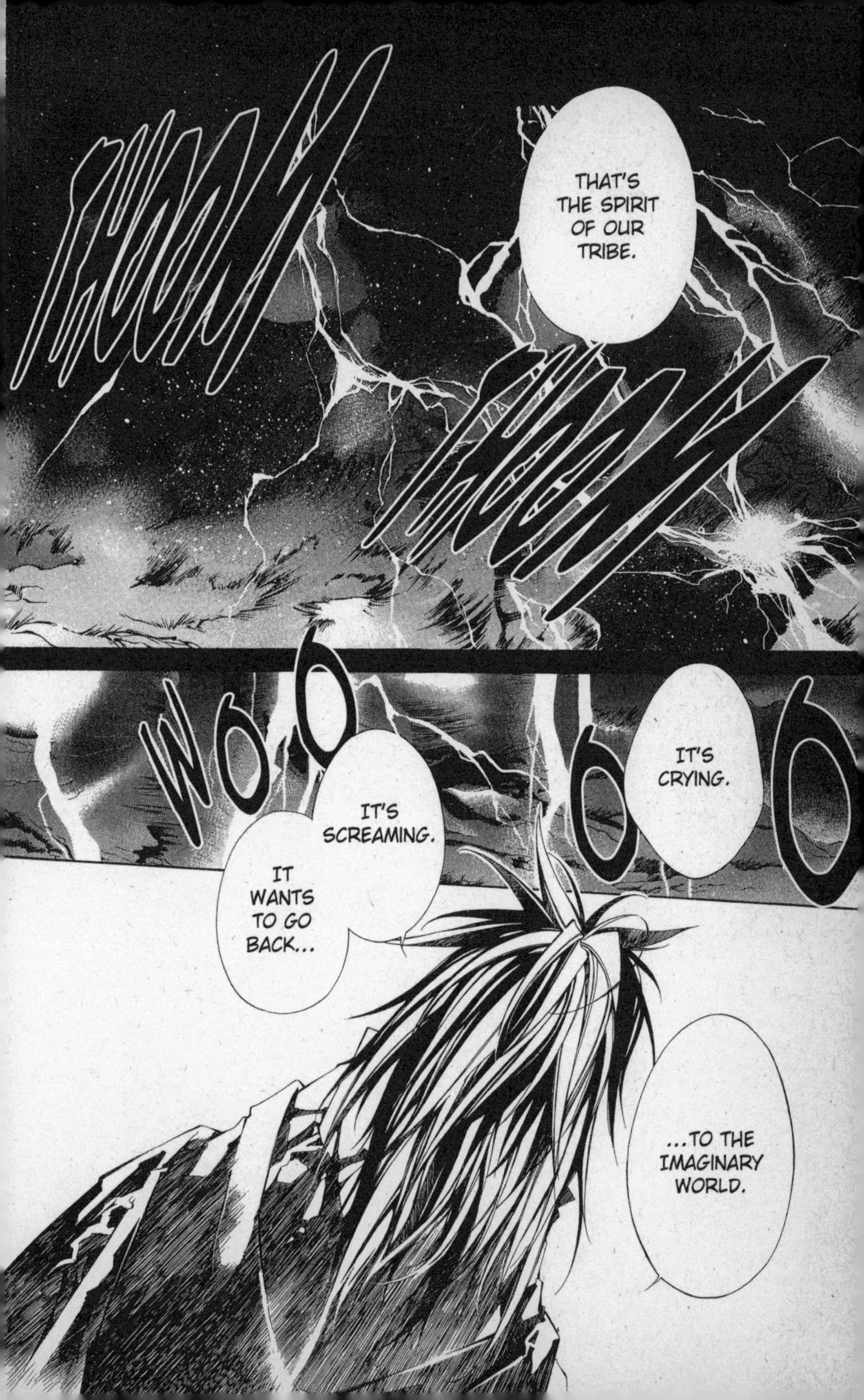
THAT'S THE SPIRIT OF OUR TRIBE.
IT'S CRYING.
IT'S SCREAMING.
IT WANTS TO GO BACK...
...TO THE IMAGINARY WORLD.

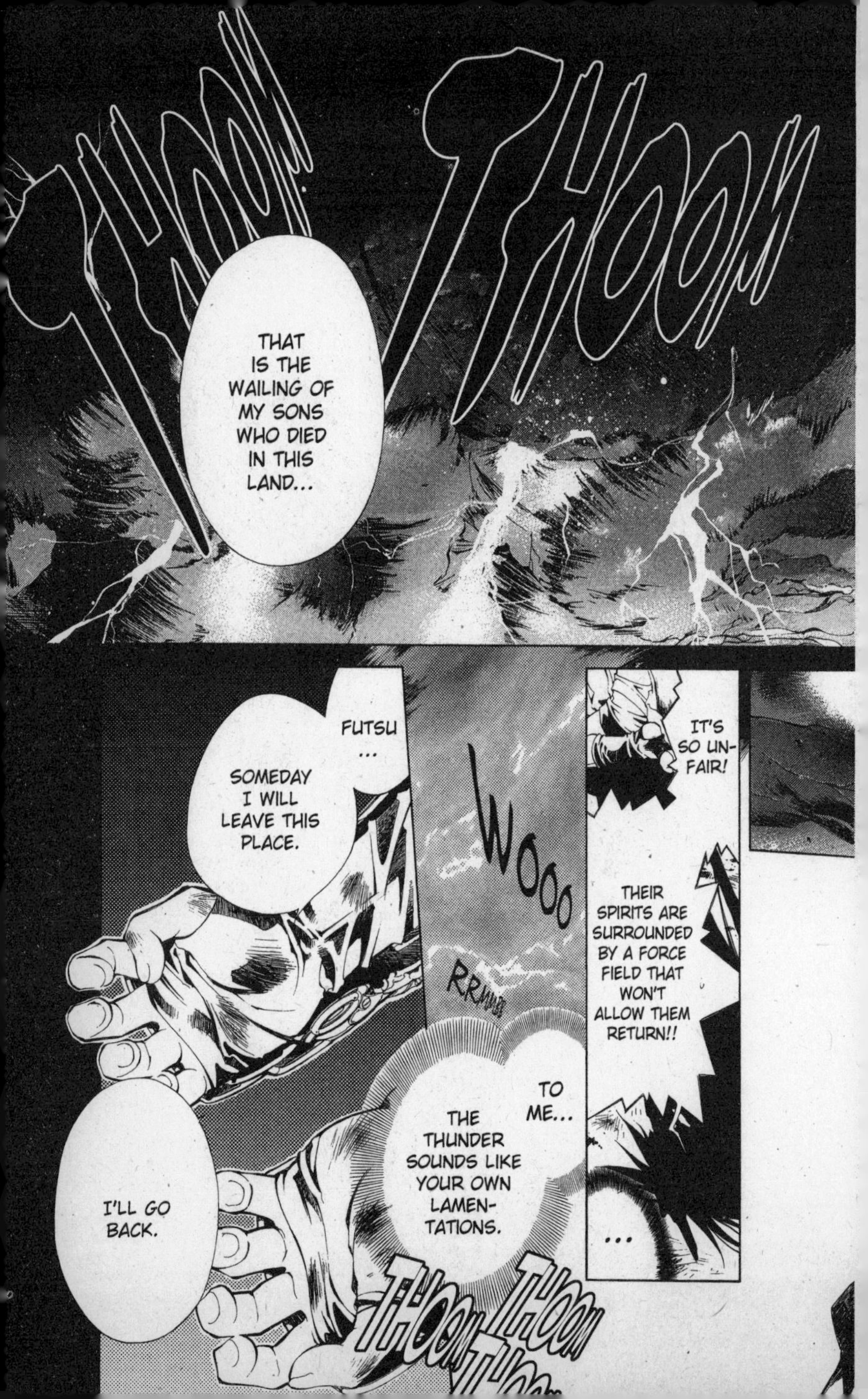
THOOM
THOOM
THAT IS THE WAILING OF MY SONS WHO DIED IN THIS LAND...
IT'S SO UN-FAIR!
THEIR SPIRITS ARE SURROUNDED BY A FORCE FIELD THAT WON'T ALLOW THEM RETURN!!
...
FUTSU...
SOMEDAY I WILL LEAVE THIS PLACE.
WOOO
RRMMM
TO ME...
THE THUNDER SOUNDS LIKE YOUR OWN LAMEN-TATIONS.
I'LL GO BACK.
THOOM
THOOM

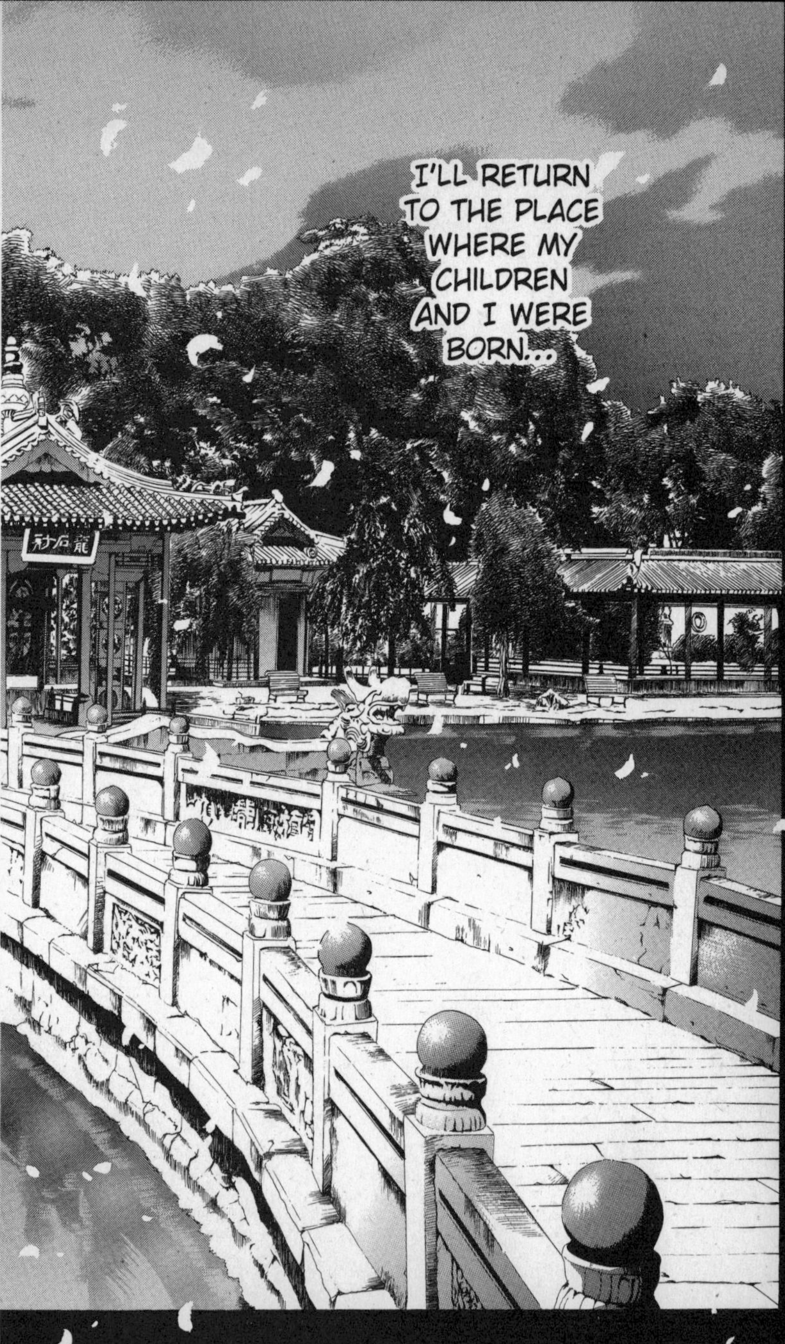
I'LL RETURN TO THE PLACE WHERE MY CHILDREN AND I WERE BORN...

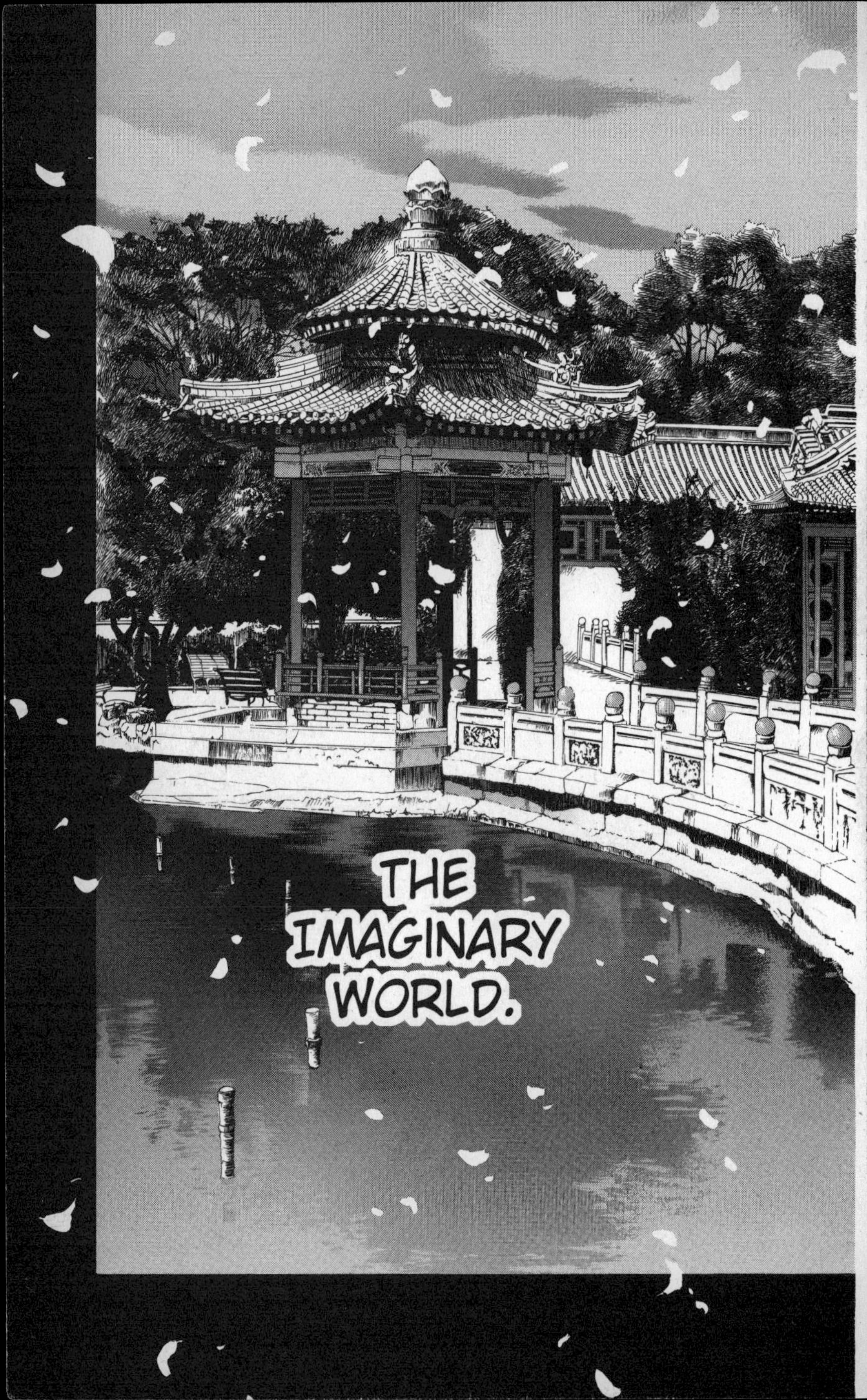
THE IMAGINARY WORLD.

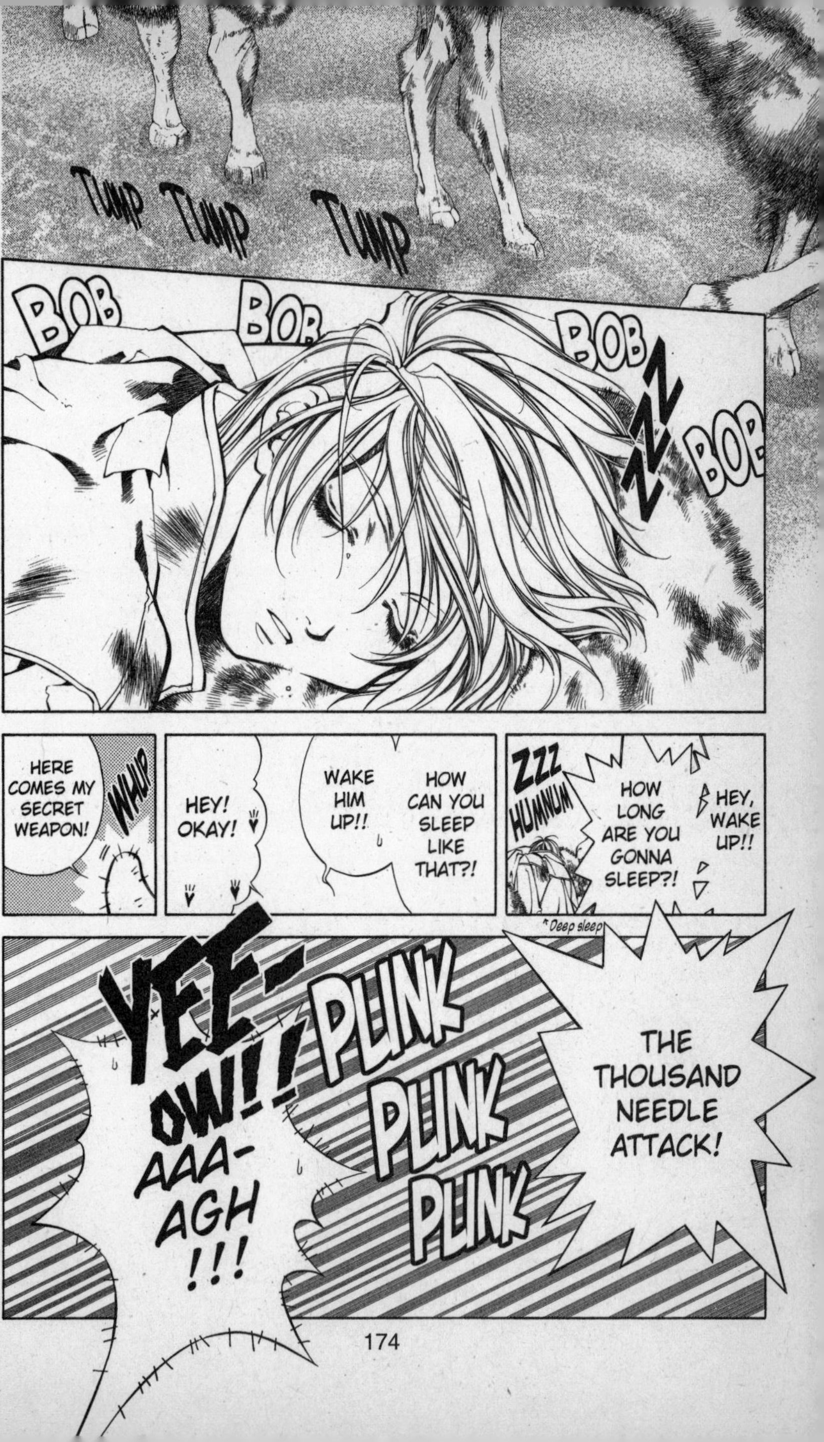
TUMP TUMP TUMP
BOB BOB BOB BOB
ZZZ
ZZZ HUMNUM
HEY, WAKE UP!!
HOW LONG ARE YOU GONNA SLEEP?!
*Deep sleep
HOW CAN YOU SLEEP LIKE THAT?!
WAKE HIM UP!!
HEY! OKAY!
WHUP
HERE COMES MY SECRET WEAPON!
THE THOUSAND NEEDLE ATTACK!
PLUNK PLUNK PLUNK
YEE-OW!!!
AAA-AGH!!!

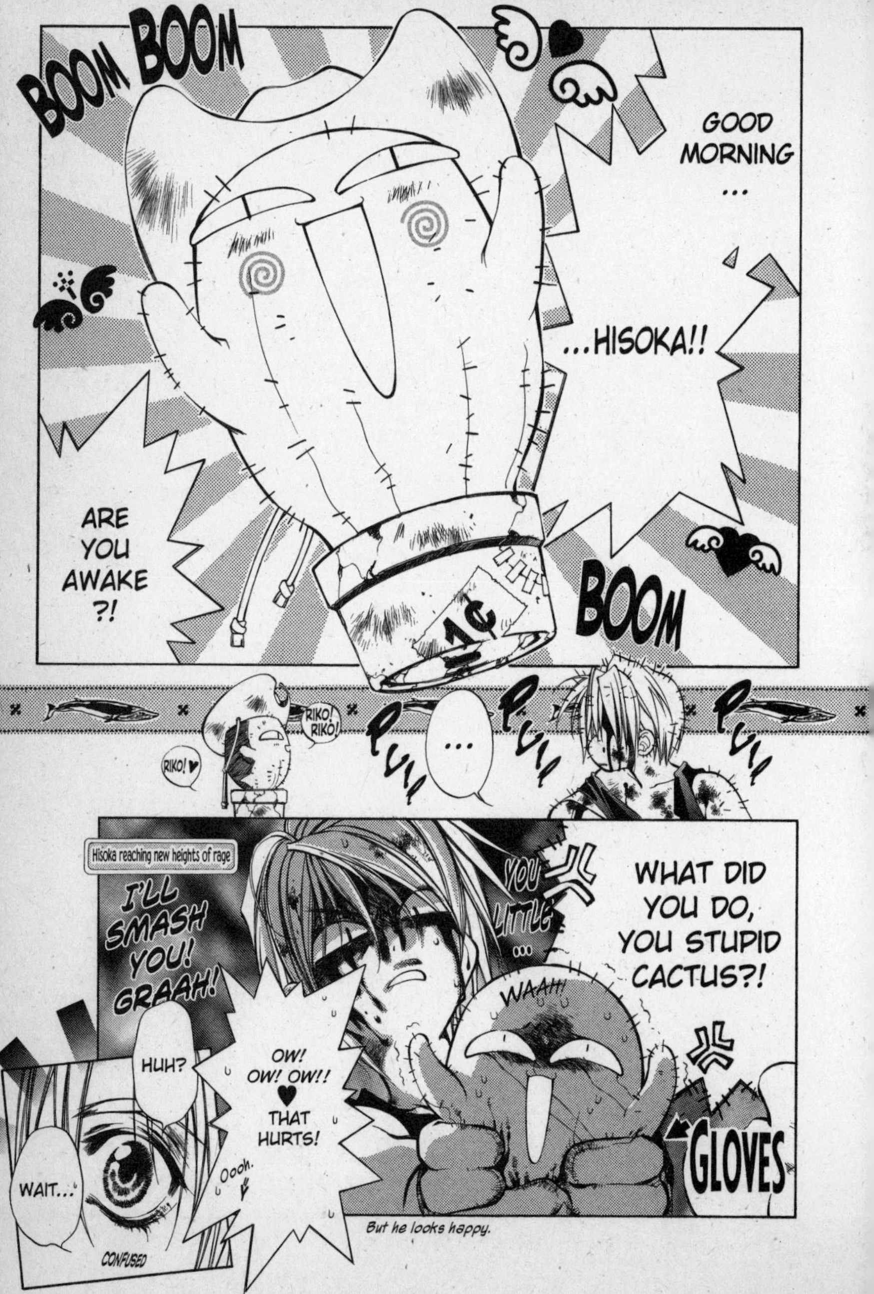
GOOD MORNING ...
...HISOKA!!
BOOM BOOM
ARE YOU AWAKE ?!
BOOM
PUIL PUIL PUIL
...
RIKO! RIKO!
RIKO! ♥
Hisoka reaching new heights of rage
WHAT DID YOU DO, YOU STUPID CACTUS?!
YOU LITTLE ...
I'LL SMASH YOU! GRAAH!
WAAH!
GLOVES
OW! OW! OW!! ♥ THAT HURTS!
Oooh.
But he looks happy.
HUH?
WAIT...
CONFUSED

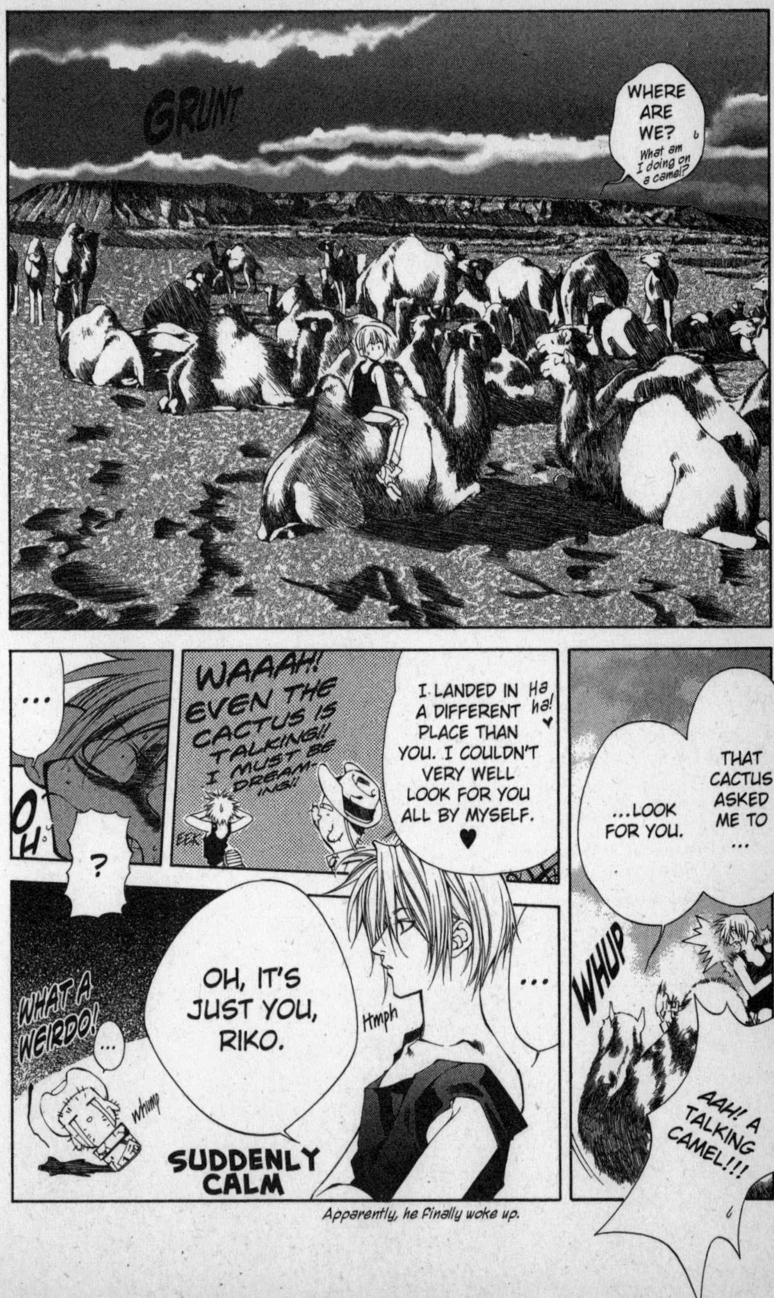
GRUNT
WHERE ARE WE? What am I doing on a camel!?
THAT CACTUS ASKED ME TO ...
...LOOK FOR YOU.
WHUP
AAH! A TALKING CAMEL!!!
I LANDED IN A DIFFERENT PLACE THAN YOU. I COULDN'T VERY WELL LOOK FOR YOU ALL BY MYSELF. ♥
Ha ha! ♥
WAAAH! EVEN THE CACTUS IS TALKING!! I MUST BE DREAMING!!
EEK
...
OH
?
...
OH, IT'S JUST YOU, RIKO.
Hmph
SUDDENLY CALM
WHAT A WEIRDO!
...
whump
Apparently, he finally woke up.

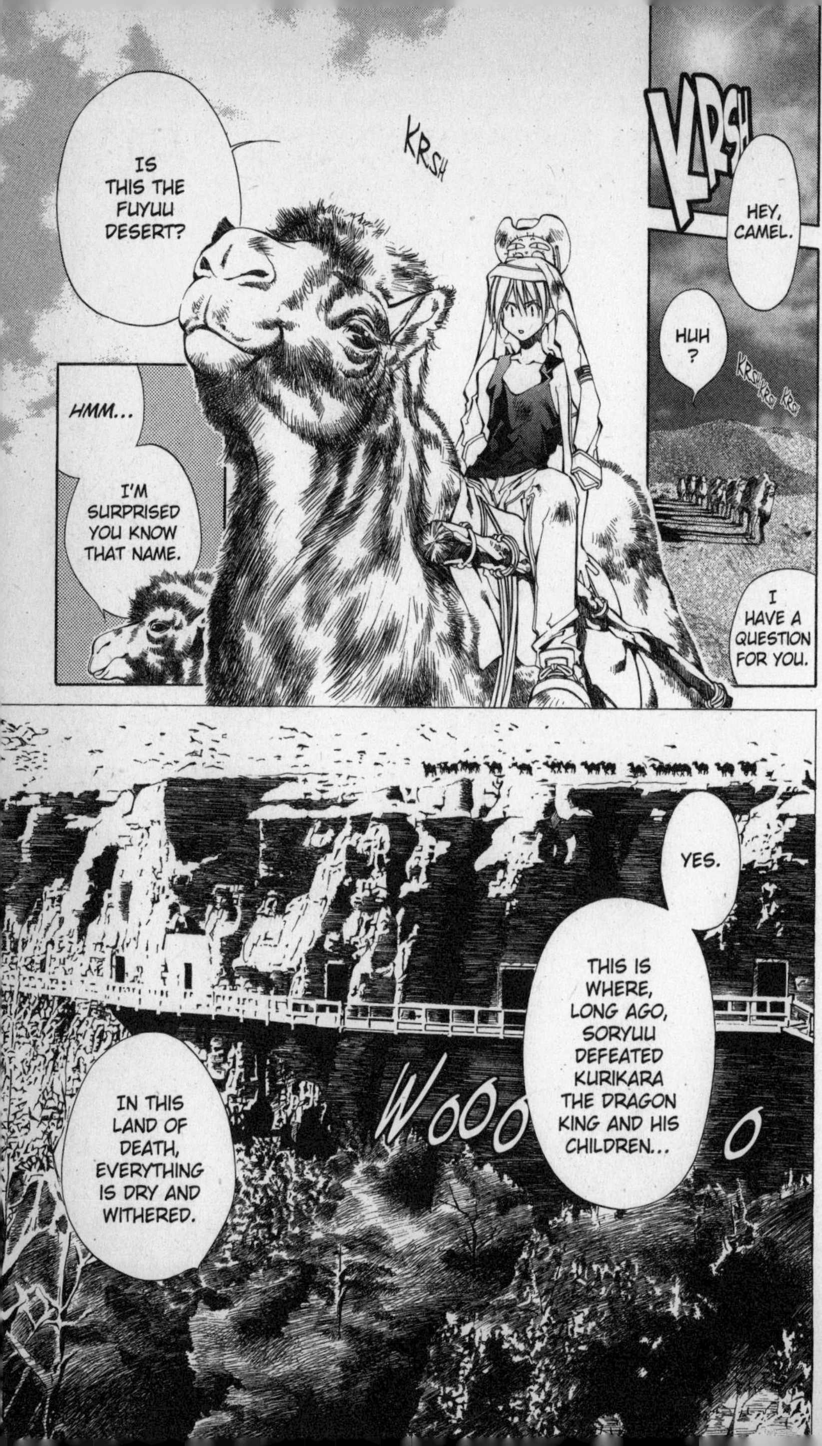
KRSH
HEY, CAMEL.
HUH ?
KRSH KRSH KRSH
I HAVE A QUESTION FOR YOU.
KRSH
IS THIS THE FUYUU DESERT?
HMM...
I'M SURPRISED YOU KNOW THAT NAME.
YES.
THIS IS WHERE, LONG AGO, SORYUU DEFEATED KURIKARA THE DRAGON KING AND HIS CHILDREN...
WOOOO O
IN THIS LAND OF DEATH, EVERYTHING IS DRY AND WITHERED.

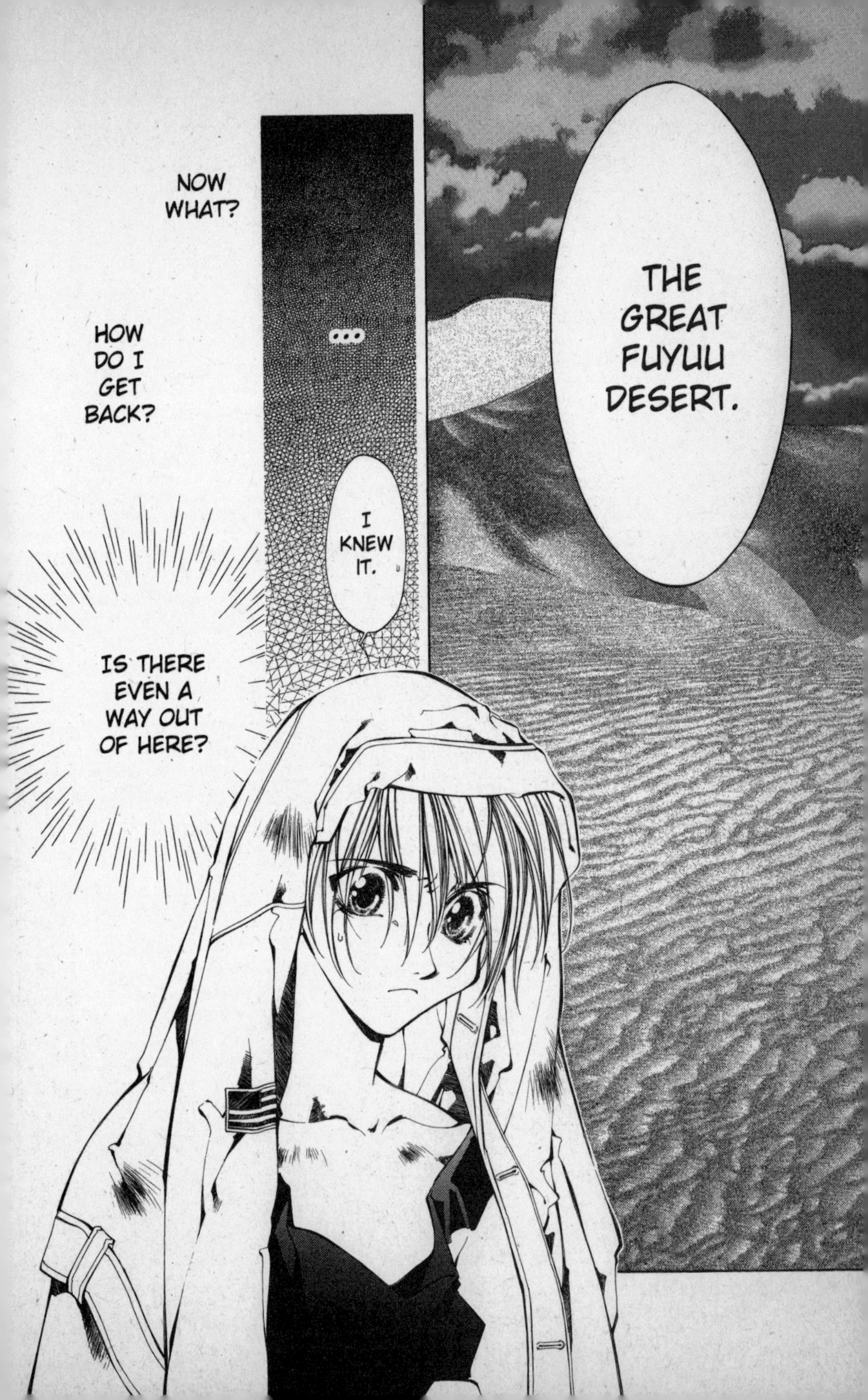
THE GREAT FUYUU DESERT.
...
I KNEW IT.
NOW WHAT?
HOW DO I GET BACK?
IS THERE EVEN A WAY OUT OF HERE?

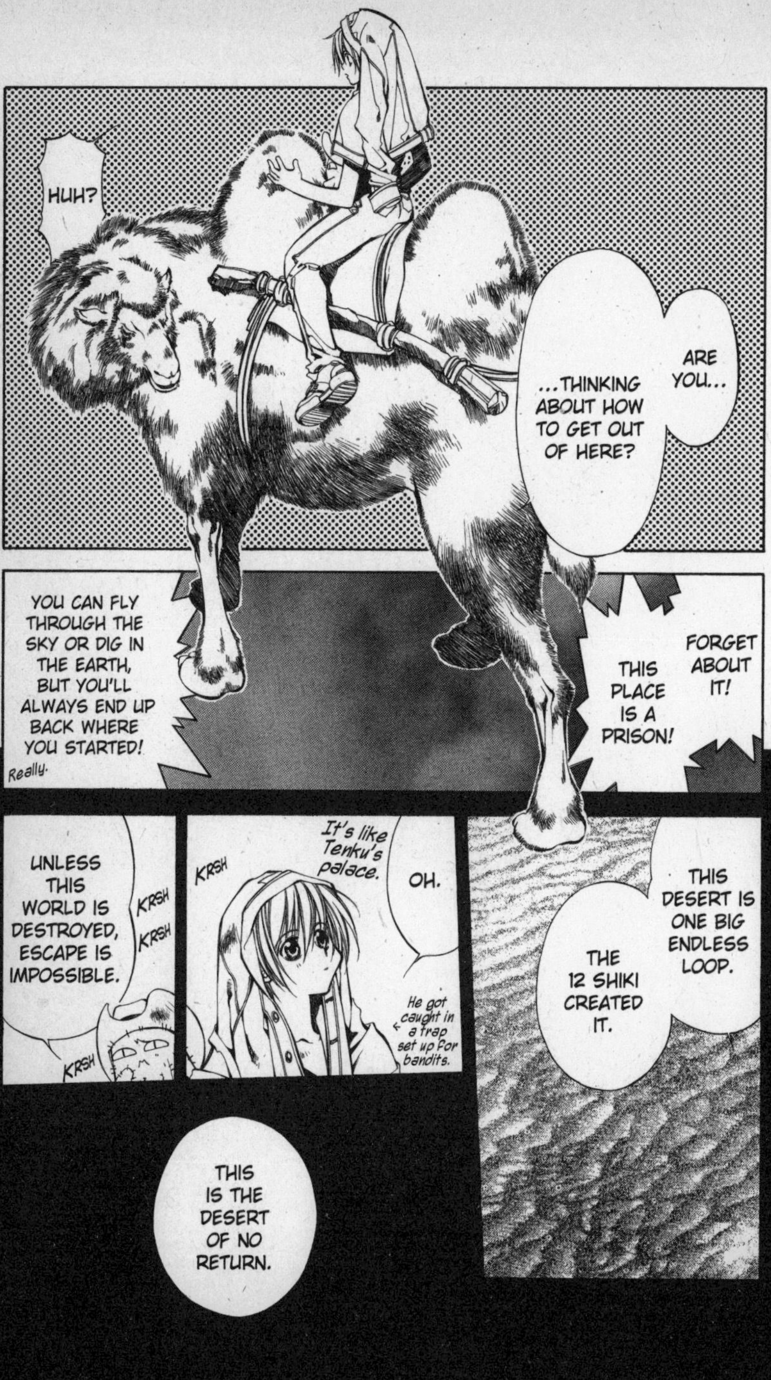
ARE YOU...
...THINKING ABOUT HOW TO GET OUT OF HERE?
HUH?
FORGET ABOUT IT!
THIS PLACE IS A PRISON!
YOU CAN FLY THROUGH THE SKY OR DIG IN THE EARTH, BUT YOU'LL ALWAYS END UP BACK WHERE YOU STARTED!
Really.
THIS DESERT IS ONE BIG ENDLESS LOOP.
THE 12 SHIKI CREATED IT.
OH.
It's like Tenku's palace.
KRSH
He got caught in a trap set up for bandits.
UNLESS THIS WORLD IS DESTROYED, ESCAPE IS IMPOSSIBLE.
KRSH
KRSH
KRSH
THIS IS THE DESERT OF NO RETURN.

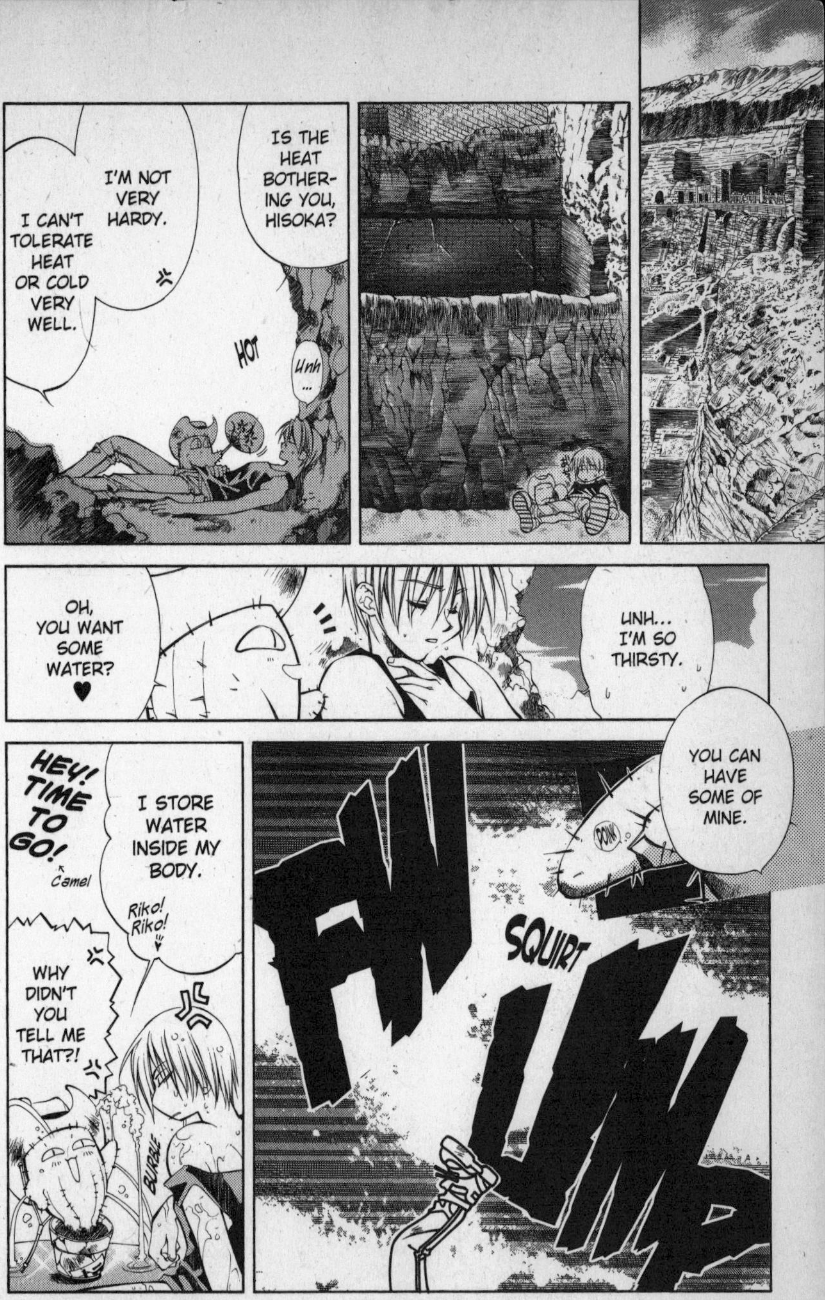
IS THE HEAT BOTHERING YOU, HISOKA?
I'M NOT VERY HARDY.
I CAN'T TOLERATE HEAT OR COLD VERY WELL.
Unh...
HOT
UNH... I'M SO THIRSTY.
OH, YOU WANT SOME WATER? ♥
YOU CAN HAVE SOME OF MINE.
DOINK
SQUIRT
FWUMP
I STORE WATER INSIDE MY BODY.
Riko! Riko!
HEY! TIME TO GO!
Camel
WHY DIDN'T YOU TELL ME THAT?!
BURBLE

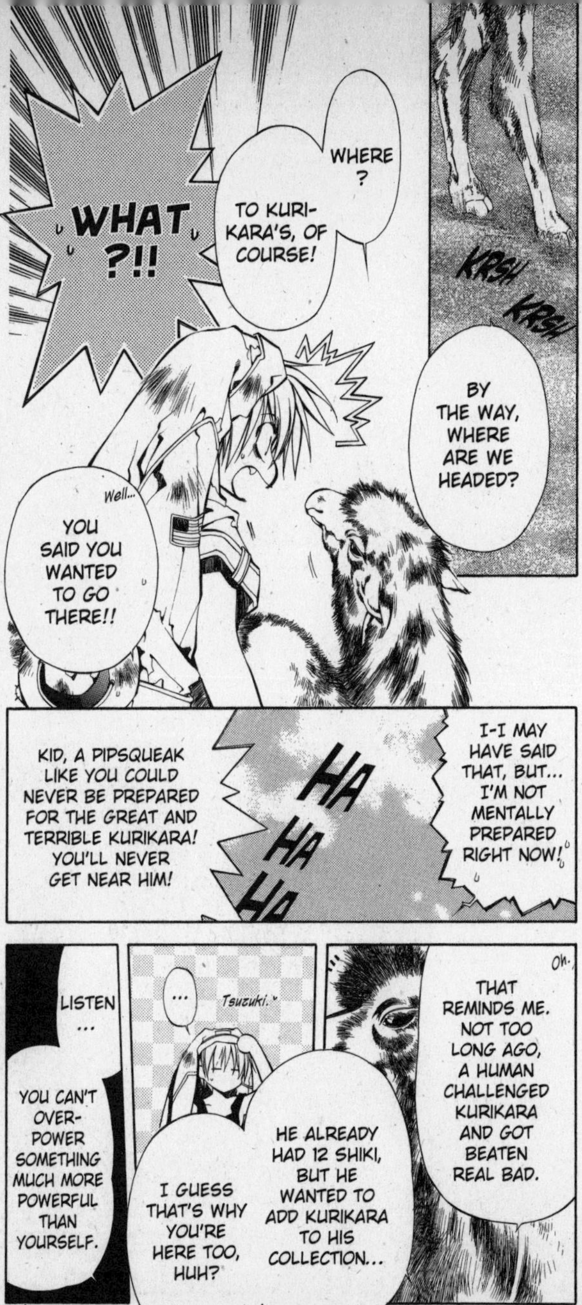
KRSH
KRSH
BY THE WAY, WHERE ARE WE HEADED?
WHERE?
TO KURIKARA'S, OF COURSE!
WHAT?!!
Well...
YOU SAID YOU WANTED TO GO THERE!!
I-I MAY HAVE SAID THAT, BUT... I'M NOT MENTALLY PREPARED RIGHT NOW!
HA
HA
HA
KID, A PIPSQUEAK LIKE YOU COULD NEVER BE PREPARED FOR THE GREAT AND TERRIBLE KURIKARA! YOU'LL NEVER GET NEAR HIM!
Oh.
THAT REMINDS ME. NOT TOO LONG AGO, A HUMAN CHALLENGED KURIKARA AND GOT BEATEN REAL BAD.
HE ALREADY HAD 12 SHIKI, BUT HE WANTED TO ADD KURIKARA TO HIS COLLECTION...
...
Tsuzuki.
I GUESS THAT'S WHY YOU'RE HERE TOO, HUH?
LISTEN...
YOU CAN'T OVERPOWER SOMETHING MUCH MORE POWERFUL THAN YOURSELF.

Topic 4: Gensou Suikoden II

Why are there so many characters in this game? That's what I thought as I tried to gather all the characters for Nanami (laugh). This game is really tough. After I beat up Eriza, I was like, "Ah, it's finally over." But then there were still all these other things I had to do. It's a game that you can play for a long time. The scenario is really good too, but it's more of a character game. I'm a big fan of Victor, a.k.a. the Bear. I love the way he throws down his enemies. I like Nanami too. There's something about the sibling attack that really gets me. And then there's Bo-chan. I wanted to see him so bad that I went looking for the earlier versions of the game. I gathered 108 stars, and then brought Gremio back to life. It was really hard to convert the data (laugh). This game is tough, but Bo-chan looks so cute when he's having a hard time. I always use his "double leader" attack to kill my opponents instantly. Anyway, it's just a very well-made game. It's really fun. I want the soundtrack.

I hope there's a sequel (laugh).

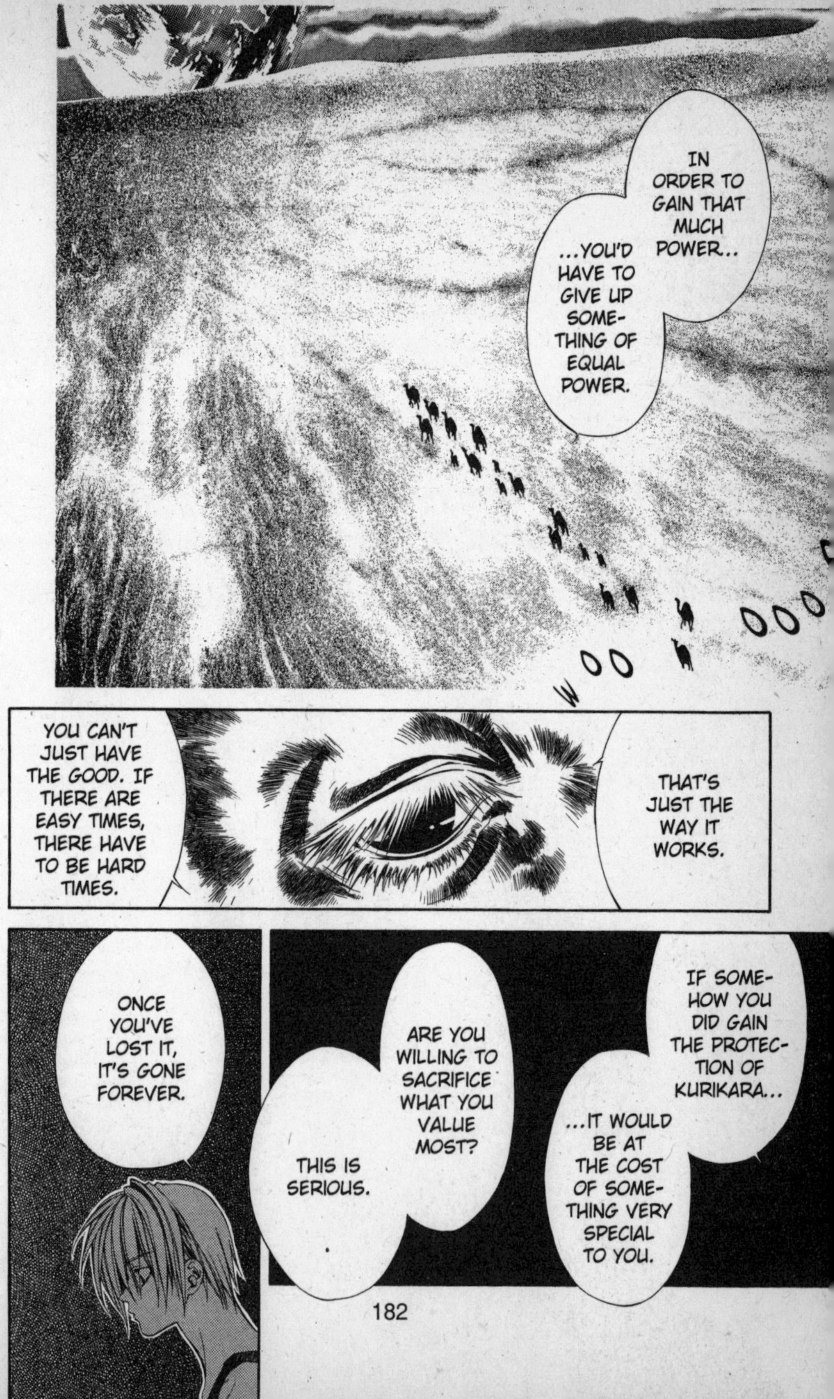
IN ORDER TO GAIN THAT MUCH POWER...
...YOU'D HAVE TO GIVE UP SOME-THING OF EQUAL POWER.
WOOOOO
THAT'S JUST THE WAY IT WORKS.
YOU CAN'T JUST HAVE THE GOOD. IF THERE ARE EASY TIMES, THERE HAVE TO BE HARD TIMES.
IF SOME-HOW YOU DID GAIN THE PROTEC-TION OF KURIKARA...
...IT WOULD BE AT THE COST OF SOME-THING VERY SPECIAL TO YOU.
ARE YOU WILLING TO SACRIFICE WHAT YOU VALUE MOST?
THIS IS SERIOUS.
ONCE YOU'VE LOST IT, IT'S GONE FOREVER.

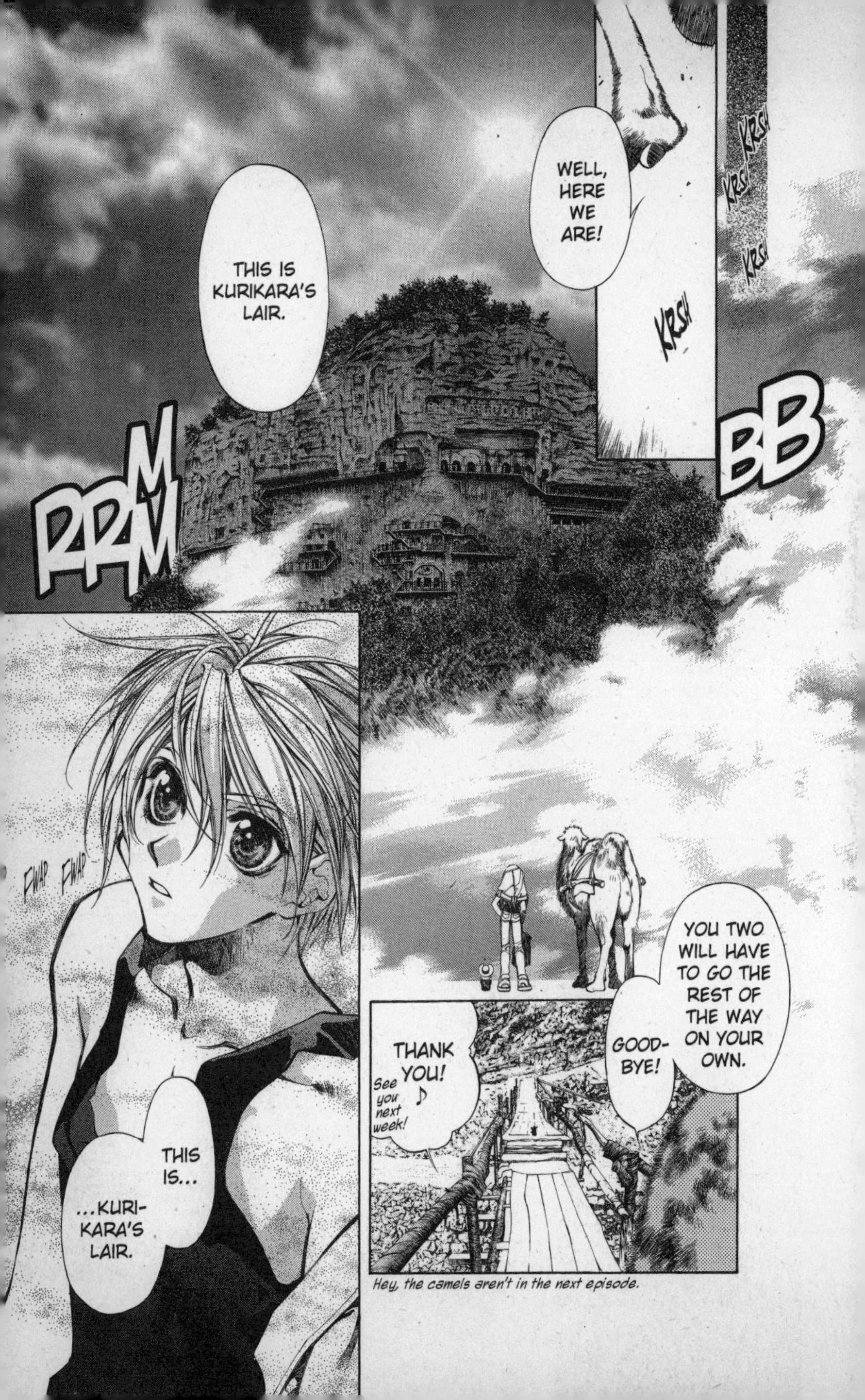
WELL, HERE WE ARE!
KRSH KRSH
KRSH
KRSH
THIS IS KURIKARA'S LAIR.
BB
RRMMM
YOU TWO WILL HAVE TO GO THE REST OF THE WAY ON YOUR OWN.
GOOD-BYE!
THANK YOU! ♪
See you next week!
Hey, the camels aren't in the next episode.
FWAP FWAP
THIS IS...
...KURI-KARA'S LAIR.

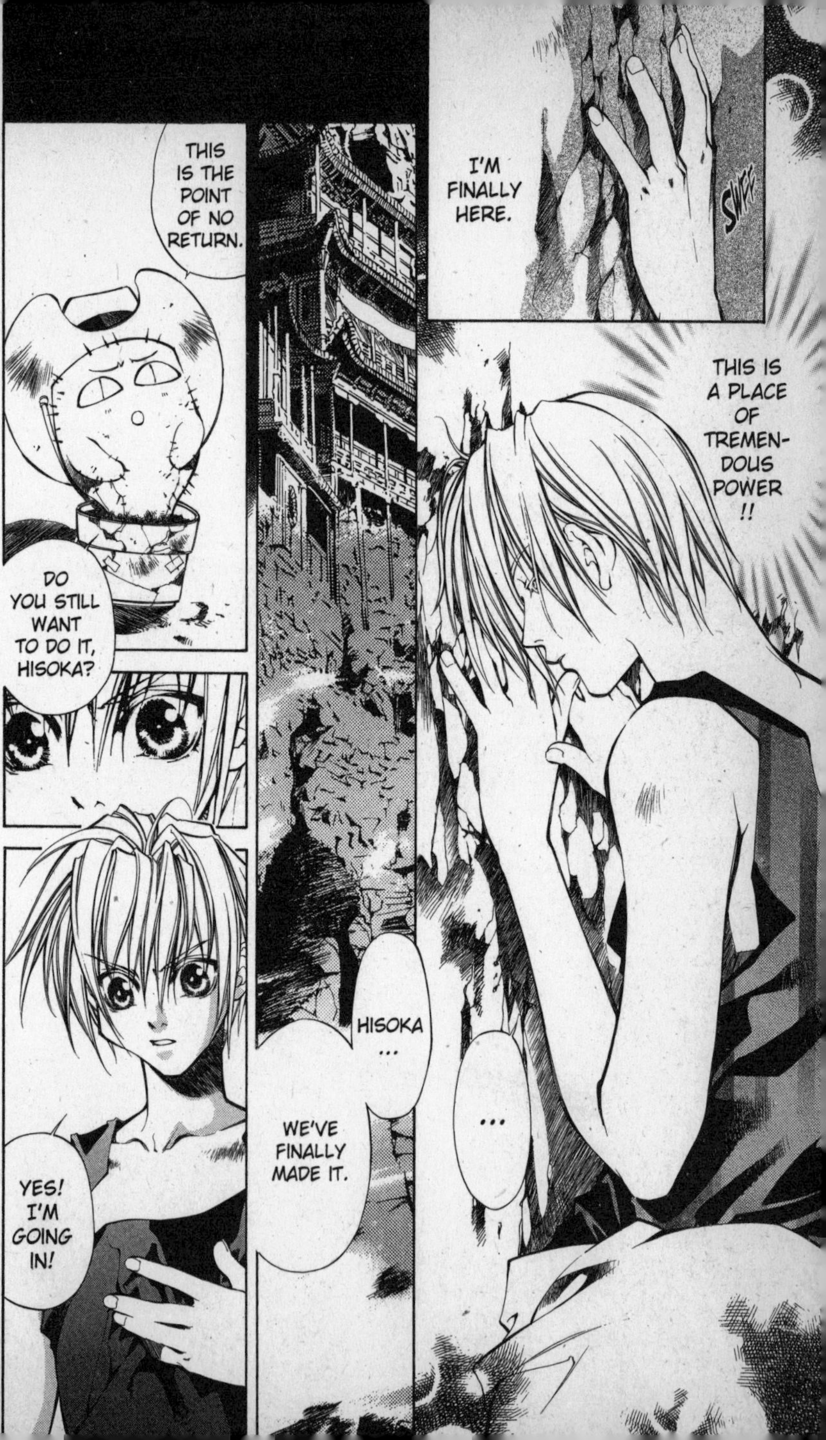

I'M FINALLY HERE.
SWFF
THIS IS A PLACE OF TREMENDOUS POWER!!
...
HISOKA...
WE'VE FINALLY MADE IT.
THIS IS THE POINT OF NO RETURN.
DO YOU STILL WANT TO DO IT, HISOKA?
YES! I'M GOING IN!

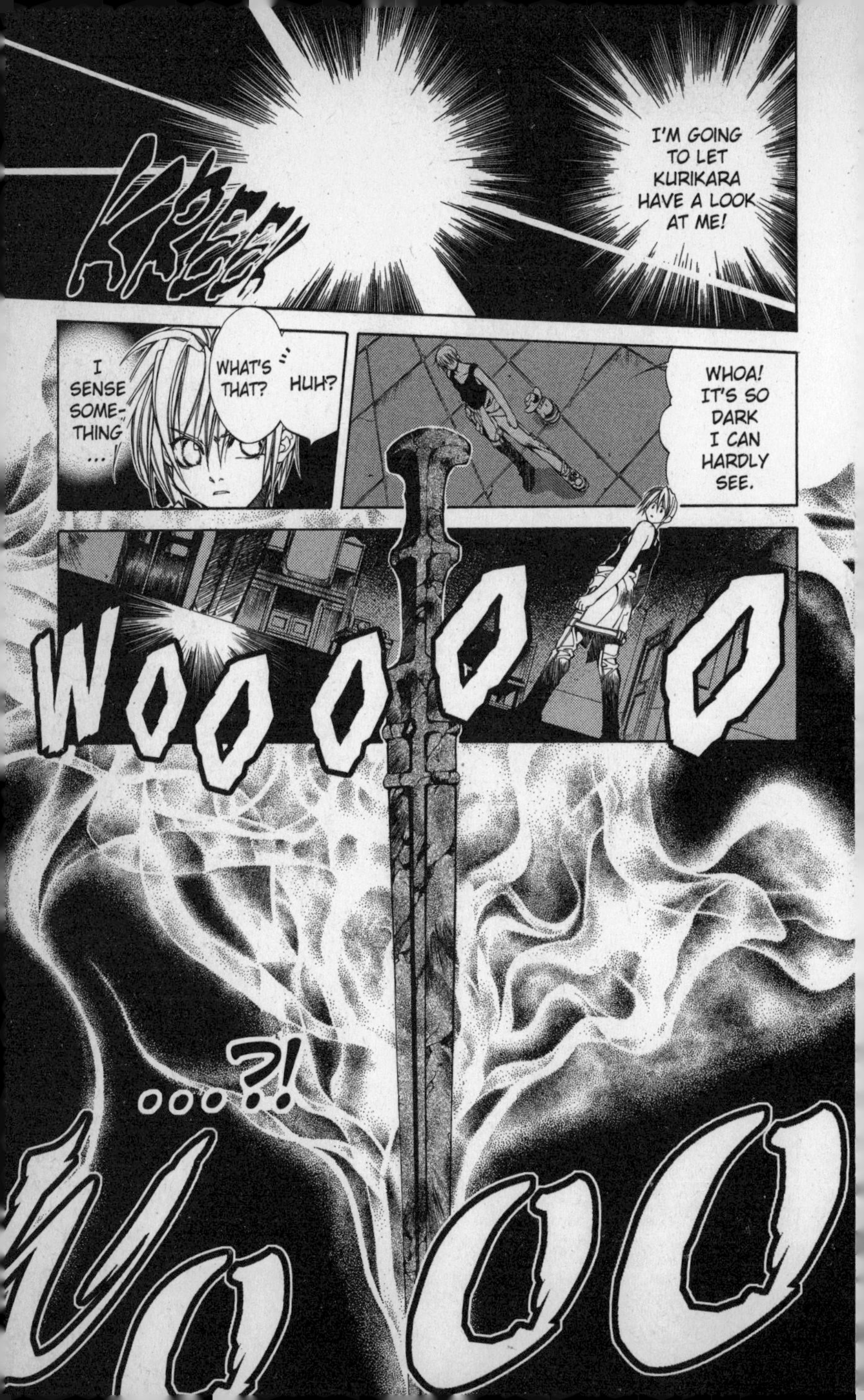
I'M GOING TO LET KURIKARA HAVE A LOOK AT ME!
KREEK
WHOA! IT'S SO DARK I CAN HARDLY SEE.
HUH?
WHAT'S THAT?
I SENSE SOME-THING...
WOOOOOO
...?!
WOOO

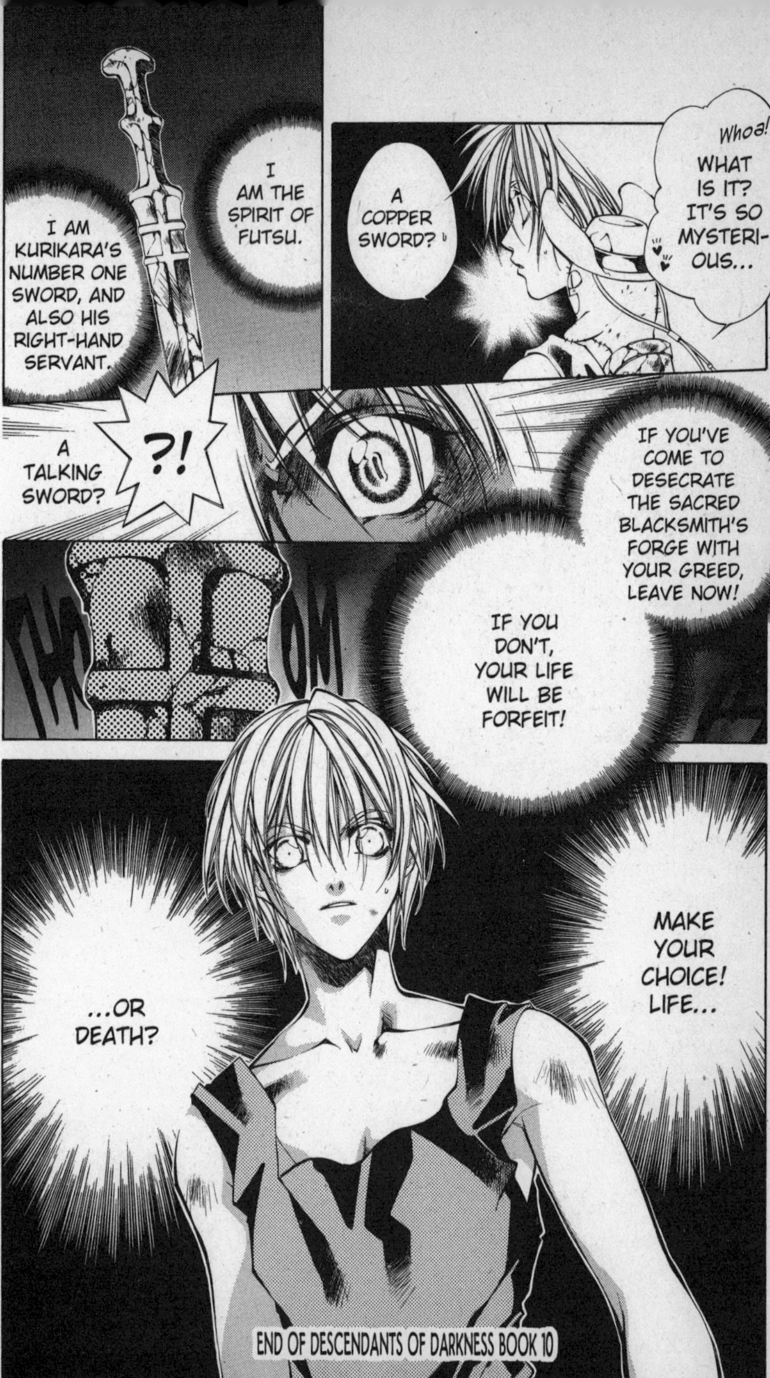
Whoa! WHAT IS IT? IT'S SO MYSTERIOUS...
A COPPER SWORD?
I AM THE SPIRIT OF FUTSU.
I AM KURIKARA'S NUMBER ONE SWORD, AND ALSO HIS RIGHT-HAND SERVANT.
IF YOU'VE COME TO DESECRATE THE SACRED BLACKSMITH'S FORGE WITH YOUR GREED, LEAVE NOW!
?!
A TALKING SWORD?
IF YOU DON'T, YOUR LIFE WILL BE FORFEIT!
MAKE YOUR CHOICE! LIFE...
...OR DEATH?
END OF DESCENDANTS OF DARKNESS BOOK 10

AFTERWORD

SO THAT WAS BOOK 10.

IT'S PRETTY AMAZING THAT
I MADE IT TO DOUBLE DIGITS
WITH MY FIRST SERIES...
AT LEAST I THINK SO (LAUGH).
WHAT DO YOU GUYS THINK?

THERE ARE LOTS OF STORIES
THAT I WANT TO DRAW, SO
I'M HOPING TO CONTINUE
AS LONG AS SALES OF THE
COMICS DON'T DROP OFF.
THANK YOU ALL FOR YOUR
SUPPORT.

STAFF

H. MIZUHO

N. RYOKO

H. YUMIKO

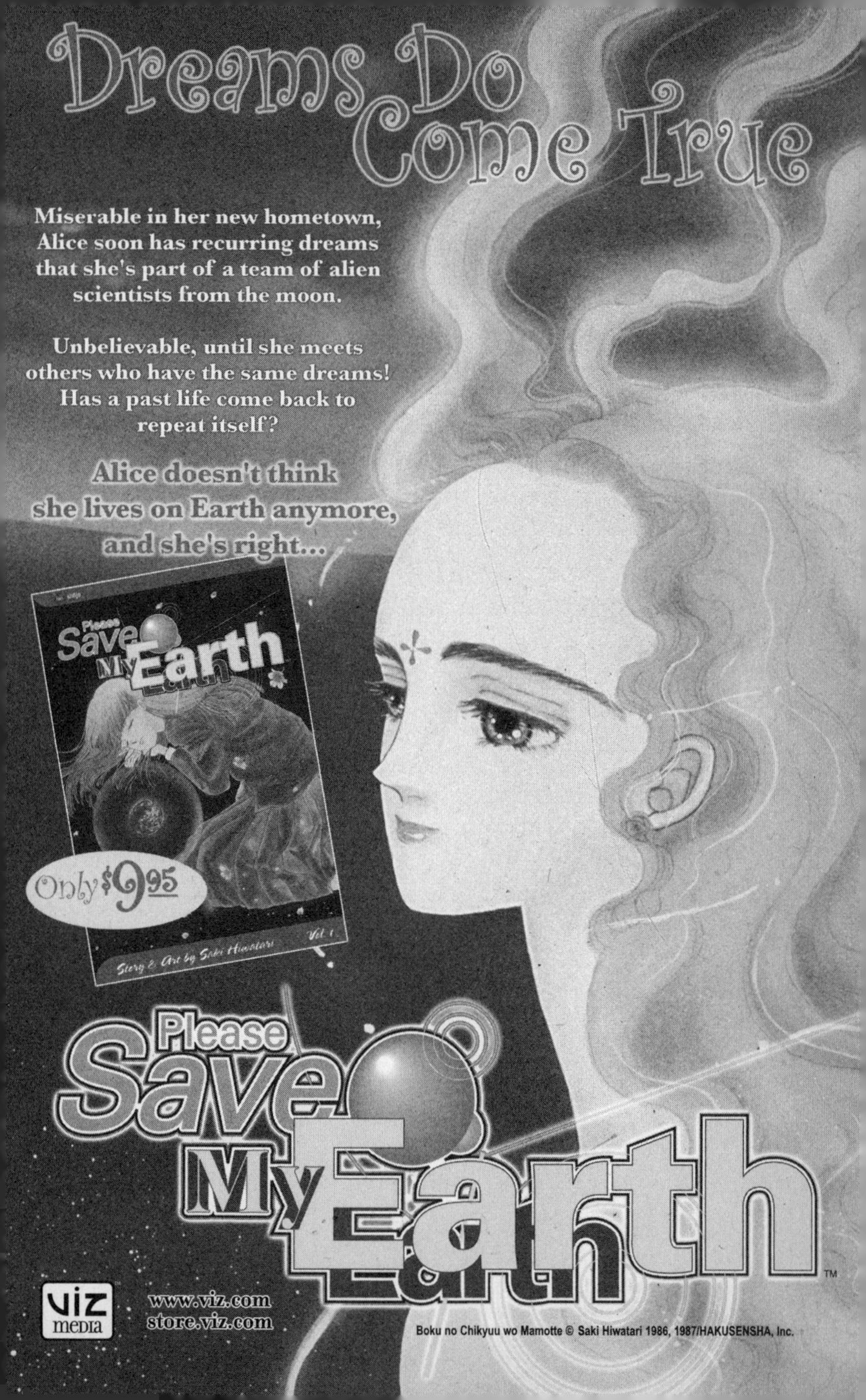
Dreams Do Come True
Miserable in her new hometown, Alice soon has recurring dreams that she's part of a team of alien scientists from the moon.
Unbelievable, until she meets others who have the same dreams! Has a past life come back to repeat itself?
Alice doesn't think she lives on Earth anymore, and she's right...
Please Save My Earth
Story & Art by Saki Hiwatari
Vol. 1
Only $9.95
Please Save My Earth™
VIZ media
www.viz.com
store.viz.com
Boku no Chikyuu wo Mamotte © Saki Hiwatari 1986, 1987/HAKUSENSHA, Inc.

LOVE SHOJO? LET US KNOW!

☐ Please do NOT send me information about VIZ Media products, news and events, special offers, or other information.

☐ Please do NOT send me information from VIZ' trusted business partners.

Name: _____

Address: _____

City: _____ State: _____ Zip: _____

E-mail: _____

☐ Male ☐ Female   Date of Birth (mm/dd/yyyy): ___ / ___ / ___   (Under 13? Parental consent required)

What race/ethnicity do you consider yourself? (check all that apply)

☐ White/Caucasian   ☐ Black/African American   ☐ Hispanic/Latino

☐ Asian/Pacific Islander   ☐ Native American/Alaskan Native ☐ Other: _____

What VIZ shojo title(s) did you purchase? (indicate title(s) purchased)

_____

_____

What other shojo titles from other publishers do you own? _____

_____

Reason for purchase: (check all that apply)

☐ Special offer   ☐ Favorite title / author / artist / genre

☐ Gift   ☐ Recommendation   ☐ Collection

☐ Read excerpt in VIZ manga sampler   ☐ Other _____

Where did you make your purchase? (please check one)

☐ Comic store   ☐ Bookstore   ☐ Mass/Grocery Store

☐ Newsstand   ☐ Video/Video Game Store

☐ Online (site:_____)   ☐ Other _____

How many shojo titles have you purchased in the last year? How many were VIZ shojo titles?
(please check one from each column)

SHOJO MANGA	VIZ SHOJO MANGA
☐ None	☐ None
☐ 1 – 4	☐ 1 – 4
☐ 5 – 10	☐ 5 – 10
☐ 11+	☐ 11+

What do you like most about shojo graphic novels? (check all that apply)

☐ Romance ☐ Drama / conflict ☐ Fantasy
☐ Comedy ☐ Real-life storylines ☐ Relatable characters
☐ Other ______________________________

Do you purchase every volume of your favorite shojo series?

☐ Yes! Gotta have 'em as my own
☐ No. Please explain: ______________________________

Who are your favorite shojo authors / artists? ______________________________

____

What shojo titles would like you translated and sold in English? ______________________________

____

THANK YOU! Please send the completed form to:

NJW Research
ATTN: VIZ Media Shojo Survey
42 Catharine Street
Poughkeepsie, NY 12601

Your privacy is very important to us. All information provided will be used for internal purposes only and will not be sold or otherwise divulged.